To Noreen, Sean, and Butch
and
To Marissa and Gabriela

CONTENTS ❧

PREFACE ∽

*T*he *Public Agenda* is best known for putting complex issues into everyday language so that students understand, care, and become intelligently involved in the policy debates. We give considerable attention to keeping the writing vivid, lucid, and personal. Our aim is to get the student's attention—and hold it. In truth, our hope is that the topics, the ideas, and the style will challenge and entertain *both* student and instructor. Reports on past editions indicate that students are more likely to read and remember this book than most other texts and that instructors are pleased that their students are intellectually engaged.

NEW TO THE FIFTH EDITION

The fifth edition of *The Public Agenda,* as with earlier editions, reflects the public mood and major public issues of the moment. The world is a very different place than when we wrote the fourth edition in 1998. It may be more accurate to say that the United States is a very different place since the September 11, 2001, terrorist attacks and subsequent steps taken by the Bush administration to combat terrorism—including domestic policies in the name of homeland security. We do not mean to imply that the world is unaffected by the terrorist attacks, but terrorism itself has been a way of life for a great many people around the world. This fact did not apply to Americans until that fateful September 11 morning.

While terrorism and the war in Iraq are uppermost in the minds of Americans, the economy and jobs topped the list of issues on voters' minds as they prepared to cast their ballots on November 5, 2002, according to public opinion polls. Terrorism and national defense rank second in importance. Both issues are discussed in this edition.

Affordable health care for every American remains an unsolved problem even though former President Clinton made it a top priority of his two administrations. The chapter on health care is updated and includes important new material. The same is true of the chapters on education and crime—issues that continue to worry most Americans.

We think longtime readers of *The Public Agenda* (it was first published in 1983) will be pleased with the substantially rewritten economy chapter, which not only places the economy in a post–cold war international trade context but also reflects the new age of terrorism and its impact on the economy. The book is shortened by one chapter, which we think will make it more attractive as a companion to an American government and/or public policy textbook.

Students have appreciated the introduction to the book for bringing the political landscape alive. Here too we have updated and rewritten the introduction to include mention of the war on terrorism and how it may affect Americans' basic civil rights and liberties. We also discuss the proliferation of lawsuits and lobbyists and ask what they cost society in lost capital and productivity. We entertain reasons why Americans remain very anxious about their futures, especially in the age of terrorism and unprecedented corporate corruption.

Several questions asked again and again in *The Public Agenda* are set forth in the introduction, as well. For example, we ask if the nation is suffering paralysis and, if so, who is responsible? Is the public to blame for the lack of political leadership? Finally, we provide students with some orienting concepts to help make sense of the complex issues that make up the public agenda. For example, we introduce Leone's Iron Law, which holds that every government action creates both winners and losers. We discuss the political and economic trade-offs to be considered in the making of public policy. And we describe the concept of a risk-free society and the costs associated with this elusive goal.

PEDAGOGY

We think that our choice and handling of these five major issues—presented simply, briskly, and perhaps a little irreverently—will challenge students to think critically and personally about politics. The chapters have been kept short, yet comprehensive and balanced in their presentation of facts and points of view. The features that worked well in previous editions remain: questions at the beginning of each chapter for students to consider and a brief, selected bibliography.

The fifth edition includes a new, and we think invaluable, feature entitled "A Closer Look" that consists of bolded and boxed questions or assignments strategically placed throughout each of the chapters. These questions or assignments are designed to help students better relate the subject being discussed to their own experience and to challenge them to further investigate what is being discussed. Easily understood tables, figures, and boxed material round out each chapter's presentation and are integral to the text, adding dimension and depth.

ACKNOWLEDGMENTS

We are indebted to Dianna Long at Wadsworth, as well as Mark Nichol, for their assistance through this project. The manuscript benefited from the thorough and thoughtful reviews by Aubrey Jewett, University of Central Florida; Euel Elliott, University of Texas at Dallas; Jill Clark, University of Texas at Arlington; and Nicholas Alozie, Arizona State University.

We both thank those who have assisted us through the researching and preparation of this fifth edition. Larry is particularly grateful to Sean for his assistance in finding relevant information on the Internet and to April Eleyce Latragna for her assistance in preparing the tables, graphs, and boxed material.

And on the personal and home fronts, we both are indebted to those close to us who have put up with and supported us through this period of tunnel-mindedness and occasional grouchiness. Larry gives his personal thanks to Noreen Barrington and to Sean and Butch for their support and patience during this writing. Genie thanks Marissa and Gabriela for their support and patience—and for giving up afternoons in the park.

INTRODUCTION ∼

On the morning of September 11, 2001, Americans learned that they no longer were immune to acts of terrorism on their soil. Life for many of us has not been the same since that fateful day. In the fourth edition of *The Public Agenda,* we wrote, "If there is a dominant emotion in the collective American pysche today, it is anxiety."[1] This statement is more true today than when we first wrote it in 1998. The reasons given then for feeling anxious had to do with worries over "paying for health care, housing, and college tuition." Many of us continue to worry about these expenses, as the costs for health care, housing, and a college education continue to soar.

The economy and homeland security top the public agenda in 2003, however. American confidence has been shaken by terrorists who seek to destroy America and corporate executives who misled investors and their own employees even as they reaped tens of millions of dollars in stock options and salaries. At this writing, the mood of many Americans has darkened as wages have stagnated and unemployment has risen to nearly 6 percent, the highest since 1996. Women and college graduates were laid off in greater numbers during the 2001 recession than in previous recessions.

The Economic Policy Institute, a liberal research group, found in its 2002 study entitled *The State of Working America* that "wages were growing at their slowest level since 1995 and that the income gap between the richest Americans and everybody else was widening again, after narrowing in the late 1990s."[2] The same study reports that "for the typical household, rising debt, not a rising stock market, was the big story of the 1990s. Household debt grew much more rapidly than household income in the last decade."[3] David S. Broder, the syndicated columnist, writes that even as most of us have become fixated on stock prices, "jobs and wages and income are a lot more vital to most people than the state of their stock portolios. That is why the economic slump of 2001 and the slow-growth economy of 2002 are the central facts of life [today]. . . . the hard-won, and often minimal, gains from the full-employment years of the 1990s are being jeopardized—and in some instances, reversed—by the current stagnation."[4]

The terrorist attacks on September 11 contributed to unemployment and falling stock prices. Understandably, the hardest-hit industries were travel and service related—the airlines, hotels, restrauants, and financial services. Unemployment and lower stock values also resulted from corporate scandals, with once high-flying companies such as Enron laying off 4,200 people, and WorldCom, the nation's second largest telecommunications company, 17,000. John Sweeney, president of the AFL-CIO, commented that "for years I've heard people talk about distrust of their employers, but something new is happening. People are really fed up and furious with corporate America."[5] (See Table I.1.)

Federal budget deficits are back again, following several years of surpluses under the Clinton administration. Increased spending on the wars in Afghanistan

TABLE I.1
Workers Upset about the Economy

Percent of workers dissatisfied with the state of the economy:	
2001	34%
2002	58%
Percent of workers with negative feelings toward corporations:	
2001	25%
2002	39%
Percent of workers with positive feelings toward corporations:	
2001	42%
2002	30%

Source: Steven Greenhouse, "Unease Marks Labor Day '02," *San Jose Mercury News,* September 2, 2002, A2.

Peter D. Hart Research Associates surveyed 900 workers, union and nonunion. The margin of error is ±3.5 percentage points.

and in Iraq, the war on terrorism, and homeland defense, coupled with reduced tax revenues as a result of the economic slowdown and President Bush's tax cuts are the reasons given for the huge deficits that are predicted to run through 2005. The bipartisan Congressional Budget Office estimated 2002 tax revenues "were about about $131 billion, or 6.6 percent, lower than last year [2001], the biggest one-year drop since the repeal of World War II surtaxes 56 years ago."[6] Deficits are forecast to run through 2005 only if surpluses accumulating in the Social Security trust fund are used to offset lower tax revenues. If the Social Security fund is left untouched, as promised to the Baby Boom generation as they prepare to retire, then the estimated deficits will be with us until 2010.[7]

In many ways, the country is a very different place than when President Clinton won reelection in 1996, the first Democrat to win a second term since President Franklin D. Roosevelt. The information-based economy faltered as dot-com companies went bust. We witnessed corporate corruption and greed on an unprecedented scale, resulting in the largest corporate bankruptcies in history. We experienced unprecedented terrorism on our shores. We are engaged in a war on terrorism that knows no national boundaries, involves an illusive enemy that hides in caves and blends into civilian populations here and abroad. Unlike World War II, which left America morally and economically stronger—and more democratic—this 21st-century war threatens to leave us a weaker and less democratic society.

On the first anniversary of the terrorist attacks, a *USA Today*/CNN/Gallup poll reflected "a country torn between the belief that government can protect its citizens and a fatalism about the likelihood of further attacks, perhaps perpetrated by terrorists living among them."[8] A question many are asking is, Are we compromising our civil liberties in exchange for a sense of security, however illusorary? A public opinion poll conducted by the *San Francisco Chronicle* on September 11, 2002, showed that 75 percent of the respondents felt that civil liberties were eroding in this country in the wake of the terrorist attacks a year before.[9] Critics of the Bush administration argue that the erosion of our basic civil liberties is unprecedented in the modern era. Whether one agrees with this position, there is little question that Attorney General John Ashcroft, and others in the Bush administration, have acted swiftly to arrest and detain hundreds of people suspected of terrorist activities.

Still hundreds of others have been deported. There is little doubt that America's noncitizens (including international students) have come under increasing pressure because of security concerns.

The Patriot Act, enacted into law on October 26, 2001, has implications for all of us, including college administrators and students. The Patriot Act allows for the detention and deportation of noncitizens who provide "assistance" for the lawful activities of a group the government now claims to be a terrorist organization, even if the group has never in the past been designated as such. Under this provision the secretary of state (or his or her appointees) can designate any group that has ever engaged in violent activity as a terrorist organization. The act also allows for the indefinite detention of immigrants who are not terrorists. Immigrants who are arrested and not found to have any links to terrorism—but have an immigration status violation, such as overstaying a visa—could face indefinite detention if their native country refuses to accept them. Furthermore, the act allows the Federal Bureau of Investigation (FBI) to secure information from Internet service providers, such as America Online (AOL), about the use of the Internet by "suspects," as well as to more easily obtain warrants to review the reading and computer habits of library patrons.[10]

Attorney General Ashcroft and the Justice Department are not totally free to act as they think necessary to protect Americans from future attacks. It was revealed in August 2002 that a secretive court created by the Foreign Intelligence Surveillance Act (FISA) ruled that "federal prosecutors, FBI agents and intelligence operatives keep intact a wall between those investigating ongoing criminal activity and those gathering intelligence on potential terrorist attacks and acts of espionage."[11] There is a very real struggle between Ashcroft and the Bush administration on one side and immigration and criminal defense lawyers, civil libertarians, and constitutional scholars on the other side. In the middle are federal judges having to decide if individual rights have been violated. In the first year since the attacks, a few federal judges ordered secret deportation proceedings opened to public hearing. U.S. District Judge Gladys Kessler wrote, when she ordered under the Freedom of Information Act that the identities of many of those who had been detained in secret be made public, that "secret arrests are a concept odious to a democratic society."[12]

In other ways, life is not that different than it was in 1998. At that time, we wrote that Clinton's reelection did not mean that Americans felt good about their country or were confident about their futures. Americans expressed dissatisfaction with the "way things are going" in the nation generally. Crime, education, health care, immigration, and the budget deficit were issues of great concern then as they are now. Perhaps even more true today than when we first reported it in 1998 is

A CLOSER LOOK

Have you or your family changed any of your behaviors as a result of the terrorist attacks or the continuing threat of attacks? If so, how? If not, why? Do you agree with the Bush administration's policies and approaches in responding to the threat of terrorism? What if anything concerns you about the path taken by the Bush administration? Why?

Americans' dissatisfaction with the way the nation's political system works. The 2000 presidential election—which many believe was decided by "hanging chads" and the U.S. Supreme Court—further undermined voter trust and confidence in the political process. Although Americans rallied around their president following the tragic events of September 11 and his popularity soared as he waged war on Osama bin Laden and the Taliban, Bush's election still was considered questionable by a significant number of Americans on the first anniversary of the terrorist attacks.[13]

A Gallup poll taken in the first week of September 2002 asked: "'Which comes closest to your view of the way George W. Bush won the 2000 presidential election: a) He won it fair and square, b) He won, but only on a technicality, or c) He stole the election.' Of the total survey of 1,012 respondents, just half—exactly 50 percent—say Bush won the election fair and square. Thirty-two percent say he won on a technicality, while 15 percent say he stole the election—making a total of 47 percent who believe that Bush did *not* win fair and square (the remaining three percent say they don't know)."[14] Not surprisingly, an overwhelming majority of Republicans polled say he won fair and square, whereas less than half of the Independents agree with that statement, and only 18 percent of the Democrats polled say he won fair and square.[15] It seems that a significant number of American voters will never view Bush's election as completely legitimate.

Many spoke of a "moral crisis" in the country during the Clinton administration. The same cry is heard today. It is in fact concern over the moral breakdown in the country that is the one recurring theme cutting across the political spectrum and that connects this edition of *The Public Agenda* with the previous one. Clinton's second term was derailed by Monica Lewinsky and his lies concerning their relationship—ultimately leading to his impeachment. Although Bush promised to return dignity and morality to the White House, his own administration has been plagued by political and legal problems related to corporate misconduct.

Unfortunately, as we begin a new century, too many children still think it normal that countless homeless people push their worldly goods in shopping carts, begging a few coins along the way, and that marauding armed gangs peddle crack and use the homes and cars of the innocent for target practice. In a first-of-its-kind study, "Child Well-Being, Child Poverty and Child Policy in Modern Nations," comparative data on child poverty are presented that include benefits and taxes not found in the "official," Census Bureau poverty statistics. The study's data also are comparable with those of other nations. "New fully comparable figures on child poverty across the industrialized world and the 50 United States show a huge disparity from country to country and state to state. While Sweden leads the world with only 2.4 percent child poverty, New York State, at 26.3 percent, ranks last in the industrialized world. California is not far behind with 25.7 percent, and in President Bush's home state of Texas, 20.7 percent of the children live in poverty."[16] Tim Smeeding, coeditor of the "Child Well-Being" study and Maxwell Professor of Public Policy at the Maxwell School of Syracuse University, points out "that despite high rates of economic growth and improvements in the standard of living in industrialized nations throughout the 20th century, a significant percentage of our children are still living in families that are so poor that normal health and growth are at risk."[17]

In 1997 former secretary of labor Robert Reich warned the nation that "the continuing gap between rich and poor threatens to blight an otherwise promising future." He went on to say that "the bridge to America's future must first traverse the chasm of inequality."[18] Reich was referring to the fact that the rich were becoming very much richer while the middle and working classes fell further and further behind each year. The gap has only grown wider in the ensuing years. Then, as now, the only way average American families maintained their standard of living was to have both parents work—which created other problems in homes and in schools. The income gap notwithstanding, former President Clinton signed into law in 1996 a landmark welfare reform bill that ended six decades of guaranteed federal help to the nation's poorest children. Why? Because the embattled middle and working classes are angry at welfare mothers—even though they collect only 1 dollar out every 30 dollars spent by the average state.

The heightened anxiety Americans feel about their futures and their growing anger toward welfare recipients, immigrants (legal and illegal), and assorted other scapegoats is the result of a great many factors. The war on terrorism and inequitable income distribution are only two factors—albeit important ones. Kevin Phillips writes that the United States in the 1990s resembles the 1890s as well as the 1930s, "the last two occasions when Americans experienced deep economic pain from global upheavals and great debt bubbles imploding after speculative booms."[19]

Michael Mandel writes that another reason Americans are anxious about their future well-being is that the new global and technology-based economy has created for us a "high-risk society." His caution to us when he wrote in 1996 has proven more prophetic than even he could have imagined, considering the wave of dot-com busts and the unprecedented degree of corporate corruption and number of bankruptcies and layoffs in the telecom and related industies. In 1996 he warned that "economic insecurity has become a fact of life for every worker and every business. In an era when giants such as AT&T, IBM, and General Motors are shedding hundreds of thousands of workers, no one can assume that today's job will still exist five years from now. In an era of rapid technological change, no one can predict which industries will grow and which will shrink ten years from now. In an era of intense international competition, no one can fore-tell which countries will dominate the global economy in the next century."[20]

Mandel goes on to say that "the old protections against uncertainty are erod-ing. No longer do companies offer employees job security in return for loyalty and commitment. Instead, corporations now create new uncertainties by cutting jobs and reorganizing work to boost productivity and profits without regard for the human costs. Promotions and pay raises have become a reward rather than a right."[21]

Mandel does not warn against changes in the business world alone. He points out that government, with considerable public support, is "gradually abandoning its traditional role as the ultimate guarantor of security to businesses and workers. Widespread deregulation means that the government is no longer protecting in-dustries like telecommunications and electric power against the rigors of compe-tition. Most elements of the safety net—welfare, Social Security, Medicare—are either under attack or in significant danger of being cut back."[22]

The dilemma for Americans in the new economy is that "prosperity and se-curity no longer go hand in hand."[23] The very factors that fuel economic growth in this fluid, global market—"open markets, deregulation, business restructuring, and technological change"—also contribute to economic uncertainty and unpre-dictability. These changes lead Mandel to conclude that "success hinges on [one's] willingness to embrace risk . . . rather than flee it."[24]

Finally, it does not help that the public lacks confidence in their government's ability to solve the many problems facing the country. It is clear that a vast ma-jority of Americans are tired of partisan politics that serve no one except the politicians themselves. Political gridlock and the constant mudslinging and scape-goating that Republicans and Democrats continually engage in have contributed to the growing popularity of third-party candidates. Voters look to the third-party candidates to focus public debate on the issues and not on personalities. Presi-dent Carter spoke about "a fundamental threat to American democracy . . . a cri-sis of confidence" back in 1979. He went on to say that "it is a crisis that strikes at the very heart and soul and spirit of our national will."[25] This "crisis of confi-dence" has only gotten worse since Carter first spoke about it—Bush's current popularity as a result of the war on terrorism notwithstanding.

It is ironic that politicians have contributed to political alienation and apathy through their own campaign rhetoric. Several decades of U.S. presidents, sena-tors, and representatives have been elected on campaign pitches that "govern-ment is the enemy." Now, it appears, many voters believe them.

IS THE PUBLIC TO BLAME, TOO?

In the late 1990s, the PEW Research Center found that, "although no single prob-lem or concern is driving public discontent with the country's course, the public is more of one mind as to who's at fault—Congress."[26] This same study found, however, that a fourth of those surveyed (27 percent) blamed "the people them-selves" for the country's problems.[27]

Public esteem for Congress has reached record-low levels. Members of Congress are viewed as part of the problem, not the solution. A great many Americans blame Congress for political gridlock. There is little indication that the "Republican revolution" has altered American antipathy toward Congress. The fact that Congress is thought of as an institution of political action committees (PACs), perks, privilege, partisanship, and paralysis has not helped its public image.

The public claims that it wants politicians who take a position and stand by it—people of strong personal belief and integrity. Politicians assert that the public wants no such thing. On the promise of anonymity, one congressman summarized the feelings of most: "People want you to tell them what they want to hear. If you tell them what they don't want to hear, you don't get much credit for courage."[28] Babying the public is tantamount to saving one's seat, as Lawrence Hansen discovered in private interviews: "The members with whom we talked admit they are reluctant to give their constituents the unvarnished truth. Based on personal experience, they have serious reservations about the public's capacity to handle the truth, but few doubts about its willingness to politically punish elected officials who test their tolerance. The result is an uneasy accommodation between people who like the truth in tiny doses and leaders who like their jobs."[29]

Although it is rare for politicians to speak candidly about their anger with the public's reluctance to hear the truth, occasionally one will speak out—usually when retiring from office. When well-respected, many-times reelected Senator Warren Rudman declined to run again in 1992, he openly aired his frustration. Congressional unwillingness to "bite the bullet" and address the deficit was no different from the public's unwillingness to accept benefit changes to moderate skyrocketing Social Security and Medicare costs. "The American people," he said, "bear some share of the responsibility for being totally intransigent to any approach on reasonable means-testing of these programs. But quite frankly, we were elected to lead. And we ought to lead."[30]

The frustration expressed by former senator Rudman is shared by a growing number of Congressional leaders. In 1996 alone, 13 U.S. senators—8 Democrats and 5 Republicans—announced that they would retire at the end of their terms—the most since 1896. While most of them gave as their reason for leaving office that they simply no longer have the same passion they once had, many also cited the now familiar complaints: "that party politics is out of control, Americans have lost faith in Washington, campaigns are too dirty and fund-raising too tedious and time-consuming."[31]

Legislators complain that the public "believes there can be gains without pains, demands instant solutions to complex problems, expects too much from government, takes its political responsibilities casually, does not understand governmental processes and is politically inattentive and disengaged. . . . It's frustrating to call town meetings and have very little attendance . . . to see that only 40–50 percent of the electorate is actually voting, as if they do not care, and to have to face an angry mob of people who demand that the budget deficit and their taxes be reduced but who won't give up their favorite programs."[32]

As we study the public policy issues presented in this book, it is important to keep in mind the role that the public—and you as a member—plays in the

---

A CLOSER LOOK

Are you cynical or disengaged from the political process? Do you vote, for example? Explore why you are cynical or disengaged, if you are. If you are engaged in the political process, then have a discussion with one of your classmates who is cynical and/or disengaged—what caused each of you to feel and act as you do politically? Can a democracy work if a majority of its citizens are disengaged?

---

process. Do we want our representatives to tell us the truth about the sometimes painful choices that must be made in areas of education, health care, crime control, taxes, and government spending, to name a few of the issues to be discussed? Are we willing to think beyond our own immediate interests and to consider what is in the national interest? Are we prepared to commit the time required to study the issues and to vote? It is easy to be cynical and disengaged. It also is counterproductive.

In a 1992 Carnegie Commission report entitled "Changing Our Ways," the United States was admonished to get its own house in order if it hopes to influence the "new world order" that is said to be emerging in the post–cold war era. The commission stressed that, while the United States faces serious challenges, we need not be defeatist. "Our government may be broke, but our country is not poor. America remains the world's foremost economic power. But we are paying a price for evading hard choices. Our crisis is essentially political, not economic."[33] Unfortunately, even fewer Americans today are exercising their right to vote. And we continue to avoid holding our political leaders accountable. Instead, we return incumbents to office election after election. As you read *The Public Agenda,* you would do well to remember the words of Carl Schurz when he spoke before the U.S. Senate in 1872: "Our Country, right or wrong. When right, to be kept right; when wrong, to be put right."

ARE WE A NATION PARALYZED?

The U.S. government was set up to stress representation over governing. The system of checks and balances was designed to prevent bold action, sharp policy changes, or the dominance of any single individual. Federalism further splintered the locus of power and governance geographically. It was a cautious democratic arrangement. As the nation developed in size and complexity, it became increasingly inefficient. But inefficiency, or even inaction, is one thing, paralysis another.

What has happened to cause this paralysis? The problem goes much deeper than simply dwelling on philosophical deadlock. It goes to the very nature of the political institutions and the origins of our system of government. Americans are disturbed to rediscover regularly that we have a fragmented, irresponsible, and ungovernable polity. Political scientist and noted author Theodore Lowi likens the government to a jellyfish that is pervasive but weak, easily captured by private interests. Where else but in America would the industrial side of the military-industrial complex be stronger than the military side?

In his interpretive study of American politics, *The Democratic Wish,*[34] James Morone argues that Americans will never solve their collective problems as long as they instinctively equate any meaningful exercise of public power as a direct threat to personal liberty. Our dread of European-style state power set us on a difficult course at the beginning. To protect against a strong central government, the Founding Fathers created a fragmented governmental system that made mobilizing for public purposes practically impossible—except in periods of national emergency like the Great Depression and the world wars. Yet public purposes have to be served. In spite of ourselves, both federal and state governments have grown in size and authority.

A paradox of American politics, according to Morone, is that the growth and power of government has come in the name of restoring power to the people. American reformers have too often been mesmerized by the myth of a citizenry that was not only virtuous but fully in accord in its understanding of the common good and capable of coherent action. But rather than empower existing institutions to take direct action to solve pressing problems, reformers have bypassed the governors with alternative institutions that promote direct democracy. The popular assemblies of the 1770s and the community action agencies spawned by Lyndon Johnson's War on Poverty were devised to cure the ailments of democracy with more democracy. But in the end, they only produced new, self-perpetuating bureaucracies.[35]

American political reformers always end up reinforcing the status quo. The central problem is that the reformers work from a narrowly conceived concept of democracy as representation—nothing more. This American belief, even conviction, that representation alone defines and ensures rational and effective policy output is simplistic and occasionally absurd as it plays itself out in the public arena. For example, clashes over equality of race or class or gender turn into sterile dickering over representation. Even radical forces contend that, for example, enough seats on the community school board will solve the dropout problem. Losing sight of the substantive forest for the procedural trees, newly legitimized groups themselves become roadblocks to more sweeping and profound change.[36]

IS GOVERNMENT THE ENEMY?

Government bashing is a long-standing American tradition. Many believe that government intervention in the affairs of business leads only to costly regulations, compromising the capitalist free-market system. They tenaciously hold on to this myth, even though the U.S. economy has always been mixed. Government plays a discreet, covert, and vital supportive role and has done so from the nation's beginning. However, our leading international business competitors, Japan and Germany, are both democratic and capitalist, and they have overtly promoted government-business partnerships. In recent years, many of the Southeast Asian countries have experienced extraordinary economic growth under a form of capitalism that allows for strong government-business ties.

The undeniable fact is that government is an essential part of doing business in the United States—just as it is in every other industrial nation. Robert Leone makes the point that "so long as governments—liberal or conservative, small or large, efficient or wasteful—collect taxes, spend revenues, or pass laws, public actions will influence private profits."[37] It is inaccurate to view government as harmful to all business. Government action creates both winners *and* losers. Leone suggests that there is an "Iron Law" at work: "For some businesses, profits increase when government acts; for others, profits fall. Who wins and who loses is by no means accidental; rather, it is the predictable consequence of the interaction among individuals, corporations, and political organizations that often knowingly and sometimes unwittingly take political and economic actions to shape these gains and losses."[38]

Leone offers a few examples of how the system works:

> A governmental agency in California succeeds in its efforts to increase the population of the endangered sea otter. Ostensibly this has little to do with business interests. Not so. As a natural predator of abalone, the revival of the sea otter population disadvantages those abalone fishermen who harvest abalone from the sea. At the same time, a new competitive opportunity is created for those aquaculturists who cultivate abalone in tanks on land. A federal agency bans the use of fluorocarbon propellants in aerosol products to protect the upper atmosphere. The resulting shift in market shares for existing products and aerosol technologies places some multimillion-dollar financial enterprises in jeopardy but creates significant growth opportunities for others. Policy makers debate the merits and demerits of natural gas price decontrol with considerable attention to the estimated redistribution of perhaps $40 billion from gas consumers to gas producers. While politicians focus on the legitimate concerns for the equity or inequity of various gas-pricing policies, the international competitiveness of several U.S. industries hinges on the outcome of these debates.[39]

We cannot study the public policy issues presented in the chapters to follow without an appreciation for the regulatory process and the responses of those parties affected by it. This process is highly political in that it responds to issues of fairness. It is quite procedural—often to the point that procedural regularity matters as much as policy outcome. And, as we will discuss in a moment, the process often tends to be myopic in its perception of relevant issues and time horizons.[40] These factors, in turn, all have competitive implications.

Initial reactions of less sophisticated business managers to public policy initiatives tend to be ideological—that is, they see them as unnecessarily intrusive and potentially damaging to their industries. In time, successful business leaders learn

A CLOSER LOOK

What role do you think government should play in our lives? Is the federal government too intrusive, or should it play an even more active role in shaping public policy and providing funding for state and local programs? Think of ways in which your family, including you, have benefited from federal programs. By your state and local governments.

to manage regulatory uncertainty, then to influence the process, and ultimately to exploit public actions for competitive gain.[41] For those savvy enough to work the political process to their advantage, government is not an enemy but an ally.

Business-government partnership or the exploitation of governmental processes does not have to be at the expense of social programs. In fact, political economists like Leone argue that the competitive forces at play in the public policy process, if properly understood and managed, can be used to advance the broader goals of society as well as more specific goals of business.

Government will not get out of business—nor will business get out of government. The birth of regional and global economies, combined with the balkanization, or splintering, of American society, makes it likely that government will become more, not less, active in its effort to shape economic growth. Whatever ideological form such policies ultimately take, they will likely fail if they are not designed with an explicit understanding of the relationship of government to business. Indeed, any policy changes will have significant competitive consequences and will create winners and losers in the marketplace.

POLITICAL AND ECONOMIC TRADE-OFFS

Leone's Iron Law reminds us that every decision to commit resources (including time, money, materials, and energy) to one project means that there will be fewer resources for another project. Political and economic systems in any country are the means by which decisions are made as to who gets what goods and services—and to what extent. Absent a Garden of Eden, goods and services must be rationed through political and economic decisions because people want more than is available. This is true of any economic system, whether it be capitalism, socialism, or feudalism. And it is true for any political system, whether democratic, autocratic, or totalitarian.

Economics exists because goods and services are scarce. Governments exist in order to help decide (authoritatively) how these scarce resources will be allocated. No matter how complex economic and political systems may become, the predicament is quite simple: there is not enough to go around. No amount of convoluted reasoning or emotionally powerful language can obscure that very simple reality. For example, the existence of unmet needs in society is used as evidence of the failure of the economic and political system. In fact, because economic systems are essentially systems of rationing scarce resources and because governments are one means of deciding who gets what among the rationed goods and services, any successfully functioning economic and political system will have unmet needs in every sector of society. The alternative would be to satisfy completely all of some category of needs, but this would still leave unsatisfied needs elsewhere.

For example, we could completely solve the downtown parking problem in every city in the country so that anyone could easily find a convenient parking space at any hour of the day or night, but the money to achieve this goal might be taken from municipal hospitals, schools, or the water supply system. The mundane fact of insufficiency must be insisted upon and restated because so many discussions of unmet needs proceed as if better policies, practices, or attitudes would solve the problem at hand without creating deficiencies elsewhere. Typical of this attitude is the comment "If we can send a man to the moon, why can't we . . . ?" followed by whatever project the speaker favors. The fact that we sent a man to the moon is part of the reason why many other things could not be done.

THE NEED FOR COMPROMISE

Since there is not enough of everything for everyone, political and economic decisions require trade-offs. It is this need to compromise one goal (or some part of it) for another that can cause political conflict. At times the conflict can be settled to almost everyone's satisfaction. At other times, the conflict is not so satisfactorily resolved. Still other times, the conflict results in paralysis.

For most of the significant issues facing the United States today, including the ones discussed in this book, meaningful compromise cannot be made. Therefore, the politics of confrontation are upon us like the plague. No one has the ability to impose solutions, and no solutions command universal agreement. Keep in mind that there is general agreement about the goals worth pursuing for most of the issues facing us: universal health care, quality education for every child, reduction if not elimination of crime, and so forth. What we cannot agree upon is the best method for reaching these goals. The reason is simple: every solution requires that someone or something be sacrificed. Not only are people with something at stake unwilling to give it up, but they understand the political system enough to fight successfully against any proposed sacrifices.[42]

Most Americans accepted the moon-landing project because the sacrifice was less obvious than, say, giving up land for a transportation system or driving their cars less in order to achieve energy independence. We did not stop to think that the resources spent on the moon project could have been spent on more earthly needs. The goal was appealing, while the technology for getting to the moon was remote and unrelated to our lives. It was, after all, the technicians' job to get us there.

DEMOCRATIC CHOICES

Looked at another way, the wide spectrum of personal values ensures that no given policy or decision will become *the* answer to a human problem. The need for health care, housing, or energy can be met in a wide variety of ways. The methods most preferred by some will be least preferred by others. Even though no political or economic system can satisfy all goals simultaneously, we nevertheless expect everything promised us when voting for a slate of politicians. Whatever the merits of democracy, it has its institutional limitations, as do all other systems, and it operates within a set of economic constraints. The open-endedness of hopes has sometimes led to the view that a majority can or should have whatever it wants—a view known as the democratic fallacy.

The democratic fallacy implies unlimited possibilities. Thus, if the majority does not get what it wants, it perceives some denial of its democratic rights. Choice through the ballot box has often been equated with a market system. But the crucial difference between ballots and prices is that prices convey effective knowledge of basic limitations while ballots do not. If I desire a Rolls-Royce and, at the same time, a continued normal standard of living, the price tag on the automobile immediately informs me that these two things are inconsistent. But if I want a large military arsenal, low taxes, a balanced budget, and massive social programs—nothing constrains me from voting for all four.

I may discover sometime later that what was promised did not materialize, but this disappointment is easily blamed on the dishonesty or incompetence of the political candidates. Personal limits on personal choices do not carry over to public limits on personal wants. Voters' disenchantment over the fact that they cannot have everything does not translate into reconsideration of what is attainable. Instead, the message received is that different choices of leaders must be made. Maybe new leaders can give us everything. Of course, this is impossible.

The question here is not whether voters have a right to choose whatever they want. Voters can only choose the candidates who make decisions, and then hope for results. Consumers, in contrast, buy results and leave the process to those with specialized knowledge of such things. There is no argument here for denying voters their democratic choices, only that the terms of the choice are usually misstated politically. Craftspeople in the art of politics are able to misstate the options while giving the appearance of satisfying competing claims that cannot be satisfied. Nearly every issue in this book has fallen into their hands.

TIME

When thinking about the democratic process and solving problems, consider time. The issues laid out in the following chapters require both short- and long-term planning. Every action taken has both short- and long-term consequences, intended and unintended. We talk about resources that are finite, such as money, but time (while ultimately finite) has different significance for different issues and for different people. For example, the Food and Drug Administration may consider six to nine years about the right time to test a potentially effective anti-AIDS drug thoroughly. The person afflicted with AIDS sees that time quite differently.

Unfortunately, most politicians have relatively short time horizons. Cynics say they think no further ahead than the next election. Although voters may have a longer time horizon than politicians, we do not always anticipate the long-term consequences of most issues at the time we are asked to vote for a candidate who champions a certain solution. Furthermore, the connection between a voting decision and our self-interest is not always clear. A decision made in Washington or our state capital, or even by our city officials, is not always clear in its implications. Finally, most of us are not used to planning very far into the future. Although we may think further ahead than the two or four years until the next election, we are not likely to think ten, fifteen, or twenty years further. Yet many of the issues facing us require that kind of long-term planning.

Planners decided in the 1950s to build an interstate highway system. Most voters, if they were even aware of the decision, thought only about the immediate benefits of faster and easier travel. Neither the voters nor the planners anticipated the increase in highway deaths, loss of land, division of neighborhoods and cities, traffic jams, or shortage of gas. Consequences of decisions usually take time to become visible. Elected and appointed officials give minimal consideration to longer-term negative consequences when making decisions.

THE VALUE OF POLITICAL PARTIES

Decisions that favor sacrificing the future for the present are less likely when the political party system is strong or when a powerful political machine holds sway and is assured of a continued run of success. However, with the rise of independent politicians who fund themselves without much party assistance, the political time horizon is bounded by the next election. The demise of party-indebted politicians has affected both national and local politics. For example, New York City's financial crisis of the 1970s grew from policies and practices adopted in the 1960s during the regime of one of its most charismatic, reform-minded, and independent mayors. Chicago, the last bastion of municipal party-machine politics, remained fiscally solvent.

A CLOSER LOOK

Do you identify with one political party? If so, what influenced you to become a member of that party? Do you vote for the candidates of that party most of the time? Do you think political parties are important to a democracy? If so, how?

Workers in a political machine have a heavy investment in its future election prospects and their own prospects of advancement to higher office. Independent, self-funded politicians are entrepreneurs who see their fates less tied to the long-run consequences of their decisions. What matters to independent politicians is how their current decisions in a current position promote their immediate prospects for voter exposure and campaign contributions for higher office. If a given set of policies enhances Governor Smith's presidential prospects, he is not terribly concerned with possible long-term damage to the state.

RELIGION AND POLITICS

Public opinion polls show that since the events of September 11, 2001, religion has become more central to the lives of many more Americans than before the terrorist attacks. Fortunately, it seems that the increased emphasis on religious life is not at the expense of Muslims or others who hold religious beliefs different from the major faiths in the United States. The PEW Forum on Religion and Public Life, for example, found in a December 2001 national poll that "fully 78% now say religion's influence in American life is growing—up from 37% eight months ago and the highest mark on this measure in surveys dating back four decades. At the same time, the public has a better opinion of Muslim-Americans than it did before the attacks."[43]

Across the United States there is a great deal of politicking going on from the pulpit, and not just in Baptist or fundamentalist churches. The role organized religion should play in American political life has changed over the years in the minds of most Americans. "In 1968, 53% of Americans opposed political expression by churches. But by 1995, majority opinion had shifted, with 54% believing that churches should indeed express their views."[44] For example, a survey conducted by the PEW Research Center in September 2000 found that "Americans embrace a role for religion in the nation's political life, but they are conflicted over the extent and contours of that involvement. Compared to a generation ago, more people are comfortable with churches expressing opinions on social and political matters, yet a solid majority of voters say they are uneasy with members of the clergy espousing their political views from the pulpit."[45] This same survey also found that a significant majority of those surveyed wanted their president to "have religious faith" but were far less comfortable with politicians discussing their religious beliefs in public.[46]

An earlier PEW Research Center survey found that 60 percent of churchgoers reported that their clergy speak out about abortion and almost as many (56 percent) speak out about prayer in schools. The issues discussed in church vary among religions. Catholics are more likely to hear about abortion and right-to-die laws. White evangelical Protestants hear about abortion, but their clergy also talk about pornography laws, prayer in schools, and laws about homosexuality. African American churches have a mixed liberal-conservative political agenda. African American ministers are more likely to discuss health care reform. Mainline Protestants report less talk in their churches about a range of contemporary political issues than do other religious groups.[47]

The bottom line is that religion plays a very important role in shaping how Americans think about politics today. The PEW survey found that for many Americans religion greatly influences their "political affiliation, political values, policy attitudes and candidate choices. Its increasing influence on political opinion and behavior rivals factors such as race, region, age, social class and gender."[48]

When race is factored into the equation, the full impact of religion on American politics is made all the more clear. Without a doubt, the most powerful religious force in politics today is conservative white evangelical Protestants. The PEW survey found that "white evangelical Protestants are not only much more conservative on policy questions that involve moral issues such as abortion, laws regarding homosexuality and family issues, but they are also more conservative on a range of values including environmentalism and beliefs about international security."[49]

HOW AWARE ARE WE?

American democracy begs its citizens to inform themselves about politics and public issues. Public schools teach civics at several different levels, then many college goers take further classes in government and political science. Politicians are always telling us to pay attention. However, most of us depend on television to pay attention for us. If we do not understand exactly what is going on, at least we get a feel for what is going wrong.

But politics is really peripheral to most of our lives—at least from our own self-centered perspective. Most of us are so insulated that we talk about how much we get back from withholding tax, rather than the extraordinary amount that the government takes. Politics happens somewhere else, affects somebody else. It is an insider game, complex and probably corrupt, or at least self-serving.

However, we can still identify the important issues of the day. Modern random telephone polling reveals a public sensitive to society's problems. Polls over recent years consistently demonstrate public concern with the economy, crime, education, health care, AIDS, immigration, and until recently, the arms race. Occasionally pollsters will ask what policies should be pursued. A significant proportion of citizens have not the faintest idea. Those who do often have frightening suggestions—at least frightening to those who seek a continuance of democracy.

Some issues do not seem to require any information or public awareness. These are moral issues. They require only personal opinion or position. In one way or another they reflect personal belief displaced onto public issues, and everybody has personal beliefs. People can get quite intense about personal beliefs. When that intensity is interjected into political decisions, controversy is boundless and heated. Over the past decade the political arena has been singed by the flames of such issues as abortion, school prayer, flag burning, the death penalty, pornography, the right to die, and affirmative action.

A CLOSER LOOK

Do you read a newspaper on a daily basis? Listen to nightly television news? Are you interested in local political events and issues? Do you read about national and international political events on a regular basis? Did your interest in political events increase as a result of the terrorist attacks of September 11, 2001?

Unlike opinions on moral issues, opinions on political issues are casually held and often mutable. For this reason, politicians are wary of public opinion as a guide in decision making. History tells them that opinions will change with the flow of events and the emergence of new conditions. Also, people often hold inconsistent views with little need to reconcile them. For example, a person may favor equal rights for women (a liberal position) yet also oppose the legalization of marijuana (a conservative position).[50]

Some issues last longer than others. President Carter's decision to boycott the 1980 Olympic Games was a short-term issue. But issues of economic policies, crime, and health care have endured. Other issues included in this book, such as AIDS, education, and immigration, promise to be similarly enduring issues.

LAWYERS AND LOBBYISTS: WHAT COST TO THE ECONOMY?

It is worth commenting on what Jonathan Rauch and others call the parasite economy. What is the parasite economy and who benefits from it? Simply put, lawyers, lobbyists, and politicians are the greatest beneficiaries as billions of dollars are "sucked from the economy that might otherwise be used for productive investment."[51] Only recently have economists begun to examine the relationship of these "parasites" to the nation's productivity. Their research shows that lawyers, lobbyists, and available politicians are costing the United States hundreds of billions of dollars every year—dollars that could produce new wealth for the nation. David N. Lasband, a Clemson University economist, argues that "our economy is absolutely infested with transfer seeking . . . it takes an unbelievable number of forms and absorbs an unbelievable amount of resources."[52]

But how is it that these parasites can suck so many billions of dollars from the economy? What does their activity have to do with the United States' diminishing productivity? Jonathan Rauch offers a thought game to explain. It goes as follows:

> You are the president of Acme Big Flange Co. and you have an additional $1 million to invest. You face stiff competition from mini-flange mills. You want the best available return on your money. What are your options?

First, you can buy a high-speed flange-milling machine or a better inventory control system. Either will improve your company's productivity, but probably not dramatically. Over a decade, you might earn 10–15 percent annually on your investment, maybe $100,000–$150,000 a year. Second, for $1 million you can hire one of the best lobbyists in Washington. The lobbyist might be able to get you a tax break, a subsidy or, best of all, a law putting many mini-flange mills out of business. Any of the above might easily be worth $10 million a year. Query: Which is the better investment? "If I throw in a million here and a million there, I might get a hundred million back," said a Washington lobbyist. "And there are probably enough cases like that so they keep throwing money in."[53]

The lobbyist, of course, was talking about transfer seeking, sometimes called "rent seeking." If you want to make yourself richer, you might invest either in producing more wealth (productive activity) or in getting a portion of someone else's wealth (transfer seeking). From the individual's point of view, the two are equivalent. But from a social point of view, the two are very different.

Each bit of energy we spend taking someone else's wealth is that much less energy spent producing more wealth. If we all spent all our time trying to get our hands into our neighbor's pockets, we'd all be very busy, and yet we'd produce nothing and eventually we would all starve. Thus, transfer seeking, in marked contrast with productive investment, is a negative-sum game.[54]

Rauch offers a second thought game to make the point that the money spent to pursue transfer seeking may cost society twice the original value sought. The problem he presents to us tells a startling tale about the potential waste of the parasite economy:

> You have $100 and I want $100. Question: In principle, how much might I be willing to spend to get your $100? Answer: up to $99. And, in principle, how much might you be willing to spend to keep your $100, once you realize I'm after it? Answer: $99 again. Adding the numbers gives a startling result: In principle, the two of us can rationally consume almost $200 fighting over an existing $100. Yet nothing would be produced.[55]

Finally, Rauch makes the point that parasites, unlike freeloaders, often force their targets to fight back. So if you are challenged in a lawsuit when lobbyists are pushing for laws that affect your industry and politicians may be influenced by those lobbyists, you have little choice but to hire your own lawyer/lobbyist and give monies to those same politicians. It is a curious fact of American life (true in other countries as well, just more prevalent in this country) that there are basically two groups of people who can take your money if you do not fend them off. One group consists of criminals, and we spend billions of dollars every year protecting ourselves from the actions of criminals. The other group includes those who use the law to go after your investment. For these people to use the law to feather their own nests, however, they require either lawyers, lobbyists, or politicians. You, in turn, must then hire your own lawyer or lobbyist to fend off the predator. There is an old joke that makes the point best: in the days of the old

West, there was only one lawyer in the territory. He was quickly going broke. A second lawyer arrived and soon after both became rich.

Why has the parasite economy become so much a problem? After all, lawyers and lobbyists are not new to the political process, nor are they unique to the United States. What is different is the sheer number of lawyers and lobbyists in Washington and elsewhere. Since the 1970s, transfer seeking has been one of the fastest-growing industries in the country. How does the United States compare with its competitors? Our primary competitor, Japan, puts far more of its dollars into research and development (R and D) and far less into personal and corporate lawsuits. In a single year, the number of new admissions to the U.S. bar often exceeds the total number of lawyers in Japan. Stephen Magee, a professor of economics at the University of Texas, plotted the prevalence of lawyers against the economic growth for 28 countries. "The Magee effect is pretty clear: Having more lawyers is associated with lower growth, a result consistent with the hypothesis that where there are a lot of lawyers, people are devoting a greater share of resources to transfer-seeking."[56] Magee also developed a corollary which holds that a nation's economic growth suffers as it increases the number of lawyers in its legislative branch of government.

We do not mean to suggest that an economy does not need lawyers. The question Rauch and others ask is, How many is too many? Furthermore, research has not determined whether lawyers are the cause or merely a symptom of the costly transfer seeking. What we have learned, however, is that we spend a considerable percentage of this country's gross domestic product in court and on Capitol Hill and not on creation of new wealth. In the end, society is worse off, not better, for the flurry of lawmaking and lawsuits.

THE DESIRE FOR A RISK-FREE SOCIETY

One last point. Most people in developed nations, including Americans, seek to make their personal world risk free—or as close to it as they can get. Government is the instrument of risk reduction.[57] Whenever possible, we want government to reduce or shift the risk carried by individuals. In his book *No Risk Society*, Yair Aharoni asserts that we have moved beyond the welfare state to the insurance state.

> The welfare state has turned into an insurance state, as all individuals are protected against a whole array of risks by shifting the burden of their consequences to a larger group or the whole community or simply by eliminating them. . . . We are insured against a variety of mishaps that range from earthquakes and other natural disasters to poor health, unemployment, and the infirmities of old age. Safety in terms of workplace and working hours is regulated; ailing firms are supported; research and development is subsidized by guarantees and grants; quality is controlled, information and social insurance supplied, foreign competition checked, extreme weather conditions and technological changes insured against, and even social status protected.[58]

Some, like Aharoni, argue that the role and size of the federal government should be limited (see Chapter 1). They blame inflation and stagnant economic growth in Western nations on government policies directed toward protecting citizens from a great number of risks. Others decry extensive government taxation, spending, and regulation but warn against the opposite extreme of complete laissez-faire.

HAVE WE GONE TOO FAR?

An increasing number of people are questioning whether we have gone too far. Abounding protections in the new society have led some to feel that they have lost rights as others have gained them. Management is less free to hire and fire workers or make decisions that have an ecological impact. Workers who are risk takers have found their right to take risks for extra compensation reduced through social and regulatory legislation. Young people who would rather spend today than save for tomorrow are constrained from doing so by, among other things, Social Security taxes. There are personal costs to some for protecting women, the elderly, the minorities, and the environment.

Big government, mounting regulations, and ever higher taxes lead some to complain that governments "route too much of income away from productive private uses, . . . high tax rates destroy the rewards of production, and capricious economic policies and tenacious inflation destroy the climate for investment to produce jobs and income."[59]

As with everything, there is a need for balance in discussions of the role of the government in solving today's problems. But all balance requires personal win/loss and a sort of leveling. Some problems are insoluble—a no-risk society is impossible. The question is whether government can selectively reduce risk without also reducing personal latitude for success and failure, across the board. However, democratic politics is wide open to the human desire for protection, if not for advantage. Selective risk reduction is a political choice made for political as well as personal ends.

THE ISSUES REMAIN THE SAME—ONLY MORE INTRACTABLE

Except for the war on terrorism, the public agenda has not changed significantly since the fourth edition of this book in 1998. The United States remains a debtor nation. We continue to suffer a balance-of-trade deficit. Our national debt just surpassed $6 trillion dollars—an increase of $1 trillion since 1998. After former President Clinton managed in his second term to create budget surpluses, the Bush administration has returned the federal government to deficit spending. Personal debt and the lack of job security remain grave concerns for most Americans.

Americans remain concerned about crime—especially violent crime—and prisons are more crowded than ever. We must either build more prisons fast or release inmates. But prisons cost money, and everybody wants them built in some-body else's backyard. Health care coverage remains elusive for many, and health care costs are still rising—even in the age of managed care. We have added a chapter on the war on terrorism to this edition of *The Public Agenda,* in the wake of the tragic events of September 11, 2001. Questions and concerns about civil liberties and rights as they relate to homeland security are also discussed.

The public agenda is not the only thing unchanged. There is still little agreement among the experts as to the best solutions to the problems. What is more clear than ever are the costs—the trade-offs—that are attached to every proposed cure to every public illness.

NOTES

1. Lawrence Brewster, *The Public Agenda,* 2nd ed. (New York: St. Martin's Press: 1987), 1.
2. Steven Greenhouse, "Unease Marks Labor Day '02," *San Jose Mercury News,* September 2, 2002, A2.
3. Ibid., B7.
4. Ibid., B7.
5. Ibid., A2.
6. Ben Torres, "Decline in Estimated Tax Revenues for 2002," *San Francisco Chronicle,* August 28, 2002, A3.
7. Ibid., A3.
8. Jill Lawrence, "Poll Shows USA's Mood Has Changed, but Not Lives," *USA Today,* September 6, 2002, 2A.
9. *San Francisco Chronicle,* September 15, 2002, A3.
10. Elizabeth Shogren, "The Patriot Act Enacted into Law," *San Francisco Chronicle,* June 23, 2002, A5.
11. Josh Meyer and Elizabeth Shogren, "Terror Inquiry Ruling Disputed," *Los Angeles Times,* August 24, 2002, A1.
12. Adam Liptak, Neil A. Lewis, and Benjamin Weiser, "U.S. Courts Weigh Liberty, Security," *San Francisco Chronicle,* August 4, 2002, A18.
13. Byron York, "Bush's Nagging Problem," *National Review Online,* November 7, 2001, http://www.nationalreview.com/york/york110701.shtml, 1.
14. Ibid., 1.
15. Ibid., 2.
16. Jill Leonhardt, "New Child Poverty Numbers Show U.S. Lag Other Wealthy Nations," February 22, 2001, http://www.maxwell.syr.edu/news/releases/child_poverty.htm, 1.
17. Ibid.
18. *San Francisco Chronicle,* January 10, 1997, A11.
19. From an interview in the *Los Angeles Times,* September 15, 1991.
20. Michael Mandel, *The High Risk Society: Peril and Promise in the New Economy* (New York: Random House, 1996), 3.
21. Ibid., 3.
22. Ibid., 3–4.
23. Ibid., book jacket.
24. Ibid.
25. Brewster, *The Public Agenda,* 1.

26. PEW Research Center, "Voter Anxiety Dividing GOP; Energized Democrats Backing Clinton," 1997, http://www.people-press.org.

27. Ibid.

28. *San Francisco Chronicle,* April 5, 1992, A3.

29. Ibid.

30. Ibid.

31. Linda Perlstein, *Washington Post,* January 15, 1996, A23.

32. *San Francisco Chronicle,* April 5, A3.

33. Carnegie Endowment National Commission, *Changing Our Ways* (1992), 8.

34. James Morone, *The Democratic Wish* (New York: Basic Books, 1990).

35. Ibid.

36. Ibid.

37. Robert A. Leone, *Who Profits: Winners, Losers and Government Regulation* (New York: Basic Books, 1986), 3.

38. Ibid., 3.

39. Ibid., 4.

40. James Q. Wilson, ed., *The Politics of Regulation* (New York: Basic Books, 1980).

41. See, for example, Sharm Oster, "The Strategic Use of Regulatory Investment by Industry Sub-Groups," *Economic Inquiry,* October 1982, 604–18.

42. For an excellent discussion of this problem in American society, see Lester C. Thurow, *The Zero-Sum Society* (New York: Basic Books, 1980).

43. The PEW Research Center, "Post 9-11 Attitudes: Religion More Prominent, Muslim-Americans More Accepted," The PEW Forum on Religion and Public Life, December 6, 2001, http://www.pewforum.org., 1.

44. The PEW Research Center, "Religion in Politics," September 2, 2000, http://pewforum.org/issues/display.php?IssueID=6.

45. The PEW Research Center, "Religion and Politics: The Ambivalent Majority," September 20, 2000, http://people-press.org/reports/display.php3?ReportID=32, 1.

46. Ibid.

47. The PEW Research Center, "The Diminishing Divide . . . American Churches, American Politics," January 7, 1997, http://www.people-press.org.

48. Ibid.

49. Ibid.

50. See Lloyd Free and Hadley Cantril, *Political Beliefs of Americans* (New York: Simon & Schuster, 1968).

51. Jonathan Rauch, "The Parasite Economy," *National Journal,* no. 17, April 25, 1992, 980.

52. Ibid.

53. Ibid.

54. Ibid.

55. Ibid.

56. Ibid., 984.

57. See Yair Aharoni, *The No-Risk Society* (Clatham, NJ: Chatham House, 1981).

58. Ibid., 1–2.

59. Editorial, *Wall Street Journal,* September 7, 1977.

One ∽

THE POLITICAL ECONOMY

What important economic issues does the current administration confront?
What economic issues face the United States in the future—how are we tied
to the futures of the rest of the world?

T he world has become a global marketplace, a place where an event in one area affects those elsewhere. A place where the closing of the stock market in Tokyo is eagerly watched by Americans waiting to see how the market will go in New York. From the cold war we have moved to a global marketplace where the battle lines have been redrawn and the nature of the game has changed. Old enemies, such as Vietnam, represent potential trade partners. What matters in today's world is a nation's economic competitiveness, not its military strength. In this new economy, the United States has many near-equals. The old allegiances based on the United States versus the Soviet Union and the "client states" of each are ever shifting. We have no dependable allies—we have trading partner/competitors instead.

The United States emerged from World War II as the world's only economic superpower. U.S. industry supplied the rest of the world with agricultural products, automobiles, chemicals, and a host of other products. U.S. multinational corporations invested abroad and spread modern technologies to other countries, making them more productive. These other countries also have helped to supply us with products such as oil from the Middle East; radios, televisions, and clothing from the Far East; and so on.

Today we are the world's only military superpower, but not so in economic terms. (See Table 1.1 for comparisons of per-capita gross domestic product among countries.) As Europe and Japan recovered from the devastation of World War II, their basic industries reemerged stronger than ever. More recently, the rates of economic growth of the industrialized countries of Western Europe, the United States, and Japan have been outpaced by newly industrialized countries such as the so-called Four Tigers (Taiwan, the Republic of Korea, Singapore, and Hong Kong) (see Figure 1.1). Besides the Tigers are Sudan, Vietnam, Ireland, Uganda, and Malaysia—each experiencing unprecedented economic growth. And of course, future superpower status will be granted to the biggest giant of all—China.

The net effect of all these developments has been an economic transformation that has profoundly touched Americans and, for that matter, the entire globe. Traditionally strong U.S. industries are now confronted with intense competition from foreign producers. Americans also have been forced since the days of Vietnam to

TABLE 1.1
Countries Rank-Ordered by Per-Capita Gross Domestic Product (GDP), 2000

Ranking	Country	GDP (in US$)
1	Bermuda	$44,060
2	Luxembourg	43,372
3	Japan	37,494
4	Norway	36,198
5	**United States**	**34,637**
6	Liechtenstein	33,394
6	Switzerland	33,394
8	Iceland	30,681
9	Denmark	30,141
10	Moldavia	29,100
10	Qatar	29,100
12	Sweden	25,903
13	Ireland	25,066
14	United Kingdom	24,058
15	China, Hong Kong SAR	23,709
16	Finland	23,377
17	Austria	23,357
18	Netherlands	23,294
19	Singapore	22,959
20	Canada	22,778
21	Germany	22,753
22	Belgium	22,323
23	Monaco	21,848
24	France	21,848
25	United Arab Emirates	20,457
26	Australia	20,298

Source: United Nations, Statistics Division, Indicators on Income and Economy Activity, 2002,
http://unstats.un.org/unsd/demographic/social/inc-eco.htm.

pay fair market value for scarce resources such as oil. The world economy has become truly international, however, and a great many countries have enjoyed increased prosperity. In this truly global economy, the United States faces serious problems, including trade imbalances and extensive foreign borrowing.

Trade imbalances create economic conflicts that threaten to erupt into trade wars—as has occurred between the United States and Japan. Japanese exports to the United States have soared in recent years, while U.S. exports to Japan have fallen. The United States has asserted that the Japanese must remove their barriers to foreign imports or face U.S. restrictions on their own exports. In return, the Japanese claim they have made considerable progress in opening their economy

FIGURE 1.1
Countries with Largest Economic Growth (over 5 percent), 1990–2000

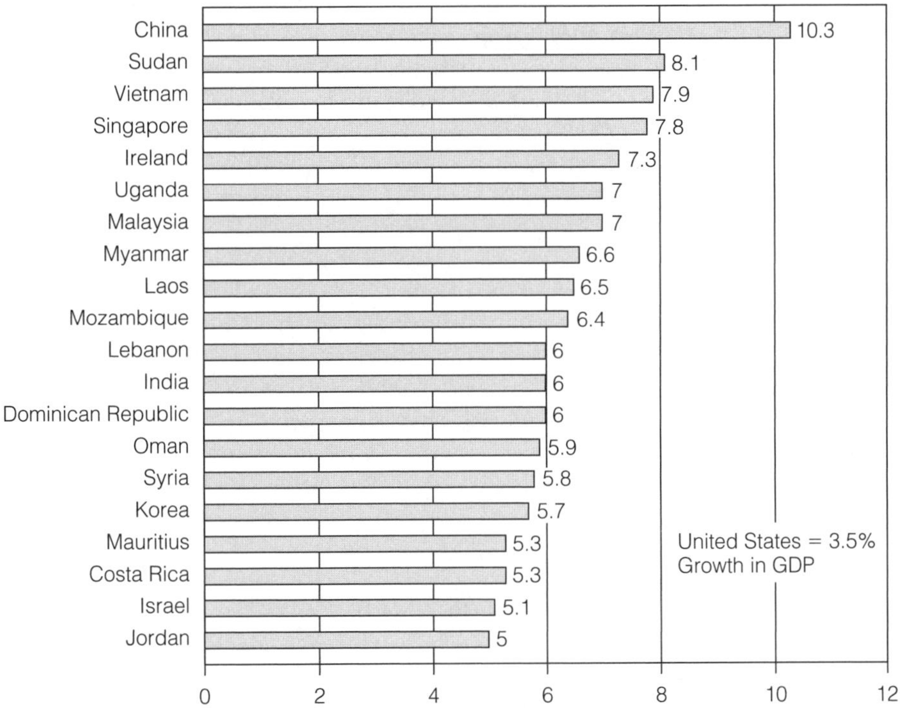

Country	Growth
China	10.3
Sudan	8.1
Vietnam	7.9
Singapore	7.8
Ireland	7.3
Uganda	7
Malaysia	7
Myanmar	6.6
Laos	6.5
Mozambique	6.4
Lebanon	6
India	6
Dominican Republic	6
Oman	5.9
Syria	5.8
Korea	5.7
Mauritius	5.3
Costa Rica	5.3
Israel	5.1
Jordan	5

United States = 3.5%
Growth in GDP

Source: World Bank, Table 4.1: Growth of Output: World Development Indicators, 2002, http://www.worldbank.org/data/wdi2002/tables/table4-1.pdf.

to foreign products and complain that the United States itself is responsible for much of the problem. In the case of China, the United States has attempted to tie trade to human rights issues. The Chinese understand that the United States can ill afford to jeopardize its trade relations with the world's largest potential market. In the end, it may be the Chinese who dictate policy to the United States. In the words of John Naisbitt, "America's moralizing may come back to haunt it. Down the road imagine a big, economically powerful China threatening to withhold Most Favored Nation status from the United States unless it does something about the slums in our big urban centers (or improves its SAT scores!)."[1]

As the world moves toward freer markets and trade—the trend of the 1990s and beyond to this new century—it is likely that the West (and, in particular, the United States) will no longer dictate the rules of the game. John Naisbitt makes this case when he writes, "Until the 1990s everything revolved around the West. The West set the rules. Japan abided by these rules during its economic emergence. But now Asians—the rest of Asia—are creating their own rules and will soon determine the game as well. Even Japan will be left behind as the countries of Southeast Asia, led by China and the Overseas Chinese, increasingly hold economic sway."[2] Clearly, this is true and becoming even more true as African nations also begin to grow and develop at the same rates as many Asian countries.

The United States also is vulnerable as a result of its extensive foreign borrowing. Beginning in early 1985, the United States became a debtor nation for the first time since World War I. What this means is that the United States owes more money to other nations than they owe to us. In the 19th century the United States was a net debtor, but the nation was in its early stages of economic development. It was appropriate then for the United States to borrow from other nations to pay for its new railroads and factories. The heavy borrowing during the 1980s was to support our military buildup and to sustain a higher standard of living during a time of slower economic growth. Unfortunately, the standard of living for future Americans was threatened as a result of decades of heavy borrowing.

These are examples of the kinds of economic and international problems that Americans face and that are considered in this chapter. We live in a time and in a society of high risk. Michael Mandel writes in his popular book, *The High Risk Society,* "Economic insecurity has become a fact of life for every worker, and every business."[3]

WHAT FACTORS SHAPE THE AMERICAN ECONOMY?

After experiencing an extended period of economic growth during the 1990s, the American economy is once more (in the early 2000s) a source of concern for many Americans even though unemployment is below 6 percent (5.8 percent in March 2003[4]) and inflation has remained below 3 percent since 1994 and, in 2002, was at a very low 1.6 percent.[5] This 1990s pattern of inflation is the best record since the early 1960s (see Figure 1.2 for historical inflation rates). However, one year after the U.S. response to the September 11, 2001, terrorist attacks (October 7, 2002), the stock market declined 18.61 percent, and the country was clearly in a recession that had begun in March 2001.[6] Add to that a growing series of scandals, corporate controversies, and corporate bankruptcies, and it is not difficult to see that American consumers had lost confidence in the American economy. In an effort to stem the tide, the Federal Reserve Board steadily reduced the federal funds rate (on November 6, 2002, it was reduced to an incredible 1.25 percent, a forty-year low), but the effect of this action remains to be seen. In addition, although the federal budget deficit was reduced and a surplus created during the Clinton administration, the effects of an enormous Bush tax cut, the September 11, 2001, terrorist attacks, and the subsequent wars in Afghanistan and Iraq were to erase the surplus and create a budget deficit once more (going from a $127 billion surplus in fiscal year 2001, to an estimated $314 billion deficit in fiscal year 2002, billions more in the red after the reconstruction of Iraq).[7] In November 2002 the signs were mixed about whether the economy was improving and that the country was moving out of the recession. However, a March 2002

FIGURE 1.2
Historical U.S. Inflation Rates, 1960–1999

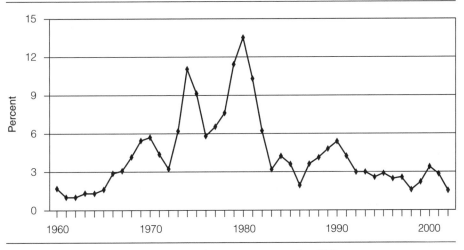

Source: Financial Trend Forecaster, Historical Consumer Price Index, 2002,
http://www.fintrend.com/ftf/html/historical.asp.

ABC poll indicated that only 37 percent of consumers felt that the economy was in good shape at that time, although confidence seemed to be holding steady.[8]

Today, the real challenge is to restore investor and consumer confidence in corporate America and in the American stock market and economy and manage the federal budget so that it does not grow out of control once more.

There are considerable data to support the proposition that the United States is becoming a nation of the super-rich and the poor, with a rapidly decreasing middle class. And while there was job growth during the Clinton administration, too many of those jobs were low paying or part-time and in the service sector. The traditional manufacturing jobs once held by working-middle-class workers are disappearing. Young people despair that they will not enjoy the American dream of home ownership. A great many working-class families have maxed out their credit cards—more than $1 trillion is owed on credit cards in this country.

A CLOSER LOOK

Do you know of anyone who has lost his or her job—or savings or retirement plan—due to the recession and decline in the stock market? What are they having to do to cope with this downturn? Is the current economic situation affecting you? How, and how are you coping with it?

We see around us every day people living on the streets and in poverty—including countless children. It is little wonder that so many Americans worry about their own and their children's futures.

INDICATORS OF A HEALTHY ECONOMY?

According to Paul Krugman, the best measures of a healthy economy are "productivity, income distribution, and employment." "If these things are satisfactory," he says, "not much else can go wrong, while if they are not, nothing can go right."[9] How healthy is the U.S. economy? At least in terms of these three indicators, the U.S. economy is a source of concern in 2002. As just pointed out, while the overall unemployment picture improved during Clinton's first term, the number of people in low-paying or part-time jobs remains high compared with America's golden years in the 1950s and 1960s. And those employed feel less secure in their jobs than in previous decades.

Unemployment

As President Bush came into office after the disputed election of 2000, the U.S. economic forecast was very positive but changed rapidly after that, when the country entered into a recession. One thing that changed was the increase in unemployment, trending up to 5.8 percent in 2001, down to 4.8 in August 2002, and back up to 5.8 in March 2003 (see Figure 1.3). The economic expansion that was expected to continue past the turn of the century did not trickle down to those whose wages remain stagnant and who remain unemployed or underemployed.

For those who still had jobs, there was some encouraging news about wages. After years of lagging purchasing power, average hourly earnings had grown to $16.23 in August 2001[10] (a 3.7 percent increase from 2000). This level fluctuated depending on whether the employment was full- or part-time, union or not, and private sector or government and by region.

One important reason for an overall downward pressure on wages (largely due to inflationary pressures over the years) is a decline in labor union membership and influence. From highs in 1945 and 1954 of 35 percent union membership across the country, the percentage of total workers belonging to unions fell to 13.5 percent in 2001. However, this level differs enormously by sector of the economy. In the private nonagriculture sector, less than 10 percent belong to unions but in the public sector, the number has increased to 37 percent and is increasing.[11] One reason for this decline in private sector membership is the decline in the very industries where unions tended to be dominant—in the manufacturing sector.

The fact that the standard of living for most Americans—the middle class in particular—has fallen steadily since the early 1970s has been largely hidden in everyday life by the growing number of women working part- and full-time. By October 2002, for example, the share of women older than twenty at work—57.8 percent—was holding steady at the highest rates since the government be-

FIGURE 1.3
Historical U.S. Unemployment Rates, 1990–2001

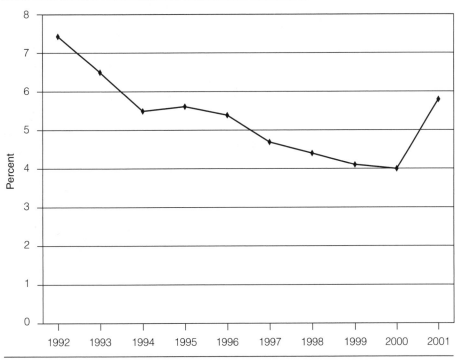

Source: U.S. Department of Commerce, Bureau of Labor Statistics, Table A-9: Unemployed Persons by Sex and Age, Seasonally Adjusted, 2002, http://www.bls.gov/webapps/legacy/cpsatab9.html.

gan keeping records in 1970.[12] This meant that in most cases the family income remained steady, but we then had "latch-key" kids, parents out of touch with their kids, and the beginning of "quality time." Since there no longer was "quantity," 15 minutes of quality time had to suffice for many middle-class parents (mothers really). The concept of quality time (applied to children and to couples) helped to justify a profound change in middle-class lifestyles.

Income Distribution

In the two decades following World War II, most American families could expect their incomes to grow from one year to the next. The median family income (adjusted for inflation) rose about a third during the 1950s and 1960s. Since most people's incomes were growing at a rapid pace, very few cared about the inequalities of wealth. After all, the rising tide of wealth in this country raised everyone's boats—rowboats and yachts alike.

This has not been true since the early 1970s, however. Even the go-go years of the 1980s did not offer everyone a piece of the action. These were party years

FIGURE 1.4
Share of Aggregate Household Income Held by Each Fifth of the Population, 1967–2001

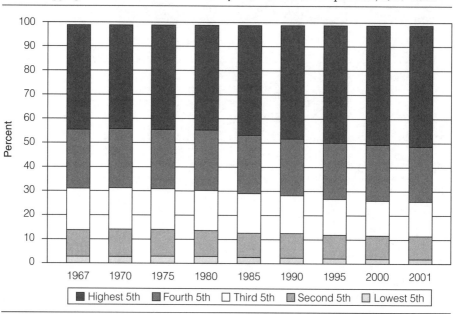

Source: U.S. Census Bureau, Table H-2: Historical Income Tables—Households, 2002, http://www.census.gov/hhes/income/histinc/h02.html.

only for those at the very top of the wealth distribution. While those in the fast lane enjoyed large increases in wealth during the 1980s and 1990s, the wealth of the rest of the population did not simply grow more slowly; it actually fell.

In 2001 the median household income was $42,228, but even over the next two years, there was a 1.5 percent real decline in the household median income due to inflation.[13] However, during the expansion of the 1990s, American prosperity was extremely uneven. Those at the top of the economic ladder enjoyed rising incomes. Families in the middle saw their incomes stagnate or slip. Young families and workers at the bottom suffered. And even though the nation was in the midst of a robust expansion, recent census statistics offer no hint that the trend toward wider inequality was slowing. Using aggregate household income, Figure 1.4 clearly illustrates that the top fifth of U.S. households earned more and more of the total income over these three and a half decades, ending up in 2001 earning more than 50 percent of households.

While the percentage of U.S. income received by the top 5 percent increased every year, poverty rates stayed relatively stable over the past decade, only slightly declining from 2000 to 2001 (and this can be attributed mostly to a difference in statistical techniques). The good news is that women's incomes have improved somewhat as discrimination has ebbed; today women earn 76 percent of what men earn, up from 63 percent in 1976.[14] As we have said, one way American fam-

FIGURE 1.5
Percent of Home Ownership by Region of Country, Third Quarter 2002

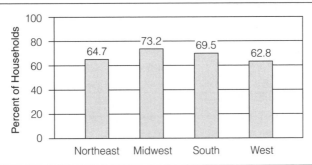

Source: National Center for Policy Analysis, Daily Policy Digest: Household Debt Levels Reach Scary Peak, October 2002, http://www.ncpa.org/iss/eco/2002/pd100902b.html.

ilies have compensated for their eroding purchasing power and standard of living is to have both parents work. Another way a great many American families managed to maintain their lifestyles while experiencing shrinking incomes was to go deeply into debt. The National Center for Policy Analysis reports that the debt for those in the top fifth of American households was actually 120 percent of their disposable income in 2002, an increase of 100 percent from 1995. The debt for those at other income levels also grew but at a slower pace and only to 80 percent of disposable income. Federal Reserve Bank data indicate that consumer debt has, surprisingly, held constant since 1980 (it was 7.84 percent during the second quarter of 2002), while mortgage debt has increased over time (6.20 percent in 2002 as compared to 4.38 percent in 1980).[15] Already, homeownership levels differ enormously according to the region of the country (see Figure 1.5), and with increasing debt levels and increased interest rates, these rates could be forced downward. While interest rates are low and incomes rising, this level of debt can be managed. But once interest rates increase, many households could find this very difficult to handle.[16]

Rate of Productivity

Unfortunately the recent track record for the United States on productivity growth is not good. In fact, productivity in the private sector has been steadily declining since the 1970s (see Figure 1.6). Paul Krugman wrote, "Productivity isn't everything, but in the long run it is almost everything. A country's ability to improve its standard of living over time depends almost entirely on its ability to raise its output per worker."[17] Krugman points out that veterans of World War II "came home to an economy that doubled its productivity over the next twenty-five years."[18] The increased productivity led to a substantially higher standard of living than that experienced by their forebears. Veterans of the Vietnam War, in contrast, returned home to an economy that increased its productivity less than 10 percent in 15 years.

FIGURE 1.6
U.S. Productivity in the Private Business Sector, 1948–2001

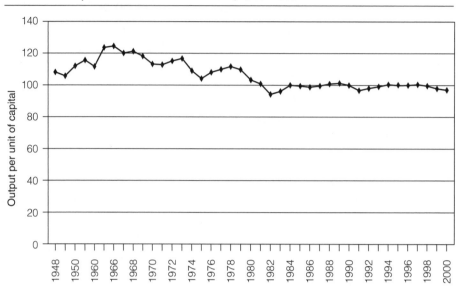

Source: U.S. Department of Commerce, Bureau of Labor Statistics, Multifactor Productivity Trends,
Table 1: Private Business Sector: Productivity and Related Indexes, 1948–2000, 2002,
http://www.bls.gov/news.release/prod3.t01.htm.

So people of the post-Vietnam era lived no better, and often worse, than did their
parents. Steven Rattner observes that "between 1973 and 1991 productivity rose
by less than one percent a year and approximately two percent annually since
1993. By contrast, productivity grew by more than three percent a year between
1947 and 1973."[19]

Today's Economy

Frank Levy, in his book *Dollars and Dreams,* suggests that Americans can divide their economic lives into two distinct periods following World War II. The
first ran from the end of World War II through 1973. During this time, inflation-
adjusted wages—for example, the average weekly earnings of all forty-year-old
men—grew by 2.5 to 3 percent per year. It was a 27-year boom. The second period extended from 1973 through at least 1985. Over this period inflation-adjusted
wages have stagnated and, in many cases, declined. This stagnation has led to a
kind of quiet depression that is responsible for many of our current problems.[20]

From our vantage point, we can see that another period extended beyond
1985 (when Levy wrote his book) to the mid-1990s. The nation had an even larger
"mountain of financial debt" and an ongoing addiction to imports and foreign
capital, as described by Levy. That economic and budgetary crisis was resolved
without fully determining whether it was the result of a fundamental structural
problem or merely represented an "episode of stagnation," as happens periodi-

cally in capitalistic economies. The Clinton administration argued, for example, that many of our problems were caused by structural flaws in the economy. The most daunting of the structural problems was the federal debt and annual deficits. The rising cost for health care was another.

Elected in a disputed election in 2000, the George W. Bush administration's Economic Security Agenda is full. The agenda

Increases trade to create better jobs and open vast new markets to create better jobs and open vast new markets to American products and services;

Makes tax cuts permanent to spur the business investment that creates new jobs;

Removes the barriers to job creation for small businesses that hire the majority of new workers in America;

Controls unnecessary government spending and regulation to return to budget surpluses and increase private investment;

Insists on corporate responsibility to bolster consumer and investor confidence and protect workers' jobs, pensions and retirement;

Puts in place terrorism insurance provisions that will allow major job-creating construction projects to go forward; and

Implements a comprehensive national energy policy that will create thousands of new American jobs and reduce our dependence on foreign oil.[21]

President Bush signed the Economic Growth and Tax Relief Act of 2001, one of the cornerstones of his presidential campaign, on June 7, 2001. The act provided tax rebates of up to $300 for singles, $500 for heads of household, and $600 for married couples, along with a tax rate cut, marriage relief, repeal of the estate tax in 2010, and other tax relief provisions.

After the tax cut was implemented, President Bush and the country were given an enormous challenge with the terrorist attacks of 2001 and subsequent wars in Afghanistan and Iraq. The budget deficits grew again, economic growth slowed, the country moved into a recession, and the stock market started a rapid decline. When the WorldCom, Enron, and other corporate scandals emerged, consumer confidence declined further and the recession moved into its second year.

Economists say that the country moved into a recession (commonly considered two consecutive quarters of a decline in economic growth) in March 2001, after ten years of the longest uninterrupted economic expansion in American history. It is unclear what precipitated this downturn—the Bush tax cut, the to-be-expected downturn in the regular business cycle, or some other factor. What is clear, the National Bureau of Economic Research believes, is that the recession grew after the September 11, 2001, terrorist attacks and the resulting short-term shutdown of the economy and long-term effects on the airlines and other industries.[22]

In 2002 the stock market declined for the third year in a row, this time by 23 percent, equivalent to a loss of a staggering $3.4 trillion dollars in wealth. September 2002 alone saw an enormous 12.25 percent loss in the Dow Jones Industrial average.[23] See Table 1.2. The collapse of the dot-com industry led the way

TABLE 1.2
Changes in Dow Jones Average Statistics, September 30, 2002

| Index | September 2002 | Year to Date | 2001 | Annualized | | | |
				1 Year	3 Years	5 Years	10 Years
Industrial Average	−12.25	−23.15	−5.44	−12.52	−8.27	0.77	11.07
Transportation Average	−4.9	−17.82	−9.3	−0.86	−8.42	−6.01	7.78
Utility Average	−11.07	−24.39	−26.27	−25.58	−6.93	1.69	8.46

Source: Dow Jones Company, Dow Jones Averages Statistics, 2002, http://www.djindexes.com/jsp/avgStatistics.jsp.

but was soon joined by numerous traditional and blue-chip stock companies post-ing losses and laying off employees. At the beginning of November, companies from United Airlines to McDonalds announced lower-than-expected earnings, and layoffs. Enormous numbers of citizens have seen their retirement plans and sav-ings go up in smoke in the massive stock market losses seen to date. The biggest bright light to date: the October 2002 record of four straight weeks with the mar-ket posting gains once again seemed to suggest that a turnaround was in order. After October 2002 the market improved then went back down again and was largely unstable.

In the midst of these economic troubles, a new scandal and market disruption occurred—the accounting scandals of Enron, a large natural gas and oil company formed in 1985 and 1986, with ties to President Bush (a close friend of Kenneth Lay, Enron's chief executive officer) and many of his administration's officials (in-cluding Vice President Cheney). Enron had created partnerships within its own or-ganization and had moved its monetary losses to those partnerships rather than having them appear on Enron's financial statements. This made it appear that En-ron was not losing money but was in fact growing enormously and making enor-mous profits (see Table 1.3 for a timeline of the scandal). The scandal ended with criminal charges filed against individuals, criminal investigations of Enron itself, and Enron's auditing firm, Arthur Andersen, being found guilty of obstruction of justice and attempting to reduce its role (as the auditing firm involved, Arthur An-dersen should have found the discrepancies and reported them in the financial statements).

Then, in 2002, WorldCom, the largest telecommunications provider in the world, announced that it was being investigated for securities fraud for manipu-lating its accounting practices and records. In July 2002, it announced it was de-claring bankruptcy, the largest in the world to date, due to the accounting scan-dal and subsequent losses.

When faced with these corporate criminal misdeeds, consumer mistrust peaks while the stock market declines. As CNN reported,

> The corporate criminals among us, the swindlers and profiteers, are now described in language once saved for bin Laden's legions. Business pro-fessors are staggered by the suicidal audacity of top executives—did they really think they would not be caught?—and marvel at the damage done. "It's as if we have given the CEOs weapons of mass destruction—at least

TABLE 1.3
Timeline of the Enron Scandal

Year	Event
1985–1986	Kenneth Lay, chairman and CEO of Houston Natural Gas, arranges for merger between two natural gas companies. Newly merged company is renamed Enron. Does both gas and oil.
1987	Enron Oil starts losing money, but real amount of losses is not revealed until 1993. Two top Enron officials plead guilty to conspiracy to defraud and filing false tax returns.
1988	Enron enters U.S. energy market and later enters futures and natural gas trade.
1991	Andrew Fastow is hired and the first off-balance-sheet partnerships are created, which are later used to hide losses and make it appear that Enron is growing faster than in reality.
1992	Enron expands worldwide and creates more businesses for selling and transporting gas. Deregulation of gas and oil in the U.S. continues, opening up more opportunities.
1994	Enron begins trading electricity and soon becomes the largest U.S. marketer of electricity.
1995	Enron expands into Europe, soon becoming major player in Britain and Western Europe.
1996	Deregulation of electricity in the U.S. continues—wholesale power transmission of electricity continues virtually without government regulation. Jeffrey Skilling becomes president and chief operating officer of Enron under Kenneth Lay.
1997	Enron continues to expand, creating more off-balance-sheet partnerships.
1999	New Houston Astros ballpark is named Enron Field. Enron enters telecommunications field, investing in broadband communications and trading bandwidth capacity. Chief Financial Officer Fastow is appointed general partner of LJM partnerships, which become company where Enron puts losing enterprises, shielding them from the rest of Enron.
2000	Enron named "Most Innovative Company in America" by *Fortune* for the fifth year in a row. Enron creates first Raptor partnership—one of several to hide $1 billion in losses. Enron's stock hits all-time high of $90 per share, and revenue is over $100 billion, making it the seventh largest company in the Fortune 500. Enron tries to sell off international assets to raise cash to cover losses. Enron uses complicated accounting strategies in order to avoid stating its losses. 80% of Enron earnings are actually due to questionable deals from controversial partnerships.
2001	Skilling becomes CEO but resigns in August; Lay remains as chairman, then CEO again. Broadband deal collapses, but Enron declares profit from it anyway. Stock price begins to decline as insiders and outsiders start to question company practices. September: Arthur Andersen, Enron's auditor, requires Enron to reverse aggressive accounting practices, causing $1.2 billion in paper losses. October: Securities and Exchange Commission starts to investigate Enron's partnerships; Enron changes 401(k) administrators, preventing employees from selling stock. Investigations continue while Enron draws on billion-dollar credit line and stock drops. December: its stock worthless, Enron declares Chapter 11 bankruptcy.

(Continued)

TABLE 1.3 (Continued)

Year	Event
2002	Criminal investigation begins. Kenneth Lay resigns, Vice Chair Cliff Baxter commits suicide, Fastow is fired and charged with criminal fraud. Arthur Andersen officials plead the Fifth Amendment when called to testify about judgement. Arthur Andersen found guilty of obstruction of justice for shredding documents.

Source: Peter C. Fusaro and Ross M. Miller, *What Went Wrong at Enron: Everyone's Guide to the Largest Bankruptcy in U.S. History,* New York: John Wiley, 2002.

economically," says accounting professor Brian Shapiro at the University of Minnesota. "The companies they run are bigger than ever. When something happens, thousands can lose their jobs—and more people than ever are invested in them. So a few can do a lot of damage."[24]

The results of the Enron and WorldCom accounting scandals are far-reaching. Not only have consumers' and investors' stock portfolios declined enormously due to both declining stock prices and the forced restatement of many companies' profits and losses, but the accounting industry itself is under scrutiny. Formerly self-regulated, accounting firms are now facing congressional attempts to reform, monitor, and regulate the way that they view and work with the companies they audit. Clearly, the damage to confidence and to the economy is deep.
"And," CNN reports,

> that damage may be lasting. A new *Time*/CNN poll finds that fewer than one-third of Americans expect the economy to improve in the next year. It is not just that we have confronted in WorldCom the worst case of fraud in U.S. corporate history; today the bluest of chips, from Merck to General Electric, are being challenged about their bookkeeping. The perception of deception is so widespread, the stakes so high and the costs so great that investors are choosing to forfeit a game they now think is rigged. The markets skidded last week straight past their 9/11 lows into the most bearish forests in a generation. The dollar sank ever lower, and the Dow dropped through 9,000 toward a 7.4% loss for one week alone. Financial planners say many people won't open their 401(k) statements; they just can't look. But as we wait in the dark, a new reality takes hold, that our lives this year are being reshaped by enemies both foreign and domestic, and while the public did unite behind its leaders in the face of the terrorist threat, we have less faith that they can protect us against the villains we planted and watered in our own backyards.[25]

Whatever the future may bring, public opinion polls report that Americans have lowered their expectations considerably. Many of us no longer expect the economy to deliver steadily rising standards of living so children will live more prosperous lives than their parents. Lowered expectations are not the traditional American attitude. The United States has always been the land of opportunity, and the good life was always assured.

It is more true today than ever before that Americans need to better understand the economy and its relationship to the political process—as well as the role that all participants play in the process, including the accountants and auditors. Since the economic system is so complex, it is tempting to leave the decisions to the experts. After all, with their fancy computer models and statistics, most economists give the impression that they know how to fix what is wrong. Even when they can offer solutions to economic problems, political expediency takes precedence over purely technical decisions.

The U.S. economy is not an engine to be correctly tuned by master technicians following a service manual. There are many different ways, but no single correct way, of solving economic problems. Through the political process, we set our priorities and determine the particular solutions we shall use. A professional economist could show that production is exceeding demand and suggest a tax cut as a solution. However, the severity of this economic problem and the question of who will get the benefit of a tax reduction are political, not technical matters. We learned in the introduction to this book that all economic decisions have costs. A tolerable cost for one person may be a disaster for another. Such a dilemma poses a political question, not an economic one.

A meaningful discussion of the political economy and how to improve a nation's economic health and performance requires an understanding of some basic concepts and tools of macroeconomics—the branch of economics that studies the national economy. The definitions and explanations of these concepts and tools follow.

THE LANGUAGE OF MACROECONOMICS

Aggregate Supply and Demand

When talking about macroeconomics, it is important to think in terms of aggregate supply and aggregate demand rather than the supply and demand of microeconomic theory. Aggregate supply is the total of all goods and services produced in an economy, subtracting exports and adding imports. Aggregate supply will increase as the labor force grows, as industry invests in new plants and equipment, as the government invests in the nation's infrastructure, and as human knowledge is advanced. Keynesian economists believe that a nation's total output or aggregate supply is determined by aggregate demand. Aggregate demand is the total spending by consumers, businesses, and government. Problems arise in a national economy when aggregate demand and aggregate supply are not balanced.

Inflation

No subject is as much discussed and as little understood as inflation. What we call "inflation" is primarily caused by an increase in the supply of money and credit. It is sometimes defined as the undue expansion (or increase) of a country's currency, especially by issuing paper money not redeemable in specie.

A CLOSER LOOK

How is inflation affecting you? What do you buy today that is more expensive than when you bought it one year ago? Is your tuition being affected by inflation? If so, how?

In recent years, however, the term has come to be used in a radically different sense. This is recognized by this more common definition: "A substantial rise of prices caused by an undue expansion in *paper money* or *bank credit*"[26] (emphasis added). Obviously a rise of prices caused by an expansion of the money supply is not the same thing as the expansion of the money supply itself. The use of the word *inflation* with these two quite different meanings leads to endless confusion.

Inflation originally applied solely to the quantity of money. It meant that the volume of money was inflated, blown up, overextended. However, because inflation is now so commonly used to mean a rise in prices, it would be difficult and time-consuming here to keep avoiding or refuting it on every occasion. The word has almost universally been used ambiguously. Sometimes it is used in the first sense—to mean an increase in money stock—but much more often it is used in the second sense—to mean a rise in prices.

Inflation has raised its ugly head at various times in history. The most serious case in recent years was in the wake of the quadrupling of oil prices in 1973, when annual inflation rates in the developed world rose as high as 25 percent. A crucial feature of inflation is that increases in prices must be sustained. A once-only increase in the rate of value-added tax (a common means of raising government revenues today) will immediately push prices up, but this does not represent inflation.

Economists argue that there are several possible causes of inflation. Demand-pull inflation, or excess demand in the economy, is the most popular explanation. Another possible cause of inflation is cost-push inflation, or higher costs for goods and services. A third cause of inflation is monetarism, or excessive increases in the money supply. These causes often amount to the same thing. For example, an increase in the supply of money leads to excess demand—thus creating inflation. The demand-pull and cost-push theories also are linked. An excess of demand causes producers to raise their prices—but this leads workers to demand higher wages to maintain their living standard; this causes higher demand, and the process begins again.

It is often argued that to attribute inflation solely to an increase in the volume of money is oversimplification. This is true. Many qualifications have to be kept in mind. For example, the money supply must be thought of as including not only the supply of hand-to-hand currency but also the supply of bank credit—especially in the United States, where most payments are done by check.

It is also an oversimplification to say that the value of an individual dollar depends simply on the present supply of dollars outstanding. The value of a dollar also depends on the expected future supply of dollars. If most people fear, for example, that the supply is going to be even greater a year from now than it is at present, then the present value of the dollar (as measured by its purchasing power) will be lower than the present quantity of dollars would otherwise warrant. Thus the expectation of inflation may be a self-fulfilling prophecy as every seller of goods and services raises prices and wages to keep ahead of expectations of increased costs. The wheel spins on and on in a process known as momentum inflation.

Again, the value of any monetary unit, such as the dollar, depends not merely on the quantity of the dollars but on their quality. When a country goes off the gold standard (as did the United States), it means that gold, or the right to get gold, has suddenly turned into mere paper. Therefore, the value of the monetary unit usually falls immediately (even if there has not yet been any increase in the quantity of money) because the people have more faith in gold than they have in the promise or the adjustment of the government's monetary managers. There is hardly a case on record in which departure from the gold standard was not soon followed by a further increase in bank credit and in printing press money.

In short, the value of money varies for the same reasons as does the value of any commodity. Just as the value of a bushel of wheat depends not only on the total present supply of wheat but also on the expected future supply and quality of the wheat, so the value of the dollar depends on a similar variety of considerations. The value of money, like the value of goods, is determined not merely by mechanical or physical relationships but primarily by psychological factors, which may often be complicated.

Deflation

The 1990–92 recession raised the fear that we could experience deflation, a phenomenon last seen 60 years ago. Although conventional wisdom holds that we should avoid inflation, it does not hold that deflation is our friend. For example, it was deflation that ruined Midwestern farmers in the late 19th century. Prices for their crops fell, making their fixed payments on loans for land, seed, and equipment all the more arduous. Home values collapsed in Texas during the oil bust in the 1980s and, more recently, home values in California have dropped. Most people and businesses make decisions on the assumption that rising prices are inevitable.

It is tempting to think of deflation as a blessing, when most goods and services become less expensive and therefore more affordable—most especially homes. The problem rests with what must happen before prices drop. Consider, for example, that it takes large-scale foreclosures, liquidation sales, corporate and personal bankruptcies, as well as high unemployment and nonqualified borrowers before prices will drop significantly. These preconditions for deflation existed in the early 1990s. How did this happen? In a word: debt. In a moment, we will discuss in more detail the problems that high debt (particularly government debt) causes the U.S. economy, including possible deflation.

If deflation becomes a reality, the results for American home owners, workers, and yes, even college students will be severe. For instance, home buyers have traditionally been willing to stretch as much as possible to make initial monthly mortgage payments. A standard mortgage has fixed payments for thirty years, so rising wages make those payments less burdensome. That assumption has less power when inflation is running at 2 percent rather than at 6 percent. It becomes a disaster when prices actually fall (deflation). The same holds for college graduates, who frequently join the workforce carrying debt loads higher than their annual income and who may also find that there is no inflation to lighten their fixed monthly payments. Inflation, according to an age-old axiom, is a friend of a debtor and the enemy of the creditor. Unfortunately, we are a nation of debtors at a time when inflation is almost nonexistent.

Stagflation

Until the mid-1970s, economists believed in something called the "Phillips Curve." The Phillips Curve showed a trade-off between inflation and unemployment: the higher inflation you had, the lower unemployment would be. Unfortunately, the 1970s revealed a fallacy. The trade-off could not be sustained beyond the short term. To keep unemployment below what economists called the natural unemployment rate required escalating inflation. The price paid for pushing the unemployment rate too low in the early to mid-1970s was rising inflation and no decline in unemployment. Stagflation was born. Fortunately, we have not experienced stagflation since the Carter years. President Reagan's economic policies defeated stagflation.

Now that we have a better understanding of some basic concepts of macroeconomics, let us look at four changes since the Great Depression that have helped us to stabilize the economy in this country. The changes are, of course, interrelated. In different ways, these all mark an increase in the importance of what happens in Washington.

STABILIZING THE ECONOMY

Government Employment

In 1929 the federal government employed 579,559 civilians. Just over half worked for the postal service. Not quite 20 percent were attached to the War and Navy Departments. Only about 30 percent of the total—180,000 people—worked for the other branches of the federal government. Counting both these civilian employees and the military (roughly 255,000 soldiers, sailors, and marines), the federal government in 1929 employed slightly less than 2 percent of the labor force. State and local governments employed another 2.5 million, or about 5 percent of the labor force. All told, 1 American worker in 15 worked for the government at some level.

FIGURE 1.7
U.S. Nonfarm Employment by Sector, October 2002

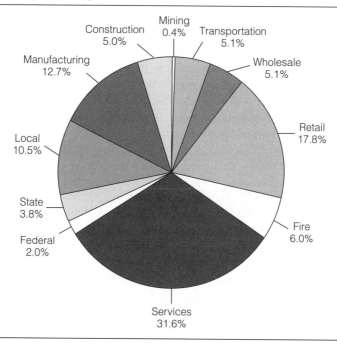

Construction 5.0%
Mining 0.4%
Transportation 5.1%
Manufacturing 12.7%
Wholesale 5.1%
Local 10.5%
Retail 17.8%
State 3.8%
Fire 6.0%
Federal 2.0%
Services 31.6%

Source: U.S. Department of Commerce, Bureau of Labor Statistics. Establishment Data, Employment, Seasonally Adjusted, Table B-3: Employees on Nonfarm Payrolls by Major Industry and Selected Component Groups, Seasonally Adjusted, 2002, ftp://ftp.bls.gov/pub/suppl/empsit .ceseeb3.txt.

Even with a downsizing of the military, the Defense Department alone employed more civilians in 1996 than did the whole rest of the federal government in 1929. The federal government as a whole employs 2.634 million civilians[27] (down in October 2002 from 3.1 million in 1990). State and local government, however, employs almost 19 million citizens (18.683 million, an increase of over 2 million since 1990).[28] Counting the armed forces, government at some level now employs about 16.3 percent of the total labor force (see Figure 1.7).

Economists see all these government workers as an immense stabilizing force on the economy. When business is slow, industries begin laying off workers. Production falls; so does purchasing power. The economy immediately looks worse than it did before. More businesses then lay off workers, and the downturn becomes more severe. Not so with the government. Business may be bad, but children are still taught, roads maintained, and criminals put in jail. Moreover, Congress may decide to fund a new project—thereby increasing government employment—precisely because business looks bad. Thus, the business cycle is stabilized or even counteracted by a large government sector. However, this strategy was more difficult for President Clinton (and for the first President Bush, before him)

A CLOSER LOOK

Go to your city or state's Web site to find out how many employees they have. Has that number increased or decreased in the past five years?

and will be even more difficult for the present President Bush, given these presidents' views about the role and size of government.

Transfer Payments

Transfer payments are federal dollars paid directly to individuals, including Social Security and Medicare. State and local government employment has grown considerably in recent years. It more than doubled, for example, between 1960 and 1990. Civilian and military federal employment, however, has increased only a little since the late 1940s and has actually fallen off in the past ten years. Transfer payments (an invention of the Franklin Roosevelt administration) have accounted for the recent growth in federal spending. In 1929 the only money the federal government paid out to individuals other than its employees went to veterans and bondholders. In 1990, transfer payments (excluding interest on bonds) were well over $500 billion, or roughly 50 percent of the total federal outlay. In the 1970s alone, transfer payments increased 76 percent in real terms.

The increase of federal spending in this area relative to state and local government spending continues despite Reagan-Bush-Clinton-Bush attempts to return authority to the states, because many of these programs are entitlements. Once individuals meet certain criteria, they can receive the funds. President Clinton's 1996 budget allowed for even greater spending in this area and so has President George W. Bush's budgets. The relative growth in federal spending was not what Reagan and Bush had in mind when they took office. Except for military spending, they advocated reducing outlays and letting states pick up affected programs. The Advisory Commission on Intergovernmental Relations, a nonpartisan research group established by Congress in 1982, attributed the federal increase in transfer payments to an aging population that has put more demands on Social Security and Medicare.

The number of people who receive some government aid is huge. In 1996, for example, the government estimated that the five major social programs each had 10 million recipients or more, and the number has grown since. People may dislike government spending and government programs in general, but when it comes to the program that aids them, their attitude suddenly shifts. Some believe that only the poor drain government resources. In fact, all layers of society "feed at the trough." Many well-off people get such tangible benefits from the government as tax write-offs or farm price supports. Some corporations are either temporary or semipermanent government wards. Chrysler, Lockheed, and Conrail are

FIGURE 1.8
Where the Federal Dollar Goes, Fiscal Year 2003

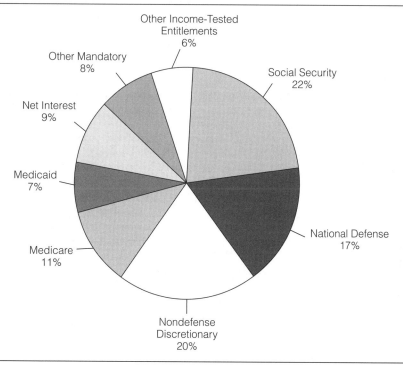

Source: U.S. Office of Management and Budget, "How Your Tax Dollars Are Spent in 2003," in *A Citizen's Guide to the Federal Budget,* 2002, http://www.whitehouse.gov/omb/budget/fy2003/ guide.html, p. 4.

giants who came to Uncle Sam with begging bowls. The savings and loan companies and banks are more recent examples. (See Figure 1.8 for the 2003 budget and where the money goes.)

From the recipients' point of view, transfer payments make retirement or lack of work a lot more tolerable than it otherwise might be. The payments also provide something of an alternative to jobs that pay too little, or jobs in which the employer tries to cut wages. For the whole economy, transfers are an important way of stabilizing purchasing power. The poor and the elderly have much more income to spend than they otherwise might. Workers who lose their jobs get unemployment benefits, giving them some money to spend. In the past, even the threat of a slump led people to cut their spending, and the slump itself might reduce their incomes to zero. Recessions can be painful (as we learned in 1982–83, in 1991–92, and again in 2001–02), but our incomes fall nowhere near as far or as fast as they once did. The downturn is apt to be less severe, and the recovery much quicker.

Having said this, we should point out that in 1996 the Republican-led Congress passed and President Clinton signed into law a landmark welfare reform law.

The new law represents a sweeping reversal of federal policy in that it ends six decades of guaranteed help for the nation's poorest children. Provisions of the welfare reform law include:

≫ States had until July 1, 1997, to submit plans for new programs to replace Aid to Families with Dependent Children, the federal program that guaranteed cash assistance for poor children.

≫ Each state receives a lump sum to run its own welfare and work programs.

≫ Lifetime welfare benefits are limited to five years, with hardship exemptions available for 20 percent of families.

≫ The head of each family on welfare must work within two years or lose benefits.

≫ States can provide benefits to unmarried teenage parents under age 18 only if the mother stays in school and lives with an adult.

≫ Food stamps are limited for adults with no dependent children.

≫ Legal immigrants do not receive most benefits during their first five years in the United States.

≫ States must provide Medicaid for all who qualify under the current law.

Fiscal Policy

Government spending of all kinds (federal, state, and local) adds up to at least one-third of the gross domestic product (GDP, the total dollar value of all goods bought for final use and for services during a year). All this spending helps anchor the economy through the business cycle, maintaining people's purchasing power during the bad times and the good. The federal budget also plays another role; it can counteract the business cycle by running in deficit when the economy is slow and running in surplus when the economy is booming. This counter-cyclical effect, as economists term it, reflects the government's fiscal, or taxing and spending, policies.

A budget surplus is easier to understand. Washington, in effect, is taking more money out of the economy than it is putting back. Thus, purchasing power is less than it would be otherwise. People buy less, workers produce less, and the economy slows down. Insofar as that eases pressure on prices and wages, inflation should slow down as well.

Deficits are a little harder to comprehend. The government is borrowing the extra money that it is spending. The factory worker who invests in savings bonds on a payroll-deduction plan and the New York bank that buys a million dollars' worth of treasury bills are both lending the government money to cover its deficit. As the government borrows, the national debt increases. Usually this is not a cause for alarm. As a company can borrow more and more every year while business is good and the firm is growing, the government can borrow more and more while the economy is growing. Between 1962 and 2002 the only budget surpluses occurred in 1999 and 2000 (see Figure 1.9).

FIGURE 1.9
The U.S. Federal Budget Deficit, 1962–2002 (estimated)

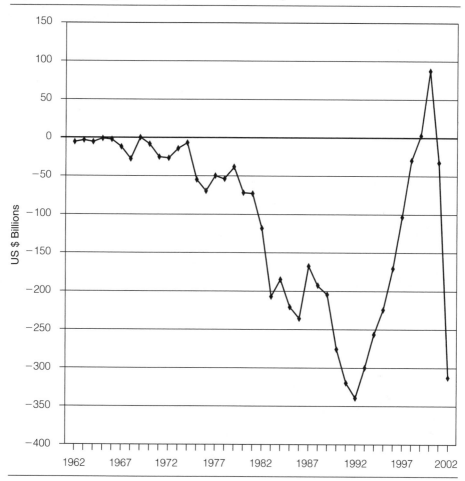

Source: U.S. Congressional Budget Office. Historical Budget Data, Table 1: Revenues, Outlays, Surpluses, Deficits, and Debt Held by the Public, 1962–2001 (in billions of dollars), 2002, http://www.cbo.gov/showdoc.cfm?index=1821&sequence=0#t1.

One of the main accomplishments of the Clinton administration was its reduction and eventual elimination of the budget deficit (see Figure 1.9), for years considered an intractable problem. With the Bush II administration and its tax cut plus the new war on terrorism, the surplus was turned into a very large deficit in the administration's very first year and deepened enormously (estimated to be $315 billion in 2002) in its second year. However, the debt burden as a proportion of GDP did not grow so steeply, since the economy grew during the 1990s.

We must ask, however, what happens when the government does not run a deficit? Without a deficit there is some chance that purchasing power (recall that the economists call it "aggregate demand") will not be sufficient to keep the econ-

---

A CLOSER LOOK

Go to your city or state's Web site to find out how it is being affected by the federal deficit and by the economy itself—is it having to make budget cuts? State and local governments are not supposed to run budget deficits, so they have to make reductions in expenditures or increase revenues—have they had to do so in your community?

---

omy going at full speed. Why this should be so is no mystery. Suppose, for example, that you make $20,000 a year. According to the way these things are figured, you have produced $20,000's worth of goods or services that somebody now has to buy. However, you may not want to spend it all. You may want to put a little in the bank or maybe buy some stocks or bonds. In good times, businesses are looking for ways to expand: building a new plant or replacing old machinery with the latest model. To do so they need to borrow money. So they sell you a bond, or they go to the same bank you put your savings in, borrow your savings, and spend them. In that case every dollar earned gets spent and the economy keeps humming.

However, suppose business looks bad and companies are not doing much investing. Your savings and everybody else's start to pile up in the banks. Now you have produced more dollars than you are spending. Everybody else who is doing any saving has done the same. Unsold goods begin to pile up on the shelves. Companies notice this and begin to cut back production. A recession threatens, and the government steps in.

If the government borrows your money (either directly or from the bank) and spends it, the money you saved will stay in circulation. Everything produced will be bought. There will be no unsold goods on the shelves and no cutbacks. In fact, business will look good. Companies too will want to borrow so they can expand, and the economy will grow. Notice, however, that the government must run a deficit to ensure this result. It must spend all it takes in taxes, borrow some more, and spend that too. It has to spend your savings as well as its "own" money. It can run a surplus only when it is willing to risk recession (to fight inflation) or when it believes that business will invest enough on its own to keep the economy moving.

The government budget's countercyclical effect varies automatically with what the rest of the economy is doing. When unemployment rises, spending for jobless benefits and other relief programs rises, but tax revenues fall, since the unemployed do not pay taxes. So the federal balance sheet tilts toward deficit spending. But when the economy is booming, tax revenues rise and spending falls, thereby creating a surplus.

In principle, whatever administration is in power sets its fiscal policy by adjusting tax and spending levels to achieve the desired effect. If recession threatens, the government should cut taxes or increase spending to boost purchasing power.

If inflation is thought to be the greater danger, the supposed cure is to increase taxes or reduce spending. In real life, of course, the choice is seldom so simple. The trade-off between inflation and recession is not always clear. Also, political considerations always impart a certain asymmetry to fiscal policy changes. Any elected official will find it easier to increase spending, to keep various interest groups and federal agencies happy, than to cut it—even in good times.

Fiscal policy therefore more often focuses on stimulating the economy than on slowing it down. Although the federal government has steadily run a deficit since Richard Nixon, it was not until the Reagan-Bush years that we experienced what can easily be characterized as runaway deficits. President Clinton managed to slow down deficit spending and in fact created surpluses in two years before stepping down from office. But the deficit is here once again.

The deficit may be the reason that the 1991–94 recession was so deep and why the recovery was so slow in coming and so disappointing once it got here. It could also play a role in any recovery from the current 2001–02 recession. First, we need to understand how the federal government tries to regulate the economy through its monetary policies.

Monetary Policies

Like an engine that runs on gasoline, the economy runs on money. If there is not enough, the economy will not run very fast and will be prone to fits and starts. By itself, plenty of money will not ensure a fast-growing, smoothly working economy. It needs people, businesses, and governments willing and able to spend that money. If, however, there is no money, there can be no spending.

The word *money* ordinarily refers to currency: bills and coins. Those who accuse the government of cheapening the dollar frequently accuse it of printing too much money, as if the presses that turn out five-dollar bills were working overtime. In reality, of course, most of what we use as money is not currency at all; it is the money that is in our checking accounts. This money is simply a bookkeeping account on the bank's ledgers. It is created, in part, by the banking system itself.

Suppose you take $1,000 in cash to a bank to open an account. You now have a brand-new checkbook, and you know that you can write checks up to a total of $1,000. Suppose your neighbor also applies to the same bank for a loan of $1,000. When she gets the loan, the bank does not give her your $1,000 in cash; more likely it also gives her a checkbook and credits her account with $1,000. Now you and she have a total of $2,000 to draw on. But the bank has only your original $1,000 in currency. As long as neither of you wants $1,000 in cash at the same time, the bank is solvent. By this process the money supply—the total deposits the banking system carries on its books plus currency in circulation— grows well beyond the volume of cash that is in circulation at any given time.

Obviously, there has to be some limit to the amount of money so created. If banks lend money to all comers, they will soon find themselves in trouble (which happened in the 1980s with the savings and loan and banking crises). Also, if the banking system creates too much money in relation to what there is to buy, the excess purchasing power will drive prices up. The dollar will be worth less because there are too many dollars in circulation.

The growth of the money supply is limited in two ways. One is the way of hard money—fiscal responsibility, reliance on the market. The other is the way of soft money and political interference with the market. By all standards of good conservatism, the first sounds preferable. When tried, however, it had two rather severe drawbacks. Coping with these drawbacks led to the inflationary monetary system we have today (although there is every sign that inflation has been whipped, at least for the moment).

Under the traditional system of managing the money supply (which was in effect in this country throughout much of the 19th century and changed only gradually in the 20th), every paper dollar was theoretically redeemable in gold. The government could issue only as much currency as it could safely cover with the gold in its vaults. Banks had to have access to enough currency or gold to satisfy any of their depositors who wanted it. The gold standard thus imposed rather severe limits on how fast the money supply could grow.

A country's gold supply depends on how much of the metal is mined and on how much is coming from other countries to purchase goods and services. A nation's need for money, however, depends on how much real economic activity there is—how much people borrow and spend. If people want to borrow and spend more money than is easily available with the existing gold supply, interest rates shoot up. Banks make fewer loans, and businesses do not invest. The supply of money can thus limit economic growth. It may even provoke a recession. That is why the Populists of the late 19th century—including William Jennings Bryan and his followers—fought so hard against the gold standard. If more money were available (if, for example, all the currency were backed by silver as well as gold), then economic booms would be longer, panics fewer. The price of this strategy— inflation—was one the Populists were willing to pay.

In a series of steps beginning with Franklin D. Roosevelt's 1933 ban on gold transactions and ending with Nixon's reunification of the international gold standard in 1971, the United States went "off gold." The particular reasons for each step were different. Ultimately, however, gold is too inflexible a standard for a rapidly growing economy. If we were still on the gold standard, we would either be limiting ourselves to a very slow rate of growth (the rate at which we could get gold) or else be constantly making the dollar worth less in terms of the amount of gold it would buy (devaluation). The former choice would be disastrous for the economy. The latter, although theoretically possible, would appear to undermine the currency repeatedly by deliberate government action. A rapidly expanding economy cannot work with a money supply fixed either by fiat or custom, any more than a growing number of automobiles can easily run on the oil produced by a fixed number of wells.

So the dollar today has no gold backing at all. Instead, limits on the money supply are set through a variety of devices by the Federal Reserve System, "the Fed." The Fed tells banks how much money they can lend in proportion to their reserves (currency and money the banks keep on deposit at the Fed). It sets the discount rate at which it will loan money to banks, influencing other interest rates. It also buys and sells government securities on the open market, pumping money into the system (when it buys) or taking money out of the system (when it sells).

Fiscal and monetary policies—tax and spending policies on one hand, regulation of the money supply on the other—fit together in an important way. In real life, there is no such thing as running a deficit exactly big enough to make sure that everything that is produced will be bought, as in the simplified explanation above. Instead, the government tries to run whatever deficit it thinks necessary to stimulate the economy. An expanding economy, however, typically requires new money, which is exactly what the Fed provides when it buys a bond from the Treasury. The Fed typically pays for its bonds by crediting the Treasury's account on its books. The effect is the same as if it paid for the bonds with newly printed Federal Reserve notes—currency. The deficit is thus *monetized,* in the language of economics, and both total spending and the money supply expand.

On the other side of the ledger, an expansionary fiscal policy ensures that expansionary monetary policy will work. In the 1930s, the money supply did not grow despite the rock-bottom interest rates: nobody was doing any borrowing. A big government deficit, though, means that new money is automatically spent. Again, total spending and the money supply increase together.

The federal fiscal and monetary policies that we have been describing are based in part on the economic theories of John Maynard Keynes (1883–1946), a brilliant economist and lecturer at Cambridge University.[29] Although many of Keynes's ideas were represented in President Franklin D. Roosevelt's New Deal, it was the Kennedy administration that made Keynesian economics accepted doctrine. Every president since Kennedy and until Reagan used Keynesian principles to guide his economic policies. President Reagan ushered in a new era when he shifted from Keynesian to supply-side economics. Although at one time Bush I denounced supply-side economics as "voodoo economics," he embraced it during his presidency. President Clinton also rejected Keynesian economics and instead opted for what is now called the "neoclassical" school of thought.

THE NEW CLASSICAL ECONOMICS

President Nixon shattered conservative orthodoxy when he announced in 1971 that he was a believer in Keynesian economics. Nixon meant he accepted the need for the government to steer the economy with fiscal policy—running larger government deficits, if necessary, to achieve full employment. The liberal-democratic faith in Keynesian economics centered on the use of government regulation and spending to curb the extremes and instabilities of the private market. Robert Kuttner puts it this way: "When the public is in a liberal mood, the polity is rendered more inclusive; and government gains expanded authority to discipline the market—a nice marriage of politics, government, and political economy."[30]

In this sense, President Clinton was seen to have abandoned the liberal cause and "stemmed the slide to the right only by moving right."[31] Clinton's shift to a more conservative center was largely in response to the 1994 congressional elections, in which the Republicans, led by Newt Gingrich and guided by the "Contract with America," won a majority in both houses. Kuttner observes, "Of course, this is no easy time to be a liberal. The market is rampant and the state constricted. The overhang of the Reagan [and Bush] debt adds further constraint. Even moderate fiscal prudence, of the kind Clinton embraced during his first two years, left little spare money for major initiatives. Clinton's acceptance of more extreme austerity after November 1994 left liberal constituencies arguing with one another over what to cut."[32]

The political and fiscal conservatism rampant in the country today is fueled by a general mistrust of government. President Clinton did little to improve the post–World War II low trust in our government and faith in the competence and value of government, which is one reason that George W. Bush instead of Vice President Gore was elected in 2000. In practice, however, Clinton's government reinvention movement was little more than a major cutting of government. The Republican-led charge to reduce government and its role in our lives (particularly our economic lives) was made easier by Clinton's claim that "the age of big government is over."

What does this have to do with supply-side economics? The term *supply-side* is as anathema to liberals as the views of the Keynesians were to fiscal conservatives. It smacks of Ronald Reagan, voodoo economics, and Arthur Laffer's idea that cutting tax rates can painlessly raise government revenues by stimulating an economic boom. Now that the economy has returned to something close to "full employment" (defined as unemployment rates of around 5 percent), the continuing challenge is to increase the U.S. economy's underlying growth in productivity.

Those who fall into the Keynesian camp worry most about taming the business cycle and preventing recessions. Supply-siders, in contrast, focus on ways to increase the economy's output. They promote incentives for greater investment in the three great building blocks of growth: physical capital (such as machines or office buildings), education, and technological progress. A major part of Clinton's second-term economic agenda was the same as his first term's: balance the budget by 2002; reduce government borrowing and free up capital for private investment; selectively cut taxes for education; and continue government spending on research and development. Bush's agenda became to cut taxes, which he did in his first year; the rest of his agenda became rapidly derailed by terrorism and homeland security, however, including dealing with the subsequent budget deficit.

The new classical economists and supply-siders reject two important assumptions of Keynesian economic theory. First, they reject the idea that government deficits are important economic stabilizers. They argue that the multiplier effects of deficit spending are much smaller than claimed by Keynesian economists. Second, new classical economists argue that the quantity of money influences prices and wages rather than standards of living and employment rates—an idea that liberal democrats find unpalatable. These convictions are based partly on a new theory of rational expectations.[33]

Rational expectations grew out of the need to explain the increasingly virulent inflation that existed in the 1970s despite high unemployment. Simultaneous high inflation and high unemployment (stagflation) contradicted traditional Keynesian principles of macroeconomic behavior. Recall that Keynesian analysis concludes that a stimulus, either fiscal or monetary, prods economic activity and a depressant slows things down. During expansions, prices rise. In contractions, prices fall or rise less rapidly. Thus, prices rise when unemployment is low and rise very slowly or fall when unemployment is high. During the 1970s, however, prices and unemployment rose together. This outcome is counterintuitive to the traditional Keynesian view.

The new classical economic analysis begins with the belief that economic fluctuations happen as a result of numerous shocks to the system. Shocks come from surprise changes in the federal budget, surprises in foreign trade, surprises in the weather, surprises in scientific inventions, and so on. These shocks cause buyers and sellers to modify their behavior in their own self-interest. The new classical economic model assumes that markets, driven from equilibrium by surprises, return to equilibrium quickly and efficiently. This means, for example, that the only time the Federal Reserve Board (the Fed) can cause real effects is when it acts capriciously and thus surprises the public. To the extent that the Fed follows a predictable course—expanding the money supply when the economy slows down, slowing down money supply growth when the economy picks up— market participants can predict and offset Fed actions.

Keynesian economists argue this is highly unlikely in that most people, including investors and business owners, do not watch the Fed closely enough to fully anticipate normal Fed actions and then to quickly change their behavior to prevent any real effects. To the contrary, new classical economists believe we will alter our behavior to compensate for actions taken by the Fed because of our rational expectations. The analogy often used to explain this principle is your favorite football team playing an opponent that consistently runs the same play on first down. It only makes sense that your team would always prepare to offset that play knowing that it is coming.

The public policy implications of new classical economics brings us back to the supply-siders. The supply-side argument goes as follows: If the fiscal deficits consistently run by the federal government from the 1970s to the late 1990s had no effect on spending levels and if monetary policy affects only price levels, then what causes fluctuations in productivity (national output)? Likewise, what causes changes in unemployment levels? Supply-side economists believe that fiscal policy has a greater impact on the incentives of producers and consumers than on spending levels—which impact, in turn, affects the level of national output and "real" spending. In public policy terms, supply-siders believe Keynesian-driven government tax, transfer, and spending policies are deterrents to work, saving, and capital formation. Supply-side economists want to see a reversal of these policies so that levels of productivity, savings, and investment will increase. In other words, they feel less government will result in real economic growth without inflation.

Most reputable economists readily admit they do not understand what went wrong in the past and thus have no magic bullet for accelerating the economy's expansion today. In his book *Peddling Prosperity,* MIT economist Paul Krugman warned that anyone who claims to have a cure for the economy's malaise is blowing smoke.

Most economists agree that a critically important step on the road to raising economic growth rates is boosting national savings, which fell from about 8 percent of GDP in the 1950s and 1960s to less than 3 percent today. Higher savings lead to higher investment and greater output of goods and services. How to accomplish that is much more controversial. Martin Feldstein, a Harvard economist, believes that fundamental tax reform and a radical program to replace Social Security with individual retirement accounts could stimulate enough savings to increase the annual rates of growth by half a percentage point.

The work of other economists casts doubt on such a rosy scenario. Alan Auerbach at the University of California at Berkeley, for example, figures that the "flat tax" probably would not affect growth by the time Congress waters it down to appease interest groups who could suffer under its provisions. Cutting governmental borrowing by cutting spending would probably do more than tax reform to help raise savings available to the private sector. But even that is no panacea. The painful fact, often ignored by some policy advocates, is that achieving higher growth is almost never costless. In simple terms, saving and investing has more to do with forgoing consumption now in the hope of consuming more later—an unpopular idea in an age of consumption and debt (see below). However, if America wants higher growth, it must practice the traditional but unpopular values of patience and forbearance. While at the moment, it appears the supply-siders have won the day, the bottom line remains the same: there are no quick and painless fixes on the road to greater prosperity.

DEBT: A PROBLEM (ONCE AGAIN) IN THE NEW CENTURY

The one fact everyone—Keynesians and supply-siders alike—can agree on these days is that the country owes far too much money. The government took on unprecedented debt and got rid of it in the past decade and now has it back (the federal debt is over $3.3 trillion and will grow considerably higher by the year 2003)[34] and therefore has much less ability to stimulate the economy (see Figure 1.9). Debt, in part, is why the economy was slow to recover from the 1991–94 recession and will also make it harder to achieve economic recovery in the early 2000s. To make matters much worse, the government was not the only one to go into dangerously high debt; businesses and individuals did as well.

In fact, many economists blamed the slow-growth economy in the early 1990s on the national and personal debt that accumulated since the 1970s. The theory held that the economy was slower than usual to recover because everyone (citizens, corporations, and government) was trying to pay back this unprecedented debt and debt-financed (for example, junk bonds) commercial real estate. These same factors are in operation in the early 2000s. Alan Greenspan, the chairman of the Federal Reserve Board, spoke about them this way:

> The normal forces of economic expansion are running up against countervailing forces that I have likened elsewhere to a fifty-mile-per-hour headwind. To a considerable extent, the factors restraining expansion are working through the financial sector. For example, a heavy overhang of debt, an accumulation of bad loans and doubts about the future have produced an unusual degree of caution.[35]

Deficit Spending

When Reagan was first elected president, the federal government was already falling into an ever deepening financial hole. For this reason, Reagan pledged in his campaign to balance the budget and reduce the deficit. Three presidential terms later, the deficit had more than tripled in size. During the Reagan and Bush administrations, the deficits grew not only in dollars but, more ominously, as a share of the country's total wealth. (See Figure 1.9 once again to illustrate this point.)

Why did presidents Reagan and Bush fail to bring down the deficit and debt? Simply put, they made the same mistake President Johnson did 20 years earlier. That is, they tried to supply both guns and butter; or in other words, they tried to stoke an arms race and to continue entitlement programs.

What was particularly disturbing was that the deficits of the 1980s persisted through a period of economic recovery and growth. The deficits, therefore, were considered structural and not temporary. As such, they posed a serious threat to the growth of the economy. Why was this so? If an economy is to grow, there must be a high level of investment in plant, equipment, and other forms of capital. To maintain this level of investment, a nation must either save an equivalent amount from its current income or get capital from abroad to foster growth. National saving is the sum of private and government saving. When a government runs a budget deficit it "dissaves," and national savings drop commensurately unless private businesses or individuals increase their savings to make up the difference, which, as we know, did not happen. From 1972 to 1981, net national saving in the United States was about 7 percent of the gross national product (GNP). In the 1990s, it was less than 3 percent. The difference is attributable to a large increase in the budget deficit on top of a fall in private saving.

This decline in national saving put upward pressure on the interest rates and would have cut U.S. investment drastically had it not been for a substantial increase in capital investment from abroad (many office buildings and U.S.-based businesses are foreign owned). Foreign investment in the United States offers us some benefits. For example, it keeps U.S. interest rates from rising higher and thereby prevents a further decline in investment levels. But it also exacts heavy costs. When foreign capital comes into the United States at the rate experienced in the 1980s, the result is an increased foreign demand for dollars and therefore a higher value for the dollar in the foreign exchange markets. The expensive dollar, in turn, creates problems for U.S. industry in remaining competitive in international markets.

Export industries (including agriculture) as well as industries that compete with imports have found their markets shrinking. Other negative results have been not only the injury to both labor and capital in industries affected by international competition but also the economy's slower growth. If continued over the long run, large budget deficits will either reduce domestic investment or force the United States to continue to rely on foreign money. In either case, the living standards of Americans will continue to fall. A reduced level of domestic investment would hold back the growth of the economy, and continued heavy foreign investment would send a larger share of the U.S. GDP overseas in payment of debt service or other returns to foreign investors.

President Clinton succeeded in bringing down annual deficit spending to the lowest level in 17 years—as a percentage of GNP—and then in creating a budget surplus for the first time in 50 years. With his tax cuts and events terribly beyond his control, President Bush is now presiding over budget deficits once again as large as those under the Reagan administration. While forecasts of the costs of the Iraqi war and reconstruction vary widely, the war and its aftermath are certain to increase deficits to a magnitude unseen even in the 1980s. The effects of this shift on the economy and beyond remain to be seen.

Personal and Corporate Debt

The federal government was not alone in spending beyond its means. A great many American citizens and corporations borrowed against the future, as well. Why did so many borrow and spend at a frantic pace, contrary to the American tradition?

To understand, we must look back to the late 1960s, when high and unpredictable inflation became a fact of life in the United States. As a result, in the 1970s, people believed that real estate was a great way to ride the wave of inflation to wealth, to borrow against the ever rising value of homes or commercial office space while repaying mortgages in devalued dollars. Then came the financial deregulation and tax giveaways in the early 1980s, which made real estate investments even more attractive. New tax loopholes made investors eager to speculate on office buildings; with deregulation, the banks and savings and loans abetted this speculation. The result was overbuilding of office space and inflation of land values. We also saw the birth of junk bonds that financed these binge years and the savings and loan mess.

Also, consumers were busy spending themselves into unprecedented debt, borrowing against the equity in their homes and using unsolicited credit cards sent to them by the dozens. For example, "about 40 percent of the growth in consumer spending during 1983–87 was financed by installment debt, including home equity loans, compared with 20 percent during earlier expansions."[36] Since people borrowed heavily to finance home purchases when construction of new homes was not strong, home prices jumped at an unprecedented rate. This process is known as "asset-price inflation." The problem is that this cannot continue forever. At some point, the cycle—debt chasing prices chasing debt—has to stop, and that is what happened in the 1990s.

Individuals were not the only ones borrowing and spending beyond their means. Corporations also were busy piling up debt. Companies can raise capital either through equity (stocks) or debt (bonds, including junk bonds). During the 1980s, companies switched from stock offerings to selling bonds in a very big way. For example, from 1982 to 1988, more than $400 billion in corporate equity was replaced by debt. Corporations and retail stores mortgaged themselves into debt through leveraged buyouts. By the decade's end, interest payments absorbed more than 21 percent of corporate cash flow.

The watchword of the 1990s was downsizing and scaled-back lifestyles, a trend that has continued into the new century. The 1980s were a time of expansion, careless spending, and greed. The Clinton administration lived up to its promise to lead us in debt reduction and thoughtful spending, and Bush is at least partly following that trend—except for the deficit spending. The Federal Reserve reports, for example, that consumer debt peaked in 1988, leveled off in 1989, declined until 1994, and has been steadily increasing ever since (to 14.04 percent in 2002).[37] The same holds for many large corporations. And, as we have said, the federal government is moving in that direction, as well.

Deficits are only one of three major problems facing us as we enter the new millennium. The other two problems, our trade imbalance and our status as a debtor nation, are not unrelated to the first problem.

Trade Imbalance and Foreign Debt

Two related problems facing the United States are its ever increasing trade imbalance and its foreign debt. The United States was in this predicament in part because of its massive budget deficits, and they will now be a significant problem again, given the return of the federal deficit. It is not only the federal government but the cities and states as well that seek foreign investment to help them through economic hard times. Total foreign investment in the United States is staggering. The deficit in the balance of trade has turned the United States from the world's largest creditor into the world's largest debtor nation. Wynne Godley writes that "if the United States continues to run current account deficits, even for only a few more years, its foreign debt and payments of interest on it will rise to an unacceptable level that would demand corrective action if the debt is not to explode."[38]

The huge inflow of money from outside the United States meant that foreign creditors financed most of the huge budget deficits of the 1980s and 1990s. To attract these ever larger amounts of foreign funds, the United States had to offer high real interest rates and accept, until recently, a dollar that was overvalued in relation to other currencies. The overvalued dollar made U.S. goods overpriced as compared with foreign products, which in turn lowered exports. The budget deficit, the soaring trade deficit, and our debtor nation status are all connected. The only way people in other countries can afford to buy so many Treasury bonds to finance the U.S. debt is with their own trade surpluses. In short, countries like Japan can finance our debt because we buy so many Toyota cars and Sony televisions. We are letting others do in reverse what we did in the first years after World War II. In those years the United States had the only undamaged, modern, working industrial structure in the world. The other industrial countries had been destroyed or exhausted by war. The whole world needed what only the United States could provide. We made it possible for others to buy by providing gifts, loans, and foreign investment. Americans lent others the money with which to support U.S. exports. Now, as we have said, other countries are lending us the means to continue buying their goods.

Just how large is our trade imbalance, and in what areas, if any, do we still manage a trade surplus? In just the second quarter of 2002, the United States had a total trade deficit of $130 billion.[39] For 2001 the deficit was $393 billion (see Table 1.4). The deficit would be even larger if the United States had not run a $68 billion surplus in services trade, which offset some of the deficit in merchandise trade. Tourism, education, and consulting expertise are the major services we sell to others. John Wilson, chief economist for Bank of America, reports that "services have by far been the biggest source of U.S. export growth. If not for them, we'd be in deep economic trouble internationally. We'd have to borrow more to pay for trade deficits, money would flow out of the country, and we'd have much higher interest rates."[40]

One main service export never leaves the country: tourism. When a U.S. business sells a service to someone from another country, the sale counts as an export, regardless of where the transaction takes place. Foreign currency used to pay for dinner, hotels, or entertainment have the same effect on the U.S. balance of payments as exports of computers or agricultural products. Other major sources of service export revenues include royalties, license fees, education, financial services, and telecommunications. Soaring enrollment of international students at American universities also is pumping valuable foreign exchange into the U.S. economy. Two of the fastest-growing sectors are health facilities management and legal services. Simply put, as the focus of the U.S. economy has moved from manufacturing to services, exports are beginning to follow. It is expected that an ever growing U.S. trade surplus in the service sector will continue into the new millennium.

An Information Technology Agreement completed in 1996 by representatives from 28 countries that conduct most of the world's $600 billion high-tech trade business may help to improve the U.S. trade balance in the critical technology sector. The agreement, sponsored by United States, would abolish import duties, or tariffs, on computers, software, semiconductors, and telecommunications equipment for countries signing the agreement. Much of the equipment necessary to construct computer networks that tap into the Internet is covered under the pact, and personal computers themselves will be cheaper. It is one of the world's biggest trade pacts and promises to open the spigot on international high-tech

TABLE 1.4
U.S. International Trade Transactions, 2001

Current Account	$Millions, Seasonally Adjusted
Exports of Goods and Services	
Exports of Goods	718,762
Exports of Services	279,260
Income Receipts	283,771
Total Exports of Goods and Services	1,281,793
Import of Goods	−1,145,927
Import of Services	−210,385
Income Payments	−269,389
Unilateral Current Transfers, Net (U.S. government grants, etc.)	−49,463
Capital Account Assets, Net	826
U.S. Owned Assets Abroad, Net	−370,962
Foreign-Owned Assets in the U.S., Net	752,806
Statistical Discrepancy (seasonal adjustment discrepancies)	10,701
Balances:	
Balance on Goods (more coming in than going out)	−427,165
Balance on Services (more going out than coming in)	68,875
Balance on Goods and Services (net—more going out than coming in)	−358,290
Balance on Income (more going out than coming in)	14,382
Balance on Unilateral Current Transfers, Net (U.S. government grants, etc.) (net—more going out than coming in)	−49,463
Total Balance on Trade Transactions (more going out than coming in)	−393,371

Source: U.S. Department of Commerce, Bureau of Economic Analysis, Table 1: U.S. International Transactions Accounts Data, 2002, http://www.bea.doc.gov/bea/international/bp_web/simple.cfm?anon = 103&table_id = 1&ar ea_id = 3.

sales—it amounts to a global tax cut. It remains to be seen what effect this will have on the trade imbalance in this area.

While European countries remain important trading partners with the United States, the most significant U.S. trade imbalance is with China, Japan, and the ASEAN nations (Association of Southeast Asian Nations: Brunei, Indonesia, Malaysia, the Philippines, Singapore, Thailand, and Vietnam). Figure 1.10 shows the United States' trade balances with individual countries and regions around the world. In 2001 the United States had positive trade balances with only four countries—Brazil, Singapore, Australia, and Hong Kong—this means that for these countries, the United States exports more goods than it imports. For the rest, the United States is currently importing more then we export. As pointed out above, this has repercussions domestically.

FIGURE 1.10
U.S. Trade Balances (Imbalances) with Selected Countries, 2001

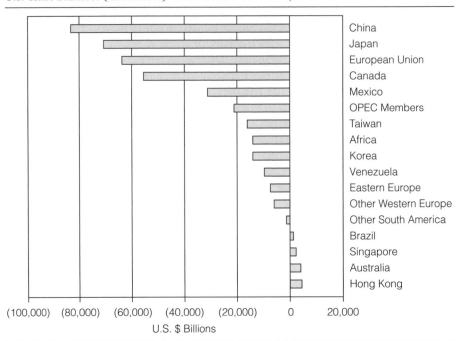

Source: U.S. Department of Commerce, Bureau of Economic Analysis, Table 2: U.S. Trade in Goods, 2002, http://www.bea.gov/bea/international/bp_web/simple.cfm?anon=570&table_id=2&area_id=3.

MERCOSUL, a trade bloc consisting of Brazil, Argentina, Paraguay, and Uruguay, will also be a major player in international trade. The real effect of MERCOSUL is geographic in that it takes Atlantic-facing nations and, via Paraguay, links them to the Pacific Coast. This means that MERCOSUL is potentially a very proximate trading partner to the Pacific Rim countries. It also encompasses the most advanced South American countries, with about three-fourths the land mass and nearly 80 percent of the population.

Protectionism or Free Trade?

Free traders win all the arguments, Mark Twain once said, but the protectionists win all the votes. Protectionist demands from various quarters of the American business and political sectors have been heard throughout U.S. history. Protectionism can take different forms, including tariffs (taxes levied on imports) and import quotas (restrictions on the quantity of a good that may legally be imported), export restrictions, and quality restrictions on imports.[41]

The very serious U.S. trade imbalance with Japan brought the issue of protectionism to the public agenda in the 1990s. The U.S. automobile and steel industries in particular felt threatened by the Japanese and demanded protection. It was only in 1990–91 that the U.S. trade policy with Japan shifted from confrontation to cooperation. U.S.-Japan trade frictions focused on three problem areas: the size of the U.S. trade deficit with Japan, the composition of bilateral trade, and the trade barriers that restricted access to Japanese markets. These same problem areas exist between the United States and other Asian countries—most notably the biggest market of them all, China.

High on the public's agenda is job protection and the prevention of jobs and companies moving overseas. This goal is supported by both protectionists and free traders—each side believing its approach is the best strategy for achieving this end. Common to the different arguments for import protection is that laissez-faire theory no longer describes today's international economy. Robert Kuttner writes, "The classical theory of free trade was based on what economists call 'factor endowment'—a nation's advantages in climate, minerals, arable land, or plentiful labor. The theory doesn't fit a world of learning curves, economies of scale, and floating exchange rates. And it certainly doesn't deal with the fact that much 'comparative advantage' today is created not by markets but by government action."[42]

On one hand, those who favor protection claim that it is required because cheap labor gives many countries greater cost advantage in the production of many goods and because the prices of many imports do not always reflect their true production costs. Protectionists would say they only want fair trade, which seems to mean the opportunity for domestic industries to compete on an equal footing (in labor costs and government subsidies) with foreign firms.

On the other hand, opponents of protectionist policies say they will not work. They argue that trade restrictions for some industries would make the country as a whole poorer and would not solve the presumed problems created by imports—lost jobs and the need to protect American industries from cheap foreign imports. Opponents also say protectionism is shortsighted and dangerous, maintaining U.S. industry's inefficiency and obsolescence. They make the point that there is unemployment in the smokestack industries in the United States not because of imports but because of delay in modernization. The American steel and automobile industries were the last, not the first, to invest in modern technology, and they were vulnerable to modernized foreign competition.

The right answer to unemployment in mines, mills, and factories and on the farm is not trade protectionism but rather speeding investment in new industries and new activities. So far, the United States has been more or less on the right track. Total employment is still rising, despite the decline in blue-collar jobs. It is difficult, however, for any politician to resist the lure of protectionism, particularly in an election year.

Perhaps the strongest argument in favor of free trade is the need for a growing world economy to support newly formed and still vulnerable democracies. Without healthy rates of growth, it will not be possible for Eastern Europe or the republics of the former Soviet Union, for example, to continue to make their painful transitions to market-based economies and for the fragile democracies of Latin America to survive the austerity normally associated with economic restructuring.

The U.S. economy is no less dependent on expanding world markets. The Carnegie Commission put it this way:

> The globalization of production and capital markets has greatly reduced America's economic autonomy, along with that of all other nations. A so-called American-made car is now composed of parts from around the world, as multinational as the American workforce is multiethnic. Our workers, consumers and businesses stand to gain much from free trade and lose much from trade wars.[43]

As Europe knit members of the European Community into a regional free-market area, the United States also became a player in the accelerating regionalization of world trade when it signed the North American Free Trade Agreement (NAFTA). Trade issues (and trade wars) are quickly replacing power and military issues in the post–cold war era. The dominant world players will be those who exercise themselves successfully in the international market. Economic alliances will replace exclusively military alliances. Foreign policy is no longer "what we do out there" but what we are able to do economically "in here." World power positions will directly reflect domestic economic policy and flexibility.

The rules of international power have shifted—rapidly. The United States may or may not be sufficiently agile to compete on an equal footing with other industrial nations. This is a new arena. There is also an sense of humiliation, after a century of political, economic, and military dominance, over suddenly having to bargain as equals. But bargain we must, and alliances we must make. It is to our tentative efforts in lining up trade partners that we turn in this next section. Issues of trade and tariffs can be complex. We will try to make our way through the often mind-boggling issues with as much clarity as we can muster.

THE WORLD TRADE ORGANIZATION

For 40 years, representatives from countries around the world have met several times a decade to discuss and revise the General Agreement on Tariffs and Trade (GATT). At their Punta del Este, Uruguay, meeting, representatives launched the eighth round of GATT trade negotiations in 1986. The unique agenda of the Uruguay Round was to consider liberalizing trade in services. Prior rounds had focused on goods and products, agricultural and industrial. Devising a multinational framework of rules to govern international transactions in services may preface a step toward liberalizing the rules for interchange of goods in the post–cold war era.[44]

It was not until 1994 that a newly revised GATT was agreed to by the participating nations. The principal result of the 1994 General Agreement on Tariffs and Trade was the creation of the World Trade Organization (WTO). The WTO was established on January 1, 1995, in Geneva, Switzerland, and is the legal and institutional foundation of the multilateral trading system, with the main goal of ensuring smoothly flowing trade between nations. As of January 1, 2002, 144 countries were members and another 26 were applying for membership; these countries account for 97 percent of the world's trade.[45] The WTO has six principal functions:

> ≫ To provide a forum for negotiations, to liberalize the trading system, and to open national markets progressively

> ≫ To oversee and enforce rules for the conduct of trade relations among most of the countries of the world

> ≫ To provide a mechanism for members to resolve trade disputes arising in areas covered by the WTO agreements

> ≫ To administer WTO trade agreements between nations

> ≫ To provide technical assistance and training for developing countries

> ≫ To cooperate with other international organizations

The World Trade Organization is the successor to the General Agreement on Tariffs and Trade, the arrangement that served as the basis for international trade from 1948 to 1995. The agreement establishing the WTO encompasses the existing GATT structure and extends it to new disciplines that were not covered in the past. The WTO agreement brings together under one institutional umbrella disciplines on government practices affecting trade in goods (the 1994 GATT), trade in services, and the protection of intellectual property rights (the Agreement on Trade-Related Aspects of Intellectual Property Rights). In addition to these main areas, associated multilateral agreements are provided for in other areas, including agriculture, textiles and clothing, and so forth.

The WTO agreement extends and clarifies GATT dispute settlement procedures. All of the Uruguay Round agreements are now subject to a single dispute settlement system. The agreement also formalized a mechanism to provide reviews of member countries' trade and economic policies that have a bearing on the international trading environment. Under the WTO, members must apply certain basic principles to trade with other members. These principles include "a non-discriminatory trading system that spells out their rights and their obligations. Each country receives guarantees that its exports will be treated fairly and consistently in other countries' markets. Each promises to do the same for imports into its own market. The system also gives developing countries some flexibility in implementing their commitments."[46]

It is expected that, by reducing barriers to global commerce, the agreement establishing the WTO will expand U.S. trade opportunities and increase U.S. economic competitiveness. If this happens, then it follows that higher real wages and living standards for Americans also will increase. For example, exports of goods and services have been steadily rising as a share of the U.S. economy's total output. An increase in U.S. export opportunities helps stimulate greater capital investment, technological innovation, higher productivity, job growth, and rising living standards.

Export growth is important not only for U.S. export producers but also for U.S. industries that provide the intermediate and capital goods used by producers of exports as well as the U.S. firms and workers supporting the export process.

A large and growing share of the U.S. workforce depends on U.S. exports for employment.

It also is expected that the substantial reductions in trade barriers negotiated in the Uruguay Round will result in lower prices for imported intermediate and final products and a greater variety of goods for American consumers. Competition in the U.S. market from increased imports stimulates U.S. industries to improve their productivity, quality, and technology; this can benefit both the producing firms and U.S. consumers who buy their goods at reduced prices. At the same time, WTO rules permit the United States to remedy situations in which unfairly traded imports have harmed competing U.S. industries.

In a speech on May 28, 1996, Renato Ruggiero, director-general of the WTO, expressed the challenge facing the WTO and its member nations in shaping the trading system of the next century:

> We have to recognize that the rapid advance of global integration has contributed to a climate of uncertainty in many societies, a situation which is ripe for exploitation by those who peddle the quack remedies of protectionism and xenophobia. What is urgently needed is for governments, the private sector and academics to work together to restate clearly and persuasively the truth that the past 50 years of our history makes so evident—that open trade within the rules of the multilateral system is the key to growth, and hence to all our hopes of a more prosperous and stable existence.[47]

However, the World Trade Organization and its goals have been exceptionally controversial, and each of its meetings around the world has been met by violent protests, some of the largest seen since the 1960s. The coalition organizing these protests has been very broad based, representing labor, environmental, and other activists—essentially the same coalition that organized unsuccessfully against the NAFTA treaties here in the United States. These activists fear that the free trade principles represented in the WTO and its activities will undercut the public policies so carefully and slowly established in individual countries to protect the environment and the rights of individual workers. The resolution of this ongoing conflict remains to be seen.

FREE TRADE AREAS: A FAVORITE OPTION

With the end of the cold war and the collapse of the Soviet empire, the world started dividing into rival trade blocs. Critics warned that the world may be heading toward an economic disaster that could rival the disaster of the 1930s. At that time, protectionist alliances destroyed two-thirds of all global trade in little more than two years, helping turn a routine recession into a staggering depression that led to World War II.

European countries—which became a single, 12-nation economic force (now 15 nations, with another 13 preparing to join) now under the name of the European Union (EU)—are not the only ones forging new trade blocs with their neighbors. The United States, Canada, and Mexico formed the North American Free Trade Agreement (NAFTA). And now there are plans for a hemispheric free-trade agreement, which would also build on existing arrangements in South America, such as MERCOSUR, the Andean Pact, and the Central American Common Market. In Asia we see ASEAN recently expanding its geographic coverage and deepening the integration process. The South Asian countries are also developing a regional arrangement. And of course, we have Asian Pacific Economic Cooperation (APEC), which, while not yet involving trade preferences among its members, embodies an ambitious vision of free trade among countries in Asia and also across the Pacific Basin to North and South America. In Africa, several regional arrangements are being developed.

The idea behind free trade areas (FTAs) is simple: eliminate barriers to trade at the border between the partner countries but keep barriers against nonpartners. It is a system of preferential access. To protect those preferences, agreements usually set out "rules of origin" to prevent goods from nonmembers being transshipped through a partner FTA country with low external trade barriers to another with higher barriers.

FTAs can be self-contained or open to additional partners. New members can be added either under the same terms of entry as the original partners or through negotiated protocols of accession. Since new members can dilute the value of preferences received by existing members, there are few examples of open-ended FTAs. Most require new entrants to make additional concessions.

A FINAL WORD

The industrial age has held disappointments for us before but perhaps none so great as the growing belief that our civilization is out of control. By every conventional measure, the postwar world born in 1945 was a huge success for most Americans. More goods were produced and sold than ever before. More people were working, and the standard of living had never been higher. The suspicion grows, however, that this era has ended—never to return. There is a pervasive sense that something is fundamentally wrong.

Every generation faces uncertainty born out of change. But few, if any, generations in the past have had to contend with the extraordinarily rapid change that characterizes our times. What makes change today different from the past and what is driving it?

In two words: globalization and technology. Change today is defined by the dramatic internationalization, or globalization, of economic activity over the past two or more decades and the profound political and social consequences that flow from this. A great many forces have come together to drive globalization.

Government policies and business practices are a part of the reason for the globalization of the economy. A more important force behind rapid global economic and social change is technology.

The most fundamental change that has happened as a result of globalization is the blurring of the lines separating production and trade. Production processes are spread across the globe. Producers must invest to trade and trade to invest. Most products entering the market today are either traded or are heavily reliant on traded components for their production. More and more jobs rely on trade. Globalization also means rising living standards in many developing countries— global economic integration has helped, and is helping, to reduce poverty and marginalization. The fear of a great many Americans is that others' rising standards of living are coming at their expense.

In this age of globalization, governments must learn to cooperate in ways they have not had to in the past. For example, many of the distinctions we used to make between domestic and international policy look increasingly facile and irrelevant. Managing the political tensions that result from linking domestic issues such as human rights to trade agreements will require political agility and deftness. As the domain of international rule making and policy coordination expands (for example, the World Trade Organization) and the notion of domestic policy assumes a narrower focus, adequate care must be taken to safeguard diversity and preserve democracy.

Managing globalization in social terms also is a major challenge. It goes without saying that international economic integration and trade liberalization will result in economic pain for some. Americans will be displaced from their jobs as a result of these changes. There will, in other words, be winners and losers. Do the efficiency gains from specialization through trade that stimulate economic activity and create jobs make up for what may be lost through job displacement? Managing this transition and dealing with the distributional consequences of change will be the real challenge for President Bush and the federal government.

Whether we like it or not, globalization is here to stay. Protectionists cannot turn the clock back. The technological genie that is driving globalization is out of the bottle, just as the atomic genie escaped its bottle. The only real question is whether the United States is able to forge domestic and trade policies that help us adapt to the reality of today's global economy without an unbearable social cost. Now that the cold war is behind us, we must learn to be competitive in an expanding global market that promises to raise everyone's standard of living and, in the process, preserve a democratic peace.

A CLOSER LOOK

How do you feel about this country's economic future—is it bright and rosy or dim and troubled? Why? What policy steps could be taken to change this future?

FOR MORE INFORMATION

Boulding, Kenneth E. *Economics as a Science*. New York: McGraw-Hill, 1970.

Bunke, Harvey C. *A Primer on American Economic History*. New York: Random House, 1969.

Congressional Budget Office. http://www.cbo.gov/Index.cfm.

Federal Reserve Board. http://www.federalreserve.gov.

Friedman, Milton. *Capitalism and Freedom*. Chicago: University of Chicago Press, 1972.

Galbraith, John Kenneth. *Economics and the Public Purpose*. Boston: Houghton Mifflin, 1973.

Harrington, Michael. *Socialism*. New York: Saturday Review Press, 1972.

Reich, Robert. *The Future of Success: Working and Living in the New Economy*. New York: Vintage Books, 2002.

Schumpeter, Joseph A. *History of Economic Analysis*. New York: Oxford University Press, 1954.

———. *Capitalism, Socialism, and Democracy*. New York: Harper & Row, 1962.

Stiglitz, Joseph. Globalization and Its Discontents. New York: W. W. Norton, 2003.

World Bank. http://www.worldbank.org

Yergin, Daniel, and Joseph Stanislaw. *The Commanding Heights: The Battle for the World Economy*. New York: Touchstone Books, 2002.

NOTES

1. John Naisbitt, *Megatrends Asia: Eight Asian Megatrends That Are Reshaping Our World* (New York: Simon & Schuster, 1996), 11.
2. Ibid., 12.
3. Michael Mandel, *The High Risk Society: Peril and Promise in the New Economy* (New York: Random House, 1996), 3.
4. Congressional Budget Office, CBO's Current Economic Projections, 2002, http://www.cbo.gov/showdoc.cfm?index=1824&sequence=0.
5. Financial Trend Forecaster, Historical Consumer Price Index, 2002, http://www.fintrend.com/ftf/html/historical.asp.
6. Dow Jones Company, The Dow Performance at the Onset of Major National Security Events, 2002, http://www.djindexes.com/jsp/events.jsp.
7. Congressional Budget Office, Monthly Budget Review, October 2002, http://www.cbo.gov/showdoc.cfm?index=3858&sequence=0; U.S. Congressional Budget Office, Table 1: Revenues, Outlays, Surpluses, Deficits, and Debt Held by the Public, 1962–2001 (in billions of dollars), Historical Budget Data, 2002, http://www.cbo.gov/showdoc.cfm?index=1821&sequence=0#t1.
8. ABC News, "MoneyScope: Confidence Steady," ABCNews.com, 2002, http://abcnews.go.com/sections/business/DailyNews/abcmoneypoll020306.html.
9. Paul Krugman, *The Age of Diminished Expectations: U.S. Economic Policy in the 1990s* (Cambridge, MA: MIT Press, 1991), 7.
10. Bureau of Labor Statistics, "National Compensation Survey—Occupational Wages in the United States, 2001," Table 2, 2002, http://www.bls.gov/ncs/ocs/sp/ncbl0449.pdf.
11. AFL-CIO, Union Membership Trends, American Federation of Labor–Council of Industrial Organizations, 2002, http://www.aflcio.org/uniondifference/uniondiff11.htm.

12. Bureau of Labor Statistics, Table for Civilian Employment-Population Ratio, 20 Years and Over, Female, 2002, series LNU02300026, http://data.bls.gov/servlet/SurveyOutput Servlet.

13. U.S. Census Bureau, Income 2001, Table 1, 2002 http://www.census.gov/hhes/income/income01/inctab1.html.

14. Bureau of Labor Statistics, Highlights of Women's Earnings in 2001: Report 960, May 2002, http://www.bls.gov/cps/cpswom2001.pdf.

15. Federal Reserve Bank, Household Debt Service Burden, 2002, http://www.federal reserve.gov/releases/housedebt/default.htm.

16. National Center for Policy Analysis, Daily Policy Digest: Household Debt Levels Reach Scary Peak, October 2002, http://www.ncpa.org/iss/eco/2002/pd100902b.html.

17. Paul Krugman, *The Age of Diminished Expectations,* 9.

18. Ibid., 11.

19. Steven Rattner, "Income Equality in U.S. Expands Dramatically," *Wall Street Journal,* June 10, 1995, 10.

20. Frank Levy, *Dollars and Dreams, The Changing American Income Distribution* (New York: W. W. Norton, 1988), 3–4.

21. The White House, The President's Economic Security Agenda, 2002, http://www.whitehouse.gov/infocus/economy.

22. CNN Money, "Economists Call It Recession," November 26, 2001, http://money.cnn.com/2001/11/26/economy/recession.

23. Dow Jones, Dow Jones Averages Statistics, 2002, http://www.djindexes.com/jsp/avgStatistics.jsp#perf; Robert J. Samuelson, "Recovery or Recession?" *MSN/Newsweek,* 2002, http://stacks.msnbc.com/news/814444.asp.

24. Nancy Gibbs, "Summer of Mistrust," *CNN News,* July 15, 2002, http://www.cnn.com/2002/ALLPOLITICS/07/15/time.mistrust/index.html.

25. Ibid.

26. The most common measure of inflation in the United States is the Consumer Price Index (CPI), a number published each month by the government's Bureau of Labor Statistics. If the CPI in January is 1 percent higher than the CPI for December, inflation (which is usually reported on a yearly basis) is said to have a high of 12 to 13 percent.

27. Bureau of Labor Statistics, B-1: Employees on Nonfarm Payrolls by Major Industry, 1951 to Date, 2002, ftp://ftp.bls.gov/pub/suppl/empsit.ceseeb1.txt.

28. Ibid.

29. For an excellent discussion of Keynesian economics, see Robert H. Heilbroner, *The Worldly Philosophers: The Lives, Times, and Ideas of Great Economic Thinkers* (New York: Simon & Schuster, 1961), and *The Making of Economic Society* (Englewood Cliffs, NJ: Prentice-Hall, 1962). For a view opposing Keynes's economic theories, see Allan H. Meltzer, "Keynes' General Theory: A Different Perspective," *Journal of Economic Literature,* March 1981, 34–64.

30. Robert Kuttner, "A Liberal Dunkirk?" *The American Prospect,* November–December 1996, 6.

31. Ibid.

32. Ibid.

33. See Arjo Klamer, *Conversations with Economists* (Lanham, MD: Rowman & Littlefield, 1983).

34. Congressional Budget Office. Table 11: Surpluses, Deficits, Debt, and Related Series, 1960–2001, Historical Budget Data, 2002, http://www.cbo.gov/showdoc.dfm?index=1821&sequence=0#table11.

35. Jonathan Rauch, "The Long Good-Bye," *National Journal,* no. 8, February 22, 1992, 438.
36. Ibid., 439.
37. Federal Reserve Bank, Household Debt Service Burden, 2002, http://www.federal reserve.gov/releases/housedebt/default.htm.
38. Wynne Godley, "A Critical Imbalance in U.S. Trade: The U.S. Balance of Payments, International Indebtedness, and Economic Policy," Public Policy Brief No. 23 (Annandale-on-Hudson, NY: Jerome Levy Economics Institute. 1995), 1.
39. U.S. Department of Commerce, Bureau of Economic Analysis, BEA News Release, 2002, http://www.bea.gov/bea/newsrel/transnewsrelease.htm.
40. *San Francisco Chronicle,* May 24, 1996, A10.
41. Roger LeRoy Miller and Daniel K. Benjamin, *The Economics of Macro Issues* (Belmont, CA: West/Wadsworth, 1997), 159.
42. Bob Kuttner, "The Free Trade Fallacy," *New Republic,* March 28, 1983, 16.
43. Carnegie Endowment Commission Report, *Changing Our Ways* (New York: Carnegie Commission, 1992), 78.
44. Marco Marconini, *The Uruguay Round Negotiations on Services: An Overview* (Washington, DC: International Bank for Reconstruction and Development, 1996).
45. World Trade Organization, WTO: The Organization, 2002, http://www.wto.org/english/thewto_e/whatis_e/inbrief_e/inbr02_e.htm.
46. World Trade Organization, WTO: The Organization, 2002, http://www.wto.org/english/thewto_e/whatis_e/inbrief_e/inbr03_e.htm.
47. Renato Ruggiero, "The Road Ahead: International Trade Policy in the Era of the WTO," The Fourth Annual Sylvia Ostry Lecture, Ottawa, Canada, May 28, 1996.

Two ~

EDUCATION: EVERYBODY'S OPPORTUNITY—NOBODY'S RESPONSIBILITY

What are the signs that the American educational system is failing to do its job? Why might the system get worse before it gets better?
Why is education so important to a nation and to its people?
How has the philosophy of American education and the extent and nature of educational opportunities changed through American history? How have American ideals influenced American education? How has religion influenced American education?
What are some of the popular school reforms today? What, if anything, do they have in common? How effective are they?
How are President George W. Bush's educational policies different from or similar to former president Bill Clinton's?

The new millennium still finds the American educational system failing to adequately prepare many of our children to become productive and well-socialized citizens. Although a few states have made some progress in improving test scores, the United States still lags behind 14 other countries in math and science scores among eighth graders.[1] In California, for example, all seniors will be required beginning in 2004 to pass an exit exam in order to graduate from high school. In preparation for this make-or-break exam, tenth graders (they will be seniors in 2004) took it in fall 2002. Fewer than half (48 percent) were able to pass both the math and language parts of the exam. Critics of the exit exam point out that once again the disadvantaged groups are most at risk of not graduating. The tenth graders with the highest failure rate were disabled students (87 percent), English learners (81 percent), African American students (72 percent), and Latinos (70 percent).[2]

The school dropout rate remains high, and schools still experience far too much disruptive and often violent behavior. Employers continue to complain that today's students cannot write or think critically, and they are ill prepared to compete in the international job market. And the problems of school failure are not restricted to the poor and the dispossessed, although they suffer the most. The inner-city schools do not have a monopoly on inadequate school facilities, drug and behavior problems, or overworked and underpaid teachers. This is why education ranked first among voters on a list of national priorities for the first time in a January 1996 national poll, with 67 percent saying it was a major concern.[3] Education was a major issue both in the 1996 and 2000 presidential campaigns.

America has been in a panic about education for more than two decades—and is right to be worried. After all, the secret of American economic and political vitality is our greatest social invention: mass education. The United States is the only country to have committed to educating all of its citizens at public expense. It did so because of a general belief that human beings are malleable and that personal and material progress is possible if people are given an adequate education. Furthermore, a well-educated and socialized citizenry is essential to a democracy. This is all the more critical in a democracy made up of immigrants from diverse backgrounds and for whom English often is a second language.

In many ways, education is the most important issue in this book. If a nation does not adequately train and socialize (enculturate) its citizens—including its immigrants—then its economy will suffer and the quality of life (measured by the health and safety of its citizens) will be seriously eroded. Education alone cannot overcome the lack of civility evidenced in everyday life. Nor can it alone shrink the growing divide between the rich and poor, the haves and have-nots. However, without an improved educational system we can be sure these troubling developments will not disappear from the American landscape.

In this chapter we discuss the social and economic importance of education and how the schools have failed to socialize our children properly or to prepare them to be competitive in a global and technologically based economy. We will look at the changing role of education in American life, how it is structured and financed, and who influences and shapes educational policy. The evolution of the reform movement begun in 1983 and its different reforms will be discussed, as well. We also touch on a few of the more emotionally charged issues such as affirmative action, school prayer, and the fundamentalist's agenda for American education.

We limit our discussion to elementary and secondary education, even though significant changes are happening in American higher education. However important the issues in higher education, we believe the country's future depends on effective reforms at the elementary and secondary levels so that children are adequately prepared for a lifetime of learning.

THE SOCIAL AND ECONOMIC IMPORTANCE OF EDUCATION

Education has an impact on all of life. Schools are the only universal public institution in the United States. Children and young adults spend a big part of their day, and critical stages in their development, in school. This is even more true today as children enter preschool at ever earlier ages. The demands of a complex and technological society make education even more important to the economic and social well-being of us all. The significance of education is further enhanced by the erosion of other primary institutions, such as the church and, especially, the family. Schools are now asked to take over activities that were once considered familial. Schools are even asked to provide health and other social services to young people—particularly underprivileged children.

Education serves two functions primarily. It helps to socialize the young into becoming "good" citizens—politically involved, neighborly, and rule abiding. Through all of American history, education as a socializing agent for the young and immigrant populations has been a powerful force in the country's political and social stability. According to education historians David Tyack and Larry Cuban:

> The political theorist Hannah Arendt argued that in the United States education has played a "different and, politically, incomparably more important role" than elsewhere, in large part because of "the role that continuous immigration plays in the country's political consciousness and frame of mind." Educational leaders have tried to transform immigrant newcomers and other "outsiders" into individuals who matched their idealized image of what an "American" should be. . . . Many groups have contested with one another to define and create model citizens through schooling, and this political debate has shaped the course of public education.[4]

Today schools are under attack in part because it appears they are failing to properly socialize the young into becoming law-abiding and civilized citizens. When asked what their concerns are about public schools, consistently parents rank very high their fear for the safety of their children at school. Apart from the greater tendency to engage in violent or threatening behavior, there appears to be a general lack of civility and greater willingness to cheat in order to "get ahead," or to disregard rules in the name of expediency. In the political arena, we find that few young adults are willing to participate in politics (voter turnout is at an all-time low). The apparent lack of role models in politics, business, sports, and even in our churches, makes it all the more difficult for educators to instill in children proper values and personal integrity. However difficult, it is critical that the educational system serve as a counterweight to the growing trend of self-serving behavior that seems not to be governed by core values and a moral imperative.

A CLOSER LOOK

Did you feel safe in your high school? If not, why not? How honest were your classmates during exams, or when writing papers? Were you tempted to cheat? How did your high school teachers or administration handle cheating? Did they take it seriously? What, if any, were the consequences for someone caught cheating?

FIGURE 2.1
High School Dropout Rates of 16-24-Year-Olds, by Race/Ethnicity, October 1972-99

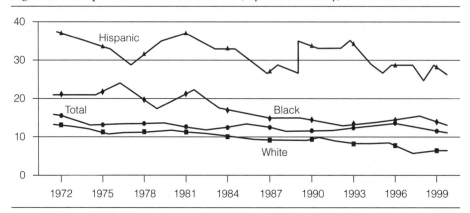

Source: Data from *Education Statistics Quarterly.*

The second function education serves is to prepare people for employment and to be generally productive citizens:

> Millennial thinking about schooling has also been a favored solution to social and economic problems. In the early twentieth century, educational elites saw themselves as expert social engineers who could perfect the nation by consciously directing the evolution of society. When Lyndon B. Johnson sought to build the "Great Society" and declared war on poverty in the 1960s, he asserted that "the answer to all our national problems comes down to a single word: education."[5]

Here too the educational system comes up short. Talk to employers and they will complain that many of their new recruits lack basic communication, analytical, and technical skills. Although America's dropout rate has declined since 1972, it was 12 percent in 1999, as compared with 8 percent in Germany and 6 percent in Japan. The dropout rates for Caucasians and African Americans have declined since 1972, while that for Hispanics has remained constant. Also, a greater percentage of Hispanics drop out as compared with all other ethnic/racial groups.[6] (See Figure 2.1.)

The school year is 180 days—60 days fewer than in some other countries. Japanese children do five times as much homework per week as their American counterparts. Even when they are working, American children are seldom stretched. The lack of a core curriculum in many schools encourages a shopping mall approach to education: pile up the soft options and leave the hard stuff behind. The result is all too predictable. American children perform poorly in international academic tests.

Simply put, a direct link has been clearly established between lack of education and an "increase in crime, a decrease in the level of personal income, limited job opportunities, and a restricted ability to compete in international markets."[7] Paul Barton, coauthor of a 1994 Educational Testing Service report on schools, suggests that tax dollars would be better spent on education and training rather than on building more prisons.

We have solid information now about how low the literacy level of prisoners is in relation to what the job market needs. And yet, over the last five years, as the prison population has expanded dramatically, more than half the states have cut back their training and education budgets. This is not a prudent approach. Education may not be the sole answer to cutting recidivism, but the evidence shows it helps.[8]

A person's lifetime earning power is greatly improved through education. Advances in technology have fueled the demand for a highly skilled labor force and transformed a high school education from a valued asset into a minimum requirement for entry into the labor market. As a result, young adults who do not finish high school are more likely to be unemployed and earn less when they are employed than those who completed high school. In addition, high school dropouts are more likely to receive public assistance than high school graduates who did not go to college.[9]

SCHOOLS: A LOCAL MATTER

American education has always been a local affair. Not so in Europe. There, education was centralized and controlled either by the government or by the church. Americans reversed this practice and placed the schools, so far as possible, under local and popular control. Thomas Jefferson strongly opposed centralization in government and education; he believed local government was the best guarantee of freedom. The U.S. Constitution does not refer to education, and consequently it has been and remains in the province of state government. In fact, however, it has been local government that has largely funded and operated public schools.

Until very recently no state took responsibility for financing public schools (in affluent districts, up to 95 percent of the school money comes from local property taxes), so the tradition of local autonomy has survived. Today, more than 95,000 citizens govern 15,000 school boards across the country.[10]

The first American schools were founded and administered by the colonists. At that time, education was not considered a responsibility of government. Schooling at all levels was essentially a voluntary matter—undertaken by families and the church. Citizens were responsible for raising money, preparing the curriculum, choosing books, hiring teachers, and building the schools. Eventually, professional administrators were hired to manage the schools, but the original citizens' committees (now called school boards) "continued to be responsible for the budget, personnel hiring and contract negotiations, the curriculum, and so on."[11] Elected school boards or local boards composed of parents and teachers continue to run public schools in the United States.

Educational opportunities for children from poor families were more limited. Other than in the home, these children could gain an education only by way of charity schools, established by religious groups or individual philanthropists. Government aid to education, though intermittent and voluntary, was not completely lacking. Still, for the most part, the federal and state governments were reluctant to provide universal education at public expense. It was not until after the Revolutionary War that many political and business leaders considered education necessary for the preservation of the new republic. Even so, it was not until about the time of the Civil War that social, political, and economic pressures led to the general acceptance of tax-supported public schools.

Industrial development, beginning in the last years of the eighteenth century and rapidly proceeding after the War of 1812, broke up the traditional agrarian social organization in most parts of the country, fostered the growth of cities, and produced new social problems. Child labor, the disintegration of traditional roles in the family, juvenile delinquency and increasing crime rates, dependence on often insufficient wages in a money economy, and other ills alarmed leaders in and out of government. Education came to be seen as an important means of providing a better life for all persons, especially those of the laboring class.

Schools in the larger cities were among the first to be supported by local property taxes. State governments were quite happy to pass legislation allowing for the use of local property taxes to pay for public schools; thereby relieving the states of this obligation. The common practice in most states was to allow for local voter approval for any school scheme involving regular taxation. As more public school districts were established, permanent state aid supplemented local effort, and the states gradually withdrew their support of private institutions. Furthermore, states ensured continuation of local taxation by making state aid contingent on the levying of a local school tax. Also, states used and still use their power over school funds to enforce compliance with requirements concerning matters of school organization and operation, such as teacher certification and the length of school terms.

This approach to education, as we have said, is quite different from that of Europe, where education is centrally run at the national level. Parents always have been more involved in the schools and their children's education in the United States than is true elsewhere in the world. "They are involved in the classroom as room parents; they do fundraising for the school, serve on committees, and run for the school board." [12] In no other country are parents so involved in their children's education.

The American approach to financing schools is not without its problems. The most pressing issues have to do with fairness and equity. The difference in spending levels between rich and poor school districts can be profound, resulting in unequal opportunity to receive a quality education for those living in the poorer school districts. In some cases, the courts have required states to take responsibility in ensuring more equal educational opportunity across local school districts.

Some policy analysts and educators are in favor of shifting more of the financial responsibility for education to the state by changing funding formulas that include a greater percentage of state taxes. There are states that are using more equitable funding formulas today. For example, approximately 70 percent of school funding in Michigan now comes from state taxes as opposed to a statewide average just a few years ago of 60 percent having come from local property taxes.[13] Chiara Nappi cites other examples: "In New Jersey, after more than ten years of lobbying by school districts, in November 1995 voters overwhelmingly approved a constitutional amendment requiring the state to pay for the school programs that it mandates. Many school districts are strangled by the requirements imposed by the state, and object to unfunded mandates especially when denied any flexibility in implementing them."[14]

The issue of who pays for public education relates to questions of control. In recent years, there has been a trend toward greater state control and state mandates. State control of elementary and secondary education is "visible not only among traditionally high-control states such as California and Florida, but also among longtime supporters of local control such as Virginia and Connecticut. In spite of the Republican theme of 'downsize and decentralize,' more state control seems to be the trend of the future in education."[15]

The push to establish and implement national educational standards is further evidence of the increasing role of national and state governments in education. A growing number of policy analysts and advocates for educational reform argue that "it is time to reconcile national needs with the tradition of local authority."[16] Chiara Nappi writes that "the prevailing notion that two school districts a few miles apart might have significantly different curricula is obviously outdated in these days of high mobility among the school population and high levels of communications. The world our students will enter is characterized by social and economic change, technological innovation, and global market competition. High standards of education are, for any country, the condition for economic stability and prosperity."[17]

States grant authority to local school boards for capital financing. School systems meet most of their capital needs by borrowing, usually through the sale of municipal bonds. A growing number of states in recent years require a two-thirds majority for passage of a school bond measure. California was one of these states until Proposition 39 passed in 2000. Former mayor of Lodi Randy Snider expressed the frustration of many voters and elected officials when he stated, "It is disturbing to me that 61.4 percent of the voters can support a school bond and it's still not enough to pass. For any political candidate, that margin of support would be considered a landslide victory."[18]

A CLOSER LOOK

Investigate how public schools are financed in your state and local community. Perhaps interview a local school board member or a principal to learn of the different sources of funding. What role do you think the federal government versus state and local authorities should play in public schools?

The passage of Proposition 39 means that only 55 percent of those voting need approve a school bond. Consequently, nearly every bond measure in the March 2002 election won voter approval—even with a near recessionary economy.[19] In most states only a simple majority is required for passage. State and federal loans and grants and public school building authorities provide additional capital resources to local school boards. Local public school districts spend most of their capital for the construction of elementary and secondary school classrooms.

Although educators are quick to credit aggressive campaign efforts by parents and other community members with the election victories, they also admit that districts are benefiting from the public's changing attitude toward schools. Concerns about falling test scores and the growing need for a highly educated workforce have raised expectations for schools. The increasing focus on education by both the federal and state governments, along with the introduction of such popular programs as class-size reductions, also have emphasized schools' needs for adequate funding.[20]

NEW IDEAS IN EDUCATION: THE PROGRESSIVE ERA

In the closing years of the nineteenth century, a group of reformers known as the progressives emerged from the new middle class. This group consisted mainly of young, educated men and women in the professions—law, medicine, social work, religion, teaching, and business—who believed they could use their expertise for the betterment of society. Repelled by inefficiency and immorality in business, government, and human relations, they set out to apply the scientific and rational techniques they had learned in their professions to the problems of the larger society.

The new preoccupation with efficiency and scientific management challenged educators to find technical solutions to the problems of modern mass society. Darwin's theory of evolution had upset traditional beliefs, immigration had replaced social uniformity with diverse nationalities, and economic change had shaken old habits of production and consumption. New ways of thinking had to be found, ways that would be meaningful for the new era yet preserve what was best in the past. A new flexibility was needed—not unlike today, as we enter the new century.

Changing patterns of school attendance encouraged these new ways of thinking. As late as the 1870s Americans attended school for an average of only four years, and educators believed their task was to cultivate virtue in children by exposing them to moralistic pieties. By 1900, however, the swelling cities and booming factories were providing the tax revenues to make extended mass education possible. Boosted by compulsory attendance laws, public-school enrollments rose from 6.9 million in 1870 to 17.8 million in 1910. During the same period, the number of public high schools grew from 500 to over 10,000.[21] By 1920, fully 78 percent of all children between ages 5 and 17 were enrolled in public elementary and high schools, and another 8 percent were in private and parochial schools.[22]

The progressives, with educational philosopher John Dewey in the vanguard, took up the cause.[23] The theory Dewey explored in *The School and Society* (1899) and *Democracy and Education* (1916) was a uniquely American phenomenon. Like American economic theory, it emphasized growth. To Dewey, it was personal growth, not mastery of a given body of knowledge, that was the goal of human existence.[24] Because people grew fastest mentally in their youth and because the family could no longer perform the educational functions it had fulfilled in an agrarian society, schools had to assume responsibility for cultivating intelligence and creativity.

Dewey and the progressives, in other words, believed children, not subject matter, should be the focus of school policy, and schools should serve as community centers and instruments of social progress. Above all, said Dewey, education should relate directly to experience. Children should be encouraged to discover things for themselves. Rote memorization and outdated subjects should be replaced by teaching techniques that make knowledge relevant to students' lives and skills useful in modern industrial society.

Education was seen as particularly important in preparing workers and immigrants for jobs in the factories. Schools were thought to be the best place to acquire the social and work skills needed to cope in the modern urban-industrial society. During this period, educators justifiably congratulated themselves for drawing more people into schools and for making instruction more meaningful. Yet few people looked beyond the increased enrollments to assess how well schools were doing their job. The faith that schools could promote equality and justice as well as personal growth and responsible citizenship underwent very little critical analysis.

SPUTNIK AND THE COLD WAR YEARS

In the years following World War II, Americans were preoccupied with education. They saw education as the key to their children's future financial success. As the baby boom became a grade-school boom, parents (particularly middle-class parents) rushed to join the Parent-Teacher Association (PTA) so that they would have a voice in the educational process. They expressed their concern that schools were overcrowded, understaffed, and aimless or that teachers were using obsolete methods. Educators encouraged their participation. "Just as war is 'too serious a matter to be left to the generals,' so, I think, the teaching of reading is too important to be left to the educators," wrote Rudolf Flesch in his best-selling book *Why Johnny Can't Read*.[25]

When the Russians launched *Sputnik,* the first earth-orbiting satellite, in 1957, education became a matter of national security. The Russian success challenged American military and technological superiority, based ultimately on the nation's school system. Critics argued that the United States needed to regain its technological leadership with a new emphasis on mathematics, foreign languages, and the sciences. In 1958 Congress responded with the National Defense Educational

Act (NDEA), which funded elementary and high school programs in those disciplines and offered fellowships and loans to college students. Parents were quick to endorse the new programs. After all, public education was the engine of democracy, a guarantee of both upward social mobility and military superiority.

To many people, it seemed that the American dream had come true. Whatever the nation's faults, it was the world's foremost land of opportunity. Americans boasted that they enjoyed political self-determination through the vote and social mobility through the melting pot. And public education, "the engine of democracy," guaranteed a better life to all who were willing to study and work hard. The obvious exceptions to the dream—the social and educational segregation, political disfranchisement, and economic victimization of nonwhite Americans—went unnoticed by most Americans, particularly those who were rushing to occupy newly built homes in the suburbs. And the lack of equal opportunity for women was concealed by an emphasis on femininity, piety, and family togetherness.

President Johnson's War on Poverty—with education programs serving as the principal weapon—was an ambitious attempt to make opportunities for the "good life" more equal for everyone. Johnson spent millions of federal dollars on education and job training programs during the late 1960s. As the War on Poverty evolved in 1965 and 1966, it included the Job Corps and Neighborhood Youth Corps to provide marketable skills, work experience, remedial education, and counseling for young people; the Work-Experience Program for unemployed fathers and mothers; Project Head Start to prepare low-income preschoolers for grade school; and Upward Bound for impoverished high school students who aspired to a college education. The landmark Elementary and Secondary Education Act, passed by Congress in 1965, provided federal aid to numerous schools. This act, along with the earlier National Defense Education Act (1958), represented an expanded role of the federal government in education. Today, the federal government's presence is felt in every schoolhouse.

The educational system experienced many changes during and after the turbulent 1960s. Court-ordered desegration of the schools and the women's movement left their imprint on the social dynamics in schools as well as on the content of textbooks and classroom instruction.

Federal funds were made available to schools to finance change and innovation. As a result, innovations such as open classrooms, team teaching, new math, individualized instruction, and alternative curricula appeared in American public schools. Educators began to emphasize thinking and decision-making skills rather than simply teaching facts. New, more realistic textbooks supplanted the "idealistic" literature previously used. These books dealt with new topics that reflected the lifestyles and attitude changes occurring in society, topics that included real-life family problems such as divorce and living on welfare, working mothers, death and dying, the changing roles of men and women, the lifestyles and practices of different ethnic groups, and formerly taboo adolescent subjects such as pregnancy, abortion, and homosexuality. The language of these books also became more graphic; street language began to be used to make the stories seem more "real." Not coincidentally, attacks on the public schools escalated.[26]

The relationship of school and religion also changed during this time. The U.S. Supreme Court took a much stronger stand against behavior such as school prayer and attempts to ban the teaching of evolution. "Although many applauded changes that occurred in public education during the mid-twentieth century, others firmly believed that public education was on a disastrous course of secularization."[27] The crisis in public education over what values and social perspectives will be taught to children and which methods of instruction are to be used is born out of the evangelical Christian fundamentalist movement.

A WARNING TO THE NATION

The first warning that American education was in trouble came in 1983, when the National Commission on Excellence in Education reported its findings in *A Nation at Risk*. The commission warned the nation of its deteriorating public school system and served as a catalyst for educational reforms. The report warned, "Our nation is at risk. Our once unchallenged pre-eminence in commerce, industry, science, and technological innovation is being overtaken by competitors throughout the world . . . [mostly because] the educational foundations of our society are presently being eroded by a rising tide of mediocrity that threatens our very future as a Nation and a people."[28]

What were some of the "indicators of risk," and are they still present after more than two decades of reforms and billions of educational dollars? The commission found that

> In 19 academic tests of international student achievement among industrialized nations, American students never placed first or second;
>
> 23 million American adults and 13 percent of all 17-year-olds were functionally illiterate;
>
> Average achievement of high school students on most standardized tests was lower than in the 1950s, and many 17-year-olds did not possess the higher-order thinking skills they should have; and
>
> Business and military leaders complained that they were spending millions on costly remedial training in such basic skills as reading, writing, spelling and computation.
>
> The average graduate of U.S. schools and colleges was not as well educated as the average graduate of 25 years ago.[29]

Although there has been some improvement in the educational system since *A Nation at Risk* was first published, most of these same "indicators of risk" exist in the new millennium. We will learn later in this chapter that educational reforms since 1983 have improved, but not yet eliminated, many of the deficiencies found by the commission in four areas of the educational process: content, expectations, time, and teaching.

The curriculum was criticized for failing to provide a clear purpose. The approach of most schools was to offer a wide choice of general-track courses in a cafeteria-style curriculum. When given the choice, students often selected the "softer" courses like health education and personal development and avoided the more difficult math and science courses.

The lack of focus or purpose in the curriculum had a negative effect on expectations, defined by the commission "as the level of knowledge, abilities and skills students should possess."[30] Lowered expectations were measured by the "declining level of student achievement, the reduced level of student effort (such as homework assignments), low diploma requirements and education standards, and access to college despite minimum competency and preparation."[31]

The commission found that students in the United States spent less time on schoolwork—in class and at home—than did students in Europe and in Asia. Furthermore, American students were able to take classes in such nonacademic areas as learning to drive and have these courses count the same as a math class toward graduation. This practice was unheard of in countries that competed against the United States in the global marketplace. Students often did not learn time management and study skills either.

The salaries and working conditions for teachers today are not much different than they were in 1983. If anything, the real salaries (after inflation) and classroom environment (safety, teacher-student ratio, and the number of students for whom English is a second language) are less desirable than a decade ago. A few states have made a special effort to improve the student-teacher ratio, such as California. The commission concluded that it was for these reasons that few talented people were interested in entering the teaching profession. The result was a shortage of qualified educators, particularly in the critical fields of science and math.

ENROLLMENTS TO HIT ALL-TIME RECORD

The educational crisis is only going to get worse as the nation continues to face record high enrollments at least until 2011 and, along with them, a shortage of qualified teachers and adequate classroom space. In fall 2001, a record 53.1 million students enrolled in K-12 schools. "It is the sixth consecutive record-breaking year," according to the U.S. Department of Education. The report also says that college enrollment reached a new high for the fourth year in a row.[32] It is predicted, however, that the enrollment growth will not be the same across the country. Some regions, such as the western states, will experience larger enrollment growth than many of the northwestern and Midwestern states. The largest growth is in high schools as the baby boomers' children move through their education.[33]

Nearly 200,000 additional teachers and at least 6,000 new schools are expected to be needed over the next ten years to accommodate what is called the "baby boom echo"—the children of the baby boom generation.[34] The report cites four factors that account for today's rising enrollments: a delay in marriage and childbearing among baby boomers, a higher birth rate among minorities, immigration, and students staying in school longer.[35]

A CLOSER LOOK

What is the average elementary and secondary teacher salary in your local area? How is your state addressing the need for more teachers? What is the average class size in your local high school? Do you think class size makes a difference in a student's education? Why? What was your experience with class sizes?

The financial demands on states and local communities will be significant as a result of this latest boom in the student population. For example, former secretary of education Richard Riley pointed out that "California can expect to add some half a million students to its high schools over the next decade, a 33 percent increase in enrollment in a state that already has one of the highest average class sizes in the country."[36] California is not the only state to face the stress of significant growth in the student population. Alabama, Alaska, Delaware, Hawaii, Maryland, Oregon, and Washington also can expect an overall jump of at least 10 percent in the number of students. In all, 33 states will have rising enrollments, mostly in the Far West and Southeast. School officials are now facing a serious challenge—how to serve significantly more students while investing in new technologies and continuing the drive toward higher academic standards and a well-prepared teaching staff.

At the same time that many states face the baby boom echo, education reformers are desperate to reduce class size. California legislators, for example, approved a plan to reward school districts in the amount of $19,500 for each class with 20 or fewer students. While this may be a good idea, it is nearly impossible to realize in those school districts that most need the additional cash. Joan Akin, principal for the new Creekland Middle School in Gwinnett County, Georgia, "knows that before she can worry about Reading, 'Riting and 'Rithmetic, she has to master the new R—Room."[37]

Simply put, there is little disagreement that serious problems in the American educational system exist. *How to fix* the problems is quite controversial, however. Virtually every fundamental aspect of the public school system now elicits quite heated, even violent, disagreement. Later in this chapter we will discuss the different reforms that have been proposed in recent years by policy makers, educators, and business interests.

EDUCATIONAL CRISIS: A FUNDAMENTALIST PROBLEM?

The Christian fundamentalist movement has challenged American public education for much of the twentieth century. When fundamentalism took center stage during the 1970s after a period of apparent hibernation, no two words better captured its public image and agenda than *Moral Majority*. In 1979, Jerry Falwell, a

Baptist minister, declared that people who were concerned about the moral decline of America were a majority waiting to be mobilized. He set out to accomplish that task, and ever since, conservative voters have been registered, rallies held, and legislators elected.

In the first 20 years of the 20th century, fundamentalists actively fought against modernism in their churches and against evolution in the schools. They eventually lost those battles but retreated and reorganized into a network of institutions that has housed much of the conservative wing of American Protestantism ever since. Fundamentalism was largely invisible on the American political scene until the 1970s. Evangelism and missions far outweighed social reform on their agendas. However, a number of things happened in the 1960s and 1970s to again mobilize fundamentalists as a social movement.

The rapid social change of the 1960s—the young rebelling against authority, women demanding equal treatment with men, the call for "free love," distrust of government, the Civil Rights Movement, the Vietnam War—looked to the "true believers" as if all of society was disintegrating. At least, the traditional and morally based society they believed in was falling apart, and rapidly. This seeming disintegration of society lent extra urgency to the evangelistic task of the fundamentalists.

The 1963 U.S. Supreme Court decision that outlawed prescribed prayers in school only confirmed in the minds of fundamentalists that the United States was fast on the road to hell. It seemed impossible that in this Christian country children should be told not to pray in school. Over the next decade, the evidence mounted in the minds of fundamentalists that the nation was being run by people intentionally hostile to their beliefs and determined to stamp out all vestiges of traditional religion in the coming generations.[38] The attacks on home, school, and church seemed so systematic that they surely must have come from a single ideological source, identified in Tim LaHaye's popular 1980 book, *The Battle for the Mind,* as secular humanism.

An important place fundamentalists have chosen to wage their battle against all that threatens their view of the world is in the schools. In a number of school board elections around the country, the fundamentalists and their supporters have won a majority of seats. In their battle to control local school boards and influence educational policy, they have resurrected the fight against the teaching of evolution by asking that "scientific creationism" be a part of the school curriculum alongside evolution. Other public school issues include efforts to reinstate prayers in the classroom and initiatives against the many forms of secular humanism to which conservatives fear their children are being exposed. And the legal strategies adopted were premised on viewing secular humanism as a religion (a premise given some legitimacy by reference to it as such in a 1961 Supreme Court opinion).[39]

So threatened are fundamentalists by the idea that children are being taught this "anti-Christ" religion called secular humanism that Carl Sommer, in *Schools in Crisis,* wrote, "Children are compelled to accept a religion contrary to their beliefs, students are trained in an environment that is hostile toward theistic religion

---

A CLOSER LOOK

Who sits on your local school board, and what are their beliefs regarding school prayer, the teaching of evolution, saying *under God* in the pledge of alligence, and other religious topics? What are your thoughts about the place of religion in public schools?

---

and prayer, the rights and liberties of the majority who believe in God are violated since they are forced to sustain a religion in which they do not believe in a tax-supported school, and schools are financing and establishing a religion in violation of the First Amendment."[40]

The age-old debate over religion and its place in the educational process is not about to go away—the very active Christian conservatives will see to that. Bush and Gore in the 2000 presidential election both played to the "religious right" in their many speeches about family values and the importance of education, as did Dole and Clinton in the 1996 election. Of course, the fundamentalists and their supporters will not be satisfied until they rid the schools of secular humanism and related liberal teachings that, in their minds, only serve to undermine the family and contribute to morally corrupt behavior among the young, such as drug use and promiscuity.

SCHOOL IS ONLY AS GOOD AS THE TEACHERS

Reduced class size, more-rigorous academic standards, better assessment tests, and improved reading instruction in American schools will not mean very much without good teachers. The National Commission on Teaching and America's Future points out that schools too often hire teachers destined to fail students because of lack of training in effective teaching methods, inadequate knowledge in subject matter—or both. In the Information Age, it is disturbing to know that "only 10 percent of public school teachers reported feeling 'very well prepared,' and an additional 23 percent reported feeling 'well prepared' to use computers or the Internet for instruction."[41]

Fewer than half of U.S. eighth graders (41 percent) are taught mathematics by a teacher trained in the subject, whereas 71 percent of their international peers are taught math by someone who majored in mathematics. Likewise, U.S. eighth graders are more likely than their international peers to be taught science by someone who majored in education, rather than, say, physics.[42] The National Center for Education Statistics reports that over a 13-year period (1987 to 2000) there was some progress in increasing the number of certified public school teachers and the percentage teaching subjects for which they were trained. Even so, "at least two-thirds of the students in middle-grade mathematics classes (69 percent) and ESL [English as a second language]/bilingual education classes (73 percent)

TABLE 2.1

Percentage of Public School Students Taught by Teachers with No Major and No Certification in the Course Subject Area, by Grade Level, 1987–88 and 1999–2000

	Middle Grades		High School Grades	
	1987–88	*1999–2000*	*1987–88*	*1999–2000*
English	64.6	58.3	38.2	29.8
Foreign language	—	60.7	—	47.6
Mathematics	69.9	68.5	37.4	31.4
Science	62.4	57.2	31.4	27.3
Biology/life science	70.0	64.2	47.7	44.7
Physical science	92.9	93.2	70.2	63.1
Chemistry	—	—	62.9	61.1
Geology/earth/space science	—	—	83.2	78.6
Physics	—	—	81.6	66.5
Social science	48.3	51.1	33.7	27.9
History	67.5	71.0	62.1	62.5
ESL/bilingual education	80.5	72.9	88.7	70.8
Arts and music	15.1	15.0	15.7	19.6
Physical education	22.2	18.9	24.8	19.1

Source: U.S. Department of Education, National Center for Education Statistics, *Qualifications of the Public School Teacher Workforce: Prevalence of Out-of-Field Teaching, 1987–88 to 1999–2000,* NCES 2002-603, by Marilyn McMillen Seastrom, Kerry J. Gruber, Robin Henke, Daniel J. McGrath, and Benjamin A. Cohen (Washington, DC: 2002), http://nes.ed.gov/ssbr/pages/field.asp.

Note: Middle-grade teachers include teachers who taught students in grades 5–9 and did not teach any students in grades 10–12; teachers who taught in grades 5–9 who identified themselves as elementary or special education teachers were classified as elementary teachers. High school teachers include all teachers who taught any of grades 10–12, as well as teachers who taught grade 9 and no other grades. Not all assignment areas were measured in each SASS administration. See source for notes and definitions of terms.

had teachers who did not report a major and certification in the subject taught. High school students are not much better served."[43] (See Table 2.1.)

    In the same 13-year period, there was not a significant change in the percentage of middle grade students taught by those without a major, minor, or certification in the subjects they were teaching. In "grades 5–8 in school year 1999–2000, between 11 and 22 percent of the students enrolled in English, mathematics, science, foreign language, social science, and the subfield of history were in classes led by teachers without a major, minor, or certification in the subject taught."[44] By contrast, the number of high school students taught by those without certification, a major, or a minor in the relevant subjects decreased significantly between 1987 and 2000.[45] (See Table 2.2.)

    While far too many students are still taught by ill-prepared teachers, the news is not all bad. "We know what to do. We know a great deal about what it takes to be a good teacher; we know what teachers need to know in order to succeed, and we know how to prepare teachers so they can be successful," reported the panel of prominent governors, business leaders, and educators who made up the National Commission on Teaching and America's Future.[46] The report offers real

TABLE 2.2

Percentage of Public School Students Taught by Teachers without a Major, Minor, or Certification in the Subject Taught, by Grade Level, 1987–88 and 1999–2000

	Middle Grades		High School Grades	
	1987–88	*1999–2000*	*1987–88*	*1999–2000*
English	19.5	17.4	13.0	5.6
Foreign language	—	13.8	—	11.1
Mathematics	17.2	21.9	11.1	8.6
Science	16.3	14.2	8.1	5.5
Biology/life science	32.9	28.8	9.3	9.7
Physical science	43.0	40.5	30.9	15.6
Chemistry	—	—	16.8	9.4
Geology/earth/space science	—	—	50.9	36.3
Physics	—	—	40.3	17.0
Social science	12.7	13.3	7.5	5.9
History	15.2	11.5	13.0	8.4
ESL/bilingual education	41.2	36.1	54.4	31.1
Arts and music	2.0	2.5	3.3	5.0
Physical education	5.8	3.4	5.6	4.5

Source: U.S. Department of Education, National Center for Education Statistics, *Qualifications of the Public School Teacher Workforce: Prevalence of Out-of-Field Teaching, 1987–88 to 1999–2000,* NCES 2002-603, by Marilyn McMillen Seastrom, Kerry J. Gruber, Robin Henke, Daniel J. McGrath, and Benjamin A. Cohen (Washington, DC: 2002), http://nces.ed.gov/ssbr/pages/field.asp.

Note: Middle level teachers include teachers who taught students in grades 5–9 and did not teach any students in grades 10–12; teachers who taught in grades 5–9 who identified themselves as elementary or special education teachers were classified as elementary teachers. High school teachers include all teachers who taught any of grades 10–12, as well as teachers who taught grade 9 and no other grades. Not all assignment areas were measured in each SASS administration. See source for notes and definition of terms.

hope because it includes a well-researched, sound, and understandable blueprint for improving the quality of the teaching force—a force that must increase by 2 million in the next decade to replace aging teachers and to meet the needs of a skyrocketing student population. For example, the commission argues that prospective teachers should have to prove to evaluators that they can design lessons, measure student progress, and teach classes effectively.[47] Other key points among the commission's 20 recommendations: every state should require teaching colleges to be accredited; nonaccredited programs should be closed; states must upgrade education programs for working teachers; and firing incompetent teachers should be made easier.[48]

The report also disputes the assumption that unqualified teachers are being hired because they are all that is available. Poor—sometimes totally absent—recruiting efforts explain some of the bad hiring. Sometimes well-prepared teachers are discouraged from applying for jobs, so the positions go to lesser-paid newcomers or younger instructors more likely to take orders. Other times bureaucratic red tape discourages good hires. "While there are shortages of qualified candidates in particular fields, e.g., mathematics and science, and particular locations (primarily inner city and rural), the nation each year produces more new teachers than it needs," the report states. A starting point, then, for many school districts, would be to overhaul their hiring processes. But that is only a tiny first step.[49]

TEACHER UNIONS AND THE PTA: OBSTACLES TO REFORM?

Teacher Unions

The two most influential teacher unions are the National Education Association (NEA) and the American Federation of Teachers (AFT). Teacher unions, like all unions, grew in size and power as it became apparent to teachers that only through collective bargaining would they see improvement in their wages and working conditions. It is interesting to note that collective bargaining in education grew rapidly beginning in the 1960s and remains strong to this day. Yet it was during this same period that unions declined in strength in industry.

As with all unions, the AFT and NEA work very hard to ensure that their members—whether unionized or not—earn the wages and enjoy the other terms and conditions of employment won through collective bargaining. In this way, teacher unions maintain their strength and raison d'être. This is why critics of teacher unions think of them as obstacles to true educational reform. Myron Leiderman writes that union efforts to stifle educational competition take many forms:

> ➢ Requiring all teachers, including teachers in private schools and home school parents, to be certified.

> ➢ Limitations on school board authority to contract out services, both instructional and non-instructional.

> ➢ Collective bargaining contracts which require school boards to employ teachers and support personnel at negotiated wage rates.

> ➢ All-out opposition to any legislation, no matter how small the scale, which could provide vouchers or tuition tax credits to parents who wish to enroll their children in private schools.[50]

In recent years, conservatives who oppose teacher unions because they are viewed as forces to maintain the status quo, concede that at least the AFT is more willing these days to consider such educational reforms as the privatization of education. Conservatives uniformly view the NEA, in contrast, as the single greatest roadblock to educational reform. However, those who support market-oriented reforms in education (for example, charter schools, vouchers, tax credits, and privatization) maintain that the only real differences between the AFT and NEA "are in the effectiveness of their opposition, not their basic hostility to any and all such reforms. Additional evidence on this is the fact that despite their differences in leadership, personnel and governance structure, the NEA and AFT overwhelmingly support the same candidates for public office and the same policies with respect to school choice and privatization."[51]

Teacher unions have significant political clout because of their financial resources and because of their large and politically active membership. Unions are not required by federal or state law to reveal their total income, and consequently, we cannot be certain of their total wealth. However, it is estimated that "their total annual revenues (local, state, federal, and overseas affiliates) are close to a billion dollars annually."[52]

A significant portion of these revenues are used to influence the political process, including supporting their political action committees (PACs). Both the NEA and AFT overwhelmingly support the Democratic Party and its candidates. The two unions, for example, made significant cash and in-kind contributions to the Gore campaign and to Democratic candidates for state and federal office in the 2000 election. In 1998–99, U.S. House Republicans received only $25,400 from the AFT, while the Democrats in the House received $1,607,200 (98 percent of AFT contributions). The NEA gave 94 percent of its contributions to the Democrats.[53]

Some speculate that the two unions will eventually merge. A vote was taken in fall 1998, but the NEA overwhelming voted against a merger at that time. Whether a merger happens, teacher unions are likely to remain a powerful political force with a vested interest in maintaining their control over *who* teaches *what* curriculum and *how* it is delivered. The union leadership and its rank and file argue they are as interested in school reform as their critics. Those opposed to the powerful teacher unions say that at best unions favor only incremental change, if not the status quo.

Parent-Teacher Associations

As we have said, parents always have been centrally involved in American education. Historically, parent-teacher associations (PTAs) were an important and trusted resource for the public, for policy makers, and for teachers. Not so today, the critics argue. Instead, many think PTAs have become ineffective and no longer are a valued resource for accurate, impartial information to help parents and policy makers understand what is happening in the educational system. Some of the reasons given for why PTAs are ineffective today include:

Teacher union influence.   National PTA policies and positions reflect the dominant influence of the teacher unions—the American Federation of Teachers (AFT) and especially the National Education Association (NEA).

Misdirected resources.   At the local level, the PTA is a fund-raising auxiliary for school districts, while its child advocacy efforts focus on social, noneducational issues.

Stifled debate.   Many PTA officials stifle open discussion of controversial issues, discourage parents from questioning the PTA's official positions, and restrict meetings to dues-paying parents and teachers.

Ignorance.   Most PTA members (80 percent in a recent national poll) have no idea of the policies advocated in their name by the national and state PTA hierarchies.[54]

National PTA leaders stated at the centennial celebration in May 1996 that their goals for the next century centered on their becoming serious players in educational policy making. In order to make this happen, they said, it is time the PTA shed its bake sale image and step up its lobbying efforts—enlarging the membership, collaborating with businesses and government agencies, and helping to train parents to become informed and effective agents for educational change.

Not everyone agrees with this new direction, however. Charlene Haar writes that

> to be effective for parents—and ultimately for children—the PTA should: Abandon its intent to become yet another group lobbying for government programs and increased government funding. Drop its union-like unified membership structure. Replace the practice of fundraising activities which are now all too often a diversion to more meaningful discussions and activities. End the practice of taking sides on issues which then eliminate parental debate. Instead, PTA should strive to become the most prestigious, unbiased, educational resource center in America by greatly expanding its role as a non-profit, charitable and educational organization. To accomplish this, PTA should support original research on issues of concern to parents. Where unbiased information already exists, PTA should translate that into parent-friendly publications useful for their use.[55]

Whatever role the PTA chooses to play in the educational system, it is clear that PTAs can and should be an important resource for informing parents of what their children are being taught in school and how. Often parents are intimidated by the educational system and do not know what to do or where to go for information. When so many others are in charge of making decisions, often there seems little for parents to decide—or at the very least, parents feel intimidated by their unequal role. Perhaps PTAs are a place where that inequality gap can be closed as accurate, unbiased information is provided and a forum for open discussion between parents, teachers, and policy makers can be created. This cannot happen as long as PTAs act as mere extensions of the teacher unions.

SCHOOL REFORMS: LET US COUNT THE WAYS

Everyone who is invested in education—parents, teachers, administrators, school boards, politicians, and community groups—are torn in many different directions by various constituencies with "divergent agendas."[56] Undoubtedly, there have been more attempts to reform schools in this country than anywhere else in the world. Over the years, the different reforms often have been at cross purposes simply because we have had, and continue to have, conflicting goals for education. Francis Schrag provides us with a few examples:

We'd like schools to offer a large array of activities utilizing the latest facilities, but we'd also like schools to be warm, family-like places that offer community and personal attention.

We'd like schools to be places where children of high academic ability can mingle with those of limited ability, each group benefiting from acquaintance with the other, but we'd also like each child to be challenged and stretched to the limits of his or her academic ability, without needing to wait for classmates to catch up.

We'd like a grading system in which grades have uniform, unequivocal meanings, but we'd also like a grading system in which children are not constantly compared with each other or made to feel superior or inferior to other children.

We'd like children to develop a love for learning, yet we'd also like to assure ourselves that they know or can do certain things we designate as essential.

We'd like athletic teams that give everyone a chance to participate and also win conference championships.[57]

Americans tend to equate progress with change and "celebrate innovation."[58] American faith in change, particularly if it is labeled innovative, certainly is evident in the literally hundreds of major and minor reform efforts in education. Some argue that the American educational system is "too trendy, that entirely too many foolish notions circulate through the system at high velocity."[59] Still others believe educators are far too resistant to change and instead are determined to use "old fashioned" and tradition-bound teaching techniques. Tyack and Cuban suggest both are true; that is, educators are vulnerable to faddism just as they are determined to teach using the tried-and-true methods. "Educators have often paid lip service to demands for reform to signify their alertness to the public will. But their demands for reform often protected school people from basic challenges to their core practices."[60]

Tyack and Cuban go on to say in their award-winning book, *Tinkering toward Utopia: A Century of Public School Reform:*

In the last generation reforms have come thick and fast, as educators can testify. Since the value of change is in the eye of the beholder, one set of innovators may seek to undo the results of previous reforms. At one time reformers thought that the graded school—which groups children by age and proficiency—greatly enhanced educational efficiency; later critics sought to create ungraded schools as a way to break the lockstep of fixed grades. Curriculum designers succeeded in substituting easy texts for classic works in English classes for "slow learners," only to find the new curriculum condemned as the educational equivalent of junk food.[61]

Above all else, politics is at the core of every attempt to reform the educational system. Once again in the words of Tyack and Cuban, "Groups organize and contest with other groups in the politics of education to express their values and to secure their interests in the public school. Conflicts in education have arisen over ethnic, religious, racial, gender, and class differences. Controversies over language policies—English only or bilingual instruction—have recurred for over a century, as did contests over racial or gender segregation or the use of the Bible and prayer in schools."[62]

Chester E. Finn Jr., writes that educational reforms in this country fall into one of four broad genres. He describes them as follows:

> By far the most common is piecemeal tinkering with the countless gears and levers of the existing machinery: upgrading teacher training programs, stiffening graduation requirements, installing technology, revamping the first grade reading program, shrinking class size, adding a period to the school day, and on through hundreds of variations.
>
> The second genre of education renewal, known within the field as "systemic" reform, tries to deal more comprehensively with this intricate machine by aligning its academic standards, curriculum, textbooks, tests and teacher training with one another. This strategy underlies President Clinton's controversial "Goals 2000" program (recently amended into near-triviality) and efforts by many educators, business leaders and governors to impose standards-based change on entire states and communities.
>
> The third genre concentrates on individual schools rather than sprawling systems. It would devolve management authority to them, empower their principals, experiment with new governance arrangements (such as Chicago's "local school councils" and the fast-spreading "charter" school idea), and devise novel designs for school structure and curriculum, such as those sponsored by the New American Schools Development Corporation, the Edison Project and Theodore Sizer's Coalition of Essential Schools.
>
> The fourth genre is more radical, better termed abandonment than reform. Voucher advocates promise that the private school marketplace will rise to the challenge of educating young America. A new organization called the "Separation of School & State Alliance" agitates for a complete end to "government compelled attendance, financing, curriculum, testing, credentializing, and accreditation." Wall Street firms hold conferences for investors in the "education industry" (which already has its own business newsletter) and corporations contemplate ambitious schemes for privatizing education, much like commercial security services in neighborhoods weary of inadequate police protection.[63]

We cannot in the space of this chapter review all, or even most, of the proposed reforms to improve American education. We will, however, touch on some of the more significant reform efforts, beginning with an attempt to establish for the first time in American history a set of national educational goals to guide us into the next millennium. (In Box 2.1 we provide a selected guide to critical educational terms. Many of these terms refer to different educational reforms. In interpreting the terms, E. D. Hirsch offers his critique.)

Box 2.1

CRITICAL GUIDE TO EDUCATIONAL TERMS AND PHRASES

At their own pace. A phrase implying that children should develop naturally rather than being forced to learn too rapidly; also called "self-paced learning." Going at one's own pace would seem to be more natural than going at someone else's, but there is no reliable evidence to support the idea of self-pacing. On the contrary, the data show that the imposition of externally set timelines, goals, and rewards greatly enhances achievement.

Authentic assessment. A laudatory term for "performance assessment," where students receive grades for their performances on realistic tasks such as writing a letter, producing a play, and solving a "real-world" mathematics problem. Such performances are also called "exhibitions." The progressive tradition has long advocated teaching and testing through "realistic" projects instead of through separate subject matters, and has long rejected tests that probe isolated knowledge and skills. To serve democratic ends, American educators have pioneered the creation of fair and accurate multiple-choice tests that probe a wide variety of knowledge and skills. The consensus among psychometricians is that these objective tests, rather than performance tests, are the fairest and most accurate achievement tests available. Performance tests, while important as one tool for classroom use, should not play a decisive role in high-stakes testing, where fairness and accuracy are of paramount importance.

Child-centered schooling. Also formulated as "student-centered schooling," to include the later grades. The phrase is a self-description of progressive education. The idea is epitomized in the injunction "Teach the child, not the subject." The opposition between child-centered and subject-centered education implies that teaching that focuses on subject matter tends to ignore the feelings, interests, and individuality of the child. Progressivists describe subject-centered instruction as consisting of lecture format, passive listening, mindless drill, and rote learning, and as directed to purely academic problems that have no intrinsic interest for children. This picture is mere caricature. Observation has shown, on the contrary, that children are more interested by good subject matter teaching than by affectively oriented, child-centered instruction.

Cooperative learning. A term describing the pedagogical method of breaking up a class into teams of five or so students who cooperate to complete a joint task or project. One of its advantages lies in its use of more advanced students to help teach less advanced ones, thus promoting the education of both groups, so long as the two groups are not too far apart in academic preparation. Cooperative learning, used with restraint, can be an excellent method of instruction when used in conjunction with whole-class instruction. It has not been effective when used as the principal or exclusive means of instruction.

Critical thinking skills. A phrase that implies an ability to analyze ideas and solve problems while taking a sufficiently independent, "critical" stance toward authority to think things out for oneself. In the progressive tradition, "critical thinking" has come to imply a counterpoise to the teaching of "mere facts," in which, according to the dominant caricature, sheeplike students passively absorb facts from textbooks or lecture-style classrooms. Critical thinking, by contrast, is associated with active, discovery learning and with the autonomous, independent cast of mind that is desirable for the citizens of a democracy. Independent-mindedness is always predicated on relevant knowledge: one cannot think critically unless one has a lot of relevant knowledge about the issue at hand. Critical thinking is not merely giving one's opinion. Common sense and cognitive psychology alike support the Jeffersonian view that critical thinking always depends on factual knowledge.

Culturally biased tests. A phrase expressing the claim that many standardized tests, such as the SAT, are culturally biased. The claim arises from the fact that different cultural groups perform differently on the tests. The difference in group performance on tests raises two distinct questions:

1. Are the tests themselves technically biased? (If so, everyone agrees they must be changed.)
2. If the tests are not technically biased, what policy decisions should be taken in light of the different group performances on the tests?

Discovery learning. The phrase refers to the teaching method that sets up projects or problems so that students can discover knowledge for themselves through hands-on experience and problem-solving rather than through textbooks and lectures. The premise is true that knowledge acquired on one's own, with difficulty and by expending lots of time and effort, is more likely to be retained than knowledge presented verbally. It is also true that knowledge gained in a realistic context as part of an effort to solve a problem is likely to be knowledge that is well understood and integrated. Unquestionably, then, discovery learning is an effective method—when it works. But there are two serious drawbacks. First, students do not always make on their own the discoveries they are supposed to make; in fact, they sometimes make "discoveries" that are not true. Hence, it is essential to monitor students to probe whether the desired learning goal has been achieved, and if not, to reach the goal by direct means. Second, discovery learning has proved to be very inefficient. Research into teaching methods has consistently shown that discovery learning is the least effective method of instruction in the teacher's repertory.

Higher-order skills. A phrase for the superior thinking skills that many current educational reforms aim to achieve. The goal is to produce students who can think and read critically, who can find information, who have mastered metacognitive strategies, and who know how to solve problems. Such students, it is asserted, will be better prepared to face the challenges of the twenty-first century than those who merely possess a lot of traditional, soon-to-be-outdated, rote-learned information. Higher-order skills are invariably and necessarily conjoined with a great deal of relevant, domain-specific information. Hence, there is no way to gain the skills without gaining the associated information. It is mere prejudice to assert that the strategies associated with using domain-specific information are of a "higher order" than the knowledge itself.

Lifelong learning. The phrase reflects a goal shared by almost all educators since antiquity. Today, when new technologies must be mastered and even new professions learned, the task of making everyone competent to learn throughout life is a primary duty of the schools. There exists, however, a disagreement about the nature of the schooling that best promotes a lifelong ability to learn. Under the tool conception of learning, students must be given not only reading, writing, and computational ability but also further abstract competencies such as "accessing skills," "critical thinking skills," and "higher order skills," in the belief that these abstract competencies can then be directed to an indefinite number of future tasks. Lifelong competencies, including reading, writing, and critical thinking, depend on the domain-specific factual and verbal knowledge spurned by many present-day "reformers."

Open classroom. A phrase for an upgraded classroom in which children of different ages can learn "at their own pace," and receive individual attention rather than follow in step with the class as a whole. In its pure form, "open" was also an architectural description—no walls between classes. Like all forms of naturalistic pedagogy, the open classroom has proved to be ineffective as a principal technique of schooling.

Outcomes-based education. A term of uncertain meaning that during the 1990s became a symbolic cause of verbal war between political liberals and conservatives. It is best understood historically. In the late 1980s and early 1990s, in the midst of public discontent with students' test scores in reading and math, some professional educators proposed that schools pay relatively less attention to methods of schooling, such as discovery learning, and more attention to results. They labeled this idea "outcomes-based education." Their goal was to correlate teaching methods more closely with results.

Portfolio assessment. A phrase for a version of performance-based assessment. In portfolio assessment, students are graded for the totality of their production. It is a device that has long been used for the teaching of writing and painting. But there its utility ceases. It has proved to be virtually useless for large-scale, high-stakes testing.

Problem-solving skills. A phrase often used in conjunction with "higher-order skills" and "critical-thinking skills." In a narrow sense, it refers to the ability to solve problems in mathematics or other specialized fields. More broadly, it refers to a general resourcefulness and skill that will enable the student to solve various future problems. The nature of this general problem-solving skill has not been scientifically defined, and it is doubtful that it exists. Work on the problem-solving abilities of specialists like doctors, chess players, and physicists has shown consistently that the ability to solve problems is critically dependent on deep, well-practiced knowledge within the special domain, and that these problem-solving abilities do not readily transfer from one domain to another.

Source: E. D. Hirsch Jr., *The Schools We Need and Why We Don't Have Them* (New York: Doubleday, 1996), 241–271. We encourage the reader to go directly to the source for the complete glossary and Hirsch's full discussion and critique of these terms.

THE IMPROVING AMERICA'S SCHOOLS ACT OF 1994

The Improving America's Schools Act (IASA) of 1994 both reauthorized and fundamentally restructured the Elementary and Secondary Education Act (ESEA) of 1965, including Title 1. The overarching goal of IASA is to support comprehensive state and local reform of teaching and learning, such as carried out under Goals 2000 (discussed below). The emphasis is on high academic standards with aligned curriculum, assessment, and professional development. Title 1 focuses on helping disadvantaged students meet the same high standards expected of all children. Specifically, the IASA supports four broad goals:

> High standards for all students

> Teachers better trained for teaching to high standards

> Flexibility, to stimulate local reform, coupled with accountability for results

> Close partnerships among families, communities, and schools[64]

Research shows that students are capable of achieving higher academic standards if only they are challenged to do so. The problem is that too often teachers neither demand nor expect that students strive to achieve higher academic standards. The IASA provides resources to states and school districts to support their efforts to help students reach higher state standards. Former secretary of education Richard Riley points out that the IASA "replaces the piecemeal structure of the old ESEA. ESEA programs will now be integrated into a state's overall school improvement efforts, focused around a core of challenging state standards. ESEA programs now promote the alignment of all education components—curriculum and instruction, professional development, school leadership, accountability, and school improvement—so that every aspect of the education system works together to ensure that all children can attain challenging standards."[65]

The IASA also recognizes that if students are to reach higher levels of achievement, it is first necessary that professional development for teachers, principals, and other school staff be provided. Funds to support professional development at the school and district level, with teachers and principals playing an important role in determining what kind of training they need, are provided through the IASA. The desire is to move away from one-time workshops and toward more lasting training efforts that are integrated into the daily life of the school.

The IASA also revises the Elementary and Secondary Education Act of 1965 to provide broad flexibility to states, school districts, and schools in their implementation of federal programs. At the same time, the IASA calls for strategies to hold school districts and schools accountable for improved student achievement. For example:

> States and school districts may choose to consolidate their federal administrative funds and to administer those funds in a coordinated way without having to keep detailed records. The law also allows states and local districts to consolidate their plans and applications when they apply for federal funds.
>
> [IASA] will ensure greater accountability through the use of state assessments that measure students' progress toward new state standards. The same standards and assessments developed by a state for all children will apply to children participating in Title 1. These two fundamental changes in Title 1—the role of high academic standards and the use of state assessments—will help ensure that Title 1 is an integral part of state reform efforts, rather than another add-on federal program.[66]

Based on evidence that meaningful, ongoing family involvement in children's learning is an essential link to achieving a high-quality education and a safe, disciplined learning environment, IASA supports greater family-school and community-school connections. In this context, it also is important for parents to work with their children to develop better time-management skills (see Table 2.3). For the first time, a federal program will actively support partnerships between schools and parents for improved student achievement through school-parent compacts. Compacts will spell out the goals, expectations, and shared responsibilities of schools and parents as partners in student success. IASA also fosters integration with other education programs, including Title VII, Head Start, Even Start, and School-to-Work Opportunities systems and, where necessary, health and social service programs to better serve the needs of students in high-poverty schools.[67]

GOALS 2000: WILL THEY WORK?

Nearly every country in competition with the United States in the global marketplace has national educational goals and a centralized governance structure; the United States has neither. In fact, of the 20 countries that participated in the 1991 International Assessment of Educational Progress (IAEP), 16 have national

TABLE 2.3
Students' Use of Time, Ages 9, 13, and 17, 1984 and 1999 (percentages)

	Watched Television 3 or More Hours Daily	Any Homework Assigned	Homework Not Done	Time Spent on Homework			Read Daily for Fun
				Less than 1 hour	1 to 2 hours	More than 2 hours	
Age 9							
1984	66.7	64.4	4.1	41.5	12.7	6.1	53.3
1999	51.1	74.2	3.8	53.1	12.4	4.9	54.1
Age 13							
1984	63.4	77.4	3.7	35.9	29.2	8.6	35.1
1999	45.9	75.9	4.5	37.2	26.3	7.9	28.2
Age 17							
1984	43.7	77.5	11.4	26.2	26.8	13.2	30.8
1999	34.3	73.6	13.1	26.4	22.6	11.5	24.8

Source: U.S. Department of Education, NCES, National Assessment of Educational Progress (NAEP): 1984 and 1999 Long-Term Trend Assessment (Washington, DC).

curricula and centralized educational systems. Only Canada, Switzerland, and Brazil join the United States in having state or provincial control of education.[68] In the absence of nationally agreed upon and clearly articulated learning goals, the thousands of local school districts in this country are able to set their own educational policies, goals, and standards virtually free from state or federal control. A report by the National Education Goals Panel states that "most countries embody their content standards in curriculum guides issued by the ministries of education, or their equivalents."[69]

The first real effort to establish national educational goals was made by George H. Bush when he was president. President Bush's agenda for American education was realized in February 1990, when the nation's governors met in a historic education summit in Charlottesville, Virginia, to establish educational goals for the 1990s. The summit had a well-defined purpose: "to establish clear, national performance goals, goals that will make us internationally competitive."[70]

One result of this summit was the six goals that make up the "Goals 2000 Educate America Act" (or simply "Goals 2000") that was signed into law by President Clinton in 1995. The six goals that make up Goals 2000 are:

≫ By the year 2000, all children in America will start school ready to learn.

≫ By the year 2000, the high school graduation rate will have increased at least 90 percent.

≫ By the year 2000, American students will leave grades four, eight, and twelve having demonstrated competency over challenging subject matter including English, mathematics, science, history, and geography, and every school in America will ensure that all students learn to use their minds well, so they may be prepared for responsible citizenship, further learning, and productive employment in our modern economy.

> ➤ By the year 2000, American students will be first in the world in achievement in science and mathematics.

> ➤ By the year 2000, every adult American will be literate and will possess the knowledge and skills necessary to compete in a global economy and exercise the rights and responsibilities of citizenship.

> ➤ By the year 2000, every school in America will be free of drugs and violence and will offer a disciplined environment conductive to learning.[71]

The year 2000 has come and gone, so we may reasonably ask how we did as a nation in achieving Goals 2000. We will find, as is usually the case in these matters, that the report card is mixed. For example, goal 1 called for all children to start school ready to learn. According to Kevin Bush Weller, project editor for Education Vital Signs and a senior editor of the *American School Board Journal,* many students are poorly prepared for school largely due to inadequate day care and preschool programs. Weller writes that "the 'atrocious' quality of day care in this country continues to be a major barrier to achieving this goal, argues Edward Zigler, director of Yale University's Bush Center in Child Development and Social Policy and widely regarded as the 'father' of Head Start."[72] Zigler points out that day care and preschool staff are often paid minimum wage and are not trained to assist children with their developmental needs.[73] Poor children are at even greater risk in that many of them do not even attend day care or preschool programs. The news is not all bad, however. Considerable progress has been made in the area of health, for example. "The percentage of 2-year-olds who have been fully immunized against preventable childhood diseases increased from 75 percent in 1994 to a record 80 percent for 1998, according to the federal Centers for Disease Control and Prevention (CDC). As a result, says CDC, disease and death from diptheria, pertussis, measles, mumps, rubella, and tetanus are at or near record lows."[74]

The second goal was to have 90 percent of high school students graduate. There has been marginal improvement in this area. "According to U.S. Census figures, the nation's high school completion rate for 18- to 24-year-olds increased 1 percentage point to 86 percent between 1989 and 1997. Already 15 states have met the 90 percent goal, with Maryland leading the pack at 95 percent. At 77 percent, Nevada has the lowest completion rate."[75]

Goal 3 would have students leaving grades 4, 8, and 12 having shown competency in several subjects, including math, English, science, foreign languages, civics, and government. On the positive side, the percentage of students proficient in math rose between 1989 and 1998 in the above mentioned grades. Unfortunately, proficiency in reading declined during the same period. Becoming a good citizen is part of this goal, and here we have had little success. "Boston University character education expert Kevin Ryan says the nation should receive a failing grade. You need look no further than the nation's high achievers—America's future political and business leaders—to appreciate the depth of the problem, Ryan says. According to a 1998 survey of 3,123 teenagers by *Who's Who Among*

American High School Students, 80 percent of the high-achievers surveyed admit they have cheated on an exam—and increasing percentages of these students say they are prejudiced against minorities and gays."[76]

Goal 4 speaks to the need to improve teacher education and professional development. Here too the report card is not as good as we hoped. "The percentage of secondary school teachers who hold a degree in their main teaching assignment has decreased. The only element of the goal in which significant progress has been made is in the number of states that have improved—seventeen."[77]

We also have not progressed as far as we would like toward achieving goal 6. While the "proportion of college degrees awarded in math and science has risen,"[78] seniors in high school still rank toward the bottom in math and science when compared with other countries.[79] We have made little progress in helping all adults to become literate (goal 6), and in creating a drug-free and safe school environment for our children (goal 7). "More than one of every five U.S. adults reads at or below a fifth-grade level, according to the National Institute for Literacy, in Washington, D.C."[80] One reason for the lack of success in helping all adults to become literate and to obtain skills necessary to compete in today's job market is the fact that school boards often pay little attention to adult education programs.[81] Drugs are more available in schools today than anytime in the past. Newspaper headlines remind us much too frequently that our schools are not safe from violence.

As a result of setting national goals that are of a general nature, there are efforts at the state and local levels to identify what students should know and be able to do within specific content areas or disciplines.[82] For example, the professional organization for mathematics teachers has identified 12 goals for mathematics education.[83] These include enhancing

Mathematical problem solving

Communication in mathematics

Mathematics reasoning

Connections between mathematics concepts

Understanding of functions

Understanding and use of algebra

Understanding of geometry from a synthetic perspective

Understanding and use of trigonometry

Understanding and use of statistics

Understanding and use of probability

Understanding and use of discrete mathematics

A basic understanding of calculus

Similarly, there are efforts by other professional organizations to identify learning goals in their areas of specialization, such as history, languages, geography, science, and social studies. The question is, Are these efforts to establish national learning goals, both general and specific, helping to solve the problems of American eduction? The answer is a qualified no.

A CLOSER LOOK

How would you rate your high school in terms of Goals 2000? Taking each one separately, think about your high school education and school environment. What grade would you give them, and why? Interview one of your classmates or college friends about their high school years in terms of these goals.

OUTCOMES-BASED EDUCATION: A GOOD IDEA GONE BAD?

Among the many reform initiatives floating around, outcomes-based education (OBE) was thought to be a surefire winner. After all, the "education president" himself, George H. Bush, first promoted it as a way to ensure all children leave school having demonstrated competencies in those subjects deemed essential to success in today's working world. Comptetency-based education is an important part of George W. Bush's education program (we discuss President Bush's No Child Left Behind Act of 2001 below). One attraction of outcomes-based education—particularly among conservatives—was the belief that it would hold educators accountable. Francis Schrag observes, "Exponents of this position will say, if we are clear about what we specifically want young people to be able to do, we will be well on our way to evaluating the success of their schooling, because it is not nearly as hard to find out what things people can demonstrate as it is to find out what they understand."[84]

Moreover, the measures used to assess outcomes were to be "criterion referenced"—based on what students needed to know in the "real world"—rather than normalized according to what the average student was doing. It was hoped this would lead to, among other things, a closing of the gap between American children and those in Germany and Japan. "Chester E. Finn, the most innovative educational thinker in the Reagan and Bush administrations, pushed hard for OBE," reports the White House Web site, "and it became part of former President Bush's America 2000 education proposals. The idea also became a part of former president Bill Clinton's education program, now enshrined in Goals 2000—the Educate America Act."[85] (OBE is the third goal in Clinton's Goals 2000 program.) Not to be outdone, President George W. Bush's No Child Left Behind Act of 2001, Schrag reports, "requires all states to set high standards for achievement and create a system of accountability to measure results."[86]

Outcomes-based education, perhaps more than any other reform, demonstrates why it is so difficult in this country to realize any significant change in how we educate our children. To say the OBE effort has been met with controversy and resistance on nearly every front and for different reasons is an understatement. The religious conservatives distrust it as an attempt to force political correctness or worse onto their children. Others argue that its educational goals are mushy and therefore difficult, if not impossible, to measure. Yet when it was first proposed, nearly everyone thought it addressed his or her particular agenda: "If OBE was a welcome answer to conservative impatience with the constant emphasis on school inputs (which usually meant demands for more money), few people noticed that it also dovetailed nicely with a major liberal agenda: to get rid of objective testing and rote learning in favor of so-called performance-based assessment—more open-ended essay questions, more problem solving, more analysis, more emphasis on 'higher-order' reasoning, perhaps even more creativity."[87]

Whatever OBE's possible benefits, the problem largely has been one of developing appropriate measures of outcome. Schrag points out that "OBE lends itself to monumental mushiness, and when state departments of education produced their new OBE guidelines for local districts, they often included such outcomes as 'positive self-image,' 'environmental stewardship,' 'openness to change,' 'appreciation of diversity in others [and] appreciation of global community,' 'interpersonal competencies,' 'a willingness to question things,' and 'holistic learning.' Those criteria not only brought the Christian right into the battle, sometimes with barrages of misinformation; they also made a great many other parents nervous. Were students going to be tested on this stuff? Were school curricula going to be based on it?"[88]

Champions of OBE contend that it "was hijacked."[89] OBE was never intended to measure such things as "values, attitudes, and psychological states like self concept and tolerance."[90] Simply put, these are not outcomes and therefore cannot be measured. The original architects of OBE saw it more as a way to encourage schools to become "free [of] the time requirements and curricular boxes that are staples of all education codes: so many years of English and math; so many hours in class."[91]

Whatever the original intent of OBE, the fact is that it has become a major political issue in many states and local school districts. It serves as a lightning rod for the Christian right and yet it was the "theoretical cornerstone of the Clinton education reform program and, depending on the definition, versions of OBE are in place in a growing number of states."[92] Furthermore, as we have said, it is an essential part of George W. Bush's landmark education act of 2001. He is particularly proud of the fact that his education program requires that school districts, teachers, and students be held accountable for performance. He demands that high standards be established and that results (or outcomes) be measured.

SCHOOL CHOICE

School choice and charter schools also are attempts to hold schools accountable for their performance. President Bush's Leave No Child Behind Act of 2001 expands the various options for parents in deciding where to send their children to school. The act, according to the White House, "empowers parents by providing unprecedented federal support for children from disadvantaged backgrounds who are trapped in low-performing schools. Students in failing schools may transfer to higher-performing public schools or get help, such as tutoring. Students in persistently dangerous schools may transfer to safer public schools."[93] The new law also mandates that states provide annual report cards that show how well schools are performing. This provision is intended to provide parents with the information they need to make informed decisions about where to send their children. The report cards evaluate teacher qualifications and their child's progress in key subjects.[94]

Charter schools are alternative public schools in which parents are empowered to make many of the critical decisions in the initial design and operation of the school. School choice is more an effort to introduce competition into public education. The assumption is that the ability of parents to choose between public schools introduces competition into an otherwise monopolistic system, which, in turn, provides incentives for schools to improve. President George W. Bush is a strong supporter of choice and therefore of charter schools as one option for parents. His Leave No Child Behind Act of 2001 calls for $200 million to support charter schools.

Charter schools are among the most popular and, for many, the most promising of all educational reforms. Between 1992 and 2002, 36 states and the District of Columbia have enacted enabling legislation and approximately 2,700 charter schools are now in operation. In 2002 alone, 393 schools opened their doors. "Since 1992, when the first charter school opened, about 160 charter schools have closed for failing to comply with the dictates of their charter, representing six percent of all charter schools ever opened," reports the Center for Education Reform.[95] In 2002 California governor Gray Davis signed into law a bill that requires greater oversight of charter schools and regulates their expansion. For example, the new law "requires charter schools for the first time in their 10-year history to stay inside the boundaries—and within oversight—of the county or school district that granted them a contract to operate. That means that approximately 200 charter school campuses currently operating outside their host counties and school districts would either have to persuade the nearest school district to grant them a charter, pick up and relocate by 2005, or shut down."[96]

While no two charter schools are alike, they share in common many features, among them that they are public schools freed of the normal state and local regulation for a period of time (usually five years) and that, in return for the freedom to run themselves according to their own distinctive educational vision, they promise to produce educational success in their students (however success may be defined). They are different from one another in that some are brand-new enterprises while others are former public schools. In some cases, teachers initiate the school; in others, parents start the school; in still others, nonprofit organizations or private firms are the organizers. The oldest charter schools have been in

A CLOSER LOOK

If you attended a charter high school, compare your experience with that of a classmate or college friend who attended a public school and also with that of one who attended a private school. Likewise, if you attended a public school, compare your experience with those of a classmate or friend who attended a charter school and one who attended a private school.

existence only about three years, so it is too early to know if this experiment will lead to higher-quality education.

Many of those who support school choice—in whatever form—are really looking for ways to capture the spirit and energy of private entrepreneurship within the context of public schools. Ted Kolderie, with the Center for Policy Studies, is among a growing number of academics who ask why school boards necessarily need to have exclusive right to operate publicly financed schools. Kolderie, for example, proposes that the "state award 'franchises' to businesses, colleges and universities, parents, teachers, and local organizations to run schools with public funds. The state would select among applicants, hold them accountable for results, and cancel the contracts of those who fail to meet agreed-upon performance standards."[97]

Other noted scholars also support plans under which most "anyone would be free to start a school and have it chartered by the state in much the same way that the states now charter private schools."[98] John Chubb, a researcher at the Brookings Institution, and Terry Moe, a professor at Stanford University, supported this approach to education in their book *What Price Democracy? Politics, Markets and America's Schools.* Edward B. Fiske describes their version of school choice as follows: "Students would receive vouchers—though that's not the word they use—to be cashed in at whatever school they selected. Children from disadvantaged areas or children with learning disabilities would carry larger scholarships, thus giving schools an incentive to take them. Transportation would be provided at public expense and parents would be assisted in making informed choices. Such a plan would extend the concept of choice as it now exists and enable private schools to compete with public ones—but within the context of overall public control."[99]

Policy Analysis for California Education, a think tank based at Stanford University and the University of California at Berkeley, issued the first-ever national study of charter schools in March 2003. The study found charter schools "rely heavily on uncredentialed teachers, fail to secure federal funds for poor or disabled kids and fare no better than traditional public schools at money management." The organization also found that "black students who attend charters are on average more racially isolated than their peers in standard public schools."[100]

While the idea of school choice may be appealing, in practice, as the above study suggests, it does not always lead to better education. For starters, the analogy with economic competition is flawed. E. D. Hirsch makes the point:

> In the economic sphere, customers tend to know what they want. Consumer preference in schooling, by contrast, is not easily determined by the consumers themselves. For one thing, the results of schooling take a long time to show themselves. Even when parents know what they want to be achieved in the long run, they rarely have a clear conception of what they wish schools to be doing day by day in order to achieve it. This mixture of long-term clarity with short-term uncertainty explains a paradoxical finding: American parents think that our schools are failing in general (because they know that the nationwide results are poor), whereas they think that their own child's school (a clean, well-lighted place where lots of activity is going on) is performing well.[101]

Hirsch goes on to make the point that there is no scientific evidence to suggest that school choice makes a difference in educational outcomes, either here in the United States or elsewhere in the world. He cites, for example, evidence from the Netherlands: "The Dutch instituted publicly financed school choice many years ago, and today the Netherlands exhibits the least consistent school quality in northern continental Europe. Today, some 16 percent of Dutch schools perform below par, compared with 1 to 5 percent of below-par schools in the *non*choice systems of Sweden, Denmark, Japan, and South Korea."[102]

Hirsch does not suggest for this reason that we abandon the idea of school choice. He, like so many others, favors it in the hopes that it will stimulate structural and substantive change in our schools. However, school choice should not be viewed as a panacea. Competition alone will not lead to more efficient and effective schools. In the words of Hirsch, "I favor . . . structural changes in the hope that they will lead to substantive changes. However, it is unlikely that any structural reform can leverage our whole educational system until the current intellectual monopoly is broken."[103]

By "the current intellectual monopoly" Hirsch refers to general trends in modern-day education that emphasize the individual child's well-being and social skills at the expense of old-fashioned knowledge-based education. That is, Hirsch believes we do children a disservice not to require them to master basic skills and subject-specific knowledge via rote learning, extensive homework assignments, and simple hard work. Consequently, he believes the greatest impediment to having school choice make a real difference in a child's education is today's general philosophy of education.

Another formidable impediment to informed parental choice: the near impossibility of choosing between schools, even those that adopt special themes, when all of them espouse the same general "philosophy" of education—the same concern for "the individual child and his or her needs," for "critical thinking," "self-esteem," "joy in learning," "respect for others," and the same pledge by the school staff to use the latest research-based pedagogical methods, such as "site-based de-cision making," "cooperative learning," "child-centered pedagogy." With such sim-ilarity of rhetoric among schools, it is a discerning parent indeed who can make a wise choice.[104]

SCHOOL-TO-WORK PROGRAMS

We have already said that business leaders are very concerned about the quality of workers they are getting from the educational system. The 1994 National School-to-Work (STW) program was one proposed solution to this particular, very seri-ous problem. The idea behind school-to-work was to start incorporating the busi-ness world into education from the earliest grade levels by exposing students to career options and aiming them toward paid work experience in conjunction with their high school education. It was felt that high school programs should help stu-dents see how what they are learning can open up a world of career opportuni-ties beyond high school. A large number of schools, employers, community col-leges, and other community partners joined forces to build bridges from school into the workplace.

While school-to-work programs varied by state and school district, most shared in common work-based and school-based learning experiences. Often the work-based learning offered a planned sequence of work-site experiences with employers and in various other settings in the community. These experiences were intended to expose students to all aspects of the business or industry they were studying. Students were expected not only to learn the aspects of their in-dustry but also to acquire general workplace competencies. Of critical importance was having the work-based learning build on and extend the knowledge and skills they were learning at school. In some programs, students were paid for their work experience.

The school-based learning was designed around high academic and technical skill standards. The program was to include career exploration and counsel-ing, and instruction in a career major (which the student generally selected by 11th grade). Often school-to-work programs included at least one year of post-secondary education (President Clinton, in his 1996 State of the Union address, called for federal support for those pursuing a two-year community college de-gree). Most school-to-work programs included periodic evaluations to identify students' academic strengths and weaknesses. School-based instruction generally challenged students to solve problems, perform tasks, and work in situations drawn from the career area for which they were preparing. Most important, class-room instruction was designed to help students apply what they are learning to the occupational area.

The National School-to-Work Act expired (through its sunset clause) in Oc-tober 2001. President Bush's Leave No Child Behind Act does not provide funds to either reinstate this program or create another similar program. Evaluations of the program showed that it was of limited success both in preparing students for college and in securing employment for them upon graduation from high school. Given its unproven success, and the limited local and state funds for such a program, the school-to-work programs are in limbo.

EDUCATION IN THE INFORMATION AGE

The dot-com bust notwithstanding, the Information Age is here, and nearly every institution has experienced profound changes as a result. Corporations, the entertainment industry, medical care, communications and publishing, banking, travel, and government are being changed by the presence of new electronic technologies. As only the most extreme futurists could have envisioned, the world has become interconnected by an electronic nervous system over which immense amounts of information flow at breakneck speeds.

The educational process has not been immune to this new technology. While it remains unclear how extensively education will be changed by the information age, we know advances in computer hardware and software, the Internet, and other related information technologies already have changed to some extent the curriculum, methods of teaching, and even the physical structure of schools. The important question is, Will the Information Age cause a truly revolutionary change in the what, how, and where of education?

President Clinton promised that every school would be linked to the "superhighway" by year 2000. One of his education goals was to have every child computer literate by age 12 and capable of accessing information via the Internet. He was not entirely successful, but there was considerable progress toward achieving his goals. President Bush's education act of 2001 is silent on the question of computer literacy.

However laudible Clinton's goals, they did not address the real issue of how these new technologies should be used in the educational process. In other words, what changes in curriculum content and, even more important, in the paradigms of instruction would be indicated if he had had his way and every school and child were connected to the "superhighway"? The role of technology in the classroom remains unclear at every level of education, including college. Millions of dollars have been spent on technology and teacher training in the use of technology and curricular redesign, yet we still do not have clear answers as to whether learning has been enhanced as a result of this investment.

At least three overlapping categories of changes suggest themselves: additions to the curriculum, notably, instruction about information itself and the technologies of information; changes in the content of the traditional curriculum; and changes in the structure of the curriculum and the style of classroom instruction. Lewis J. Perelman, the noted author and specialist in educational policy, calls for the most revolutionary changes in the educational process in his popular book, *School's Out: A Radical New Formula for the Revitalization of America's Educational System.*

He states, for example, that the new technology "has blown the social role of learning completely inside out."[105] Perelman, in the passages below, describes what he calls "hyperlearning" and claims this is today's reality and the way of future learning.

> Learning used to be a distinctly human process. Now learning is a transhuman process people share with increasingly powerful artificial networks and brains. Even today, expert systems and neural networks are being "trained" by human knowledge engineers; the machines' automated expertise in turn is providing "just-in-time learning" for car mechanics, power plant operators, and a growing legion of other workers.
>
> Learning was an activity thought to be confined to the box of a school classroom. Now learning permeates every form of social activity—work, entertainment, home life—outside of school. For what piano lessons would cost, you now can buy an electronic piano that will teach you to play it. Only a quarter of American adults know how to program a VCR; a new model will teach you how in any of six languages. The fastest growing cable TV networks—The Discovery Channel and The Learning Channel—are devoted to learning. Of the more than sixty million Americans who learned how to use personal computers since 1980, most learned from vendors, books, other users, and the computers themselves, not in schools. Learning was presented as the result of instruction: a linear, hierarchical process in which an "expert" teacher would pour knowledge into the empty head of an obedient student. With knowledge doubling every year or so, "expertise" now has a shelf life measured in days; everyone must be both learner and teacher; and the sheer challenge of learning can be managed only through a globe-girding network that links all minds and all knowledge.
>
> Learning or education was a task of childhood in preparation for entering adult life and work. Now learning is literally the work of the majority of U.S. jobs and will be what virtually all adults—whether employed, unemployed, or "on welfare"—will do for a living by the early years of the twenty-first century.[106]

Perelman is calling for a true revolution in how we structure education and in how we think about the learning process. He argues that this new technology should be viewed not as a mere tool to aid in traditional instruction but as a way to move beyond the conventional boundaries of the educational system.

At its root, this technological revolution puts learning and education on a collision course. The essence of education is *instruction*—something some people do to other people, usually with required "discipline." The word *pedagogy* comes from a Greek verb meaning "to lead," and *education* itself is from the Latin word meaning "to lead forth"—both imply the active leader herding a flock of passive followers. But the essence of the coming integrated, universal, multimedia, digital network is *discovery*—the empowerment of human minds to learn spontaneously, without coercion, both independently and cooperatively. The focus is on learning as an action that is "done by," not "done to," the actor.[107]

While not everyone agrees with Perelman's radical vision for the educational system, most agree the educational process will never be the same thanks to the new technology. At the very least, distance learning technology allows educators to reach a wider audience—certainly in higher education—who may live in remote areas or who simply may not want to travel to a central campus. Paul Starr makes the point that the new technology has caused a rebirth of progressive education, which places the student at the center of learning. In his article "Computing Our Way to Educational Reform," he quotes a 1995 report by the National Academy of Sciences entitled, "Reinventing Schools: The Technology Is Now!":

> Postindustrial society "calls for a new, postindustrial form of education"—one that puts students in a more central, active role in their own learning, helps them learn "to ask many questions and to devise multiple approaches to a problem" instead of forcing them to come up "with one right answer," and encourages "critical thinking, teamwork, compromise, and communication."[108]
>
> . . . Computer-based technology in education raises questions of equity in addition to the issues of how it should be used. The fact is, poorer school districts and the families within those districts do not have the same computer resources that are available to wealthier families and schools. Proponents of increased use of information technology in education argue that the falling costs of these technologies will make them more affordable for every school in the country. Perhaps. But so far, possession of computers (and of network connections) has continued to grow more rapidly among high-income than among low-income households, thus widening the disparities.[109]
>
> . . . Skeptics of technology and its eventual impact on education make the point that "ultimately, the qualities of education that we care most about are not technological; they are matters of educational philosophy and practice and in turn depend on broader moral and political judgments. In thinking about education, we ought not to be preoccupied with computers at all, and if the technological transition is successful, we will not be. Because of all they make possible, we must make computers part of education. Then they should "disappear."[110]

DOES "ONE SIZE FITS ALL" EDUCATION WORK?

As we have said, Thomas Jefferson, among others, argued that a democratic nation-state required children to be taught a shared body of knowledge. This philosophy gave birth to the American "common schools," which provided all children with a common grade-school education that would lead to a literate and independent citizenry. This democratic approach to education also would serve to breed future leaders. "It would be a place where every talent would be given an equal chance to excel, where 'every fibre would be eradicated of ancient and future aristocracy; and a foundation laid for a government truly republican.'"[111]

While the goal of a comprehensive education for every child—including a common core of knowledge—is laudable, the recent American experience suggests it may not work. Simply put, perhaps it is a mistake to require every student to take essentially the same academically oriented curriculum in lieu of opting for one of several tracks. An educational approach that insists "one size fits all" denies innate differences in people. Take, for example, the very successful and highly respected German educational system. What makes the Germans' system so successful?

For starters, they do not insist every child follow the same educational track but instead encourage students to pursue one of three directions, depending on their talents and interests—in other words, it allows for flexibility and choice. German "employers like it [the flexible approach to education] because it churns out skilled workers as well as state-of-the-art scientists."[112]

What are the different approaches to education available to German students? There are three choices for parents and their children to choose among: grammar schools, technical schools, and vocational schools. It is interesting to note that socialist-inspired attempts to introduce comprehensive schools in the 1960s— similar to American schools—provoked much hostility.[113]

This division lets schools tailor their teaching to the abilities and aspirations of their pupils. Grammar schools can challenge academic children without discouraging their less able contemporaries. Technical schools can motivate their students by introducing them to general principles through practical examples. The most striking achievement of this system—more striking even than its success in grooming the elite—is its ability to engage the enthusiasm and test the abilities of the mass of tomorrow's skilled workers.[114]

The most crucial element of the German system is the equal respect accorded to each of the options available to students. Those who choose a technical school are as respected as those who decide to go the university route.

An important distinction in the German model is its dual system. Those students who do not want to go to university instead attend a three-or-more-year apprenticeship. An apprenticeship combines on-the-job training in a local factory and theoretical education in school (anywhere from two to three days a week). Those who are successful are guaranteed a job in a local factory, while those less successful are still likely to be able to put their training to good use.

The beauty of this system and the real lesson for American education is that adolescents who were bored by school find their enthusiasm reignited, partly because they start to see the links between learning facts and earning a living. The cost of training is divided between the *Lander,* which provide the vocational schools; the employers, who contribute 2 percent of their payroll costs to training; and the apprentices, who work for a relatively small salary. This model of education allows for a smoother transition from school to work, which is not usually the case in the United States. Most important, the German system of education supports a culture "in which training is cherished and skilled workers revered. For many Germans, an apprenticeship is simply the first step on a learning escalator that can turn them into trainers *(Meisteren)* in their own right."[115]

We are not suggesting that the German educational system is not without its own difficulties or that the United States should adopt this model. We are saying there is ample evidence to suggest that many American students are bored with school as it is currently structured and/or are ill-suited for a purely academic curriculum. The evidence is found in the relatively high dropout rates, poor performance on SAT tests, and other indicators of academic standing, as well as the many discipline problems in school. Why not consider a multitrack system of education that would allow parents and students to select the path most suited to their temperament, intellect, and career ambitions? If we do move away from "one size fits all" education, it is important that equal respect be accorded whichever path a student takes.

THE EDUCATIONAL SYSTEM:
A BATTLEGROUND FOR AFFIRMATIVE ACTION

Affirmative action programs have become a sensitive and controversial political issue—especially on college campuses. There are some critics who would eliminate all forms of affirmative action, while others argue programs that currently target individuals by race and ethnicity should instead focus on other definitions of disadvantage—for example, economic or social class. These "class-based" affirmative action proposals have become particularly important in college admissions in the wake of a recent Supreme Court decision suggesting that race-based scholarships may be unconstitutional.

There is every indication that the public and the courts are ready to do away with racial preferences in favor of some other means to promote equal opportunity. Examples of recent voter initiatives and court decisions that either eliminate or significantly restrict affirmative action programs include the California voter-approved Proposition 209, known as the California Civil Rights Initiative (CCRI). Proposition 209 was passed in November 1996 by 54 percent of California voters. In 1997 the CCRI was upheld by the California State Supreme Court as constitutional. The new amendment to the state constitution reads: "The state shall not discriminate against, or grant preferential treatment to, any individual or group on the basis of race, sex, color, ethnicity, or national origin in the operation of public employment, public education, or public contracting."

The Fifth Circuit Court of Appeals in *Hopwood v. State of Texas* ruled that race may not be considered as a factor in the admissions process for the purpose of achieving diversity. This opinion appears to be in conflict with the Supreme Court's earlier opinion in *Bakke v. University of California, Davis,* which stated that race could be used as one factor in admissions decisions for the purpose of achieving diversity. The Supreme Court in July 1996 refused to review the Hopwood case. *Bakke* is still considered the law of the land outside the Fifth Circuit (Texas, Louisiana, and Mississippi)—at least for now. The California Civil Rights Initiative is thought by many to be a direct challenge to the *Bakke* decision.

The Third Circuit Court of Appeals in *Taxman v. Board of Education for Piscataway Township* ruled on the question of hiring and firing of teachers. In this case, the school board in Piscataway, New Jersey, was facing financial troubles and was forced to lay off one of two teachers. The two teachers were deemed to be equal in every respect. One teacher was black and the other was white. The school district decided to keep the black teacher in order to promote diversity. The Third Circuit Court of Appeals ruled that this action violated Title VII of the Civil Rights Act of 1964. Race may be considered only to specifically remedy past discrimination. The school district has appealed the case to the U.S. Supreme Court. This case may be very influential in affirmative action issues outside the labor and employment area, including college admissions.

The initial breakthrough civil rights cases in the 1950s and 1960s targeted discrimination in education. An important reason education has been consistently a central focus of civil rights efforts is that it serves as the gateway to opportunity and material well-being. Greater educational opportunity has in some important ways revolutionalized education, although gaps persist. While the enrollment of women in higher education has risen steadily, with women now earning more than half of all bachelor's and master's degrees, they earn only one-third of doctorate and professional degrees and continue to lag in math, engineering, and the physical sciences at both the undergraduate and doctorate levels. However, women are attending college in greater numbers, while male attendence is in decline.

Student aid programs and aggressive recruitment and retention programs have helped to increase the numbers of college-going African Americans. In 1977, for example, the college-going rate for African Americans and whites who graduated from high school was about the same. Since 1977, however, the proportion of African American 18- to 24-year-old high school graduates enrolled in college has not kept pace with that of white students. The story is similar for the Hispanic enrollment rate.

Diane Ravitch, a senior research scholar at New York University, sums up the feelings of many when she writes that "affirmative action is a good idea that went bad. It began as a means of achieving the purposes of the Civil Rights Act of 1964, which banned discrimination on grounds of race, color, religion, sex, and national origin. But time and politics have converted it into a vast, covert, and deeply unpopular system for distributing rewards and burdens on those very grounds."[116]

Ravitch, like so many other critics of affirmative action, argues that the only way to ensure equal opportunity is to provide everyone with the same high-quality education from grade school forward. She writes:

> The original definition of affirmative action remains valid. By that, I mean it is important in a pluralistic society like ours to make every effort to identify talented and able black candidates for jobs, promotions, or places in college. But standards for advancement should be well defined and consistently applied. For example, students who read at a sixth-grade level should not be admitted to college; instead, they should receive supplementary instruction that enables them to meet admission standards that apply equally to all. Additional resources should be redirected to inner-

city schools; extraordinary efforts must be made to improve the education of black Americans, including the use of alternatives such as charter schools, management of schools by contract, and means-tested parental choice. Such efforts should continue until blacks are graduating from high school and attending college at the same rates as the rest of the population.[117]

Will Marshall, president of the Progressive Policy Institute, also argues for improving the quality of education that minorities receive beginning in preschool. He believes that the gravest injustice of all is the incredibly poor quality of education provided to the minority community—particularly to those living in inner cities. His solution to racially based inequities is not affirmative action but improvement in the early educational experience of all children.

The impact of racial prejudice pales in comparison to the damage done to black aspirations by scandalously bad urban schools. The problem is not lack of resources but a sclerotic school bureaucracy that sets expectations for minority students too low and puts the interests of adults in the system ahead of those of the children they are supposed to educate. The solutions include higher standards; an apprenticeship option that forces links with local employers, thereby giving students more reasons to finish high school; and charter schools, to break the bureaucratic monopoly in public education.[118]

The social policy goal is the same for those who support affirmative action programs as for those who advocate an alternative strategy that places greater emphasis on improving educational opportunities and adequate preparation for a college education and employment in the Information Age: to provide everyone—regardless of sex, race, or ethnic origin—an equal opportunity for upward social and economic mobility.

On one hand, those who argue for a shift in public policy initiatives away from race-based strategies (such as affirmative action) to a class-based strategy believe this will focus the debate on a growing underclass made up of people ill prepared for an Information Age economy and, in turn, will be more likely to help "restore a sense of justice and fair play to social policy . . . than the current racial spoils system."[119] On the other hand, defenders of affirmative action claim that it is unrealistic to expect, at least in the short term, that there will be significant improvements in the early educational experience of minority children—particularly in the inner cities and older and deteriorating suburbs—to allow them upward mobility. While it may be true that current affirmative action programs need fixing (former president Clinton and President George W. Bush argue this position), nevertheless they must be retained.

A FINAL WORD

The educational system serves as a battlefield for a great many issues that divide this country. Two of the more emotionally charged issues are affirmative action and school prayer. Schools today also represent all that seems to be wrong in

America. Public education is blamed for the country's weakened economic position in the world. The greater propensity for young people to engage in dishonest or criminal behavior (including violence) and to display a general lack of civility is in large measure blamed on the schools, as well. Yet for all that may be wrong with American public education, it remains the greatest achievement in American history. We remain the only country committed to educating all of its citizens at public expense.

Why does public education shoulder so much of the blame for the social and economic ills plaguing American society? Why do conservatives feel so strongly about school prayer or, in the case of many fundamentalists, the teaching of "secular humanism" and the theories of evolution instead of creationism? The answer is simple. The educational system is a significant force in the socialization of the young. Education is second only to the family in influencing a person's values, attitudes, and behavior, and as more families are headed by two working parents—or one parent, working or not—it may well become the most important influence in a person's life.

Beginning with the Industrial Revolution, education became more than a social instrument, it was critical to the national economy and a ticket to secure and rewarding employment. The ability of people to find and keep well-paying jobs and of the nation to compete in the international marketplace is, in the Information Age, even more tied to quality education. It is in fact the economic role of education that has taken center stage in policy debates in recent years. As Tyack and Cuban point out, "The underlying rationale of most recent reforms—to use schooling as an instrument of international economic competitiveness—is not new, but its dominance in policy talk is unprecedented."[120]

Educational reforms have come and gone and come again throughout American history. The one constant in all of these efforts is the principal goal of educational reform: to improve learning so that students will "grow intellectually and mature as persons."[121] In other words, quality education involves more than producing high test scores and successful employment for its graduates. A complete education involves the "intellectual, civic, and social development" of every student.[122] It strikes us that many of today's reforms place undue emphasis on market-driven skills at the expense of the intellectual, civic, and social dimensions of education. In the words of Tyack and Cuban, "when the purposes of education become narrowed to economic advantage, and the main measure of success is higher test scores, an easy next step is to regard schooling as a consumer good rather than a common good."[123] It is in this context that such reforms as school choice—with its emphasis on market forces and competition rather than on the common good—gain in popularity.

Tyack and Cuban further observe that "in the last generation, discourse about public schooling has become radically narrowed. It has focused on international economic competition, test scores, and individual 'choice' of schools. But it has largely neglected the type of choices most vital to civic welfare: collective choices about a common future, choices made through the democratic process about the values and knowledge that citizens want to pass on to the next generation. 'While public education may be useful as an industrial policy,' Deborah Meier says, 'it is essential to healthy life in a democracy.'"[124]

In thinking about your own educational experience, undoubtedly the greatest influence and fondest memory is that teacher (or those teachers) who awoke in you an intellectual curiosity and challenged you to realize your potential as a person, citizen, or a professional. Reforms in whatever form—school choice, technology, competency-based education, and so forth—are only as good as the teachers charged with implementing them. Too often, teachers are among the last to be included in the design of educational reforms and poorly supported (in training, equipment, and other essential resources) when asked to implement them. It is for this reason the National Commission on Teaching and America's Future in its 1996 report proposed that "by the year 2006, America will provide all students in the country with what should be their educational birthright: access to competent, caring and qualified teachers."[125]

It is time the teaching profession gain respect and financial support commensurate with other professions and the status of teachers in other countries. Unlike the United States, most other countries invest most of their education dollars in teachers—ensuring they are well prepared and properly rewarded for their training and work. In this country, at least half of the dollars spent on education go toward supporting "staff and activities outside the classroom."[126] So long as entrenched administrators insist on maintaining their offices and support staff at the expense of the frontline educators—the teachers—there will be little hope of significantly changing educational outcomes.

The National Commission on Teaching and America's Future makes the point best when it writes:

> On the whole, the school reform movement has ignored the obvious: What teachers know and can do makes the crucial difference in what children learn. And the ways school systems organize their work makes a big difference in what teachers can accomplish. New courses, tests, and curriculum reforms can be important starting points, but they are meaningless if teachers cannot use them well. Policies can only improve schools if the people in them are armed with the knowledge, skills, and supports they need. Student learning in this country will improve only when we focus our efforts on improving teaching.[127]

Public education for the masses and not simply for the elites is the greatest gift Americans have given to themselves. In a land of immigrants, it is an important means to the goal of socializing and integrating a diverse citizenry. In the days of Horace Mann and the common school, public education was expected to create "literate, moral citizens capable of fulfilling the millennial hope of making the United States God's country."[128] Later, thinkers and writers like John Dewey advanced our "understanding of the links between democracy and education."[129] In the years following the Supreme Court's 1954 *Brown v. Board of Education* decision, "Americans ardently discussed how public schooling could promote racial and economic justice."[130]

As the long tradition of debating the direction and form the educational system should take continues, we can only hope that a more inclusive view of education—its social, civic, and economic purposes—will prevail. It is a mistake to allow the politics of education to be dominated by special interests who seek to achieve their more limited goals at the expense of the public good.

Likewise, in our concern about the crisis in American education, we should not embrace every reform or technology as a panacea to magically transform the system. Although the ideal educational system has yet to be achieved, the enterprise is hardly rotten. In pursuing change in educational policy and practices, we should not lose sight of the broader purpose of education, and we would do well to preserve the best of past practices.

FOR MORE INFORMATION

Education Week. http://www.edweek.org.
Moe, Terry M., ed. *A Primer on America's Schools.* Stanford, CA: Hoover Institution Press, 2001.
National Center for Education Statistics. http://nces.ed.gov.
Spring, Joel. *American Education,* 9th ed. Boston, MA.: McGraw Hill, 2000.
Wishnietsky, Dan H.. *American Education in the 21st Century.* Bloomington, IN: Phi Beta Kappa Educational Foundation, 2001.

NOTES

1. National Center for Education Statistics, *The Condition of Education 2001* (Washington, DC: U.S. Department of Education, Office of Educational Research and Improvement, June 2001), 26.
2. *San Francisco Chronicle,* October 1, 2002, A1.
3. *Washington Post,* January 22, 1996, A6.
4. David Tyack and Larry Cuban, *Tinkering toward Utopia: A Century of Public School Reform* (Cambridge, MA: Harvard University Press, 1995), 2.
5. Ibid.
6. National Center for Education Statistics, *The Condition of Education 2001,* 43.
7. Mercedes M. Viana, "The Federal Government: 21st Century Standard Bearer for Education," *G. W. Policy Perspectives* (George Washington University), vol. 1, no. 1 (1996), 62.
8. Ibid., 63.
9. National Center for Education Statistics, *The Condition of Education 2001,* 43.
10. Chiara R. Nappi, "A Tale of Two School Systems," *Dissent,* spring 1996, 61.
11. Ibid.
12. Ibid.
13. Ibid., 64.
14. Ibid.
15. Ibid.
16. Ibid.
17. Ibid., 65.

18. Corinne Chee and Jason Kruger, "Two Thirds Vote Requirement Once Again Fails Lodi Kids in Overcrowded, Aging School Facilities," Let's Fix Our Schools? September 30, 1999, http://www.letsfixourschools.org/presscenter/pr_93099_lodisj.html, 1.

19. Alan Richard, "New Law, Civic Spirit Bolster California Bond Measures," *Education Week,* March 13, 2002, http://www.edweek.org/ew/newstory.cfm?slug=26bonds .h21, 1.

20. *San Francisco Chronicle,* March 6, 1997, A1.

21. Francesco Cordasco, *A Brief History of Education* (Totowa, NJ: Littlefield, Adams, 1970), 124–126.

22. Ibid., 136–138.

23. Newton Edwards and Herman G. Richey, *The School in the American Social Order: The Dynamics of American Education* (Boston, MA: Houghton Mifflin, 1947), 732–735.

24. Ibid., 732–733.

25. Rudolf Flesch, *Why Johnny Can't Read* (New York: Harper Collins, 1985), 2.

26. Barbara B. Gaddy, T. William Hall, and Robert J. Marzano, *School Wars: Resolving Our Conflicts over Religion and Values* (San Francisco: Jossey-Bass, 1996) 14.

27. Ibid., 14.

28. National Commission on Excellence in Education, *A Nation at Risk: The Imperative for Educational Reform* (Washington, DC, 1983), 5.

29. Ibid., 8–9.

30. The Conference Board, *Ten Years after* A Nation at Risk, report no. 1041 (New York, 1993), 10.

31. Ibid., 10–11.

32. Joetta L. Sack, "K–12 Enrollment Sets Another Record, but Dip by 2011 Forecast," *Education Week,* September 5, 2001, http://www.edweek.org/ew/ewstory.cfm?slug= 01stats.h21&keywords=K%2D12%20Enrollment%20Sets%20Another%20Record, 1.

33. Ibid.

34. U.S. Department of Education, National Center for Education Statistics, *Digest of Education Statistics* (Washington, DC: 1996).

35. Ibid.

36. "Record K–12 Enrollments Forecast for Fall 1997," Internet Press Release, August 21, 1996, http://www.csun.edu/~hfoa102/csun.edu/csun97_98/csun968_97/Features/ Record.html.

37. *Newsweek,* September 16, 1996, 81.

38. Gaddy, Hall and Marzano, *School Wars,* 34.

39. Ibid., 35.

40. Ibid.

41. National Center for Education Statistics, *The Condition of Education 2001,* 66, 70.

42. National Center for Education Statistics, "Out of Field Teaching," http://nces.ed.gov/ ssbr/pages/field.asp, 1.

43. Ibid., 3.

44. Ibid.

45. Ibid.

46. National Commission on Teaching and America's Future, *What Matters Most: Teaching for America's Future* (New York, 1996), 8.

47. Ibid., 68–69.

48. Ibid., 62–65.

49. Ibid., 94–96.

50. Myron Leiderman, "Teacher Unions: Is the End Near? How to End the Teacher Union Veto over State Education Policy," briefing paper no. 1994-37 (Claremont, CA: The Claremont Institute, Golden State Center for Policy Studies, December 15, 1994), 2.
51. Ibid., 3.
52. Ibid.
53. John C. Bowman, "100,000 New Teachers, or 100,000 New Union Members?" Children First, http://childrenfirsttn.org/newteachr.shtml.
54. Charlene K. Haar, "The PTA: What Should Its Role Be in Its Second Century?" Harte-Hanks Community Newspapers, North Dallas, June 30, 1996, 1.
55. Ibid., 2.
56. Francis Schrag, *Back to Basics: Fundamental Educational Questions Reexamined* (San Francisco: Jossey-Bass, 1995), 147.
57. Ibid., 148.
58. Tyack and Cuban, *Tinkering toward Utopia,* 4.
59. Ibid.
60. Ibid.
61. Ibid.
62. Ibid., 8.
63. Chester E. Finn Jr., "Can the Schools Be Saved?," Fordham Foundation, http://www.fordhamfoundation.org/library/canthe.html, 7.
64. U.S. Congress, H.R. 6, "The Improving America's Schools Act of 1994," http://www.ed.gov/legislation/ESEA/index.html.
65. Richard W. Riley, "The Improving America's Schools Act of 1994," U.S. Department of Education, http://www.ideas_classroom.org/conferences/title_1/home_title, 1.
66. Ibid.
67. Ibid.
68. National Education Goals Panel, *Promises to Keep: Creating High Standards for American Students* (Washington, DC: National Education Goals Panel, November 15, 1993), C(L)-5.
69. Ibid., i, xii–xiii.
70. Gaddy, Hall, and Marzano, *School Wars,* 78.
71. Kevin Bush Weller, "Does Our Reach Exceed Our Grasp?" December 1999, http://www.asbj.com/evs/99/goals.html, 1.
72. Ibid.
73. Ibid., 2.
74. Ibid.
75. Ibid., 3.
76. Sharon Cromwell, "Goals 2000: How Are We Doing?" *Education World,* http://www.education-world.com/a_admin/admin106.shtml, 2.
77. Ibid.
78. Weller, "Does Our Reach Exceed Our Grasp?" 4.
79. Ibid., 5.
80. Ibid.
81. Gaddy, Hall, and Marzano, *School Wars,* 79.
82. Ibid.
83. Schrag, *Back to Basics,* 6.
84. Francis Schrag, "The New School Wars: How Outcomes-Based Education Blew Up," *American Prospect,* winter 1995, 53.

85. "President Bush Signs Landmark Education Reforms into Law," The White House, January 8, 2002, http://www.whitehouse.gov/infocus/education, 1.
86. Schrag, "The New School Wars," 54.
87. Ibid.
88. Ibid.
89. Ibid., 55.
90. Ibid.
91. Ibid.
92. Ibid.
93. "President Bush Signs Landmark Education Reforms into Law," 2.
94. Ibid.
95. Center for Education Reform, "Growth in Charter Schools Reflects Increasing Demands for Choices," *Education Reform,* http://www.edreform.com/press/2002/charternumbers.htm, 1.
96. *San Francisco Chronicle,* September 30, 2002, A1.
97. Edward B. Fiske, *Smart Schools, Smart Kids: Why Do Some Schools Work?* (New York: Simon & Shuster, 1992), 200.
98. Ibid., 201.
99. Ibid.
100. Meredith May, "Report Critical of Charter Schools," *San Francisco Chronicle,* April 8, 2003, A15.
101. E. D. Hirsch Jr., *The Schools We Need, And Why We Don't Have Them* (New York: Doubleday, 1996), 61.
102. Ibid.
103. Ibid.
104. Ibid., 62.
105. Lewis J. Perelman, *School's Out: A Radical New Formula for the Revitalization of America's Educational System* (New York: Avon Books, 1992), 22.
106. Ibid., 22–23.
107. Ibid., 23.
108. Paul Starr, "Computing Our Way to Educational Reform," *American Prospect,* July–August, 1996, 56.
109. Ibid., 59.
110. Ibid.
111. Hirsch, *The Schools We Need,* 17.
112. *The Economist,* November 21, 1992, 11.
113. Ibid.
114. Ibid.
115. Ibid.
116. Diane Ravitch, "Recalling the Original Intent," *New Democrat,* May–June 1995, 32.
117. Ibid., 34.
118. Will Marshall, "Rebuild America's Civil Rights Consensus," *New Democrat,* May–June 1995, 21.
119. Joel Kotkin, "The Hot Zone: Why Did the New Affirmative Action Debate Erupt in California?" *New Democrat,* May–June 1995, 10.
120. Tyack and Cuban, *Tinkering toward Utopia,* 136.
121. Ibid.
122. Ibid.

123. Ibid., 140–141.
124. Ibid., 140.
125. National Commission on Teaching and America's Future, *What Matters Most,* 5.
126. Ibid.
127. Ibid., 6.
128. Tyack and Cuban, *Tinkering toward Utopia,* 141.
129. Ibid., 142.
130. Ibid.

Three ~

HEALTH CARE IN CONTINUING CRISIS

Why has personal health become a political issue?
Why are we spending so much for health care in the United States?
How are the major players making out in the megabuck health industry?
How has government intervention affected health costs and quality of care?
What are the initiatives to cut costs, increase quality, and provide care to
  everyone?

T he escalating U.S. health care bill has reached such proportions that political policy makers have been forced to respond. The spiraling increases
in health costs reached crisis proportions during the profound economic
recession that set in during the early 1990s and the economic and stock market
downswings during the early 2000s. Layoffs, wage freezes, and labor force reductions, which reached up into the white-collar classes, coupled with the return to
deficits at every level of government, resulted in spending cutbacks for all public
services. Both private sector employee health benefits and government-subsidized
care for the elderly and the poor became major targets for reduction. The patchwork quilt of health care funding and delivery frayed visibly as its costs became
staggering.

By the early 1990s, none of the players in the health care game—from the
providers (doctors and hospitals) to the payers (employers and private and public insurers)—was happy with the overall system of health care in the United
States. The consumer was not happy either. A Harris Interactive/Health Care Research poll reported in August 2002 that 31 percent of the public believed that
"the health care system has so much wrong with it that we need to completely rebuild it."[1] Eleven percent of physicians, employers, and hospitals agreed with the
same statement; 9 percent of health plans agreed. Forty-nine percent of the public believed that fundamental change was needed, and a majority of physicians
(70 percent), employers (74 percent), hospitals (79 percent), and health plans
(81 percent) agreed with them.[2] A January 2001 Gallup poll found that 27 percent
of the public was somewhat dissatisfied and 22 percent was very dissatisfied with
the quality of the medical care they had received.[3]

While, as one analyst has observed, "health policy has looked like political quicksand, not pay dirt,"[4] political candidates at both state and national levels started to exploit the health care crisis in the 1992 election cycle. Harris Wofford's upset victory in the Pennsylvania race for the U.S. Senate was attributed to his near single-issue campaign theme of radical health care reform. Democratic presidential candidate Bill Clinton did not miss the significance of rising disenchantment with health care cost and delivery. His party convention platform called for "universal access to quality, affordable health care—not as a privilege, but as a right."[5] The Democrats promised government reform that would do that. The Republicans promised a health plan to remedy problems of cost and access but reiterated their historic position: "Republicans believe government control of health care is irresponsible and ineffective."[6] But by 1996 both political parties were screechingly silent about health reform, for reasons that will soon become evident.

Political rhetoric and motives aside, there are profoundly serious and very basic problems with our health care apparatus. Compared to the other major industrialized nations in the world, our uneven patchwork of health delivery (1) costs more per person,[7] (2) delivers lesser results based on international standards of success like infant death rates and adult longevity (the United States is virtually at the median of other OECD [Organization Economic Cooperation and Development] countries),[8] and (3) serves fewer of our citizens. In this chapter we will look at the issues of cost and access to health care, the evolution of government involvement in its financing and delivery, and periodic attempts at reform. Then we will look at the policy alternatives that have been proposed as solutions to the current costly disarray in delivering health care to the nation.

THE ESCALATION OF HEALTH COSTS

It is difficult to depict the costs of health care to the reader in a way that has personal impact. Most of our readers are college-age students who (1) by virtue of age are usually healthy, (2) have access to college health centers for minor problems, and (3) are likely to have medical insurance coverage through a parent's workplace. In short, most are insulated from direct payment for their limited health needs. But so has the average American family been protected from the escalating costs of health care over the past several decades. Whether underwritten by an employer or the government, health insurance has shielded most Americans from the sobering experience of paying the actual billed cost for a doctor's visit, a hospital stay, or prescription drugs.

However, employers have become less and less willing to absorb the steepening medical insurance costs, and government programs that insure the aged, disabled, and poor are strained to the maximum. "My insurance will cover it," is becoming a less familiar phrase. Increasingly, workplace-insured health consumers are making greater out-of-pocket contributions to their care bills. Between 2000 and 2001, monthly health insurance premiums for employers increased by 11 percent; they had increased by 8.3 percent only a year earlier.[9] Insurers are now increasingly passing on their costs to employers or are making other significant changes in how they are managing their costs. As an example, CalPERS, one of the two largest purchasers of health insurance in the nation, was faced with drastic increases in their premiums for 2002. It rejected early bids with increases of 13 percent, negotiating much smaller increases but only by passing on increased costs for prescription drugs and office visits. For 2003 CalPERS dropped several health plan alternatives from its menu offered to customers, reducing the number of plan options to four.

How fast have health costs increased? In 1991 alone, they skyrocketed—nearly four times that year's rate of inflation. Between 1988 and 1993, the yearly increases in national medical outlay were three times the annual increases in the overall cost of living, declining slightly in recent years to two times the annual rise. This rate of growth slowed significantly in the mid-1990s, with hospital inpatient costs even declining during that period (and until 1998). But by the end of the decade, fueled by large growth in prescription drug costs and hospital outpatient costs, growth had increased again to 7.2 percent in 2000 and an estimated 7.7 percent in 2001.[10] In real dollars, the yearly per-capita (per-person) expenditures for health care had increased by just short of 25 percent between 1990 and 1999 (from $3,495 to $4,358 per person).[11]

Although the yearly per-capita increases are hefty by any measure, they are staggering when viewed in a national context (see Table 3.1). Health care costs as a personal issue become a public issue when they affect the national economy. That is the case with our present costs, which are gobbling up a disproportionate share of the nation's annual gross domestic product (GDP), the total dollar volume of goods and services that the country produces. How much of our yearly national income does health care eat up? In 1999, medical expenditures devoured 12.9 percent of the GDP.[12] Thirty years ago, they constituted only 5 percent. At the present rate, health costs will consume 15 percent of the nation's income by 2005.[13]

Table 3.1 illustrates the fact that the United States spends more on health care per capita ($4,358 in 1999) and spends a greater percentage of its GDP on health care (12.9 percent) than any other of the OECD countries. Two other countries, Switzerland and Germany, also spend more than 10 percent of their GDP on health care, and Canada and France spend over 9 percent, with Belgium, Iceland, the Netherlands, and Australia close to that. In 1999 the United Kingdom spent only 6.9 percent and Japan spent 7.5 percent.

Table 3.2 presents the health outcomes for several Western democracies, including the United States, after spending these kinds of dollars on health care.

Why are health care costs increasing? Many factors are cited,[14] including:

Demographic trends—the population is aging since people are living longer; this results in more need for health care since people use more health care as they age.

TABLE 3.1
Health Spending (U.S. dollars) in 30 OECD Countries, 1990 and 1999 Ranked by Percent of Gross Domestic Product (GDP) Spent on Health Care

| | Health Spending per Capita | | Percent of GDP Spent on Health, |
	1990	1999	1999
United States	3,495	4,358	12.9
Switzerland	2,275	2,853	10.4
Germany	2,045	2,361	10.3
Canada	2,142	2,463	9.3
France	1,940	2,115	9.3
Belgium	1,592	2,181	8.8
Iceland	1,756	2,287	8.7
Netherlands	1,791	2,259	8.7
Australia	1,882	2,085	8.6
Norway	1,740	2,388	8.5
Denmark	1,855	2,275	8.4
Greece	902	1,198	8.4
Austria	1,538	2,014	8.2
New Zealand	1,196	1,505	8.1
Italy	1,881	1,832	7.9
Sweden	1,904	1,732	7.9
Portugal	754	1,203	7.7
Japan	1,381	1,795	7.5
Czech Republic	735	983	7.4
Spain	1,040	1,189	7.0
United Kingdom	1,236	1,569	6.9
Finland	1,649	1,547	6.8
Hungary	652	782	6.8
Ireland	1,016	1,534	6.8
Slovakia		668	6.3
Poland	329	535	6.2
Luxembourg	1,897	2,543	6.1
Korea	474	868	5.4
Mexico	332	419	5.3
Turkey	218	316	4.8
Median	1,592	1,764	7.9

Source: Derived from Uwe E. Reinhardt, Peter S. Hussey, and Gerard Anderson, "Cross-National Comparisons of Health Systems Using OECD Data, 1999," *Health Affairs: Trends in Health Tracking* May–June 2002, http://www.healthaffairs.org/freecontent/v21n3/s21.htm, Exhibit 1.

TABLE 3.2
Comparative Health and Life Expectancy Data, 2001

	Total Fertility Rate	*Life Expectancy at Birth*	**Probability of Dying before Age 5 (per 1,000)**	
			Male	*Female*
Canada	1.6	79.3	6	5
France	1.8	79.3	5	4
Germany	1.3	78.2	5	4
Great Britain	1.6	77.5	7	6
Italy	1.2	79.3	5	5
Japan	1.4	81.4	5	4
United States	**2.0**	**77.0**	**9**	**7**

Source: World Health Organization, Annex Table 1: Basic Indicators for All Member States, 2002, http://www.who.int/whr/2002/whr2002_annex1.pdf.

Advances in biomedical technology, which are typically more expensive techniques and are not replacing an even more expensive, older technique (as they often do in other industries). So costs increase even further from the technology itself, and then operators must be trained to use the technology.

Developments in new drugs—prescription drug expenditures are the fastest growing segment of health care costs, and many of the new drugs have been known for their high costs.

Hospitals and other health care providers consolidated, which gave them additional bargaining power to achieve better reimbursements from insurance companies for the services they provide.

Health care labor pressures for increased wages, as in many other industries.

Managed care reduced the increase in health care costs during the mid-1990s, but today, more and more consumers are moving to health insurance plans that allow more choice and provide insurance companies less control—over treatment and over costs.

Figure 3.1 illustrates the growth in health costs by highlighting the components of that growth. Clearly, hospital inpatient and outpatient costs are the culprits in the recent increases in health care costs, followed by the costs of prescription drugs. Figure 3.2 highlights the relative size of each component of overall health care costs. Hospital costs are 37 percent, while physician costs are 29 percent, followed by nursing care and prescription drug costs, both at 9 percent. Clearly, when hospital and drug costs increase, they will have an enormous effect upon overall health care costs.

FIGURE 3.1
Growth in Health Care Cost Components, 1991–2001

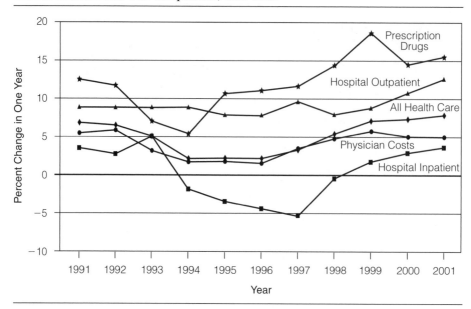

Source: Bradley Strunk, Paul B. Ginsburg, and Jon R. Gabel, "Tracking Health Care Costs: Hospital Spending Spurs Double Digit Increase in 2001," Center for Studying Health System Change, September 2002, http://www.hschange.org/CONTENT/472/table1.shtml.

FIGURE 3.2
Components of Health Care Expenses across the United States, 1998

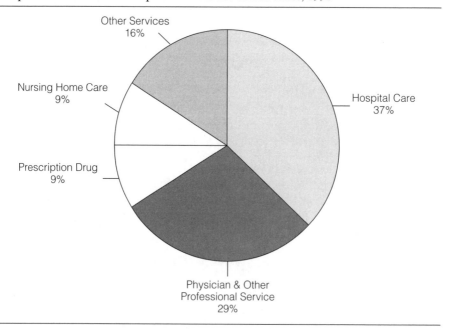

Source: Kaiser Family Foundation, "State Facts, 1998," 2002, http://www.statehealthfacts.kff.org.

A CLOSER LOOK

How much have your own health insurance premiums increased in the past two years? Are you paying more for doctor's visits? For each drug prescription? Or maybe you do not have insurance at all or get it through your university—what will happen between semesters and after you graduate?

INSURING HEALTH: THE AMERICAN PATTERN

Health care delivery in the United States has developed very differently from that in all other industrialized democratic nations. Access to medical care in this country has been seen traditionally as a private transaction between individuals and their care providers. The extent and quality of care turns on the ability to pay. An American citizen's access to quality health care is perceived as a privilege, not a right. Finally, our assumption is that individual health is unrelated to the public good, an attitude that contrasts sharply to that held in all other industrialized countries.

By the turn of the twentieth century in Europe, the health of the working man was seen as essential to national economic growth. German chancellor Otto von Bismarck initiated the first compulsory health insurance program for his industrializing nation in 1883. Most other European democracies had some form of mandated "sickness insurance" by 1914.[15] Early government-initiated health insurance in European countries had strong political motivation as well as an economic rationale. The perceived threat of Marxist economic ideas, coupled with a multiparty system that gave socialist parties easier access to power, forced nonsocialist moderates to address the needs of the workers. Once in place, programs to ensure worker health care through insurance became an assumed and expected function of government.

Health insurance in this country had different origins. The absence of a domestic socialist threat and a two-party system that foreclosed any representation of the tiny Socialist Party doomed any serious political initiative addressing the workingman's health. The first health insurance plan in the United States was an economic response by private hospitals to declining patient admissions in the first years of what became known as the Great Depression. In 1929 a Texas hospital enrolled a group of Dallas schoolteachers in a prepaid hospital plan for which each participant paid a premium of 50 cents a month. The group prepayment kept the hospital solvent during lean times—and Blue Cross, still the major insurer for hospital coverage in the country, was born. Although other insurers entered the health field offering limited coverage, only 12 million Americans had any health insurance by the time we entered World War II. That number increased two and a half times by the end of the war.[16] Another private insurance provider, Blue Shield, later became part of this system.

On the face of it, one could speculate that the war somehow affected American attitudes toward life, death, and health. The simple reality is that Franklin Roosevelt's wartime economic policies required cooperation between employers and employees under his administration's watchful eye. One outcome of this cozy relationship was the creation of tax incentives to employers who provided health insurance to workers. Employers were allowed to deduct the full cost of employee health insurance premiums from their yearly taxable revenues as a cost of doing business. Their employees did not have to declare the benefits as income. The government did not have to take any direct hand in providing medical care. Everybody won. Tax breaks continue to this day as the primary incentive for voluntary employer-financed health insurance. Of course, for every carrot there is a stick—as employers discovered in the postwar years when the National Labor Relations Board decided that *not* offering health insurance was, under certain conditions, a violation of "fair labor practices." Consequently, employer-paid health insurance for workers, and often for their dependents, became commonplace over the following decades.

This health care pattern is very much within the American political tradition of covertly promoting certain public policies through subsidizing private-sector growth and profit. One is hard-pressed to find a single developing segment of the American economy, from early government transport subsidies (rail, then air) to recent urban redevelopment schemes, that has not been subsidized to further public policy goals. The political genius of the American approach has been to remove elected officials and government bureaucracies from direct responsibility for the failure or inefficiencies of programs, projects, or services that they have covertly promoted through subsidies and incentives. Our tradition of individualism and free enterprise is the face we paint over the helter-skelter mosaic of government intervention and subsidy. As a consequence, we lack the targeted directions that national policy can provide. Erratic and uneven health care delivery would have remained just another aspect of this American fabric had it not, in a very brief period, become so expensive to employers, workers, and to government-funded programs for the elderly, disabled, and poor.

This system of subsidized health care was further developed in the 1960s with the development of the federal government's systems for providing assisted health care for the elderly (Medicare) and the poor (Medicaid). This step completed the creation of a three-tiered system of providing financing for health care—private specialized health care insurance providers, publicly assisted health care, and insurance providers operating as health maintenance organizations (HMOs) or preferred provider organizations (PPOs) utilizing selective contracting out to networks of health providers. This is the system still in place in the United States today.

HEALTH MONEY: WHERE DOES IT COME FROM, WHERE DOES IT GO?

The *crisis* of health care in this country is not the crisis of access—who can get it and who cannot. Nor is it a crisis of quality—how good is our health care really? It is a crisis of cash. President Clinton, in a first-term preinauguration economic conference on the deficit, exploded: "We are kidding each other . . . if we think we can get control of this budget if we don't do something about health care. It's going to bankrupt the country."[17] Issues of access and quality are central to the consumers of health care and to public health academics. However, the major players in the health care game are primarily interested in maintaining and increasing their respective economic advantages within the existing system.

Paying America's health bill has traditionally fallen to what is termed a third-party payer—a financial agent who assumes the risk of medical and hospital expenses incurred by the *first party,* the insured patient. The *second party* is the physician, hospital, pharmacist, or other health care provider from whom the patient obtains services. The third party (insurer) reimburses the second party (provider), in full or in part, *after* services are provided. Known as fee-for-service, this process of reimbursement is the predominant one in the American health care delivery system and is still the model preferred by most consumers. Under this traditional insurance system, the insurance company pays, or reimburses, a health insurance claim when the claim is filed by the patient (the insured party) or by the patient's health care provider. The financing of the health care service is kept totally separate from the health care service itself.

Making recent, rapid strides toward becoming the new model for health delivery is the prepaid, inclusive care system employed by health maintenance organizations. HMOs are a type of health insurer but, unlike traditional insurers, they do more than provide financing for health care. They also directly provide or arrange for health care to patients by providing access to a limited number of health care providers. The HMO model of managed care at a preestablished price has gained momentum among health care academics and politicians as a cheaper alternative delivery system that has potential for reducing health cost inflation. Preferred provider organizations are another method of providing service. A PPO is "a managed care system in which you use doctors, hospitals, and providers that belong to the network. You can use doctors, hospitals, and providers outside of the network for an additional cost."[18]

Managed care is a method of contracting "with select providers who share financial risk for the cost of care (as is typically done in HMOs) or who accept negotiated discounts in fee-for-service payments (as is typically done in PPOs). Providers' compensation may be tied, at least in part, to their own pattern of clinical decision-making and/or resource utilization. Managed care strategies include various forms of utilization review . . . and case management. Moreover, managed care organizations employ internal, and often external, quality assurance processes."[19]

HMO enrollments have boomed and the trend is moving away from private providers; in the 1990s, many large employers moved their employees into HMOs or PPOs—by 1998, 78 million people were enrolled in HMO plans,[20] slightly less than 80 percent in 2001.[21] The shift occurred because of moves to Medicaid provision, away from private insurance providers (fee-for-service), and away from receiving health insurance as a benefit for employees and because of the increased numbers of individuals with no health insurance at all.

Aside from the general trends in overall health costs, another perspective is offered by examining the health care dollar. (1) How is each health care dollar presently divided among the providers? And (2) who pays how large a share to reimburse them? Taking the most recent figures calculated by the Health Care Financing Administration (HCFA), we find that over half (56 cents) of every dollar paid out went to the two central providers, hospitals and physicians. Where did the other 44 cents go? A little over half of it (24 cents) was paid in about equal parts for drugs, dental care, and other health services such as home health care, orthopedic appliances, and eyeglasses. Of the remaining 20 cents, 12 went to miscellaneous spending, including public health, medical research, construction, and insurer administrative costs, leaving 8 cents to pay for nursing home care. Who paid for these health care services? The consumer's direct out-of-pocket costs constituted 18 cents of each dollar. Government (federal and state together) footed 45 cents of the tab. Private health insurers were liable for 32 cents, and the remaining 5 cents was paid by other private sources.

The *relative* shares of the health dollar spent for services and the respective shares of those footing health costs has not shifted much over the past decade; what has increased dramatically is the overall expenditure, the "size of the pie," from $355 billion in 1983 to over $1.3 trillion by 2001. But to understand who ultimately pays the nation's health bill, we have to examine the money trail a little more closely. What we discover is that federal and state government payments (Medicare and Medicaid) to health providers come from nonvoluntary contributions (taxes) levied on employed workers by government for redistribution to those not employed (elderly, disabled, or dependent). Private insurance premium payments to providers come from both employee and employer pockets. But the employer share is subsidized by government (and thus the taxpayer) through tax deduction incentives. Too, employer benefit packages are calculated to compensate for lower employee wage structures, and any excess costs of benefits are passed on to the consumers of products and services. Fundamentally, although indirectly, working persons are paying 100 percent of the nation's health bill. But they are personally insulated from that reality by third-party payers, who pick up 82 percent of billed costs.

HOW GOVERNMENT GOT INVOLVED

The traditional American pattern of health care financing has been a work-based group insurance undertaking, promoted through tax incentives, funneling money through private third-party insurers to reimburse providers' fees. Historic and economic events over the several decades after World War II brought about a new third-party payer: federal and state governments and HMOs.

As the country got back to work in the post–World War II era, the economy boomed, the birth rate increased, and the movement to suburbia began. The "affluent society" was born; "organization men" exercised economic power. It was the full flexing of corporate America. The government balanced budgets regularly. Taxation and inflation were low. Public expenditures for education and health increased in the decade and a half after the end of the war, but its bite of the GDP was low since the economy was expanding at a boisterous 6 percent a year through the 1950s into the 1960s.

It was within this national context of rising middle-class affluence, generous funding of education and other public services, and balanced governmental budgets that proposals to increase access to health care fell on more receptive ears. What about the elderly, no longer in the workforce and unprotected from health crises? What about the unemployed and those in poverty for whatever reason? Should a bountiful society subsidize their access to medical care?

Isolated legislative attempts were made earlier in this century to provide health care access to all citizens through universal compulsory insurance. Each attempt was successfully rebuffed through lobbying efforts by a coalition of insurance companies and medical service providers. They branded calls for universal health insurance before World War I as *unAmerican* and *pro-German*—a reference to Bismarck's national health plan. The stigma of imitating the enemy culture sank the earliest health reform proposals.

This early success of the Germanizing gambit in discrediting a national health plan was repeated in the late 1940s, when President Harry Truman pursued his goal to universalize medical access. This time our enemy, in the cold war, was the "Communist menace" that (it was proclaimed by Representative Richard Nixon and Senator Joseph McCarthy, among many others) threatened to subvert American institutions from within. National health insurance was branded as the first step toward a Communist takeover in the United States. An editorial in the official publication of the American Medical Association made the connection clear when it asserted that "politically controlled medical care supported by a compulsory tax is an early but essential part of the development of a socialized nation, the forerunner of various forms of collectivism. This fight is not that of medicine alone; it is a fight of all America." [22] The major players in the health establishment exploited the growing public hysteria over claims that every American institution was threatened by infiltration of Communist ideas. In the midst of the McCarthy era, the call to resist what the medical establishment labeled "the socializing of medical care" forced Truman to abandon his national health policy efforts.

The truly radical intervention of the federal government in 1965 as the third-party insurer for the country's elderly and its poor was the result of a historic political and economic coming together. Fifteen years of excellent economic times in the United States engendered a spirit of beneficence and social concern by the early 1960s, and that spirit radiated through every aspect of American life. It was also the first time since the New Deal administrations of Franklin D. Roosevelt that both houses of Congress as well as the presidency were in the hands of the Democrats. Lyndon Johnson, who had worked up through congressional ranks to become vice president to John F. Kennedy, was thrust into the Oval Office following the JFK assassination in 1963.

With a nation in mourning and repentance, Johnson thrashed the Republican candidate, Barry Goldwater, in the 1964 elections. Goldwater was, for the 1960s, an ultraconservative for whom the specter of socialism was tightly and ideologically welded to any form of federal government initiative in social programs. His resounding defeat was taken as the go-ahead for healthy Democratic majorities in both houses of Congress to move rapidly in amending and approving a version of the Forand health care bill, which had been lingering in congressional committees for eight years.

In summer of 1965, President Johnson signed the legislation that ensured hospital and physician services to the nation's elderly and poor. He considered it the cornerstone of his plan for the Great Society, a vision of a humane America where no one should lack necessities or equal opportunity for advancement. Within two years, the economic and political capital necessary to carry out the remainder of his Great Society agenda dissipated in the jungles of Vietnam.

Radically expanding access to basic health care, the legislation established two separate programs: Medicare and Medicaid. Medicare addressed the needs of the elderly and disabled and was to be administered through the Social Security Administration, which had exhibited efficiency in handling Social Security pension programs. Medicaid, the companion program to serve the health care needs of the nation's poor, would be financed jointly with the states. It left to them the task of determining eligibility, benefits, and administering payments to providers. This time around, the health care establishment did not mount a concerted campaign to fight off direct government funding for the elderly and the poor. Why did health care interest groups, which had successfully rebuffed any intrusion on the prevailing pattern of coverage for more than 40 years, suddenly relent? Were they, too, caught up in economic good times and social beneficence? Or were they just tired out from years of obstructionism?

Neither. Their years of lobbying and testifying and backroom negotiating on health care proposals had legitimated them as participants in the final shaping of the Forand bill. Both the providers and existing third-party payers emerged from the negotiations intact—and enriched by an enlarged client base. Medicare and Medicaid would reimburse doctors on a fee-for-service basis. Hospitals negotiated a combination of fees plus additional imbursement for capital expenditures on facilities and equipment. Private insurers would contract with federal and state governments to process medical claims. Old-fashioned American capitalism, and a heavy dose of government benefit parceling, triumphed over the specter of socialism.

The only stumbling block thrown up by the American Medical Association was its position that only the *poor* elderly, lacking private insurance coverage, should be eligible for Medicare. It wanted means-testing, proof that the elderly fell below the poverty level, similar to that projected for recipients of Medicaid benefits. Physician-providers feared that elderly patients with generous private insurance benefits would shift to Medicare with its lower reimbursement rates. For physicians that meant the same number of patients but less money. Labor unions fought ferociously, and successfully, to block any form of means-testing for the elderly. Their fight was not motivated by issues of access to care, fairness, or sentiments of charity. The unions' goal was to unload employer payments for retired workers' medical insurance onto Medicare. This shift of medical liability would allow the unions to press employers for higher wages for active working members to be paid out of the resultant cost savings.[23]

FIGURE 3.3
State Health versus State Nonhealth Expenditures, 1999

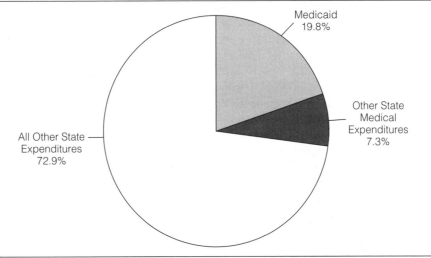

Source: Milbank Memorial Fund, the National Association of State Budget Officers, and the Reforming States Group, 1998–1999 State Health Care Expenditure Report, March 2001, http://www.milbank.org/1998shcer/index.html#states.

In summary, the federal and state governments simply became another third-party insurer in the eyes of the providers. The legislation provided them with a sizable new client group of formerly unserved or minimally served senior citizens and the never served poor of all ages. Paid access to medical care for these new clienteles could only enrich the providers. It was a whole new market. But the rules of reimbursement remained the same: fee-for-service paid to the provider after the service is performed.

GOVERNMENT AS A THIRD PARTY

With that 1965 stroke of the pen, government instantly became the single largest third-party payer in the United States. By 2001, Medicaid and Medicare payments alone accounted for $351.6 billion, or 18.9 percent, of the federal budget.[24] In addition, in 1998–1999, 27.1 percent of states' total expenditures were for Medicaid (19.8 percent) or other health care expenses (7.3 percent) (see Figure 3.3).

Medicare

Medicare is an entitlement program administered through the Health Care Financing Administration, a division of the Social Security Administration. Elderly and disabled persons eligible to receive Social Security benefits are automatically eligible for Medicare health coverage. Since Social Security is an insurance system into which workers have paid a percentage of their income, matched by equal employer contributions, the retiree is considered *entitled* to benefits. This contrasts with other social programs that are means-tested. For instance, those seeking state Medicaid coverage must prove how poor they are to qualify for assistance.

Medicare coverage is composed of two parts: Part A pays hospital costs, care in a skilled nursing facility, and hospice and some home health care, while Part B covers physicians' expenses and outpatient care. This separation is significant because the two components are financed in different ways. Hospitalization (Part A) for the elderly and disabled of all ages (now numbering 38 million Americans) is paid out of the Medicare Trust Fund. Monies that move through that fund for hospital costs are collected as a stipulated part of Social Security taxes on wages. Currently, employers and employees each pay 1.45 percent each on wages that goes directly into the Hospital Insurance Trust Fund to pay for Medicare Part A benefits.

The hospital insurance works like this: the patient pays for the first day ($812 deductible under the present schedule), Medicare pays for the next 59 days. After the 60th day, the patient pays $203 daily until the 90th day, then $406 per day from the 91st to the 150th day.[25] Part A pays only hospital care, not physician services. During 1999 alone, over 29 million Medicare recipients received a reimbursed service.[26]

Physician services (Part B) are optional for beneficiaries and are funded out of general federal tax revenues, rather than a specific Social Security tax, and by the participants in the plan, who pay $54 per month (in 2002, about 25 percent of the premium), although they are often not aware of it since it is deducted from their monthly Social Security checks. This contribution does not go far in defraying the mammoth costs of those services for this segment, which, by virtue of aging and infirmity, needs more frequent medical attention. After a $100 annual deductible is met, Part B pays 80 percent of the bill for physicians and related services. Unpredictable bouts of ill health put a sizable dent in the monthly Social Security allotment of an elderly person who must pay 20 percent of all health costs, except for 59 days of hospitalization. Consequently, a great number of the elderly enroll themselves in MediGap insurance programs, which supplement and extend basic Medicare coverage, for which they pay monthly premiums ranging from about $80 to over $200 a month depending on their region of residence and the terms of the supplemental plan chosen.

Medicaid

In 2001, 34.3 million citizens, including one-quarter of all children,[27] participated in Medicaid, a means-tested entitlement health insurance program (meaning that individuals are entitled to participate in the program if their income, or means, fits certain criteria) funded by both the federal and state governments. In 2003 the nation spent an estimated $280 billion on Medicaid programs alone ($159 billion is the federal government's share).[28] The federal government's share of costs ranges from at least 50 to 77 percent; Mississippi has the highest rate for 2003 at 76.62 percent. These rates are evaluated annually and are based upon states' per-capita incomes averaged over three years. Since state economies had improved during the 1990s, the reimbursement rates for 29 states went down in 2001, just as the economy began to decline again in 2002. These states will lose an approximate $565 million in reimbursements from the federal government as a result.[29] Further, Medicaid enrollments declined until mid-1998, when they began to increase again.[30]

Under the 1965 Medicaid enabling legislation (Title XIX of the Social Security Act), the states were handed the mission of setting up a health insurance program for the unserved poor. Under this cooperative program between the federal and state governments, each state:

Establishes its own eligibility standards;

Determines the type, amount, duration, and scope of services;

Sets the rate of payment for services; and

Administers its own program.[31]

Therefore, the program varies from state to state.

What a state named "the program" and defined as poor and the range of services it provided were left to its own discretion. These are some examples of the types of groups that are eligible for coverage:[32]

≫ Low-income families with children

≫ Supplemental Security Insurance (SSI) recipients—the aged, blind, and disabled

≫ Babies born to Medicaid-eligible women

≫ Children under 6 and pregnant women whose family income is at or below 133 percent of the federal poverty level

≫ Recipients of adoption and foster case assistance

≫ Some Medicare beneficiaries

≫ Some other protected groups

Figure 3.4 shows the total share of various groups participating in the Medicaid programs—children are by far the largest share (51 percent); they are followed by adults under the poverty level (20 percent) and the blind or disabled (18 percent). In 1998 a new Medicaid program, the State Child Health Insurance Programs (SCHIP) Medicaid was implemented, which also contributes to the health care needs of children.

Medicaid plays an important role for Medicare recipients by ensuring access to health care. The state Medicaid programs modeled themselves along Medicare lines. They offered eligible recipients hospital and physician services paid on a fee-for-service basis to the providers. Some states extended benefit coverage to dental and eye care and prescription drugs. Others kept to minimal coverage. Since Medicare did not cover long-term nursing-home coverage for the indigent

FIGURE 3.4
Populations Served by Medicaid Programs

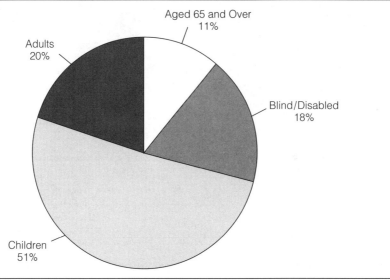

Source: U.S. Department of Health and Human Services, Centers for Medicare and Medicaid Services, *2002 CMS Statistics* (Washington, DC: U.S. Government Printing Office, 2002), 11.

elderly, that costly program fell to the state Medicaid programs. At present, Medicaid is the largest purchaser of nursing home and long-term care services[33] and is the only public program providing ongoing nursing-home care. An untold number of ailing, elderly citizens have had to "buy down" to qualify for long-term nursing care, shedding their assets to fall within state eligibility limits for Medicaid coverage. More recently, increasing numbers of debilitated young AIDS sufferers have exhausted personal finances and become eligible for nursing-home care under Medicaid programs.

Not only do state programs vary in items covered and level of provider reimbursement, but eligibility ranges widely. Although federal guidelines for Medicaid programs are rather vague in most respects (typical of most matching-fund schemes devised by Congress), they are overly specific in others. For example, in the early 1990s urban Democratic representatives shepherded a bill through Congress that ordered state Medicaid programs to exempt pregnant women and children under seven years of age from means-tested eligibility. It was the sort of bill that even a fiscally minded president could not veto. The effect of the federal action was to open access to health care for sizable new clienteles, with little concern over its impact on state resources. Then, the U.S. Public Health Service ordered state Medicaid programs to test children up to three years of age for lead poisoning and to phase in a more precise (and expensive) test for the purpose.[34]

And as a final example, several U.S. Supreme Court decisions have held that states are *not obligated* to perform abortions at public expense, which led the federal government, via the Hyde Amendment, to deny all Medicaid matching funds to states that do fund abortions. In each of these instances, state resources were at the mercy of a national political agenda.

"Medicaid has become a dumping ground," according to the president of the Kaiser Foundation.[35] Between congressional and federal agency requirements for specific programs, increased responsibility for crack babies, nursing home care, and sheer numbers of poverty-level Americans, states are trapped with an inherently expensive patient load. The response of state Medicaid programs, caught in the upward spiral of provider costs coupled with burdensome clienteles, was to cut hospital cost payments and reduce physician fees over the past several years. General administrative inefficiency of some state Medicaid systems caused payments to linger for many months before finding their way to provider pockets. Providers responded by refusing to treat Medicaid patients, shifting the care of such patients to public facilities. Those facilities, usually local government teaching hospitals affiliated with medical schools, started to set quotas on the number of Medicaid patients they would admit.

As hospitals were squeezed by declining Medicaid reimbursements on the one side and increasingly stringent contracts with private insurers on the other, they resorted to court action. They claimed that Medicaid legislation required hospitals to treat the poor and that it promised to pay for those services. Neither state nor federal government has fulfilled that agreement, they asserted. The U.S. Supreme Court (1991) agreed with them, holding that hospitals can sue state governments in federal court to obtain "reasonable and adequate" reimbursement for treating needy patients. The decision also opened the door for public hospitals funded by local government (county or city) to sue their own states for adequate Medicaid reimbursement.

Medicare has increasingly moved to a managed care system to provide services for its recipients (56 percent of its participants are in some sort of managed care arrangement), and all states have some of their recipients in these types of systems.[36] The Balanced Budget Act of 1997 allowed states to mandate enrollment in managed care organizations (MCOs) for Medicaid recipients without special permission, or waiver, from the federal government. The managed care system here relies upon primary care providers and coordination of patient care as a way to reduce health care costs and unneccessary procedures.

Two primary models exist for providing this care—the risk-based model, with approximately 80 percent of all beneficiaries participating, and a fee-for-service primary care case-management model. Under the first, the managed care organization receives a monthly fee for each beneficiary (the capitation) and must provide services for that fee. Under the second model, the primary care provider coordinates the care and attempts to keep costs low, although they do not have the financial risk of the managed care organization itself. There is a great deal of financial risk for managed care organizations in Medicaid-only organizations, as

---

A CLOSER LOOK

Do you have family or friends on either Medicaid or Medicare (particularly elderly relatives)? Ask them about their experience with either program—are they satisfied? Why or why not? Are they having problems holding on to their health care provider? How much do they pay for their prescription drugs?

---

they do not have higher-income individuals with which to balance out their risks and costs. For these organizations, the capitation rate is the critical factor in their continuing to participate in these programs.

EFFORTS AT COST CONTAINMENT

As the single largest insurer and underwriter in the health care business, the federal government wields the heaviest club in controlling provider costs. The Medicare program has undertaken several initiatives to limit hospital and physician costs. The response of providers has been to devise ways around the limits. State Medicaid programs are in desperate straits; some claim they are a hopeless mess. However, the crisis in Medicaid has brought forth some radical proposals for change from several states and has set off a renewed national debate on the merits, perhaps the necessity, of a simplified and cost-efficient national health care system.

Hospital Costs

Hospital expenses are the largest component of health care expenses today. Spending on hospital care rose more than 12 percent in 2001, comprising 37 percent of the total change in health care costs.[37]

Federal subsidies for hospital construction, begun in the mid-1940s, continued under another guise with the passage of Medicare. Medicare adopted the prevailing Blue Cross payment system for hospital costs, covering billed charges for room, tests, supplies, and drugs. However, hospitals were also allowed to build in an additional overhead charge to cover costs of facility improvements and construction. Heavy overbuilding and underutilization of facilities led to increases in daily rates to make up for empty beds. Medicare paid for the increase in beds, then paid again to cover the costs of empty rooms. The higher cost engendered by this cost-plus arrangement were also passed on to plans administered by private health insurers.

Several unsuccessful efforts to contain hospital costs were tried during the 1970s. President Nixon's economic stabilization program at the beginning of that decade included price controls. Riddled with exceptions and erratic application, controls made no dent in health care costs. Another approach, under the Health Planning Act (1974), set up health systems agencies (HSAs) in each state to monitor and regulate hospital construction and major equipment expenditures with the power to issue (or deny) certificates of need (CONs). The HSAs were phased out early in the Reagan administration. However, that administration delivered a one-two punch to hospitals in the early 1980s. Its first action limited increases in hospital reimbursement for Medicare patients (under the Tax Equity and Fiscal Responsibility Act). The second initiative was a more basic change in the fee-for-service arrangement and sent hospital administrators scurrying to develop alternative facility use. The new protocol, the prospective payment system (PPS), paid flat fees to hospitals for Medicare patients based on diagnosis. A hospital was free to keep patients as long as it wished—but it was only paid for the total hospitalization cost that Medicare established for each of 467 diagnosis-related groups (DRGs). Within two years the average number of inpatient days for Medicare recipients fell 22 percent.

Declining admissions spurred resourceful hospital administrators to begin promoting outpatient procedures and services. In particular, they targeted rehabilitation and psychiatric programs that had no Medicare limits and were amply covered by most private insurers. Today, the consumer is barraged by advertisements on radio and television and in the print media promoting drug and alcohol rehabilitation programs as well as one-day outpatient surgeries. Hospitals have additionally recouped losses of inpatient income by doubling daily facility charges for outpatient procedures.

Hospitals also began to court the privately insured consumer through graphically slick newsletters promoting staff doctors, special programs, and symposia for every possible health concern. They touted innovations in medical technology from CT (computed tomography) scans and MRI (magnetic resonance imaging) to the latest laser surgery miracles. This direct marketing of technology and procedures to affluent, well-insured potential patients has escalated demand among all segments of the population for more sophisticated (and much more expensive) levels of medical attention. Aggressive hospital administrators have more than compensated for the DRG limits with new consumer strategies.

Keep in mind that hospitals are reliant on doctors for admissions. The marketing strategies directed toward consumers have also been effective in promoting doctor loyalty. Doctors like high-tech medicine. Sophisticated diagnostic technology can save them time in pursuing targeted therapies. It can also help them avoid "bad calls"—machine-assisted diagnoses are useful in malpractice defense. Too, doctors like affiliations with hospitals that have been successful in creating a positive community reputation through effective marketing.

What overall effect have the DRGs and the changes they set in motion had on hospital costs? The intent was to (1) limit the length of stay to cut Medicare costs and (2) force competition between hospitals in filling empty beds, thus reducing prices for everyone. Either free-market capitalism has some basic flaw, or hospitals are exempt from the law of market forces, because costs were higher in communities with competition than in communities without.

And what has been the effect of Medicare hospital cost containment on reimbursement practices of private insurers? Most private third-party payers have instituted (1) fixed-fee schedules for reasonable costs, (2) requirements of second opinions for many procedures requiring hospital admission, and (3) preferred provider organizations (PPOs).

The PPO is actually the Medicare cost-containment plan in private disguise. Major insurers contract with hospitals to serve their insured on a fixed-fee, procedure-based structure. The insured has a choice not to patronize a preferred hospital, but the insurer will typically cover only 60 percent of the non-PPO provider's bill. For example, a $10,000 hospital stay (three to four days) billed in the traditional way is settled up by a PPO for about $3,000. An insured patient opting for a non-PPO hospital would personally have to pay $4,000 as the cost for exercising free choice. An uninsured individual would be liable for the full cost. The question this example raises, of course, is how much does hospitalization actually cost? Were the real costs in this hospitalization example $10,000 or $3,000? Or, one wonders, does a *real cost* exist in the present health delivery system?

But whether real or fictional or done with mirrors, we know this: it all costs more than state Medicaid programs can afford to spend. As state budgets have tumbled into severe deficit, Medicaid reimbursements to providers are continually cut. Hospitals have particularly suffered; they claim they actually lose money on Medicaid admissions. As a result, increasing numbers of hospitals simply refuse to admit Medicaid patients. The consequence of that refusal is to "dump" these patients on public hospitals that already have their hands full with the *totally* uninsured, who have no coverage of any sort. The alternative tactic is to make up the loss on Medicaid admissions by increasing billed costs to private insurers.

Hospital emergency and trauma units in urban areas have been the first fatalities of falling Medicaid payment levels coupled with increasing numbers of working poor families who have no insurance whatever. Gunshot and stab-wound victims have a low probability of being privately insured. They are routinely routed to public facilities or else are first stabilized and then dumped. Medicaid recipients are also, as a group, more likely to use emergency units for routine medical complaints. Recognizing the first signs of illness, making and keeping appointments, planning transportation, and arranging child care all require patience and planning. The easier alternative is to use emergency rooms as 24-hour clinics. For hospitals that keep an eye on bottom-line economics, the easiest alternative is to close their emergency rooms.

Doctor's Fees

Physicians charge a lot and they make a lot. The American public has been led to believe that they should. Medical association lobbying stresses that they deserve to—reciting the costs and time spent preparing for medical practice. Physician services comprise 38 percent of the total increase in health care costs in 2001.[38] But do they deserve an average salary of from $150,000 to $430,000 de-

A CLOSER LOOK

Go to http://www.salary.com and, using their Salary Wizard, select *Health Practitioner* under the "Select a Job Category" dropdown wizard. Then enter your own zip code or select the state/metropolitan area in which you reside; click on the *Search* button. Select *Physician* from the dropdown menu on the next screen when asked to "Select the Job Title Closest to Yours" and select *Basic Salary Report* under "3. Create Your Report" to find physician salaries in your area.

pending upon their specialty?[39]—several times over the median salary of the people they treat?

As the health cost vise turns more directly on consumers, media attention is likely to illuminate excessive salaries as the tip of the compensation iceberg. Physicians are often shareholders in hospitals into which they admit their patients, encouraging hospitalization when none might be needed. More commonly, they have financial interests in laboratories, rehabilitation and therapy practices, and nursing homes to which they refer patients.

Medicare was slower to act in limiting physician fees than in controlling hospital costs. It followed the private insurer formula that calculates fees on the "usual and customary" charges for a given procedure based on prevailing rates in the geographic area where the procedure is performed. All fees in major urban areas, for example, are higher than the cost of the same procedures in medium-sized cities, and both are costlier than rural care. The obvious problem with the "usual and customary" standard is that this year's fee increases by physicians in an area become next year's "usual and customary" charges. The less apparent loophole has been the frequent introduction of new procedures that have no established, customary fees. Until new treatments have a track record, the sky is the limit for billed charges—although third-party payers are becoming tougher negotiators on costs for innovative procedures.

A more critical scrutiny of overall physician billing practices was developed in the late 1980s and continued into the 1990s under managed care. Preapproval and second opinions before performing major surgical procedures were instituted. Medicare introduced billing schedules (limits) for nearly 7,000 different physician procedures. Those basic schedules, with more generous limits, have become widely used by private-insurer preferred provider organizations. Physician response to this cost-control squeeze play depended on the nature and type of practice. Specialty medicine practitioners and surgeons were hit harder than family practice providers. Those in PPO networks were less affected, since they could compensate for fee reduction through greater volume. Health maintenance organization (HMO) physicians, paid on other than a fee-for-service basis, were unaffected.

"Creative billing seminars" constituted the major response by physician providers. Surgeons were taught to *unbundle* a procedure into several billable components. For instance, a $2,900 gastrectomy (removal of part of the stomach) could be unbundled and billed for a total of $6,900.28. Dermatologists (skin specialists) learned to delay billing for removing a mole until the lab biopsy showed whether it was cancerous or not. The mole, of course, was already gone, but a malignant mole fell under a higher billing code. All physicians were advised to schedule extra, chargeable follow-up visits.

Medicare's counterresponse was part of the 1989 Omnibus Budget Reconciliation Act (OBRA). A new national fee schedule, adjusted for geographic variations in physician office expenses and malpractice insurance, was phased in over a four-year period (1992–96). Called the *resource-based relative-value scale* (RBRVS), it also set target limits for annual cost increases. Its overall goal was to reduce the range of compensation, clustering physicians more closely around the overall median. Toward that end, Medicare increased office visit payment rates to primary care physicians, the "gatekeepers" of health delivery, and decreased specialist fees.

In the longer run, the most profound impact on the medical profession may be the research institute established and funded under OBRA: the Agency for Health Care Policy and Research (HCPRA). Both Medicare and private insurers have developed huge patient procedure–cost databases. With additional physician-supplied patient information, HCPRA can determine the relative effectiveness of different medical protocols in the treatment of specific ailments. The goal of this *outcomes evaluation* is to establish which treatments are most effective, have the lowest risk to the patient, and are the least expensive to provide. Once established, insurers are not likely to pay for more expensive, less effective procedures. Outcomes evaluation could prove to have the greatest direct effect on the actual practice of medicine.

Drug Costs

Prescription drug costs are statistically lumped under "other personal health care" by the Health Care Financing Administration. Hefty cost increases have set off several congressional investigations. The General Accounting Office (GAO), the budgetary adviser to Congress, reported that prices for 19 of the most commonly prescribed drugs increased by more than 100 percent between 1985 and 1991. In the past 15 years, the cost of the average prescription has risen 300 percent. The increases in prescription drug costs peaked in 1998 with increases per capita of 18.4 percent; by 2002 that per-capita increase was still high but was estimated to be a smaller 13.0 percent.[40]

The Pharmaceutical Research and Manufacturers of America (PhRMA) estimates that the costs of developing new drugs introduced today is from $500 million to $600 million in total and the time to develop drugs has grown from an average of 8 years in the 1960s to 14.2 years in the 1990s.[41] An estimated $30.5 billion is being invested. Figure 3.5 illustrates where the share of the development dollar goes—it is highly significant that, even though the PhRMA highlights the re-

FIGURE 3.5
Where Do Pharmaceutical Companies' Drug Development Dollars Go?

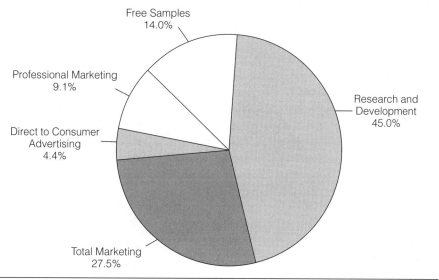

Source: Based on Pharmaceutical Research and Manufacturers of American, Figure 8: Research-Based Pharmaceutical R&D in Comparison to Marketing, 1997–2000, *Pharmaceutical Industry Primer 2001,* 2002, http://www.phrma.org/publications/publications/primer01/figure/figure8.html.

search and development costs, their own data illustrate that over one-half (55 percent) of all development expenses goes to marketing and advertising costs.

The top three areas of research are on diseases like cancer and diabetes, diseases affecting the central nervous systems (Alzheimer's disease and Lou Gehrig's disease), and on infectious and parasitic diseases (the flu, AIDS [autoimmune deficiency syndrome]). Figure 3.6 shows pharmacy company expenditures on drug research.

The insured consumer who is responsible only for a small copayment is oblivious, for example, to the actual retail costs for drugs. Even doctors, who have free manufacturer samples available to them and are usually unaware either of the drug or laboratory test costs, are under increased pressure by insurers to give attention to drug costs. Prescribing generic formulas, if available, instead of brand-name pharmaceuticals is now a Medicare requirement. The cost of providing evidence that a generic drug is equivalent to a nongeneric is approximately $1 million, only a fraction of the cost of developing a new drug. It is small wonder that the generic drugs' share of the market rose to 47 percent in 2000, as compared to 18.6 percent in 1984.[42]

The cost of physician-administered drugs has come under heavy scrutiny by Medicare. The elderly are most apt to have heart disease or cancer. Drug therapy is employed in various stages of both to avoid expensive, high-risk surgical procedures. The drug industry, in response to these cost-containment measures, has moved from heavy advertising in medical journals to broader, consumer-directed

FIGURE 3.6
Pharmaceutical Company Investment in Drug Research and Development,
by Type of Drug Product

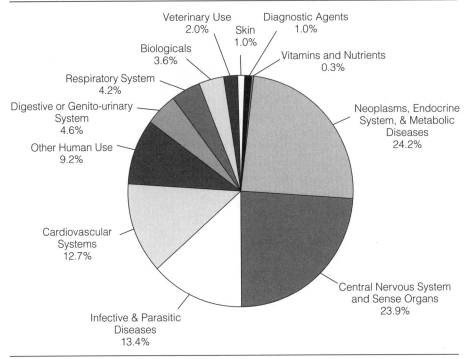

Source: Based upon Pharmaceutical Research and Manufacturers of American, Figure 3: Company-Financed R&D by Product Class, Ethical Pharmaceuticals, Research-Based Pharmaceutical Companies, *Pharmaceutical Industry Primer 2001,* 2002, http://www.phrma.org/publications/publications/primer01/figure/figure3.html.

advertising for prescription drugs. Just as the hospitals used a flanking response in undertaking mass marketing, the drug industry is targeting consumers who, they hope, will pressure physicians to prescribe a media-hyped miracle drug to cure their chronic ailments. It is the rare mass circulation magazine that does not carry at least one full-page prescription drug pitch per issue.

Squeezing the Employer

While insured workers have been traditionally insulated from rising medical costs, employers have begun to balk at the astronomical increases in their share of health-benefit insurance premiums. Employers' use of managed care plans in the 1990s eased the strain to some extent, but the costs are rising again (by 13.6 percent for 2002).[43]

At present, only 62 percent of all U.S. firms are offering health insurance benefits to their workers. This breaks down to 99 percent of all large firms and

FIGURE 3.7

Percentage of American Firms Offering Health Insurance Benefits to Their Workers, by Size of Firm

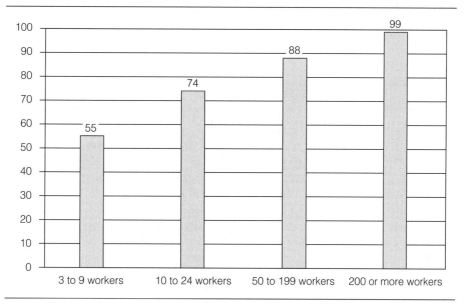

Source: Kaiser Family Foundation, Chart 11, Percentage of Firms Offering Health Benefits, by Firm Size, 1996–2002, "2002 Employer Health Benefits Survey," 2002, http://www.kff.org/content/2002/20020905a.

only 61 percent of all small firms (up to 199 workers) (see Figure 3.7). Only 74 percent of firms with 10 to 24 workers provide a health insurance benefit for their workers—and the percentage declines with the size of the firm. And even in those firms that offer coverage, not all employees are eligible—typically, temporary and part-time are ineligible. Only those who work full-time or, in some cases, close to full-time are eligible to receive the benefit.

Since the 1980s the service sector of the U.S. economy has far outstripped the growth of the manufacturing sector. It is often not recognized that employment practices in the service sector, even among the chain operations, are really small business practices. An increasingly common practice is "short-scheduling"— keeping employees short of the 40-hour work week, which would entitle them to health and other benefits.

Smaller business operations often contract for group health plans that allow employees to have health coverage at premiums lower than they would pay for individual insurance coverage. Most employers do not contribute toward the employee premium; some may pay a token amount. Under these conditions, many workers choose to forgo health plan enrollment because the monthly premiums are too high and often the benefits too limited to compensate for the decreased modest take-home pay.

Accelerating cutbacks in health benefits by larger American businesses must be seen within a broader economic context. Although it is a fact that health costs have escalated seemingly out of control, it is also a fact that workers for large companies are no longer organized and represented so that they can effectively protest benefit reductions. During the heyday of economic growth (the 1950s and 1960s), over one-third of American workers were represented by labor unions, but today, unions are far less powerful, and in fact, many of the existing unions are considered by members and employers to be powerless.

The severe recession of the late 1980s through the early 1990s forced millions of American businesses into bankruptcy. Many major corporations filed for protection under Chapter 11, the provision in the bankruptcy laws that allows companies to reorganize while continuing to do business under federal court supervision. Countless major corporations have used the Chapter 11 reorganization provision to reduce workforces, cut wages, and reduce all benefit packages, including health benefits, and this practice continues today.

Major employers seeking to continue some level of paid health coverage for their employees are pursuing different avenues. Many have simply reduced the scope of their coverage, either by dropping some peripheral services (drugs, dental care, eye care) or by increasing the amount of deductibles and copayments. For example, the cost of hospital premiums is reduced if the policy covers only 80 percent of the daily rate, leaving a 20 percent copayment for the employee. Raising the yearly deductible (the amount the employee pays out of pocket before coverage kicks in) to $500 or $1,000 similarly reduces the premium. Another method for reducing employer costs is to negotiate health insurance coverage with a lower payout limit. This strategy puts a cap on the dollar amount of total benefits available to the employee, as a lifetime maximum amount and/or an allowable maximum amount for a single illness. This reduces the liability of the insurance carrier for serious ongoing health conditions (for example, AIDS or kidney dialysis) as well as for catastrophic occurrences. Alternatively, employers may choose to offer fuller coverage but to pass on a larger part of the monthly premium to the insured employee. As health premium costs increase, employers are phasing in one or several of these cost-cutting measures.

Reduction in coverage and premium cost sharing are not as imaginative as programs developed by many large companies that have decided to self-insure. On one hand, by self-insuring, the company assumes the fiscal risk that would otherwise have been incurred by a private insurance company. On the other hand, the company's insuring practices do not fall under ordinary state laws regulating insurance companies. For example, one large company-owned chain of convenience stores self-insured and immediately denied health benefits to an employee who developed symptoms of AIDS. Existing law in that particular state would not have allowed a similar action by a private insurer.

More adventurous self-insured companies have developed their own managed care plans, shopping their communities for health providers and negotiating reduced fees with local doctors, medical groups, hospitals, and even HMOs. Some have set up their own pharmacies at the workplace to reduce drug costs. Others have their own X-ray facilities. Still others have in-house clinics for minor ail-

---

A CLOSER LOOK

Check the Web site of your own HMO or that of your friends for information about the HMO, their costs and premiums, how they deal with
those costs, and their policies on appeals and other policies.

---

ments. Nearly all require annual checkups and run preventive health programs for
employees and dependents. In effect, these corporations have taken over the
functions that private insurers have exercised through PPOs.

A major drawback is that self-insured employers are tempted to take a past
health record into consideration when hiring or, in the case of layoffs, to take an
employee's expensive health history with the company into consideration. Private
insurers, by contrast, can respond to high-claim companies by increasing premiums or by refusing to continue company coverage, but they cannot discriminate
against an individual employee in bad health nor against a single disease or serious ailment.

Uninsured

The Kaiser Family Foundation estimates that 14 percent of the American population are uninsured while only 59 percent are covered through their employers
(see Figure 3.8). Many of the uninsured are the working poor, those employed in
low-paying service and unskilled-labor jobs but whose incomes are marginally
above state-defined eligibility for Medicaid. In some states, the percentage is
much higher (New Mexico has 24 percent uninsured; Texas, 22 percent). The
numbers of the uninsured working poor are higher in the West and Southwest,
where over one-quarter of the population is without health coverage.

FOR TEMPORARY RELIEF

As we have seen, in their efforts to circumvent cost containment, medical providers sought relief from extra burdens through shifting costs, risks, and access to
care. These reactive machinations have done nothing to control the nation's
health expenditures and have given the players only temporary respite. The cu-
mulative effect has been to damage public perception of health care quality and
the character of health providers and insurers.

Cost Shifting

From a rational perspective, cost shifting is not a remedy for anything. But
to the health care providers, it is the most expedient solution to immediate cash-
flow problems. Cost shifting is simply the unloading of one player's burden onto

FIGURE 3.8
Insurance Status of U.S. Population, 1999–2000

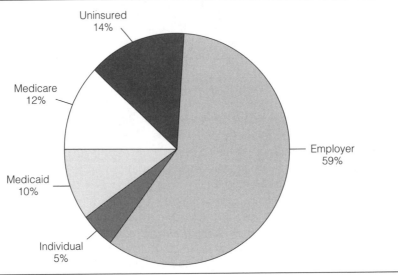

Source: Kaiser Family Foundation, State Health Facts Online, 2002, http://www.statehealthfacts .kff.org.

another. Hospitals and doctors shift costs by taking low-reimbursement Medicaid and Medicare patients, then increasing fees billed to higher-paying, privately insured clients. Insurers pass the increases on to employers who, in turn, pass it on to the insured worker through reduced coverage of increased out-of-pocket costs.

Then there is cost shifting between federal and state governments. As noted, the federal government shifts partial costs of new access programs to the states by exempting certain classes of people from Medicaid eligibility requirements or by mandating that a particular service be offered to a specific segment of the population. There is even cost shifting from one federal government agency to another. For example, the Veterans Administration (VA) actively tries to move ailing, indigent veterans from federally financed VA hospitals to Medicare and Medicaid programs.

Although Medicare has taken several steps to contain provider costs, it has been repeatedly blocked from shifting the increasing cost burden to Medicare recipients for several reasons. First, Americans over 50 years of age vote regularly and at a high rate in all elections. Political tinkering with Social Security or Medicare benefits is a personal survival issue to elderly voters, who can be persuasive at the ballot box when aroused. Conversely, Medicaid cuts are much easier to make since the poor and the indigent are marginal participants in the electoral system. Second, the largest membership interest group in the United States is the American Association of Retired Persons (AARP). It maintains a high profile in Washington, D.C., and tight communication with its membership. It follows all health legislation expertly and closely. When the Reagan administration pushed passage of legislation to introduce an additional Medicare premium–generating program (catastrophic health benefits), the AARP considered the potential benefits to be less than the extra cost to its members. Swift and relentless pressure was exerted. The proposed legislation was buried by congressional committees almost overnight. Frequent suggestions that the more affluent elderly should pay higher Medicare costs, either through higher premiums or an upper-income cap to limit eligibility, have met with solid resistance by the AARP.

As the U.S. population ages, protection of the elderly becomes a more politically volatile issue. But the economics of elderly support are sobering. In 1960, there were 11 people under 65 for each citizen over that age. By 1990 there were only 7. Clearly, the "graying of America" is creating a significant cost shift from the increased numbers of senior citizens onto the shrinking ranks of younger working people.

Risk Shifting

The insurance industry is a lucrative profit-making entity. Profits issue from gambling on the risk level of the insured. Those profits from premiums, after paying liabilities, are then invested in other segments of the economy. Insurance companies became heavily invested in the commercial building frenzy of the mid-1980s. Their profit margins were endangered by the collapse of that sector in the early 1990s. These reverses, coupled with increased litigation and large court judgments unfavorable to them, caused insurers to look more closely at the risk probabilities of those whom they insured. Those companies that offered health policies were experiencing the simultaneous escalation of medical costs. Short of leaving the field, their alternative was to offer coverage only to healthy people. Particularly among medium-sized and smaller companies, insurance carriers became much more discerning about health histories of individuals eligible for group coverage. The companies often required long health inventories and physical examinations and consulted computer databases to establish whether they were assuming liability for any potentially expensive preexisting condition.

It is not generally known that the insurance industry has access to the medical histories of over 15 million Americans through the Medical Information Bureau (MIB). Anyone who has had, or who has applied for, health insurance or life insurance has signed a contract allowing the release of medical information and records to the insurer. A national data bank, second in size only to the Medicare recipient database, is available to member insurance carriers to check medical histories of applicants for coverage. Since insurers are not regulated by the federal government, the use of MIB information is restrained only by state law and its application by generally weak state regulatory agencies.

Using this body of personal information, common insurer practice within larger companies is to exclude individuals with preexisting conditions from coverage. A medium-sized or smaller business applying for worker coverage is often rejected outright if it employs individuals who have preexisting medical conditions or who have high-risk medical profiles. Alternatively, these employers may be granted policy coverage that has restricted yearly dollar limits and stringent life-time dollar caps. These limits and exclusions greatly reduce insurer liability for any serious chronic illness or procedure. Often, the monthly premium cost for minimal and restricted coverage is set so high that the small employer simply cannot afford it. Once insured, a smaller employer is under heavy scrutiny by the insurer. Overall company claims, as well as extensive individual claims, are calculated when policies are renewed. Burdensome companies find their premiums raised astronomically at renewal, or their group coverage is canceled. If these actions result from one ailing employee, the employer is often forced to consider sacrificing the one to preserve benefits for the rest. A national repository of individual health histories makes it difficult for the sacrificed employee to find new employment even across state lines.

It is ironic that, at the same time that private insurers are shifting costs and reducing their risk exposure in writing employer group policies, they are financially relieved from insuring the most significant consumers of health care, the elderly and disabled, who are underwritten by Medicare.

CUTTING OVERHEAD: FRAUD, ADMINISTRATION, AND OVERUSE

Another approach to fiscal relief is the reduction of waste. Estimates are that fraud, excess administrative costs, and unnecessary procedures account for nearly $200 billion, or about one-quarter of our annual health expenditures.

Punishing Fraud

The General Accounting Office (GAO), an investigative arm of Congress, reported that the U.S. Department of Justice recovered $1.2 billion in civil health care fraud through the False Claims Act that it administers.[44] Although Medicare and Medicaid abuses are often most blatant, they are also more likely to be prosecuted than similar abuses against private insurers. But the costs to investigate, document, indict, and try fraudulent providers is usually far in excess of any monies recovered. The only public satisfaction gained is to see providers put through long criminal or civil litigation. However, the costs versus benefits of making an example of a fraudulent provider cannot be calculated, and criminal action against one provider that is aimed to dissuade others from abusing the health care system is often undercut by the vagaries of the criminal justice process.

Cutting Administrative Costs

Excess administrative overhead is not easy to calculate; the actual costs of administering health insurance are not clear-cut. For example, should a hospital's or physician's clerical costs in claims preparation be included as an administrative cost, or is clerical cost defined solely as the insurer's claim processing.

A reduction in administrative overhead is a simple way to save health care dollars. One proposal has floated around the insurance industry and congressional health care committees for years: design a single form for all health care claims using standard codes for all procedures and services. Medicare has already codified much of medical practice into billable pieces. Yet both providers and the private insurers have resisted standardizing claims reporting.

Eliminating Unncessary Procedures

Overuse of medical services by consumers and ordering of unnecessary procedures by providers are consistent concerns about the health care system. Although DRGs have encouraged limits on hospitals stays, there is still a way to go in moving toward less expensive outpatient treatment.

Physician overuse of expensive diagnostic procedures is encouraged by their availability and by the willingness of insurers to reimburse. Three-dimensional computer scanning technology (CT, MRI) produces startling pictures of human flesh and bone. In many cases, a simple, old-fashioned X-ray film would be sufficient. The cost difference is significant.

Surgical procedures, in spite of increased insurer oversight, are too often a first, and very expensive, medical intervention in the United States. Within this country there are variations in the frequency of surgery for different conditions depending on where the patient lives. This phenomenon of "small area variations" was first detected, and repeatedly confirmed, by John Wennberg and his colleagues. They discovered that physicians who interact with one another in an area come to share similar attitudes toward treatment, particularly surgical intervention. From a cost perspective, not to mention a care perspective, are routine tonsillectomies effective medicine? The same regional variations are found in physician attitudes toward all types of surgical intervention.

While abuse, unnecessary procedures, and expensive paper shuffling would seem the first targets for reducing health costs without impairing quality of care or limiting access, they are not likely to be aggressively addressed within the present delivery system. Reform in any of these areas infringes too closely on provider prerogatives. Outright provider fraud in fake billing is only a step away from sophisticated unbundling of a single procedure. Questioning an unnecessary surgical intervention is construed as interference in physician judgment and his or her relationship with the patient. Private insurers consider their administrative costs as an issue between them and the stockholders to whom they report. The political clout of professional provider associations and insurance interest groups has been powerful enough to prevent concerted government action in curtailing health cost excesses.

Rationing Care: The Oregon Plan

The most controversial plan for health cost relief has come out of the state Medicaid mess. Termed the *Oregon Plan,* it is really no plan at all. Rather than continue to reduce Medicaid provider fee reimbursements in Oregon, the plan proposed limits on the treatments for which Oregon would pay. State Senator Dr. John Kitzhaber, the architect and leading proponent of the rationing plan, justified the rationing of procedures on what he termed the mistaken assumption "that all medical interventions are of equal value, in spite of this enormous body of research that suggests that a whole lot of what we do in the name of medicine . . . doesn't have an impact on people's health."[45] At the core of the plan is a list of 709 procedures ranked by their potential to improve the health of the individual. Current Oregon Medicaid funding levels provide treatment for a certain number of conditions on the priority list. For example, a child can get a liver transplant, but an alcoholic suffering from cirrhosis of the liver cannot. Treatment in the early stages of AIDS would taper off to "comfort care" as the disease advanced. Expensive, "heroic" measures to sustain life with a marginal rate of success are at the bottom of the list. For example, babies born within 23 weeks of gestation weighing a pound or less would be allowed to die. But then, colds and sprains that get better by themselves are below the cutoff, as well.

Rationing medical procedures is justified as the lesser of evils. The alternative, according to Kitzenhaber and others, is to continue to underfund *all* procedures or to limit access to every kind of care by dropping the income eligibility level even lower than it is. The cost savings from rationing are reallocated to increase health care access to poor Oregonians by raising the state's income eligibility level up to the federal poverty level. Companion legislation to the rationing scheme requires all employers to provide health insurance plans to accommodate health needs of the working poor. It also forbids private insurers from denying group health policies to businesses employing high-risk individuals.

The Oregon Medicaid rationing plan, as with all state modifications of Medicaid benefits, required federal approval before implementation. Although the plan had received widespread community and political approval in Oregon, it became a political hot potato for the federal executive branch in Washington, D.C. On one hand, it was the first innovative, reasoned solution to setting priorities in order to contain state health care costs gone berserk. On the other hand, it conjured up images of dying babies and old people left to wither. Those were not attractive pictures to an incumbent chief executive up for reelection. Faced with the opportunity to approve the Oregon Plan in the 1992 election year, President Bush rejected it on the grounds that it appeared to violate the Americans with Disabilities Act. Oregon resubmitted the plan, virtually unchanged, to Clinton health operatives in the initial months of his first administration. Desperate to provide interim relief to state Medicaid programs, implementation of rationing in Oregon was immediately approved.

Still troubled by their health care system, Oregon voters in 2002 continued to seek ways to deal with increasing health care costs and the problem of the increasing numbers of uninsured citizens. They took the opportunity to place an initiative (Measure 23—the Oregon Comprehensive Health Care Finance Plan) to reform their health care system and move toward a single-payer system of health care provision that would cover benefits for all Oregon citizens. A study commissioned by the American Association of Health Plans estimated that Oregon currently spends $5,375 per capita to provide health care. The new system was estimated to increase this by $600 to $1,800 per resident. This would be primarily due to the increased benefits and the elimination of the copayment and coinsurance requirements.

FOR LONGER-LASTING RELIEF

Other proposals for health reform abound. The most thoroughgoing ones address both access and cost by making the federal government the only third-party payer—in other words, national government health insurance for every citizen. The least revolutionary propose increased access to health care by those presently uninsured but do little or nothing to contain skyrocketing costs. Somewhere in between are the advocates of managed care, who believe that substituting a flat-rate structure for provider reimbursement can prove cost-efficient and also achieve the goal of universal coverage without massive government intervention.

Play or Pay

Different versions of what is termed the play-or-pay approach to health care reform have bounced around committees of both the House of Representatives and the Senate. Details vary, but the approach targets employers as the responsible parties in providing employee health coverage. If they choose not to offer coverage, then they must pay into a national insurance fund that will provide it. Play-or-pay plugs the Medicaid gap, guaranteeing some health coverage to the working poor. Hardly an innovative approach, laying responsibility for health coverage on employers has been enacted in several states and is on the legislative agendas of many others. The states wish to close the gap between the Medicaid-covered and the employee-covered populations for two reasons. First, they are under political pressure to provide equity in health coverage to part-time and full-time workers employed in uninsured or underinsured sectors of the economy (small business, the self-employed, agricultural workers, the retail and service sectors) so that working people may receive benefits equal to the poor and unemployed, who are covered by Medicaid. Second, by requiring employer coverage, state- and county-funded public clinics and hospitals will be relieved from the crushing burden of care for the increasing numbers of uninsured residents.

The specifics vary from state to state, but two alternatives to national play-or-pay proposals have emerged. The Oregon plan called for employers to provide minimal group coverage to all employees without the choice of paying into a state insurance plan. The other approach, instituted in Minnesota, bypasses the employer in guaranteeing health care access to the uninsured. The Minnesota plan subsidizes coverage for its estimated 370,000 uninsured residents through a tax on health care providers and an added cigarette tax. Eligibility for state health insurance is determined by a means test, and the insured person pays premiums for coverage based on a sliding scale. Those who are eligible and working but uninsured pay more than those unemployed. The plan emphasizes preventive health services and places a $10,000 yearly cap on in-hospital expense.

A case unto its own, Hawaii boasts nearly 100 percent health coverage for its residents. Hawaii started early with its Prepaid Health Care Act, which required employers to provide coverage for all full-time workers. Under that 1974 legislation, employers pay at least one-half of a worker's health care premium, limiting the worker's share to 1.5 percent of gross wages. For the "gap people," a means-tested state subsidized plan similar to Minnesota's is in place. Both Hawaii and Minnesota have strong traditions of health maintenance organizations. In Hawaii, two insurer-providers (Kaiser and Blue Shield) control 70 percent of the health market, which allows them to lever provider costs more easily.

MANAGED COMPETITION

Health policy was the first priority of the incoming Clinton administration in January 1993. Clinton's 500-member task force, guided by his wife, Hillary, turned out a lengthy, detailed, comprehensive national health policy plan that started through the legislative process. It was ravaged in congressional committees, where it encountered heavily organized and unified opposition from health providers, insurers, and employer groups. Clinton's first-year plummet in public opinion polls rating his job performance was attributed in some part to his administration's confused and clumsy handling of health care reform. Having been drubbed by nearly every political faction, including a sizable segment of his own party, Clinton withdrew his health care proposals in late 1993. Republican party majorities took over both houses of Congress in the 1994 off-year elections, bringing with them clearly articulated ideas for new directions in domestic policy, the "Contract with America." Major health reform was not one of the contract's provisions.

For the record, the proposed health policy was vintage Clinton: an eclectic array of big ideas and little ideas, none of them terribly bad and none earth-shatteringly bold. The basic intent was to be certain that every citizen would always have a core of central health coverage; the major instrument in achieving this end was to be the employer. In many respects the proposal was a retread of state play-or-pay programs on a national basis. Employers would be required to pay 80 percent of core coverage premiums, offering employees a choice of plans (fee-for-service, PPO, HMO). In order to keep coverage affordable, the government would assist in managed competition, alliances of employers that would bargain for the best prices from competing providers. Finally, the proposal guaranteed continued coverage to (1) every person regardless of present or past medical condition and (2) those who became unemployed or who changed jobs. In the final days of the 104th Congress (1996), legislation was passed and signed by Clinton requiring "portability" of health insurance and disallowing exclusion from coverage of those people with "preexisting conditions." That is what survived out of over 1,000 pages of administration-proposed legislation for universal health care.

Managed Care

Managed care comes in various forms, but the strategy is to manage patient health in an organized, efficient, and cost-effective way. The phrase intimates an approach that joins personal quality care with cost containment. The purest form of managed care is the Kaiser Foundation health maintenance organization, a consolidated provider of both hospital and physician services. Subscribers pay a flat fee for total medical care; medical staff is generally salaried. For decades Kaiser has stood alone as the model for managed care. The Kaiser philosophy emphasizes preventive health care. Assignment to a primary care physician charged with keeping the subscriber healthy is central to cost containment. Regular examinations and health education programs are designed to reduce the high costs of late intervention in disease. Kaiser physicians develop house protocols for many aspects of patient care; there is a rather consistent mode of treating major ailments as well as agreement on specific prescription drug appropriateness. There is a Kaiser way of doing things. Table 3.3 provides a description of the enrollments of the largest managed care plans.

At the other, permissive end of managed care stand the preferred provider organizations. As we discussed earlier, the PPOs are primarily a cost-containment strategy developed by the major private insurers to negotiate reduced fee-for-service rates of physicians and hospitals. While they manage costs through these fee arrangements and attempt to institute some control mechanisms on providers (preauthorization and second opinions for surgery), they do not manage patient

TABLE 3.3
Enrollments in U.S. Managed Care Plans

Health Plan	Total Managed Care Enrollment (millions)
Blue Cross Blue Shield plans	81.5
Aetna U.S. Healthcare	15.0
Cigna HealthCare	14.3
Kaiser Foundation health plans	8.3
United HealthCare Corporation	8.4
Humana	6.5
PacifiCare Health Systems	3.3
HealthNet	3.8

Source: MCOL, 2003. "Managed Care Fact Sheets: Major Managed Care Plans," http://www.medicare.hmo.com/mc.mno.htm

care, nor do they manage the treatment protocols of physicians. By penalizing subscribers who seek non-PPO care with 40 to 50 percent copayments, the insurance carriers have been very successful in bringing providers into their cost-controlled provider organizations.

Nevertheless, the PPO is still a fee-for-service arrangement and the employer premium costs plus subscriber copayments total to more than the inclusive care premiums offered by managed-care operators. Although the new breed of managed care organization is commonly called an HMO, its structure of provider payment and patient practices differ from the Kaiser health service model. The new breed controls cost but does so by reviewing and often overruling the medical judgment of the subscriber's primary care physician. Some of the practices of these HMOs have earned them cover stories in major mass circulation news magazines and investigative reports in newspapers and on television in which both subscribers and participating physicians relate medical horror stories of calculated patient neglect; a *New York Post* series was headlined "HMOs: What You Don't Know Could Kill You."

In what basic ways do these new, managed-care operators differ from the early model of the health maintenance organization? First, there is a significant difference in the relationship between the operator and the participating physicians. Kaiser, everyone's example of the classic HMO, generally hires physicians, both primary care and specialist. Those physicians practice out of Kaiser-owned clinics, prescribe drugs out of Kaiser pharmacies, order laboratory tests from Kaiser labs, and admit patients into Kaiser-operated hospitals. The primary care physicians, the gatekeepers, are apt to be familiar with the specialists and surgeons to whom patients are referred because they work within the same physical setting. Too, Kaiser administrators spend considerable energy in encouraging staff interaction, usually deferring to staff's collegial decisions in determining medical protocol and practice.

The aggressive new breed of HMOs, usually publicly held (stockholder) corporations, recruit and pay physicians in a very different manner. Generally, they approach individual and small-group family practice physicians in a community to join their managed-care network; occasionally they will cannibalize a smaller managed-care operation. For every subscriber choosing or assigned to a specific primary care physician, that practitioner is paid a capitation rate—a flat monthly fee to handle the subscriber's medical problems. The monthly capitation rate per subscriber varies geographically and according to age. Commonly, the physician receives about $8 a month for a young, healthy person; up to $28 a month for an elderly subscriber. The subscriber can visit the doctor every day of the month, or not set foot in the office for years—the physician still receives the monthly capitation. Very often, the primary care physician is a member of several managed-care networks, a member of one or more preferred provider organizations, and serves government-insured Medicare and Medicaid recipients as well. In those areas of the country in which HMO subscriber rolls are booming, family practice physicians are being forced into HMO participation to survive as their traditional client base is being levered into managed care by cost-conscious employers.

The local list of specialists and surgeons to whom a managed-care patient can be referred by the primary care physician is generally limited. Specialists who agree to take HMO patients also agree to take greatly reduced fees. To make up for reduced compensation, the HMO limits the number of approved physicians in each specialty, thus increasing the volume of patients that each receives. Unlike the Kaiser model, primary care physicians in the new mananged care networks often are not familiar with the specialists to whom they refer their patients. And the primary care doctor must get approval from HMO administrators before a patient may be referred, sometimes having to submit patient case histories. If and when a patient gets clearance, the wait time between HMO approval and actually seeing a specialist can often be lengthy since the specialist serves a number of third-party payers. Even then, action on the part of the specialist in ordering expensive diagnostic tests or surgical intervention is carefully monitored and requires clearance by HMO headquarters. Clearly, the HMOs want to cut unnecessary costs through their extensive preapproval requirements. Interestingly, their long-term cost-cutting objective does not wholly issue from denying the recommendations of primary care physician or specialists; rather, their demands for justification in the preapproval process and delays in giving the green light discourage the efforts of many member physicians in pursuing expensive interventions, often forcing the conscientious HMO physician into a "patient-advocacy" role against a reticent HMO. As a consequence, many HMOs have considerable turnover in member physicians.

Although HMOs may have contracts with major hospitals in a given community, generally they utilize smaller facilities, usually for-profit operations that have experienced a greater occupancy loss as a result of reduced insurer reimbursements and admissions review than their neighboring larger, nonprofit facilities. In many instances, HMO contracts have saved fewer-bed facilities threatened by insolvency; increasingly, the bigger managed care operators are buying financially ailing hospitals outright.

The receptiveness of the health care consumer to managed care is variable. Although in the past, HMOs enjoyed strong consumer approval and even loyalty, the recent relationship between HMOs and the public has been much rockier. The several Kaiser HMOs across the nation and several small, local HMOs topped the list in customer satisfaction. The larger and more publicly aggressive managed care operators did not fare so well at the hands of their patients.

Significantly, the need for protecting patients rights ranked fourth (12 percent) on the list of the most important health care issues today in a July 2002 Health Care Index poll (see Figure 3.9). The most important was helping citizens pay for health insurance, the next most important was helping the elderly pay for their prescription medicines, and third was making Medicare more financially sound. The fact that the need for protecting patient rights ranked even fourth on a list of issues as important as these indicates just how important the need for patient rights is considered to be in this era of managed care and dealing with HMOs.

The lack of trust is also indicated in Figure 3.10, which reports the results of a June 2002 poll on the confidence consumers have in American institutions. Asked

FIGURE 3.9
What Americans Considered the Most Important Health Care Issues in 2002

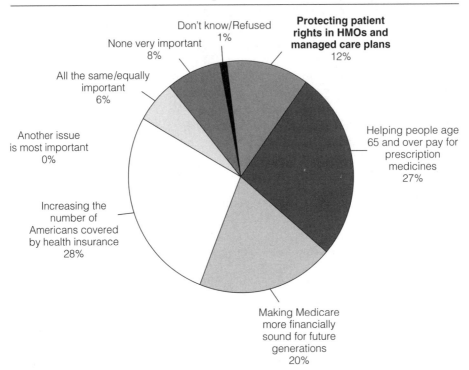

Source: KaiserNetwork.org, July 2002 Health Poll Search, http://www.kaisernetwork.org/ health_poll/hpoll_index.cfm.

Question: "Which of the following (health care) issues you say are very important (for the President and Congress to deal with) do you think is most important? . . . Protecting patients' rights in HMOs (Health Maintenance Organizations) and managed care plans, helping people age 65 and over pay for prescription medicines, making Medicare more financially sound for future generations, [or] increasing the number of Americans covered by health insurance?"

about their level of trust in HMOs, 42 percent reported very little trust, 36 percent some. Only 5 percent reported a great deal and 8 percent quite a lot.

Some of the managed care excesses in cost-cutting have had to be addressed by state and federal statute. Congress has attempted to halt what is called the "drive-through" delivery of babies: the increasingly common managed care limit of a one-day hospital stay for new mothers. National legislators also attempted to get a handle on gag-rule provisions in managed care operator contracts with providers, which forbid discussion of treatment options with patients who fail to get clearance for physician-recommended care through the HMO. More serious treatment issues are beginning to surface among the elderly, who may now choose HMO enrollment instead of the traditional Medicare fee-for-service plan. Entering an HMO relieves the fixed-income, elderly population from copayments and hos-

FIGURE 3.10
How Much Confidence Consumers Have in HMOs, 2002 Survey

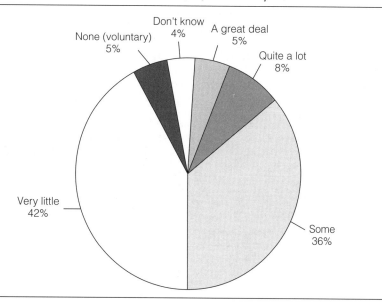

Source: KaiserNetwork.org. June 2002 Gallup/CNN/*USA Today* Poll, http://www.kaisernetwork.org/
health_poll/hpoll_index.cfm.

Question: "Now I am going to read you a list of institutions in American society. Please tell me how
much confidence you, yourself, have in each one—a great deal, quite a lot, some, or very little?
How about . . . Health Maintenance Organization, also known as HMOs?"

pitalization limits and from paying for additional MediGap coverage. However,
the elderly need more regular and more costly medical intervention. Under existing Medicare rules, an elderly person denied treatment believed to be necessary
may appeal to the secretary of health and human services. However, several
lower-court reviews have found that HMOs are reticent to inform the elderly of
their rights and also fail to provide reasons for denial of care in their often lengthy
review and appeal processes. Many of the same issues are arising in states that
are encouraging Medicaid recipients to enroll in managed care organizations.

PATIENT BILL OF RIGHTS

As an attempt to protect consumers from what were perceived as the excesses of
managed care and HMOs, there have been many attempts by the U.S. Congress
to pass a patient bill of rights. While President George W. Bush did not initially
support these efforts, he did come out with his own proposals on the topic. At
this writing, there are bills pending in the 107th Congress on this important issue.
Box 3.1 presents the American Hospital Association's Patient's Bill of Rights.

Box 3.1

THE AMERICAN HOSPITAL ASSOCIATION'S PATIENT'S BILL OF RIGHTS

These rights can be exercised on the patient's behalf by a designated surrogate or proxy decision maker if the patient lacks decision-making capacity, is legally incompetent, or is a minor.

The patient has the right to considerate and respectful care.

The patient has the right to and is encouraged to obtain from physicians and other direct caregivers relevant, current, and understandable information concerning diagnosis, treatment, and prognosis.

Except in emergencies when the patient lacks decision-making capacity and the need for treatment is urgent, the patient is entitled to the opportunity to discuss and request information related to the specific procedures and/or treatments, the risks involved, the possible length of recuperation, and the medically reasonable alternatives and their accompanying risks and benefits.

Patients have the right to know the identity of physicians, nurses, and others involved in their care, as well as when those involved are students, residents, or other trainees. The patient also has the right to know the immediate and long-term financial implications of treatment choices, insofar as they are known.

The patient has the right to make decisions about the plan of care prior to and during the course of treatment and to refuse a recommended treatment or plan of care to the extent permitted by law and hospital policy and to be informed of the medical consequences of this action. In case of such refusal, the patient is entitled to other appropriate care and services that the hospital provides or transfer to another hospital. The hospital should notify patients of any policy that might affect patient choice within the institution.

The patient has the right to have an advance directive (such as a living will, health care proxy, or durable power of attorney for health care) concerning treatment or designating a surrogate decision maker with the expectation that the hospital will honor the intent of that directive to the extent permitted by law and hospital policy.

Health care institutions must advise patients of their rights under state law and hospital policy to make informed medical choices, ask if the patient has an advance directive, and include that information in patient records. The patient has the right to timely information about hospital policy that may limit its ability to implement fully a legally valid advance directive.

The patient has the right to every consideration of privacy. Case discussion, consultation, examination, and treatment should be conducted so as to protect each patient's privacy.

The patient has the right to expect that all communications and records pertaining to his/her care will be treated as confidential by the hospital, except in cases such as suspected abuse and public health hazards when reporting is permitted or required by law. The patient has the right to expect that the hospital will emphasize the confidentiality of this information when it releases it to any other parties entitled to review information in these records.

The patient has the right to review the records pertaining to his/her medical care and to have the information explained or interpreted as necessary, except when restricted by law.

The patient has the right to expect that, within its capacity and policies, a hospital will make reasonable response to the request of a patient for appropriate and medically indicated care and services. The hospital must provide evaluation, service, and/or referral as indicated by the urgency of the case. When medically appropriate and legally permissible, or when a patient has so requested, a patient may be transferred to another facility. The institution to which the patient is to be transferred must first have accepted the patient for transfer. The patient must also have the benefit of complete information and explanation concerning the need for, risks, benefits, and alternatives to such a transfer.

The patient has the right to ask and be informed of the existence of business relationships among the hospital, educational institutions, other health care providers, or payers that may influence the patient's treatment and care.

The patient has the right to consent to or decline to participate in proposed research studies or human experimentation affecting care and treatment or requiring direct patient involvement, and to have those studies fully explained prior to consent. A patient who declines to participate in research or experimentation is entitled to the most effective care that the hospital can otherwise provide.

The patient has the right to expect reasonable continuity of care when appropriate and to be informed by physicians and other caregivers of available and realistic patient care options when hospital care is no longer appropriate.

The patient has the right to be informed of hospital policies and practices that relate to patient care, treatment, and responsibilities. The patient has the right to be informed of available resources for resolving disputes, grievances, and conflicts, such as ethics committees, patient representatives, or other mechanisms available in the institution. The patient has the right to be informed of the hospital's charges for services and available payment methods.

The collaborative nature of health care requires that patients, or their families/surrogates, participate in their care. The effectiveness of care and patient satisfaction with the course of treatment depend, in part, on the patient fulfilling certain responsibilities. Patients are responsible for providing information about past illnesses, hospitalizations, medications, and other matters related to health status. To participate effectively in decision making, patients must be encouraged to take responsibility for requesting additional information or clarification about their health status or treatment when they do not fully understand information and instructions. Patients are also responsible for ensuring that the health care institution has a copy of their written advance directive if they have one. Patients are responsible for informing their physicians and other caregivers if they anticipate problems in following prescribed treatment.

Patients should also be aware of the hospital's obligation to be reasonably efficient and equitable in providing care to other patients and the community. The hospital's rules and regulations are designed to help the hospital meet this obligation. Patients and their families are responsible for making reasonable accommodations to the needs of the hospital, other patients, medical staff, and hospital employees. Patients are responsible for providing necessary information for insurance claims and for working with the hospital to make payment arrangements, when necessary.

A person's health depends on much more than health care services. Patients are responsible for recognizing the impact of their life-style on their personal health.

Conclusion

Hospitals have many functions to perform, including the enhancement of health status, health promotion, and the prevention and treatment of injury and disease; the immediate and ongoing care and rehabilitation of patients; the education of health professionals, patients, and the community; and research. All these activities must be conducted with an overriding concern for the values and dignity of patients.

Source: American Hospital Association, *A Patient's Bill of Rights,* 2002, http://www.hospitalconnect.com/aha/about/pbillofrights.html.

A CLOSER LOOK

Does *your* health care provider have a patient bill of rights? If so, what rights do you have?

TOWARD A NATIONAL HEALTH POLICY

Ducking, dodging, and shifting responsibility to avoid taking the health care crisis in hand is typical of the way the United States has handled other complex domestic problems. Some say it is a crisis of leadership. Others suggest a crisis of imagination. Still others maintain that the too little, too late response to domestic problems is to be expected from a government structure constitutionally divided and set against itself.

Ruminating over the whys, though always an interesting exercise, does not alter the reality that this nation has not developed coherent policies to address any of the profound social issues of the late twentieth century. The unabating deterioration of the social fabric, of the working person's compensation and benefit levels, and of the physical environment is evident to even the most apolitical citizens. The disarray in health care access and delivery, and the piecemeal tinkering that has brought it to crisis proportions in both cost and quality, is little different from the pattern of political response in every other area.

It is not difficult to locate options to our present inadequate health delivery system, since we are the only industrialized country in the world without a national health plan. Although each of the major reference systems is different in funding and structure, (1) all provide universal access to low-cost or no-cost medical care, (2) they do so at much less cost per person, and (3) they perform more effectively in preserving and prolonging life.

WHAT DIRECTION FOR THE UNITED STATES?

Reference systems from abroad and state experiments from within this country are instructive in assembling components that work and rejecting those that compound present problems. Also, the distinctive American political culture and economic tradition must be understood as the context for public acceptance of a government-guided health system. Finally, the nation's leadership must be willful and assertive in making necessary and basic change.

Health as a Right

The first preliminary requirement is that we, as a nation, accept universal access to health care as an entitlement, similar to our acceptance of public education as a right. It is not necessary that entitlement be based on some philosophic justification that health care is an inherent right; it is quite enough that it be based on the mundane fact that we already pay dearly for state-subsidized health care in large part because we do not embrace the first premise. However the argument is made, it must be simple and cogent to achieve citizen consensus.

Workplace-Based Funding

The second issue is how a national plan would be funded. France and Germany fund national health out of employer-worker contributions that also subsidize the nonworking population. Canada and Britain tax and fund health directly.

The success of workplace funding for health must take account of the workplace in the historical context of any national culture. The American tradition contrasts sharply with French and German experiences and attitudes. Both have strong traditions of organized worker associations and a cultural celebration of work as honorable and useful. Private companies offer extensive paid vacations, recreational opportunities, and other benefits. Workers are not viewed as easily replaceable or expendable. They are considered human resources worth nurturing. This workplace culture is rare in the United States today. The well-being of workers, from hazard protection to various types of discrimination to job security, has not been a central concern to the American industrial-corporate culture. Protections gained have been fought through the political and legal systems. Our upwardly mobile cultural values engender disdain for workers and laborers. In fact, one's personal progress in the workplace is measured by one's distance from hard, physical work. Constant infusions of cheap labor from less-developed countries, an expanding employment base, and a postindustrial service economy have contributed to the lack of loyalty in the workplace. Employers have not cultivated or nurtured a workforce; employees are expected to move on to greener fields.

Although it is politically, as well as administratively, easy to bind compulsory health insurance to the workplace in the United States, it can be accomplished only through endless statute and regulation in order to ensure employer conformance. Unlike France and Germany, the United States does not traditionally respect workers, and employers have no sense of responsibility to the employee as a whole person. Over the past decade, employers have used every opportunity, including bankruptcy and reorganization, to rid themselves of workplace health and retirement commitments. As the American production apparatus strains to compete in the international market while maintaining profit levels, employment practices are bound to become even more brutal. Tying health care to an unwilling employer culture with an unorganized and nonunionized workforce promises the necessity for greater rather than lesser government regulation and enforcement if worker's health care needs are to be met.

Provider Compensation

The third issue is the right of the health provider to exercise professional judgment and receive fair compensation. All the reference systems except the British have preserved physician independence and patient-centered treatment. Because fees are negotiated and agreed to by physician organizations, they are by definition fair and reasonable to both parties.

Medicine in this country flows from our entrepreneurial tradition. Doctors expect to be wealthy, and their patients expect them to be. Money is a substantial motivation to attend medical school, just as it is to attend law school. The free-market concept in the professions means charging whatever the traffic will bear. Like our employer culture, our medical culture lacks any encompassing sense of its mission as a part of an interdependent community.

The Better Option

The Canadian system is the most talked-about clear alternative to our health system. Most American doctors are now receiving fees for services that have been set by third-party payers without being involved in setting those fees. In practical terms, their position would differ little under a single-payer plan. Actually, it would be enhanced through physician inclusion in annual fee negotiations as well as through economic relief from multiple third-party billing costs.

While the major player fatality in adopting the Canadian approach would appear to be the private insurer, that is not actually the case. Since the Canadian system is really "Medicare for All," private insurers would likely be contracted to administer claims along present Medicare lines. Insurers could gracefully exit the health field they already have marked as expendable. Hospital administrators could

---

A CLOSER LOOK

What do *you* think should be done to improve the American system of health care? What would be the difficulties of achieving your plan? Who would benefit and who would lose under such a plan?

---

focus on inpatient care with a predictable annual budget instead of racing to fill empty beds by inventing short-term cash solutions.

It is the general conclusion of most experts that the Canadian system is the cleanest funding mechanism for universal access. Single-payer systems such as Medicare are administratively cost-efficient for all parties. The Canadian model preserves local geographic control and involves providers directly in both fiscal and medical protocol issues. It delivers managed care, but it preserves wide consumer choices of primary care providers. It also allows direct specialist consultation, for an additional out-of-pocket charge, to the individual who wants to bypass the primary care gatekeeper.

A FINAL WORD

The failure of the Clinton administration to design and sell national health policy reform has brought an onslaught of for-profit managed care operations that understand baseline economics: competitive cost-cutting requires limits on provider compensation and reduction in the extent of health services to the subscriber. The first cuts squeezed the providers and resulted in a temporary slowing of health cost increases. In the second wave of cuts the HMOs reduced the extent of coverage and raised even more roadblocks in approving expensive procedures. In their all-out battle to woo new subscribers, the new HMOs began to accept a patient load (Medicare, Medicaid) that was considerably more expensive to maintain. Traditionally, three-quarters of HMO subscribers had been under 45 years of age—younger, healthier, employed people. Having cut the providers to the veritable bone, the HMOs had only two options: cut services or raise premiums. In order to compete among themselves, the first move was to skimp on services. Next, the cash-rich HMOs began to buy out competitors and merge, along with making reduction in coverage to Medicare patients. The net effect will be a reduction of managed care operators with resultant lack of competition, informal price-fixing, and resumption of increases in health care premiums. Market economics predicts this progression of events. One must be very clear that the primary goal of the new managed care operators is profit, not health. Government will have only three options: dust off antitrust laws to fight health care monopoly, legislatively regulate excessive cost-cutting practices on a piecemeal basis (which has already begun), or massively intervene with a national health plan.

Let us recall that the central issues addressed in balancing an approach to health care reform are cost, access, and quality. HMOs have capitalized on the cost issue. The failure of the Clinton health initiative leaves the access issue unaddressed. Quality of care is going by the boards; judgments as to quality of care are increasingly removed from provider hands and placed in profit-conscious HMO administrative hands. Consumer choices of health delivery (HMO, PPO, fee-for-service) are limited by employer-offered options. Increasingly, those options are between competing HMOs, not among different types of delivery models. Choice is disappearing in many parts of the nation.

Actually, health care delivery has begun to emerge as a popular *political* issue, one that engages the attention of the average citizen, but other issues (the economy, war, terrorism) have largely forced it from the forefront of the policy agenda. The economics of health care can be a little abstract for the general public, but personal and family experiences, as well as media revelations of death and dying through delayed or denied treatment, could still return the health delivery issue to the top ranks of public concern. Should the economy become more stable and sustainable, concerns over terrorism ease, and the crime rate continue to de-escalate, there will be room at the top for the growing public concern about changing practices in health care delivery.

FOR MORE INFORMATION

Centers for Disease Control. http://www.cdc.gov.

Garrett, Laurie. 2000. *Betrayal of Trust: The Collapse of Global Public Health*. New York: Hyperion.

Kaiser Family Foundation. http://www.kff.org.

Kaiser Family Foundation. State Health Facts. http://www.statehealthfacts.kff.org.

Lundberg, George D. *Severed Trust: Why American Medicine Hasn't Been Fixed*. New York: Basic Books, 2000.

Robert Wood Johnson Foundation. http://www.rwjf.org/index.jsp.

U.S. Department of Health and Human Services. http://www.hhs.gov.

World Health Organization. http://www.who.int/en.

NOTES

1. Harris Research/Health Care Interactive, "Attitudes towards the United States' Health Care System: Long-Term Trends," *Health Care News*, vol. 2, no. 17 (2002), http://www.harrisinteractive.com/news/newsletters/healthnews/HI_HealthCareNews2002Vol2_Iss17.pdf.

2. Ibid.

3. January 2001 Gallup poll cited in "Health Poll Search on Health Care Industry—Quality of Health Care," Kaiser Network, 2001, http://www.kaisernetwork.org/health_poll/hpoll_index.cfm.

4. Robert P. Huefner, "Designing a Health Care System," in Robert P. Huefner and Margaret P. Battin, eds., *Changing to National Health Care* (Salt Lake City: University of Utah Press, 1992), 258.

5. *Los Angeles Times,* August 17, 1992, A16.

6. Ibid.

7. Uwe E. Reinhardt, Peter S. Hussey, and Gerard Anderson, "Cross-National Comparisons of Health Systems Using OECD Data, 1999," *Health Affairs: Trends in Health Tracking,* May–June 2002, http://www.healthaffairs.org/freecontent/v21n3/s21.htm.

8. Ibid.

9. Adele Kirk and Susan Ettner, "Health Care Costs: Trends and Relationship to Insurance Premiums," University of California Academic Senate Current Issues, 2002, http://www.ucop.edu/senate/hccosts.pdf.\

10. Bradley Strunk, Paul B. Ginsburg, and Jon R. Gabel, "Tracking Health Care Costs: Growth Accelerates Again in 2001," *Health Affairs: Trends in Health Tracking,* vol. 20, no. 6 (Sept. 2001), http://www.healthaffairs.org/images/Strunk_Exhibit1.gif, Exhibit 1.

11. Reinhardt, Hussey, and Anderson, "Cross-National Comparisons of Health Systems Using OECD Data, 1999," http://www.healthaffairs.org/images/Reinhardt_Ex1.gif.

12. Ibid., http://www.healthaffairs.org/freecontent/v21n3/s21.htm.

13. Robert Wood Johnson Foundation, "Health Care and Health Care Forecast," chapter 1 in *Health and Health Care: 2010—The Forecare, the Challenge,* 2002, http://www.rwjf.org/publications/publicationsPdfs/iftf/index.htm.

14. Ibid.

15. Kenneth E. Thorpe and Paul B. Ginsburg, "Factors Driving Cost Increases. Health Care Costs: Why Do They Increase? What Can We Do?" Workshop Brief for State and Local Policymakers (Agency for Healthcare Research and Quality, 2001), http://www.ahcpr.gov/news/ulp/costs/ulpcosts1.htmk; AETNA Foundation, "Alliance Rising Star Series on Controlling Healthcare Costs," June 3, 2002, http://www.aetna.com/foundation/news/articles/2002/pr_20020603.htm.

16. Harold Bauman, "Verging on National Health Insurance," in Huefner and Battin, *Changing to National Health Care,* 31.

17. Ibid.

18. Quoted in *Los Angeles Times,* January 6, 1993.

19. U.S. Centers for Medicare and Medicaid Services, Glossary, 2002, http://cms.hhs.gov/glossary.

20. Congressional Research Service, *Managed Health Care: A Primer* (Washington, DC: U.S. Library of Congress, Congressional Research Service 1997), CRS-6.

21. Robert Wood Johnson Foundation, "Health Insurance—The Three Tiered Model," chapter 4 in *Health and Health Care.*

22. Medicare HMO, Medicare Fact Sheets/Managed Care National Statistics, 2002, http://www.medicarehmo.com/mcmnu.htm.

23. John W. Cline, "The President's Page: A Special Message," *Journal of the American Medical Association,* vol. 148, no. 208 (January 19, 1952).

24. Paul J. Feldstein, "Why the United States Has Not Had National Health Insurance," in *Changing to National Health Care,* 57.

25. Centers for Medicare and Medicaid Services, *2002 CMS Statistics* (Washington, DC: U.S. Department of Health and Human Services, 2002), http://cms.hhs.gov/researchers/pubs/CMSStatisticsBlueBook2002.pdf.

26. Medicare.gov, "Medicare Premium Amounts for 2002," 2002, http://www.medicare.gov/Basics/Amounts2002.asp.

27. Centers for Medicare and Medicaid Services, *2002 CMS Statistics.*

28. Ibid.

29. U.S. Office of Management and Budget. *The President's 2003 Budget,* 2002, http://www.whitehouse.gov/omb/budget/fy2003/bud15.html.

30. Center on Budget and Policy Priorities, "Federal Aid to State Medicaid Programs Is Falling While the Economy Weakens," October 21, 2001, http://www.cbpp.org/10-11-01health.htm.

31. Kaiser Commission on Medicaid and the Uninsured, Medicaid Enrollment in 50 States, 2000, http://www.kff.org/content/2000/2210/ES2210.pdf.

32. Centers for Medicare and Medicaid Services, Medicaid Eligibility, 2002, http://cms.hhs.gov/medicaid/eligibility/criteria.asp.

33. U.S. Office of Management and Budget, *The President's 2003 Budget.*

34. New York Times Service, *Long Beach Press-Telegram* (CA), September 13, 1992.

35. Quoted in *Los Angeles Times,* December 20, 1992.

36. Kaiser Commission on Medicaid and the Uninsured, Medicaid and Managed Care, December 2001, http://www.kff.org/content/2001/206803/206803.pdf.

37. Bradley C. Strunk, Paul B. Ginsburg, and Jon R. Gabel, "Tracking Health Care Costs: Hospital Spending Spurs Double-Digit Increase in 2001," Data Bulletin no. 22 (Center for Studying Health System Change, 2002), http://www.hschange.org/CONTENT/472.

38. Ibid.

39. Based on a survey by Physician Search, 2002, http://www.physicianssearch.com/physician/salary2.html.

40. Strunk, Ginsburg, and Gabel, "Tracking Health Care Costs," Table 1: "Annual Spending and Premium Trends, 1991–2002," www.hschange.org/CONTENT/472/table1.shtml.

41. Pharmaceutical Research and Manufacturers of American, *Pharmaceutical Industry Primer, 2001,* 2002, http://www.phrma.org/publications/publications/10.08.2001.528.cfm.

42. Ibid.

43. Aetna, Health Care Costs, accessed November 2002, http://www.aetna.com/public_policy_issues/healthcarecosts.htm.

44. U.S. General Accounting Office, "Medicare Fraud and Abuse," GAO-02-546, 2002, http://www.gao.gov.

45. From an interview in *Los Angeles Times,* January 19, 1992.

Four ⌒

CRIME AND THE (IN)JUSTICE SYSTEM

How has crime changed in recent years?
What importance should we give to white-collar crime?
Do we expect too much of the American criminal justice system?
What are the traditional methods for solving the crime problem?
    What are alternative approaches?

M any Americans have little confidence in their criminal justice system. Inept, if not racially motivated, police; egotistical lawyers who are more interested in winning than in finding truth and justice and who, more importantly, are willing to use the system's maze of formalities and technicalities as barriers to the truth. Increasingly, the decisions of judges and juries violate common sense and, in some cases, decency. It seems that the procedural dotting of every *i* and crossing of every *t* has become more important than the crime's substance. Judge Harold J. Rothwax, in his controversial book *Guilty: The Collapse of Criminal Justice,* concludes with what many of us feel today: "The bottom line is that criminals are going free. There is no respect for the truth, and without truth, there can be no justice."[1] We will learn, however, that more people are in prison today than at any time in our history, and the average length of time served, at least for violent offenders, has increased in the past few years. Acts of terror, such as the September 11, 2001, attacks, the mailing of anthrax to individuals and government offices, and the recent sniper attacks in the Washington, D.C., area have contributed to generalized fear and anxiety and a lack of confidence in law enforcement for many Americans.

Reported violent crime figures declined slightly beginning in 1991. That trend was reversed in 2001, when serious and violent crime increased. The FBI's annual Uniform Crime Report showed that "murder, the crime that is best measured because it is least likely to go unreported, rose 2.5 percent nationwide over the figure for 2000. At the same time, robberies climbed 3.7 percent, burglaries 2.9 percent, petty thefts 1.5 percent and motor vehicle thefts 5.7 percent."[2] (See Table 4.1.) Rape also increased slightly during this period. The weak economy, high unemployment, the increase in prison inmates returning home, and an increase in the number of teenagers (a group more prone to commit crime) are some of the reasons given for the increase in reported crime.[3]

167

TABLE 4.1
Crime Increased in 2001

According to the FBI's compilation of reports from nearly 17,000 law enforcement agencies in the United States, there were 11.8 million serious crimes in the United States in 2001, up 2.1 percent from the previous year. Here are the breakdowns for different classes of crime:

	Number Reported	*% Change*
Murder	15,980	up 2.5
Robbery	422,921	up 3.7
Aggravated assault	907,219	down 0.5
Rape	90,491	up 0.3
Burglary	2.1 million	up 2.9
Larceny	7.0 million	up 1.5
Auto theft	1.2 million	up 5.7

Source: Cox News Service, http://www.statcan.ca/Daily/English/010719/d010719b.htm-35k.

Even when crime was on a slight decline during the 1990s, most Americans still did not feel safe in their homes, at work, in school, or on the streets. It is the need to feel safe—a universal emotion—that accounts for the willingness of taxpayers to support building more prisons and "get tough measures" like three-strikes laws. There also is growing support for fundamental reform of the criminal justice system—including greater protections for victims, doing away with unanimous jury verdicts, limiting the number of appeals (particularly for capital offenses), and closing technical loopholes through which attorneys help their "guilty" clients escape.

All crimes are corrosive to society. The most costly crimes in terms of dollars and the most damaging to the moral fiber of society are so-called white-collar crimes. White-collar crime (including corrupt political and business practices and computer crime) cost society much more in dollars than other crime—either in direct loss or indirectly through high insurance rates, through tax-supported bailouts, and in court costs. The corporate greed and corruption exposed in recent years—2001 and 2002—including Enron Corporation, the Arthur Anderson accounting firm, WorldCom, and many others, are dramatic examples of how damaging this form of white-collar crime is to the economy, individual lives, and public trust in the political and economic systems. The 2001–02 stock market crash

---

A CLOSER LOOK

Go to the Internet to learn what the crime rate is in your local community. Has violent crime increased or declined in recent years? How about other crimes, such as theft? Does your sense of personal safety improve as crime rates decline? If not, why?

was in part caused by the lack of trust in corporate financial statements. Widespread use of drugs and alcohol in the home and on the job also cost society far more in dollars—through lost productivity and health—than crimes against property and persons. Yet it is not these crimes that we are most concerned about as individuals. Crimes against persons (especially when they involve potential violence) and property (for example, when houses are broken into and cars are ripped off) cause us to be afraid and, in some cases, to alter our behavior.

However important, crimes against businesses or government often seem remote and not very personal. They may be costly to society, but they do not engender fear. The exception is those who lost their life savings and/or jobs as a result of the practices of corporate officers in companies like Enron, Arthur Anderson, and WorldCom. The victims fear for their future and the future of their loved ones. Fear, not cost, is the real motivation for most Americans to seek reform of the criminal justice system. Simply put, this is why we are willing to fund every prison proposed—even though the cost is astronomical and the benefits are negligible. If you think about it, the job of government, its essential raison d'être, is making its citizenry secure from external and internal threats. A secondary purpose of a democratic government is to ensure the free exercise of all basic rights protected under the Constitution. The assumption is that you cannot have freedom without security. This is why, for example, leaders in places like China and Singapore are critical of American human rights policies. They believe there is only one basic human right: to be safe in your home and on the streets at all times. All other rights are of little importance if one's safety is in jeopardy. They claim this basic right exists in their countries and not in the United States.

Greed, corruption, and violence have always been a part of the human condition. However, the unfettered greed that began in the 1980s and continues to the present has been a low point in the history of American capitalism. The savings and loan, BCCI International Bank, Wall Street, and more recent scandals, such as those involving Enron and the Arthur Anderson accounting firm, are examples of what happens when people become fixated on money, power, and ostentatious lifestyles. Even the common citizen—unable to "steal" on the scale of high-ranking business or political leaders—was encouraged to seek his or her more limited fortune through questionable lawsuits. What message did this send to young people? For starters, many believe they do not need to take responsibility for their actions, nor must they suffer serious consequences. These lessons also play out in the schools, where cheating is commonplace and the consequences nearly nonexistent. Consequences are particularly light for violent youth offenders. It is true that the average time served in prison has increased since 1999, but most offenders serve little more than half their prison sentence (see Table 4.2).

The American justice system is thought by many to be extremely punitive, yet the Bureau of Justice Statistics demonstrates that this image does not always match reality. For example, even with a rapidly growing prison population, many convicted felons are not sentenced to state prisons. In 2001 the odds that a person arrested for a felony would eventually be sentenced to prison for a year or more was about three in ten, and for violent felonies about two in eight. The median sentence for violent crimes in state prisons around the United States is 100 months,

TABLE 4.2

Percentage of Prison Sentence Served for all Release Types, Fiscal Years 1994–2001

	1994	1995	1996	1997	1998	1999	2000	2001	% Change 1994–2001
All Offenders	33.9	41.8	44.4	47.4	50.4	53.0	57.1	56.5	66.7
Violent Offenders	45.2	53.9	59.2	64.7	68.1	71.6	74.7	73.2	61.9
Aggravated Offenders	46.2	55.2	65.2	70.5	73.7	77.4	79.6	78.7	70.3

Source: Texas Department of Criminal Justice—Data Services, http://www.cdcj.state.tx.us/statistics/stats-home.htm.

TABLE 4.3

Average Maximum Sentence Length (in months) for Felons, 1998

Most Serious Conviction	*Total*	*Prison*	*Jail*	*Probation*
All Offenses	39	57	6	40
Violent Offenses	77	100	7	47
Property Offenses	31	44	5	39
Drug Offenses	31	47	5	38
Weapons Offenses	29	42	6	35
Other Offenses	25	40	6	40

Source: U.S. Department of Justice, Bureau of Justice Statistics, 1998, http://www.ojp.usdoj.gov/bjs/sent.htm.

Note: Means exclude sentences to death or to life in prison. Sentence length data were available for 921,328 incarceration and probation sentences.

and for drug offenses it is 47 months[4] (see Table 4.3). A person convicted of a crime in Los Angeles can expect to serve on average only 23 percent of his or her sentence if it is a first offense; in New York City, those convicted and sentenced to jail will serve an average of 70 percent of their time. Why? In a word, overcrowding. In many parts of the country, there are not enough cells to house inmates. Consequently, the system has become a joke among career criminals—they know that doing the crime does not mean doing the time—at least not very much time.

There are, of course, exceptions to this rule. In 1999 Florida enacted legislation that requires mandatory sentencing of at least 10 years for possession of a gun during a crime. This same law requires a minimum sentence of 15 years if a semi-automatic weapon is used in the crime.[5] Texas and California, among other states, also have enacted harsher sentencing laws for violent crimes in recent years. It is not surprising that Texas and California have the largest prison populations in the nation.

This chapter looks at the issue of crime and the criminal (in)justice system. We will identify many of the reasons why a growing number of Americans think the system is not working and what, if anything, can be done to make it more functional. We will discuss issues such as victim rights, due process, gun control, drugs, and sentencing laws. We begin with a brief discussion of crime statistics and the different types of crime. We end with President George W. Bush's agenda for solving the crime problem and how it compares with President Clinton's approach. As you think about the American justice system, it is important to keep in mind that nearly all of court time in this country (approximately 90 percent) is spent on civil, not criminal, cases: the vast majority of criminal cases are heard at the state level and under state law, not in federal courts under federal law; consequently, the disposition of cases varies considerably from state to state.

THE UNITED STATES: A DANGEROUS PLACE TO LIVE

Even though tougher laws and increased dollars spent fighting crime have slightly lowered the crime rate, America remains a dangerous place to live. A comparison of the 1996 and 2000 crime clocks (see Figure 4.1) shows a slight reduction in crime, but the difference is insignificant. The 2000 crime clock shows that a violent crime

FIGURE 4.1
Crime Clock, 2000

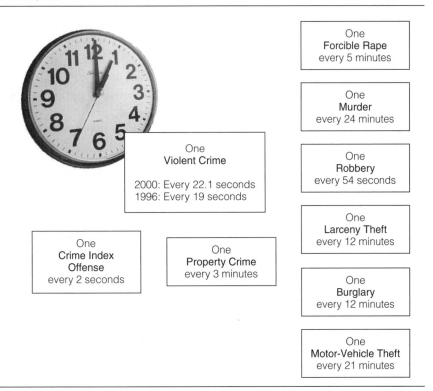

One
Forcible Rape
every 5 minutes

One
Murder
every 24 minutes

One
Robbery
every 54 seconds

One
Larceny Theft
every 12 minutes

One
Burglary
every 12 minutes

One
Motor-Vehicle Theft
every 21 minutes

One
Violent Crime

2000: Every 22.1 seconds
1996: Every 19 seconds

One
Crime Index
Offense
every 2 seconds

One
Property Crime
every 3 minutes

Source: Howard Hulen, Top Tips, 2000, http://www.toptips.com/crimeclock.htl.

TABLE 4.4
FBI Uniform Crime Reports, 1999–2000 (percentage change)

Population Group	All Crimes	Violent Crime	Property Crime
Total	**0.0**	**+0.1**	**0.0**
Cities by Population			
More than 1,000,000	−0.5	−0.2	−0.6
250,000 to 499,999	+0.1	+1.7	+0.4
50,000 to 99,999	−1.1	+0.4	−1.3
10,000 to 24,999	+0.1	+1.2	+0.0
Area			
Suburban	+0.7	+0.2	+0.8
Rural	−0.8	−0.7	−0.8
Cities outside Metro Areas	−0.6	−0.9	−0.6
Regions			
Northeast	−2.4	−1.7	−2.6
Midwest	−1.1	−0.7	−1.2
South	+1.0	+0.7	+1.0
West	+1.1	+1.2	+1.0

Source: U.S. Department of Justice, accessed October 2001, http://www.homestore.com/news/06-05-01/crime.asp.

happens every 22.1 seconds and a property crime every 3.1 seconds. Someone is murdered every 33.9 minutes and raped every 5.8 minutes. A crime of some sort is committed every 2.1 seconds in this country. More than 10 percent of all crimes involve violence or the threat of violence to individuals, and nearly a third of all crimes violate people's homes or cars. However, an individual is more or less at risk of becoming a victim depending on where he or she lives. Those living in the western United States are more likely to experience a violent or property crime.[6] (See Table 4.4.)

Until recently, there had been a significant increase in the murder rate in major cities in the United States. New York City, for instance, had a record number of killings in every year between 1989 and 1994. In fact, more than a dozen cities had record-setting years, including Boston, San Antonio, San Diego, Oakland (unfortunately, Oakland bucked the national trend of lowered murder rates in 2002, a record-breaking year), and Phoenix.[7] The rise in homicides was generally attributed to several factors: guns, drugs, gangs, and an increasingly casual attitude among young people toward violence. For example, criminal justice statistics show a dramatic increase in murders committed by 14-to-17-year-olds and 18-to-24-year-olds between 1976 and 2000. In this same period, there was a decline in murders committed by people 25 years and older. It seems "life is cheap" for many young people today.

Those record-setting years may help to explain why Americans still fear violent crime even though recent figures show they are experiencing it less. Violent crimes (murder, forcible rape, robbery, and aggravated assault) have declined steadily since 1994. In 2001 violent crimes reached the lowest level ever recorded by the National Crime Victimization Survey.[8] However, the proportion of violent crimes committed with firearms has remained relatively stable since the mid-1990s.[9] Furthermore, it is the random and unpredictable nature of many violent crimes, such as street gangs and drive-by shootings, that frightens most Americans today.

Even with the slight decline in reported crimes, at current rates, almost everyone will be a victim of crime during his or her lifetime. It is estimated, for example, that five-sixths of us will be victims of attempted or completed violent crimes during our lives. The risk is greater for males than females and for African Americans than for whites. Nearly three-fourths of Americans age 12 and over will be assaulted in their lifetime, and a third of them will be robbed. Two of every five Americans will be injured in an assault or robbery. Eight percent of American women will be raped. In general, violent crime is more likely to happen during the day, although rape and sexual assaults most often occur at night. Most murders are committed with guns, especially handguns.[10]

The most disturbing aspect of the growth in street crime is the increase in violent, vicious crime among young criminals. A public defender spoke of "a terrifying generation of kids" that emerged during the late 1960s and early 1970s. When she began practicing law, adolescents and young men charged with robbery had, at worst, pushed or shoved a pedestrian or storekeeper to steal money or merchandise; members of the new generation kill, maim, and injure without reason or remorse.[11] The good news is that juveniles committed fewer murders in 2000 than anytime since the mid-1980s. Likewise, juvenile arrests for rape, sexual assaults, robbery, property crimes, larceny theft, and burglary declined in the 1990s.[12] However, this trend is not likely to hold as the number of young people increases significantly over the next ten years.

Violent crimes remain far more common in the United States than in Europe, Canada, Australia, and New Zealand. Murders, rapes, and robberies were reported to the police at rates four to nine times higher in the United States than in Europe beginning in the 1980s. Rates for other crimes also were higher in the United States, but the difference in property crime rates was not as great.[13] This trend continues into the 21st century. Not surprisingly, such statistics are matched by rising concerns about personal safety. Recent public opinion polls show that a majority of Americans believe crime is a bigger problem than in the past. We must remember that the fear of crime affects many people, even those who have never been victimized.

The groups at the highest risk of becoming victims are not the ones who express the greatest fear of crime, however. Women and the elderly generally express a greater fear of crime than do people in groups who face a much greater risk. Studies show that these fears are in part related to the stories of crime reported in newspapers and elsewhere, which emphasize crimes against

A CLOSER LOOK

Why do you think America is a more violent country than all other industrialized nations? Interview a classmate who was raised in another
country regarding their experience with crime. Ask if they feel more
or less safe in the United States than in their own country. Ask them to
explain.

the elderly and women. These same stories may influence women and the elderly to change their behaviors to reduce their risks, thus contributing to their low
levels of victimization.

People are taking more responsibility for self-protection at considerable cost
to themselves. For example, the Victimization Risk Survey in 1984 asked households about what measures had been taken to prevent crime. Of the households
that responded, 25 percent had engraved valuables to help identification, 38 percent lived in areas with neighborhood watch programs, and 7 percent had in-
stalled burglar alarm systems. In addition, two-thirds of employed respondents reported at least one security measure in their place of work. The measures most
often used were a receptionist to screen persons entering the work place (42 percent), a burglar alarm system (33 percent), and guards or police (30 percent).[14]
Americans were even more prone to these types of preventive behavior in 2002—
particularly in the wake of terrorist attacks and increased workplace and school
violence.

HOW MUCH DOES CRIME COST?

There will never be a satisfactory answer to the question, What is the total cost of
crime to society? Estimating the cost of crime involves many variables that consider both direct and indirect costs of crime. Economist David Anderson wrote in
the *Journal of Law and Economics* that the total annual cost of crime in this country is $1.7 trillion. How did he arrive at that staggering figure?

He begins by looking at the percentage of the U.S. economy devoted to all
the goods and services that we would not have to buy if we lived in a crime-free
society. Think of all the money spent on locks and safes ($4 billion), police pro-
tection ($47 billion), surveillance cameras ($1.4 billion), jails ($35 billion), com-
puter virus screening and security ($8 billion), airport security ($448 million), and
even guard dogs ($49 million). The biggest part of this production is due to drug
trafficking ($160 billion). A crime-free society would mean that we would not need
federal agencies to fight crime ($23 billion) and we would not need the medical
care to treat victims of crime ($8.9 billion) or children born with exposure to co-

caine and heroine ($28 billion). The total cost of these and other subcategories adds up to over $397 billion annually.[15]

We know that Anderson's estimated costs for airport security and other security measures put in place since the terrorist attacks on September 11, 2001, have greatly increased.

Anderson goes on to suggest that there are opportunity costs to consider, as well. Opportunity costs include the time we spend securing our homes, cars, and other possessions when we could be doing something more productive. Anderson calculates that "2 minutes a day is a reasonable estimate for the average time spent per person per day, and that people spend on average another 2 minutes looking for their keys."[16] While this may not seem a lot of time, when you consider that "there are 365 days a year and around 200 million adults in the country,"[17] this adds up when you calculate the average hourly value of a person's time. Anderson figures that this particular opportunity cost comes to $89.6 billion in lost time.[18]

Anderson goes on to say that if there were no criminals, then these individuals would not be sitting in jail or prison but would be contributing to society and their own lives. He calculates that the lost productivity of criminals costs society another $35 billion. The total cost to society for lost opportunity is $130 billion. Anderson estimates that another $574 billion is lost through medical expenses and deaths due to crime, including the $8.9 billion spent on treating victims and the $28 billion spent on cocaine- and heroine-exposed children.[19]

Finally, Anderson includes the cost of property and money stolen through fraud. "Included in this category are fraud at work ($203 billion), unpaid taxes ($123 billion), health insurance fraud ($108 billion), auto theft ($8.9 billion) and many others. In case you were wondering, coupon fraud racks up $912 million annually."[20] Table 4.5 summarizes the total costs of crime. While some may take issue with how Anderson defines and calculates the cost of crime, few will argue that crime is very costly in dollars and lost time and productivity.

TABLE 4.5
Estimated Total Cost of Crime in the United States

	Value ($ billions)
Crime-Induced Production	397
Opportunity (time) Costs	130
Risks to Life and Health	574
Transfers	603
Gross Burden	1,705
Net of Transfers	1,102

Source: David A. Anderson, "The Aggregate Burden of Crime." Journal of Law and Economics, vol. 42, no. 2, 1999, http://economics.about.com/library/weekly/aa041300.htm, Table 7.

Note: Transfers are the result of money or property taken from one individual or organization through robbery, burglary, theft, embezzlement, or fraud. This money or property is "transferred" to the offender.

Although reasonably accurate figures are known for some of the component costs of crime, many of the elements cannot easily be measured. For example, it is difficult to measure the higher costs for consumers from organized crime's involvement in legitimate businesses or to assign a dollar value to the pain and suffering of crime victims, their families, and their friends. Many crimes are undetected, such as successful fraud (for several years we were unaware of the billions of dollars that were being lost as a result of fraud in the savings and loan industry during the 1980s, or the more recent cases involving some of the world's largest corporations—such as WorldCom, Enron, Telco, Arthur Andersen, and many others), embezzlement, and arson for profit. Still other crimes go unreported because victims are afraid to report (blackmail), are embarrassed (con games), or are involved in the illegal activity (gambling).

Direct Costs of Crime

Too often we think only of money or the value of objects stolen when we think about the direct costs of crime. These costs are only the tip of the iceberg, as Anderson suggests. Other costs directly attributed to victimization include medical costs because of injuries suffered; lost productivity because of death and medical or mental disabilities resulting from crime; time lost from work by crime victims; damage to property; lower property values because of crime in the neighborhood; the cost of operating the criminal justice system; and the costs of private security services and devices, such as locks and burglar alarms.

Involuntary Transfer Costs

In addition to direct costs, involuntary transfers occur when resources (money or property) are taken from one person or organization and acquired by another but still remain in society. For example, the dollar value of cash and property lost through robberies, burglaries, theft, embezzlement, and fraud is "transferred" to the offender. Consumers also pay a higher price for goods and services to cover the retailers' and manufacturers' losses from crime.

Underground Economy

A third category involves the underground economy, which consists of consensual crimes in which both parties agree to participate in the illegal activity. Examples of the underground economy are illegal gambling, prostitution, drug trade, knowingly buying stolen property, and so on. The underground economy also represents money that does not get reported to the Internal Revenue Service (IRS).

Costs Are Different for Different Groups

Crime has costs for all of society, but to different degrees. A study on the economic cost of crime shows that the dollar loss from crimes involving money, property loss, or destruction of property rises with income. For example, median losses were higher for middle-income households than for lower-income families. We also know, however, that minorities (particularly blacks) suffer proportionally greater loss than whites.[21]

TYPES OF CRIMES

Too often we think of crime in general terms and stereotype both crimes and criminals. When most of us, for example, think about or are asked about the crime problem, we lump all criminal acts together. Actually, the words *crime* and *criminal* are too broad to be useful. Because criminal acts and lawbreakers are varied, no one term can account for the wide range of behaviors that are illegal, nor can one term meaningfully describe all people who break the law. After all, how many of us have broken a law or two and yet wish not to be labeled a criminal? It is useful, therefore, to review some important types of crime and who is likely to commit them.

Violent Crime

Violent crime refers to such events as homicide, rape, and assault that may result in injury to a person. Robbery is also considered a violent crime because it involves the use or threat of force against a person. Although robbery occurs most often between strangers, murders are very often a result of violent disputes between friends or relatives. (There has been a significant increase in murders at the hands of strangers in recent years, however.) At least traditionally, because murders were often committed by someone known to the victim, they were considered unpremeditated acts and not a result of criminal intent. There also has been an alarming increase in violent crimes committed by persons under the influence of alcohol or drugs. The U.S. Department of Justice reported that in 2000 more than one-third of violent crime victims reported that their assailants were under the influence of alcohol or drugs. Victims of rape and assault were more likely than victims of other crimes to report that the offenders had used drugs or alcohol.[22]

The proliferation of guns and gun violence has burdened health care facilities in its impact on trauma and intensive care units. A large number of the victims are poor inner-city dwellers who either are not covered at all by a health plan or are on Medicaid (known as Medi-Cal in California). *U.S. News & World Report* disclosed in an October 1996 article that gunshot violence alone costs this nation $20 billion annually.[23] One-fifth, or $4 billion, of this amount is for medical services alone. Eighty percent of gunshot victims are uninsured or on Medicaid. Currently, almost 160,000 people sustain gunshot wounds every year. Approximately 40,000 die of their wounds, and the figure is rising rapidly. It is anticipated that by 2010 gun violence will be the leading cause of injury deaths. The remaining 120,000 victims are hospitalized. One-third of them suffer lifelong disabling injuries, and more than one-half of them are under age 30. The United States has the dubious distinction of having more guns per capita than any other industrialized nation.

Property Crime

Property crimes are unlawful acts with the intent of gaining property without the use or threat of force against an individual. Larceny, burglary, vandalism, shoplifting, and motor-vehicle theft are examples of property crimes.

Although some property crime is committed by professional thieves, many are the acts of the so-called occasional offender. Occasional offenders are not likely to associate with habitual lawbreakers and do not consider themselves criminals. In fact, many consider themselves respectable law abiders who excuse their behavior because what they steal has little value and their victims are usually large impersonal organizations.

White-Collar Crime

The investigation of white-collar crime remains one of the top national priorities of the Federal Bureau of Investigation (FBI). The FBI dedicates more resources to this crime problem than any other criminal program within its jurisdiction. The FBI defines white-collar crime "as those illegal acts which are characterized by deceit, concealment, or violation of trust and which are not dependent upon the application or threat of physical force or violence. These acts are committed by individuals and organizations to obtain money, property, or services; to avoid the payment or loss of money or services; or to secure personal or business advantage."[24]

The white-collar offender is far removed from the popular stereotype of a criminal. Few of us think that a conservatively dressed lawyer or stockbroker living in an affluent suburb with a well-paying, high-status job is likely to engage in illegal activities. It is difficult to think of these offenders as criminals because of their respectable appearance. Yet these so-called respectable citizens are costing society billions of dollars each year. Although numbers are scanty, the data show white-collar crime is both frequent and expensive. Conservative estimates of its cost are $300 billion per year.[25] One study estimates that fraudulent car repairs alone cost consumers $9 billion a year, deceptive grocery billing $14 billion, and lack of competition in the auto industry $16 billion.[26] Banks lose about five times as much to fraud (mostly by their own employees) as to robbers. Organized crime costs society about $20 billion a year and causes a great deal of violent crime.[27] Even we gourmet coffee drinkers are vulnerable to others' greed. It was reported in November 1996 that multimillionaire Michael Norton passed off cheap Central American coffee beans as expensive Kona beans from Hawaii. His get-rich-quick scheme duped coffeehouses and coffee drinkers across the country and netted Norton several millions of dollars in excessive profits.[28]

As a nation, we are still recovering from the greed and corruption of the late 1990s and early 21st century—dwarfing in dollars the corruption of previous decades. As we have noted, the corporate scandals that bankrupted some of the largest corporations in the world—Enron, WorldCom, Tyco—and nearly closed the doors of one of the big five accounting firms, Arthur Andersen, cost billions

---

A CLOSER LOOK

Investigate on the Web just one of the recent major corporate scandals in terms of the financial and human cost. What, if anything, has happened to the corporate officers responsible for the corrupt practices? Why do you think too often the top leadership escapes serious punishment?

---

of dollars and tens of thousands of jobs and wiped out many people's retirement savings.

The more recent scandals came in the wake of the savings and loan scandal in the 1980s, which cost more than $200 billion. The S&L collapse put tremendous strain on a federal budget already in deficit, forced President George H. Bush to renege on his fatuous "no new taxes" pledge in the 1988 presidential campaign—costing him reelection in 1992. It also fueled the 1991–93 recession through higher taxes and the lost liquidity of the now defunct S&Ls. It is worth noting that the 2000–01 recession and the dramatic stock market decline during this same period were largely in response to the scandals mentioned above. The 1980 S&L collapse was followed by the equally troubling BCCI scandal, costing Americans billions more in lost dollars and investment opportunities.

White-collar crime cannot be measured in dollars alone, however. Corruption of public officials undermines the public trust in government, tearing at the very fabric of American society. Environmental crimes, such as illegal dumping of toxic waste, contaminate our environment, endanger public safety, and often cause irreparable harm. The theft and piracy of intellectual property discourages creativity and can cripple a business. Finally, the substitution of inferior parts and products can jeopardize the lives of everyone.[29]

Because white-collar crime is so costly to Americans—in dollars and in lost confidence in the institutions that bind society—it is important to identify its many forms.

Government Fraud

Fraud against the government means big dollars. Even with reduced defense spending in the last decade, the Department of Defense alone spent more than $700 million dollars every day. The department deals with more than 60,000 prime contractors to meet its requirements for items ranging from basic supplies and equipment to major weapons systems. The size of the defense budget makes the potential dollar impact of contractor fraud enormous. President George W. Bush has promised to spend billions more on homeland defense and increased military spending in waging war on terrorism. In addition to substantial costs to the government, many frauds imperil the safety and capabilities of our armed forces.

Another department that spends billions of dollars every year and serves millions of Americans is the Department of Health and Human Services. Examples of fraud within the health care provider industry involve physicians, laboratories, nursing homes, hospitals, pharmacists, chiropractors, durable medical equipment companies, and others. The usual criminal activity includes mail or wire fraud statutes, bribery/kickbacks for referring business, or simply false statements on Medicare or Medicaid forms.

Other vulnerable areas of the federal government are the Veterans Administration and the Department of Housing and Urban Development (HUD). For example, single-family housing programs have historically been victimized by investors, speculators, fee appraisers, real estate agents, and others who have devised myriad criminal schemes to profit from program abuse. Typically, these schemes result in the government's insuring of mortgages for unqualified or "straw" applicants, who undercollateralize the loans and cause their defaults. Usually, all participants in these straw mortgages profit at the expense of the taxpayer, as was true with the HUD scandal during the Reagan years.

Environmental Crimes

The United States has the largest petrochemical-industrial complex in the free world. The safe disposal of by-products generated by this industry has become a major national problem. This problem is one of increasing concern to the American public, particularly the illegal disposition of hazardous wastes. In the early 1980s, Congress passed the Resource Conservation and Recovery Act (RCRA), while the Environmental Protection Agency (EPA) began strengthening regulations governing the handling of toxic substances. The result was a massive increase in the costs associated with the handling and disposing of these substances. With cost-avoidance incentives, the incidence of environmental crimes increased dramatically. The EPA estimates that as much as 90 percent of the hazardous waste in this country is illegally handled or disposed. The crimes involved with illegal toxic-waste handling range from illegal storage, transportation, and disposal by corporations to corruption of public officials and the infiltration of the disposal industry by organized crime.

Public Corruption

A broad definition of this form of white-collar crime holds that corruption occurs when a public servant—elected, appointed, or otherwise owing a duty to honest and faithful public service—asks, demands, solicits, seeks, accepts, receives, or agrees to receive something of value in return for influence in the performance of an official act. Public corruption ranges from the health inspector who "puts the arm" on the restaurant owner, the police officer who "shakes down" the drug dealer, the councilman who extorts money from lobbyists to influence legislation or contracts, to the judge who takes bribes to "fix" the outcome of cases.

Public corruption is particularly egregious, not only for the specific act of misconduct itself, but because it may affect the reputation and sincere efforts of public officials who seek to properly and honorably carry out their responsibilities. Allegations of official misconduct erode the public's confidence in its executives, lawmakers, and courts, thereby undermining government's ability to maintain a stable society.

The fact that Bob Dole was unable to make President Clinton's character and the many scandals that plagued his first administration a viable issue in the 1996 presidential election may indicate that the public has resigned itself to political corruption. Public opinion polls suggest that at the very least the public resents the millions of dollars and thousands of hours spent on investigating our leaders—as was the case with Clinton—only to have the investigations end with few, if any, convictions. Often these investigations are thought to be politically motivated and inconsequential to the things that matter most to the public, such as jobs, affordable health care, and public safety.

Financial Crimes

Financial crimes are schemes to defraud, embezzle, or misapply the money, funds, securities, or credits of individuals, businesses, and/or financial institutions by manipulation, misrepresentation, falsification, or deceit. Although variations of financial crimes are endless, the most common crimes include bank fraud and embezzlement. For example, the epidemic bank and savings and loan failures that occurred in the 1980s and early 1990s contributed to dramatic increases in bank fraud and embezzlement.

Identity theft is a serious and growing problem in this country. It is estimated that at least 700,000 people every year are victims of this crime. Identity crime costs hundreds of millions of dollars each year. Linda Foley, executive director of the Identity Theft Resource Center in San Diego, California, comments that "it's an extreme feeling of powerlessness. You can lock your house. You can lock your car. How do you protect yourself from something like this?"[30]

Bankruptcy Fraud

The federal bankruptcy laws were written to allow the honest debtor who is overwhelmed by debts a chance to make a fresh start in life. However, it is a condition of this relief that all assets owned, except as exempted by law, be turned over to the court for distribution to the creditors. Criminal action relating to bankruptcy fraud involves intentional concealment of some of the assets belonging to the debtor or the furnishing of false information to the courts. Most bankruptcy fraud consists of planned bankruptcies known as bust-outs. Bust-outs occur when a business and a good credit record is established and extremely large orders for the business's product or components are purchased on credit. Once the large inventories are received, the goods are shipped to associates and the suppliers are unpaid. Often records are destroyed, fires set, and robberies faked in an effort to hide what actually took place. The business files for bankruptcy, and the crime is completed.

Computer Crime

Since the 1970s a new form of white-collar crime involving high technology has brought sensational accounts of computerized "heists" by sophisticated felons seated safely behind computer terminals. The specter of electronic penetration of the nation's financial assets has spurred widespread interest in computer security by both business and government. In recent years, we have learned just how vulnerable we have become to sophisticated criminals invading every aspect of our personal and financial lives by collecting information on us through our discarded mail, scanning the cellular airwaves and the Internet, and then electronically penetrating our bank and credit card accounts, retirement accounts, and just about every other part of our lives. And, as we will learn later in this chapter, computer crime is not limited to adults in the workplace; teenagers in the privacy of their bedrooms are using their computers to vandalize or worse.

Unwarranted Lawsuits: A Form of White-Collar Crime?

Americans' individualistic attitude of taking risks and accepting responsibility often appears to have been replaced by a sue-everyone-in-sight reaction to any accident. The types of lawsuits filed range from the questionable to the outrageous—with more tilting in the direction of the outrageous. For example, a woman was awarded more than $1 million in damages because her alleged psychic powers were lost as a result of a CT (computed tomography) scan used to diagnose her brain tumors. Of course, had the physicians not ordered the CT scan, she undoubtedly would have sued for malpractice—assuming she lived long enough. Other examples include several lawsuits filed against coastal cities on behalf of swimmers injured while surfing. Their claim: the cities should have warned them that swimming could be dangerous to their health. Or there's the woman who lost thousands of dollars gambling in Reno and then sued the casino because they should have realized she was an incompetent cardplayer and therefore not allowed her to lose so much. While these are extreme examples, they help to make the point, and sadly, they are becoming more commonplace every day. But perhaps the most insidious examples include those who trip and fall because they are not watching where they are going and then sue; or the hundreds of car-accident victims who claim soft-tissue damage when in fact there is none.

It is easy to assign blame for the many and expensive lawsuits now prevalent. Insurance companies are blamed for too quickly settling out of court rather than fighting claims that are obviously weak or false at best—and in turn raising their premiums (passing the cost on to the rest of us) to make their profits. In very recent years, some insurance companies have begun to fight even minor auto-accident claims in an effort to discourage these types of lawsuits.

A CLOSER LOOK

Do you think we are too quick to sue in this country? What are the positive and negative consequences of living in a litigious society? What are some of the steps we might take as a country to reduce the number of lawsuits?

Aggressive trial lawyers (the United States has two-thirds of all the lawyers in the world today), inventive judges, and softhearted juries are blamed for twisting legal concepts of negligence into novel shapes to justify excessive damage awards to people who claim personal injury. Avaricious lawyers, critics argue, seek outrageously high damages for clients who have flimsy cases to gain a higher contingency fee. Still others blame the clients who see others collecting settlements and say, "Why not me too?" Regardless of who is to blame, almost everyone agrees the underlying source of the problem is plain old-fashioned greed.

The simple fact is that this latest means to a quick (and often painless) buck is costing all of us a great deal of money. Every American pays: doctors and their patients, ski slope operators and their customers, municipal governments and their taxpayers, and those who take the buses and those who drive them. Even more seriously, the problem threatens the very character of American life, from city-sponsored recreation programs to events like the 1993 Great Peace March across the United States, which came apart only a few weeks after it began because they lacked liability insurance. Factory owners seeking to launch new products, young entrepreneurs seeking to set up shop: all are running into an obstacle far harder to surmount than high taxes and interest rates in their pursuit of the American dream. Because of increasing lawsuits and huge settlements, liability insurance has become a crippling cost.

Drugs on the Job and in the Home

Changing human behavior is like reshaping concrete. The material is stubborn. Over the past three decades government agencies and private corporations and foundations have spent billions of dollars trying to blunt destructive habits that create grim casualty lists. Alcohol and drug abuse is not a new problem in the United States, although the scope and cost to society have grown exponentially. Politicians would like to avoid this issue because it is so intractable, but the public will not allow them that luxury. Consequently, every presidential election the out-party, Republican or Democratic, claims the incumbent president's drug policies a failure, which in turn compels the sitting president to renew his war on drugs and appoint a new drug czar. Bob Dole made the claim against President Clinton during the 1996 presidential campaign, and sure enough, he soon thereafter announced the 1996 U.S. National Drug Control Strategy and appointed General Barry R. McCaffrey, a retired four-star army general, the new drug czar. At the time Clinton announced his new strategy, he stated, "We are going into a world of enormous possibility for our people, dominated by global trade and high technology. But you also know that the more open our borders are, the more freely people can travel, the more freely money can move and information and technology can be transferred, the more vulnerable we are to people who would seek to undermine the very fabric of civilized life, whether through terrorism, the weapons of mass-destruction, organized crime, or drugs—and sometimes through all of the above."[31]

Unfortunately, Clinton's new drug strategy offered little that was different from every other administration's attempt to control the sale and use of drugs. His proposed strategy offered the same menu as that of his first term in office: "educating young people about the dangers of drugs, offering treatment for drug abusers, interdicting drugs at the border, breaking up sources of supply in the countries where illicit drugs are produced, and reducing the social and economic costs on U.S. society, which Mr. Clinton pegged at $69 billion in 1995."[32]

George W. Bush criticized the Clinton-Gore administration on its drug policy during the 2000 president campaign, promising his own version of how to win the war on drugs. And so goes the merry-go-round of drug politics. While drugs garner headlines, alcohol is far more costly in absenteeism from work, high medical bills, and reduced work quality. Alcoholism alone costs the U.S. economy tens of billions of dollars each year. MADD (Mothers against Drunk Driving) made Americans aware that alcohol is the greatest cause of death on the highways and has successfully pressured the courts and state legislatures to take drunk driving more seriously.

Drug addiction among teenagers and adults—particularly cocaine and its derivative, crack—has profoundly affected home life and the workplace since the 1970s. The costs of drug abuse on the job alone are staggering. The consequences range from accidents and injuries to theft, bad decisions, and ruined lives. Studies have found that employees who use drugs are far less productive than their coworkers and miss ten or more times as many workdays. Drug abusers are three times as likely as nonusers to injure themselves or someone else. Moreover, addicts with expensive habits are much more likely to steal cash from a company safe, products from a warehouse, or equipment from a factory.

Illicit drug use in American society has become so important a political issue that President Clinton elevated the nation's drug czar to a Cabinet-level position during his first administration. He claimed credit during the 1996 presidential election for an overall reduction in drug abuse among people of all ages during his two terms in office. Yet George W. Bush in his campaign against Al Gore argued that crime statistics showed an increase in drug use among teenagers during the Clinton-Gore years in office. Of course, both Gore and Bush supported stiffer sentences against drug dealers and a national drug strategy to reduce teenage drug abuse by half—the specific strategy was never articulated, however.

The latest wrinkle in the debate over drugs is the recent passage of initiatives in California and Arizona that permit the use of marijuana for medical purposes. In allowing for the medical use of marijuana, California and Arizona voters have touched off a nationwide battle between Americans who want to hold the line against illegal drugs and those who want to challenge other longstanding prohibitions against drug use. Passions are fierce on both sides, and the votes have stirred a dialogue about drugs and the potential, or risk, of broader policy changes. Drug Czar General McCaffrey and Attorney General Janet Reno pledged to prosecute under federal law anyone dispensing marijuana for medical reasons. General McCaffrey complained that "just when the nation is trying its hardest to educate teenagers not to use psychoactive drugs, now they are being told that marijuana and other drugs are good, they are medicine. The conflict in messages is extremely harmful."[33] The Bush administration has taken a similar position, arresting those who dispense marijuana for medical purposes.

The initiatives mark probably the first time since the repeal of Prohibition that the public has approved a pullback in the war on drugs. The votes in California and Arizona may represent an increasingly cynical and jaundiced public when it comes to drug-war politicking. Proponents of the initiatives portrayed the referenda as acts of compassion meant to help the chronically or terminally ill by letting them use an illegal drug to ease pain, relieve nausea from cancer treatment, or otherwise alleviate their condition. Critics contended voters were tricked into approving measures that pave the way for broader use of marijuana. There are those who argue the next step is toward a more rational drug policy. This includes making hypodermic needles available to stop the spread of AIDS among addicts sharing needles, increasing access to the heroin substitute methadone, and reversing mandatory minimum sentences for drug offenders.

Victimless Crime

Most crimes by far fall into the so-called victimless crime category. These crimes include prostitution, homosexual activity, gambling, drug addiction, drunkenness, vagrancy, disorderly conduct, and traffic violations. They are quite often called victimless crimes because they cause no physical harm to anyone but, allegedly, the person committing them. Society considers them crimes because they violate the order or customs of the community and are considered socially harmful. Some "victimless" crimes, such as homosexuality, gambling (particularly as more states adopt the lottery—a form of legalized gambling), and prostitution are granted a certain amount of tolerance.

People who commit any of these acts rarely consider themselves criminals or their actions crimes. The behavior and activities of prostitutes and controlled-substance users, however, tend to isolate and segregate them from other members of society, and these individuals may find themselves drawn into criminal roles. As we just learned, for example, one reason there is growing concern about drug abuse among workers in industry and government is that they will be forced to commit crimes (usually against their own company or the government) to feed their habits. Some critics object to the term *victimless* in general. They point out, for example, that members of the family of an obsessive gambler are, in a real sense, victims.

Hate Crimes

The presence of hate crimes in the United States today is sobering. There is nothing that tears up the fabric of a community more than hate crimes—crimes against others because of their race/ethnicity, religion, or sexual preference. Hate crimes increase dramatically when the economy is weak—minorities and immigrants are easy scapegoats for all that ails the nation. Tensions are particularly high since the terrorist attacks on September 11, 2001, between Americans and immigrants from the Middle East. Some murders have been directly attributed to hate crimes against immigrants in retaliation for the terrorist attacks.

The FBI reported that 60 percent—three of every five—of hate crimes in 1995 were motivated by race. African Americans were targets in three of five of the racial attacks.[34] Religious bias was the second most frequent motivation (16 percent), with Jews the most frequent target. Sexual orientation was the motivation in 13 percent of hate crimes. Ethnicity and national origin were behind 10 percent of all hate crimes. Latinos were targets in 63 percent of these cases.[35]

Crimes that stem from bias vary widely, from a swastika daubed on a synagogue to the beating of a white youth waiting for a bus in an African American neighborhood. During times of economic insecurity and political turmoil in particular, people need to affirm a sense of their own value. The socioeconomic and political tensions evident in the past few years shake many people's identity. Those threatened attempt to recreate a positive view of themselves and the group in which they are rooted. In fact, the definition of oneself as a member of a group includes enmity toward another group.

Reports of violence, vandalism, and threats motivated by bias continue to increase. According to FBI reports, white supremacist groups number more than 200. Law enforcement and civil rights groups are more troubled, however, by the growing number of skinhead gangs that have been discovered in at least a hundred cities. These groups are noted for their obsessive violence and a willingness to attack a broad range of assumed enemies—African Americans, Asians, Latinos, homosexuals, transgender people, Jews, and rival skinheads. In response to the dramatic increase in hate crimes, more than 40 states have laws banning such activities as paramilitary training and religious desecration. Federal officials are using civil rights laws to prosecute skinheads who attack minorities. In March 1990 the first such case resulted in five Dallas skinheads being convicted of civil rights violations, sentenced to long prison terms, and ordered to pay reparations to a synagogue and Jewish community center that they had vandalized.

Courts are awarding large sums to victims or their heirs. Rallies by the Ku Klux Klan and other hate groups often bring out more counterprotesters than members, indicating growing public awareness and revulsion. Although comprehensive statistics are unavailable, reports from around the country indicate the problem is escalating. Even more disturbing is the age of those committing hate crimes. For example, 70 percent of those arrested for bias crimes in New York City are younger than 19, and 40 percent are under 16 years of age. It is the work not just of organized hate groups but of individuals working alone as well—the kid down the street or the next-door neighbor acting out of bias can do as much harm to the fabric of a community.

The growth in hate crimes and the inability to accurately report such crimes led to the passage of the federal Hate Crime Statistics Act in April 1990. In the first two months after passage of the act, the federal hate crime hotline took more than 1,800 calls. Under the act, murders, assaults, arson, robberies, thefts, threats, and vandalism spurred by hatred toward a person's race, religion, or sexual preference are to be counted by the FBI as part of its Uniform Crime Report survey of state, local, and federal law enforcement agencies. Misleading police reports are a problem, because hate crimes frequently go unrecognized. It is also true that law enforcement officials are reluctant to label a crime as a "hate crime."

Although hate crimes are still a small part of the total crime picture in this country, they are particularly disturbing because, in the words of Democratic Senator Paul Simon of Illinois, they represent "a growing poison in the land, a growing hatred."[36] We cannot underestimate the psychic toll of hate crimes. It is terribly unsettling to be reminded that people seethe with hatred simply because someone has a different skin color, religious belief, or sexual preference and are capable of venting their bias in so many repugnant and violent ways.

Organized Crime

Unlike many other types of crime, organized crime is not wholly predatory. Rather, the syndicate supplies goods and services many people want but cannot get legally. Without the public's desire for gambling or drugs, for example, organized crime's base would collapse. As the president's Commission on Organized Crime concluded, "Organized crime will not be defeated in the United States until its customers change their ways."[37]

Crime organizations of the sort depicted in movies such as *The Godfather* are losing power as new faces emerge, such as Asian and Latino gangs. Law enforcement agencies report at least five distinct Asian cartels trafficking in drugs in the United States alone. Police in some parts of the country think that Asian organized crime could become the country's most intractable crime problem. These Asian crime organizations mainly traffic in heroin, and they run large gambling, extortion, and prostitution rackets. These groups also are known for their extreme violence.

The most grievous of all the organized crime developments in the last few decades relate directly to cocaine traffic. The demand in the United States for cocaine and for its even more dangerous derivative, crack, has emboldened the Colombian drug cartels and their drug-trafficking subsidiaries in the United States. It is estimated that nearly $2 billion in cocaine profits were laundered in 2001, as compared with $70 billion in marijuana and $35 billion in heroin.

The latest twist in the politics of illegal drug trafficking is the recent knowledge that terrorist groups have used drug profits to fund their operations. Asa Hutchinson, U.S. Drug Enforcement Agency (DEA) administrator, spoke about a strong connection between Afghanistan's drug trade and Al-Qaeda's terrorist activities when he testified before Congress on October 3, 2001. Al-Qaeda, headed by Osama bin Laden, is the group responsible for the terrorist attacks on September 11, 2001. Mr. Hutchinson testified that "Bin Laden's group, unlike terrorist groups from Colombia, benefits directly from Afghanistan's opium trade—driven economy. DEA intelligence confirms that presence of a linkage between Afghanistan's ruling Taliban and the Al-Qaeda. Although DEA has no direct evidence to confirm that Bin Ladin is involved directly in the drug trade, the sanctuary enjoyed by Bin Laden is based on the Taliban's support for the drug trade. The Taliban directly taxes and derives financial benefits from the opium trade, as evidenced by their provision of receipts for collected drug revenues."[38]

Since the time Mr. Hutchinson testified the United States has gone to war against the Taliban in Afghanistan, defeating them at least for now. Unfortunately, we have not been successful in dissuading Afghans from raising poppies (the source of opium). It is simply too lucrative a crop in a land where people struggle to survive. Not everyone is convinced that the worldwide illegal drug trade funds terrorism. Kevin Zeese, director of Common Sense for Drug Policy, a Washington-based nonprofit organization, says that "this connection is blown out of proportion. They [the Bush administration] are trying to tie the unpopular drug war to the more popular terrorism issue."[39]

The United States is home to more than 100,000 street gangs with a combined membership of well over 1 million youths and adults. Los Angeles County alone is the base for some 750 of these gangs, with a total membership of roughly 85,000. The police in Los Angeles estimate that long-standing Latino gangs have about 35,000 members. These "home boys" (*cholos*) are known for heroin trafficking, high levels of deadly violence in defense of neighborhood turf, and crack sales, primarily to African American users. These Los Angeles–based gangs also have been given considerable attention in films such as *Boyz N the Hood*. The most infamous of these gangs are the Crips and the Bloods. Though these two gangs are endlessly at war with each other, they also fight among themselves, and account for most of the gang-related killings in Los Angeles County. This is true for most other major cities. Tragically, an uncertain number of the victims—estimates run as high as 50 percent—have been innocent bystanders.

A relatively new development in gang membership is the rapidly increasing number of female members. Women always have been associated with gangs as sex objects or have played a secondary role in gangs. Not so today. Serious criminal behavior committed by female gang members has steadily increased over the past two decades and is becoming more common.[40] As female gang members became more liberated and independent beginning in the 1980s, they took on roles more comparable to male gang members. According to C. S. Taylor, "Female gang members now are hard-core and deadly."[41] Female gang members today have become more entrenched, more violent, and more and more oriented to male crime. Early literature on delinquency associated teenage girls with status criminal behavior (for example, truancy, shoplifting, violating curfew, and writing graffiti), while teenage boys more often committed more serious crimes. Today, a significantly greater number of teenage girls engage in serious criminal activities such as drive-by shootings, armed robberies, muggings, automobile thefts, and drug sales and distribution.[42] One explanation for the increase in violent criminal behavior among female gang members is the easy availability of guns. In the past, gang fighting was done with fists and knives, and female members could be at a disadvantage. No matter how big and muscular the opponent, using a gun evens out the odds.

How big is the problem of organized crime? Like every other type of crime, it is difficult to say with certainty. Some estimates, however, show organized crime's annual revenues from legitimate and illegitimate enterprises to be as high as $150 billion.[43] In addition to drugs, gambling, and prostitution, organized crime has piled up enormous profits from pornography, entertainment, labor unions, construction, trucking, loan-sharking, vending machines, garbage and toxic waste disposal, banking, stock fraud, insurance, and extortion.

JUVENILE OFFENDERS: ARE THEY THAT DIFFERENT FROM ADULTS?

For the past three decades, there has been increasing concern about juvenile offenders. One reason is teenage criminals seem far more violent (indeed, deadly) than their predecessors. There is a significantly greater number of teenage criminals (even preteens) today who are armed with handguns and automatic weapons and who are willing to use them. It has become far too common for juveniles to engage in random acts of violence—drive-by shootings, car hijackings, muggings, and even killing for pleasure.

We also are seeing more children engage in vicious bullying. An example is the case of a 13-year-old boy in Mountain View, California, who was kidnapped and tortured by other teenagers. During a two-hour attack, the boy was handcuffed, beaten, stripped, shot in the stomach with a BB gun, forced to eat coffee grounds and drink toilet water, had hot wax dripped on him, and was sexually abused. The boy reported that he had been picked on for more than a year before the attack but out of fear had never told anyone. Although bullying has always existed, it is the frequency and viciousness of today's attacks that have authorities so concerned. It seems groups of teenagers (and younger) have taken to acting out in ways not too unlike the boys who run amok on a remote island in William Golding's 1954 novel, *Lord of the Flies*.

It is for these reasons that public attitudes about juvenile offenders have changed dramatically in the past 15 years. Today, there is strong public support for prosecuting and sentencing juveniles (at least those who commit violent criminal acts) as adults. Even the term *juvenile delinquent*—which somehow implies it is a passing and relatively harmless phase in the maturation process—is heard less often when talking about teenage criminals. In fact, a closely divided U.S. Supreme Court refused on October 21, 2002, to reconsider a ruling allowing executions of juvenile murderers. Although one of the dissenting justices called the ruling "shameful," there is growing support across the country for treating violent juveniles as adults—even if it means a death sentence.

One positive development is a recent drop in the arrest rate for violent juvenile crime. In 2001 the number of youths between ages 10 and 17 arrested for violent crimes—murder, rape, robbery, and aggravated assault—fell to the lowest level since the mid-1980s.[44] However, Attorney General Janet Reno was quick to warn against becoming complacent or confident that this trend will continue. "What is so important is that we not relax and we not take credit for victory yet, because the number of young people is going to increase significantly in the next fifteen years. So, the actual number of crimes, unless we work real hard, is going to go up."[45]

Despite the drop in violent crimes committed by juveniles in the past five or so years, the fact is the overall crime rate for teens increased dramatically in the 1980s and early 1990s, while the crime rate for adults steadily dropped during the same period. "Between 1990 and 1994, the rate at which adults age 25 and older committed homicides declined 22%; yet the rate jumped 16% for youths between 14 and 17, the age group that in the early '90s supplanted 18- to 24-year-olds as the most crime-prone. And that is precisely the age group that will be booming in the next decade."[46] That is why Northeastern University criminologist James Alan Fox warns that "so long as we fool ourselves in thinking that we're winning the war against crime, we may be blindsided by this bloodbath of teenage violence that is lurking in the future."[47]

Numbers alone do not tell the whole story. For example, the current crop of teenagers have grown up in a new era of the American family. These are the kids known as the "home alone generation." Left alone, they spend far too much time hanging out on the streets or watching violent television. The 2000 Census shows that both parents work in most families, leaving their children to the care of others. Generally, young people today are more street savvy than the adolescents of the baby boom era. Drive-by shootings, AIDS, and greater uncertainty about their future financial security help to define their world. In addition to putting more pressure on the education system, the growing number of teenagers will strain an already pressured juvenile justice system.

A growing number of today's preteens are growing up in abusive or broken homes and with few positive role models—for example, too frequently superstars are busted for drugs, wife abuse, or unlawful possession of guns. These same kids as teenagers will have easy access to guns and drugs, making them all the more vulnerable to committing acts of violence. They are vulnerable because teenagers are, in James Alan Fox's words, "temporary sociopaths—impulsive and immature."[48] John J. DiIulio Jr., a professor of politics and public affairs at Princeton University, warns "about a new generation of 'superpredators,' youngsters who are coming of age in actual and 'moral poverty' without 'the benefit of parents, teachers, coaches and clergy to teach them right or wrong and show them unconditional love.'"[49]

It is the willingness of a growing number of young people to engage in random and often gratuitous acts of violence that is most disturbing and the reason many people support treating juveniles as adults in the criminal justice system. It is difficult to comprehend, but some atrocious crimes in America are being committed by those who should be the most innocent—the young. The soul of soci-

FIGURE 4.2
Percentage of Juvenile Victims for Each Type of Crime

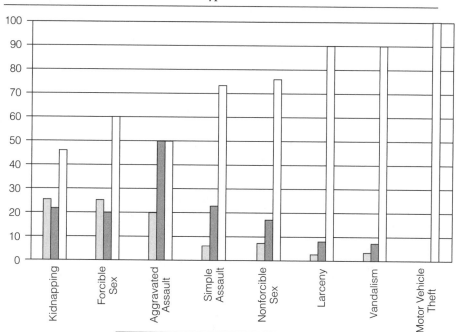

Source: U.S. Department of Justice, Federal Bureau of Investigation, Crimes against Children Research Center, National Incident-Based Reporting System (NBRS) (Washington, DC, 1997), 4.

ety has been shaken by the rise in brutal crimes by the young. Of course, teenagers have never been angels. Adolescence is often a troubled time of rebellion and rage. From *West Side Story* to *Rebel without a Cause,* the violence of youth has been chronicled on stage and screen. But today juvenile crime is more widespread and vicious.

It is also important to know that a greater percentage of teenagers are victims of violent crimes than are persons aged 20 and older. The Bureau of Justice, for example, reported that in 2001 juveniles made up 12 percent of all crime victims. In the case of sex offenses and kidnapping, juveniles made up a disproportionate number of crime victims (see Figure 4.2). Teenagers were twice as likely as adults to be a victim of robbery and nearly three times as likely to suffer violent crime (see Box 4.1). About half of all violent crimes against young people occurred on school property or in school buildings, or on the street. At least another million violent crimes against teenagers, including those acts committed in the home, were not reported to the police.

The young offenders are mostly male, but as we have learned, girls too are capable of vicious crime. Most important, violence-prone young people are found among all races, social classes, and lifestyles. Contrary to most assumptions, a

---

Box 4.1

THE RISK OF VICTIMIZATION DEPENDS
ON A COMBINATION OF FACTORS

Who are the victims of crime?

Victims of crime are more often men than women.

Younger people are much more likely than the elderly to be victims of crime. But the elderly have greater fear of crime and may restrict their lives in ways that reduce their chances of being victimized.

African Americans are more likely to be victims of violent crime than whites or members of other racial groups.

The divorced and the never married are more likely than the married or the widowed to be victims of crime. These differences may result in part because of the age differences of people in various marital-status groups.

Violent crime rates are higher for people with low incomes and those with high incomes.

Students and the unemployed are more likely than women who are full-time homemakers, retirees, or the employed to be victims of crime.

Rural residents are less often crime victims than are people living in cities.

Young African American males have the highest crime rates; elderly white females have the lowest rates.

Source: National Council of Juvenile and Family Court Judges, January 2002, http://www .ncjfcj.unr.edu/homepage/g3.html.

1991 study found that teenagers who work after school are more likely to break the law and court trouble than those who do not have jobs. The study concludes that teenagers who work before graduating from high school are about 1.5 times more likely to commit criminal offenses and use alcohol and are more than twice as likely to experiment with marijuana. Delbert Elliott, the study's principle researcher, thinks that the national survey showed that "a job may replace interest in school. Then what happens is a decline in educational aspiration . . . and in activities surrounding the school."[50]

Many different answers are given to the question, Why is there so much violence among young people? The reasons offered range from physiological and psychological abnormalities to family and cultural decay. By themselves, none of the explanations are satisfactory. But each of these factors may contribute to at least some of the violence. Studies show that violent youths frequently have neurological problems and learning disorders, many of which result from brain injuries inflicted in beatings by parents and others. Yet many experts argue that it is too easy to say that biology is destiny and that all violent youths are simply captives of their physiology or raging hormones.

Society attempts to control and channel aggressive impulses through its basic institutions—home, schools, and church. But these moral pillars of society appear weakened. A 1991 study conducted by Stanford University economists showed that American children are worse off than at any time before in our history. They found, for example, that children are more likely to commit suicide or be murdered and have a harder time reading and writing than their parents did 30 years ago. The study concluded that the nation's children are in a state of crisis.[51] There is little reason to believe that conditions 20 years later have improved for the nation's children and teenagers. In the minds of many, the crisis is as real in 2002 as it was in 1991, at the time of the study.

Too many children are growing up in families headed by one overburdened parent, usually the mother. Even when two parents are present, both often have demanding jobs, and they are absorbed in their own concerns. The 2000 Census shows, for example, that a significant majority of families with 6-to-17-year-olds have both parents working outside the home, as compared with slightly less than half in 1970. Sometimes the parents are addicted to alcohol or drugs. The result is that children do not get the nurturing, guidance, or supervision necessary to instill a set of values and a proper code of behavior. Children normally learn to trust and to develop attachments to people within the first two years of life. By then they have also gained a sense of compassion and empathy for others. They have been taught the difference between right and wrong and that hurtful actions have consequences. Many children, though, fail to acquire those early curbs on conduct. Later, when children misbehave, indulgent parents make excuses and forgo punishments.

The neglect is frequently compounded by abuse. Studies show that children today are raised by more and more disturbed parents. Parents abuse each other verbally and physically and frequently do the same to their children—a condition more pronounced in times of economic hardship or uncertainty. Records show that most violent children have been physically, and often sexually, abused by parents, relatives, or others. Research found that nearly every female gang member had experienced sexual and/or physical abuse and usually beginning at a very early age.[52] In the words of one 17-year-old woman, "I remember this one Thanksgiving dinner. As usual, everybody got real drunk and . . . started fighting. My uncle was yelling at my stepdad and cousin about some shit, and he pulls out a gun and shoots it right there in the house. I was so scared. I thought, 'Shit, he's gonna kill somebody right here,' and I was hoping it was gonna be my stepdad. If my uncle had known what that son-of-a-bitch had done to me [sexual abuse], he would have blown his head off right there."[53]

As a consequence of indifference and abuse, children are left emotional cripples, self-centered, angry, and alienated. Fated to repeat the chilling lessons they have learned, they often abuse their own children, and society must share the continuing costs of neglect. Even the children not abused in the home learn lessons that do not bode well for society. After all, what have been the lessons and who have been the role models for so many of the young in America today? For many, the message has been one of greed and self-centeredness—getting rich and wanting instant gratification. We have become more and more a nation whose role models, presidents, and leaders on Wall Street have set a tone in the country of "I'm going to get mine." The thinking may go, if the big-shot investment banker can take what he wants, often by illegal or unethical means, then a teenager may think he can grab the spoils in the only way he knows how.

The question asked most often is, What, if anything, can be done about violent youngsters? Many Americans are calling for stronger laws and punishments. They argue that juveniles should be prosecuted as adults and that prison sentences should be longer. Others have offered an even more radical idea: locking up parents. California, for example, is trying to do just that. Under a 1988 statute, parents can be held responsible for the criminal activity of their offspring. However, such solutions offer only illusory security. Parents often contend that they cannot control their children. And, not unlike adults, most youngsters released from jail return to society more hardened than before.

Those who argue for harsher punishment believe that juveniles above all must learn there are limits to permissible behavior—that acts such as robbery, rape, burglary, and assault cannot and should not be tolerated. The other side of the argument holds that because they are less mature—less able to form moral judgments, less capable of controlling their impulses, less aware of the consequences of their acts—juveniles should not pay so high a price as adults. In a word, they are less responsible, hence less blameworthy, than are adults.

The diminished responsibility of juveniles flows from another, equally important consideration, so the argument goes. The socialization of the young is an obligation of the whole society, not just of parents; school attendance is compulsory, for instance, and courts have the power to take children away from parents who neglect or abuse them. Thus, society bears a responsibility for young criminals that it does not have with adults. Their acts must be condemned; but society has an obligation to do more than merely punish them for their offenses. It is their capacity for change, even more than their diminished responsibility, that creates the need for a different and more lenient sentencing policy. As their stake in society increases, so do the pressures to conform to societal norms. Since most juvenile offenders do in fact grow out of crime, it makes sense to respond to juvenile crime with that possibility in mind.

The problem is that, as young people have armed themselves with guns, including military-style automatic weapons, their impulsive behavior too often results in the death of innocent people. Among a growing number of juvenile offenders, we no longer are talking about relatively harmless pranks, petty thefts, or fistfights. It is this growing and exceedingly dangerous group of teenagers (and even preteens) that most scare the public. The growing number of murders committed by teenagers at their schools has been cause for alarm among parents, teachers, and students. The deadliest school shooting in U.S. history happened on April 20, 1999, at Columbine High School. Fourteen students and one teacher were killed on that fateful day. While the deadliest, it is only one of many such shootings to happen in the nation's middle and high schools (see Box 4.2).

Box 4.2

A TIME LINE OF RECENT SCHOOL SHOOTINGS

Feb. 2, 1996,
Moses Lake, Wash.

Two students and one teacher killed, one other wounded when 14-year-old Barry Loukaitis opened fire on his algebra class.

March 13, 1996,
Dunblane, Scotland

16 children and one teacher killed at Dunblane Primary School by Thomas Hamilton, who then killed himself. 10 others wounded in attack.

Feb. 19, 1997,
Bethel, Ala.

Principal and one student killed, two others wounded by Evan Ramsey, 16.

March 1997,
Sanaa, Yemen

Eight people (six students and two others) at two schools killed by Mohammad Ahman al-Naziri.

Oct. 1, 1997,
Pearl, Miss.

Two students killed and seven wounded by Luke Woodham, 16, who was also accused of killing his mother. He and his friends were said to be outcasts who worshiped Satan.

Dec. 1, 1997,
West Paducah, Ky.

Three students killed, five wounded by Michael Carneal, 14, as they participated in a prayer circle at Heath High School.

Dec. 15, 1997,
Stamps, Ark.

Two students wounded. Colt Todd, 14, was hiding in the woods when he shot the students as they stood in the parking lot.

March 24, 1998,
Jonesboro, Ark.

Four students and one teacher killed, ten others wounded outside, as Westside Middle School emptied during a false fire alarm. Mitchell Johnson, 13, and Andrew Golden, 11, shot at their classmates and teachers from the woods.

April 24, 1998,
Edinboro, Pa.

One teacher, John Gillette, killed, two students wounded, at a dance at James W. Parker Middle School. Andrew Wurst, 14, was charged.

May 19, 1998,
Fayetteville, Tenn.

One student killed in the parking lot at Lincoln County High School three days before he was to graduate. The victim was dating the ex-girlfriend of his killer, 18-year-old honor student Jacob Davis.

May 21, 1998,
Springfield, Ore.

Two students killed, 22 others wounded in the cafeteria at Thurston High School by 15-year-old Kip Kinkel. Kinkel had been arrested and released a day earlier for bringing a gun to school. His parents were later found dead at home.

June 15, 1998,
Richmond, Va.

One teacher and one guidance counselor wounded by a 14-year-old boy in the school hallway.

April 20, 1999,
Littleton, Colo.

14 students (including killers) and one teacher killed, 23 others wounded at Columbine High School in the nation's deadliest school shooting.

Eric Harris, 18, and Dylan Klebold, 17, had plotted for a year to kill at least 500 and blow up their school. At the end of their hour-long rampage, they turned their guns on themselves.

April 28, 1999,
Taber, Alberta, Canada

One student killed, one wounded at W. R. Myers High School in first fatal high school shooting in Canada in 20 years. The suspect, a 14-year-old boy, had dropped out of school after he was severely ostracized by his classmates.

May 20, 1999,
Conyers, Ga.

Six students injured at Heritage High School by Thomas Solomon, 15, who was reportedly depressed after breaking up with his girlfriend.

Nov. 19, 1999,
Deming, N.M.

Victor Cordova Jr., 12, shot and killed Araceli Tena, 13, in the lobby of Deming Middle School.

Dec. 6, 1999,
Fort Gibson, Okla.

Four students wounded as Seth Trickey, 13, opened fire with a 9mm semiautomatic handgun at Fort Gibson Middle School.

Dec. 7, 1999,
Veghel, Netherlands

One teacher and three students wounded by a 17-year-old student.

Feb. 29, 2000,
Mount Morris Township, Mich.

Six-year-old Kayla Rolland shot dead at Buell Elementary School near Flint, Mich. The assailant was identified as a six-year-old boy with a .32-caliber handgun.

March 2000,
Branneburg, Germany

One teacher killed by a 15-year-old student, who then shot himself. The shooter has been in a coma ever since.

March 10, 2000,
Savannah, Ga.

Two students killed by Darrell Ingram, 19, while leaving a dance sponsored by Beach High School.

May 26, 2000,
Lake Worth, Fla.

One teacher, Barry Grunow, shot and killed at Lake Worth Middle School by Nate Brazill, 13, with .25-caliber semiautomatic pistol on the last day of classes.

Sept. 26, 2000,
New Orleans, La.

Two students wounded with the same gun during a fight at Woodson Middle School.

Jan. 17, 2001,
Baltimore, Md.

One student shot and killed in front of Lake Clifton Eastern High School.

Jan. 18, 2001,
Jan, Sweden

One student killed by two boys, ages 17 and 19.

March 5, 2001,
Santee, Calif.

Two killed and 13 wounded by Charles Andrew Williams, 15, firing from a bathroom at Santana High School.

March 7, 2001,
Williamsport, Pa.

Elizabeth Catherine Bush, 14, wounded student Kimberly Marchese in the cafeteria of Bishop Neumann High School; she was depressed and frequently teased.

March 22, 2001,
Granite Hills, Calif.

One teacher and three students wounded by Jason Hoffman, 18, at Granite Hills High School. A policeman shot and wounded Hoffman.

March 30, 2001, *Gary, Ind.*	One student killed by Donald R. Burt Jr., a 17-year-old student who had been expelled from Lew Wallace High School.
Nov. 12, 2001, *Caro, Mich.*	Chris Buschbacher, 17, took two hostages at the Caro Learning Center before killing himself.
Jan. 15, 2002, *New York, N.Y.*	A teenager wounded two students at Martin Luther King Jr. High School.
Feb. 19, 2002, *Freising, Germany*	Two killed in Eching by a man at the factory from which he had been fired; he then traveled to Freising and killed the headmaster of the technical school from which he had been expelled. He also wounded another teacher before killing himself.
April 26, 2002, *Erfurt, Germany*	13 teachers, two students, and one policeman killed, ten wounded, by Robert Steinhaeuser, 19, at the Johann Gutenberg secondary school. Steinhaeuser then killed himself.
April 29, 2002, *Vlasenica, Bosnia-Herzegovina*	One teacher killed, one wounded, by Dragoslav Petkovic.

Source: Society and Culture Law Enforcement and Crime—Crime Data, Infoplease.com, http://www.infoplease.com/ipa/A0777958.html.

Even so, many experts remain adamant that the best way to head off today's young offenders from becoming tomorrow's adult criminals is to offer them rehabilitative services early in life. These experts argue that the more sensible long-term solution to crime is to offer rehabilitative treatment when a person is more likely to change—that is, when he or she is young. However unpopular this approach may be today as juveniles have become more violent and aggressive, and no matter that rehabilitation has largely failed, the remedy is not to abandon the effort. The voices in favor of programs to rehabilitate young offenders argue that we must try to understand why past efforts have failed and to intensify the search for approaches that offer some hope of working. Though we may not know enough to help every troubled juvenile, we do not know so little that we should stop trying.

In fact, communities across the country are trying a variety of rehabilitative programs. The programs often call for individual and group therapy for the offender and sometimes for the family. The strategy is to get violent youngsters to recognize the inappropriateness of their actions and to accept responsibility for their actions—as difficult a task with youngsters as it is with adult offenders.

In some programs, the young inmates write up or discuss their own cases to identify the behavior pattern or situations that are liable to trigger hostile actions. For example, young sexual offenders may recognize their susceptibility to hostile actions when they are around young children. They may then be advised to avoid baby-sitting. The treatment centers also try to elicit a sense of empathy.

For example, juveniles convicted of murder or attempted murder may be asked to keep daily journals of their feelings and to act out their crime, taking the roles of both their victim and surviving family members. Sexual offenders may be asked to meet with groups of victims every few months. The California Youth Authority, for example, runs voluntary classes in which inmates study property crimes, domestic violence, sexual assault, child abuse, homicide, and victim rights. Although there is anecdotal evidence that some offenders do eventually express remorse, statistics are unavailable to show definitively the success or failure of these programs.

Even if data were available to show that these programs worked, they are indisputably too late. Violence-prone youths need to be identified and helped before they explode in rage. It is argued, for example, that reporting of sexual and physical abuse should be encouraged, if not mandated. In many states, therapists, social workers, and teachers are required to report such abuses. There is no question that the earlier the intervention, the greater the chance of success. Many favor improved sex-education programs in the schools as well as courses in preventing violence such as those offered in Boston, Detroit, and Denver schools.

Still others say that no matter the lessons taught in school or by parents, children and teenagers are bombarded with messages of violence and sexuality on television, at the movies, and on their stereos. Consequently, there is a growing band of activists who lobby television, movie, and record producers to reduce the level of sex and violence in entertainment. Americans for Responsible Television is one such group that calls on networks to devote the first two hours of evening programming to family shows and also has asked major advertisers to avoid sponsoring programs that they find objectionable. Another group, Parents' Music Resource Center, successfully pressured the Recording Industry Association of America to create a rating system that alerts parents to sexually explicit lyrics. Warning labels are now printed on CD covers. The group also provides printed lyric sheets and encourages parents to complain to radio and television stations about raunchy and violent programming.

President Clinton called on the entertainment industry to reduce the violent and sexual content of their programming, especially for television. On February 8, 1996, Clinton signed the first major overhaul of telecommunications law in almost 62 years. Among its many provisions, the Telecommunications Act requires television manufacturers to provide "V-chips" for all new sets so that parents can block certain programming, thereby giving them the ability to protect their children from television violence and other age-inappropriate broadcasts.

Even the activists admit, however, that removing all sex and gore from the media would do little to solve the problem. Fundamental changes in society are needed for a significant reduction in crime, particularly violent crime. George W. Bush, and his father and Clinton before him, has argued for more money and stronger laws directed at the selling and using of drugs. Others, including Bush and Clinton, say that more attention should be given to reducing poverty and racism and that more money should be spent on education, day care, and recreational opportunities for the young. Still others say that adults, especially parents, should take a long look in the mirror. The values of today's youth merely reflect the values of their elders.

CRIMINALS: WHO ARE THEY—WHY ARE THEY?

The age-old question of why some people act outside the norms and laws of society still awaits a satisfactory answer. This is particularly true, as we have said, when trying to understand and predict the more violent members of society. This is not to say that theories of criminal behavior do not exist. Emile Durkheim, a sociologist, offered one of the earliest and still relevant macrosociological approaches to criminal behavior.

Durkheim argued that when the various parts of the social system lose their integration (that is, cease to mesh together), people may fall into a state of normlessness or confusion (termed by Durkheim anomie) that may cause rates of criminal activity to increase. Durkheim believed these behavioral changes are particularly widespread during times of rapid change, when values, technology, and social structure are shifting at different rates. A high crime rate, Durkheim would say, is almost always a product of rapid economic development (and not just an economic depression) and social change. A sudden rise in prosperity, for example, creates what he called overweening ambition—that is, people develop unreasonably high expectations. In their rush for material gain, some play by the rules while others ignore them.[54] This may help to explain the greed and unlawful or unethical practices undertaken by so many beginning in the 1980s.

DEMOGRAPHIC FACTORS

Other criminologists and sociologists think the high prevalence of crime in the United States is due to demographic factors. Demographic changes swelled the numbers of persons between ages 15 and 24 beginning in the 1960s. In 1950 there were only 24 million people in the United States in this age group; by 2000 there were nearly 40 million. Since most crimes are committed by young people, usually males, under the age of 24, it is tempting to blame the sharp increase in reported crime that began during the 1960s on the coming of age of the postwar baby boomers (see Table 4.6).

If this is true, then the drop in overall crime rates during the 1990s may be explained by the fact that in that decade, for the first time since the baby boom of the 1950s and 1960s, there was an increase in the median age. This is the result of the baby boomers becoming middle-aged and their having put off having children until their late twenties and early thirties. However, the future may not be so rosy given that in 1995 there were 39 million children under the age of ten, more than at any time since the 1950s. The rise in serious and violent crimes reported in 2001 may be the start of an upward trend as the children of the baby boomers increase the number of 15-to-24-year-olds.

TABLE 4.6
Profile of Age Characteristics for the United States, 2000 and 1990

	2000 Census Data		1990 Census Data	
	Number	%	*Number*	%
Total Population	281,421,906		248,709,873	
Sex and Age				
Total Male	138,053,563	49.1	121,239,418	48.7
Total Female	143,368,343	50.9	127,470,455	51.3
Under 5 years	19,175,798	6.8	18,354,443	7.4
5 to 9 years	20,549,505	7.3	18,099,179	7.3
10 to 14 years	20,528,072	7.3	17,114,249	6.9
15 to 19 years	20,219,890	7.2	17,754,015	7.1
20 to 24 years	18,964,001	6.7	19,020,312	7.6
25 to 34 years	39,891,724	14.2	43,175,932	17.4
35 to 44 years	45,148,527	16.0	37,578,903	15.1
45 to 54 years	37,677,952	13.4	25,223,086	10.1
55 to 59 years	13,469,237	4.8	10,531,756	4.2
60 to 64 years	10,805,447	3.8	10,616,167	4.3
65 to 74 years	18,390,986	6.5	18,106,558	7.3
75 to 84 years	12,361,180	4.4	10,055,108	4.0
85 years and over	4,239,587	1.5	3,080,165	1.2
Median age (years)	35.3		33	
18 years and over	209,128,094	74.3	185,105,441	74.4
Male	100,994,367	35.9	88,655,140	35.6
Female	108,133,727	38.4	96,450,301	38.8
21 years and over	196,899,193	70.0	173,378,573	69.7
62 years and over	41,256,029	14.7	37,629,695	15.1
65 years and over	34,991,753	12.4	31,241,831	12.6
Male	14,409,625	5.1	12,565,173	5.1
Female	20,582,128	7.3	18,676,658	7.5

Source: U.S. Administration on Aging, February 12, 2002, http://www.aoa.gov/aoa/STATS/Census2000/2000-1990-Pop.html.

The truth may not be so simple. The 1967 report of President Lyndon Johnson's Commission on Law Enforcement and Administration of Justice puzzled over why the rise in reported crimes was much larger than the growth in the size of the crime-prone age groups in the U.S. population.[55] The authors of the report showed, for example, that if the arrest rate for teenagers had been the same in 1965 as it was in 1960, the number of teenager arrests in 1965 would have come to 536,000. The actual figure was 646,000.

This study shows that changes in the crime rate cannot be simplistically explained by isolating one variable or another. Yet a correlation between rising crime and a rising (or more recently, declining) proportion of young people in the population is too clear to dismiss. The same holds for explanations of decreasing crime rates in certain categories. For example, no one cause explains the decline in the rates of larceny theft, burglary, or for that matter, murder and rape during the 1990s. Similarly, there is no one explanation for why these crimes increased in 2001. Criminologists offer a number of explanations for the decline in crime during the 1990s, including the greater number of people convicted of crimes who are in prison (especially due to a growing number of states and the federal government that have adopted three-strikes laws), the decreasing size of the teen and young adult population, and the growth of citizen crime-prevention activities such as neighborhood watch and community policing programs.

It is worth noting that one reason offered for the recent increase in crime is the growing number of inmates who are returning home. In other words, the large number of men and women who were incarcerated during the 1990s are coming home, many of them without jobs or an education. Consequently, many return to a life of crime and will eventually be sent back to prison.

Recognizing that many factors contribute to the rise and fall of crime in society, there is no doubt that shifting demographics play a significant role. Mathematical models incorporating rather basic demographic information have proved to be highly accurate in predicting future crime rate trends.[56] Suffice it to say that the decline in crime beginning in 1991 may not continue (as 2001 crime figures indicate) as the 39 million offspring of the baby boom generation become teenagers.

Race and Class

Virtually all data on race and crime, regardless of locale or year, show that a large proportion of offenders come from minority groups. Within the minority population, the arrest rate of African Americans for most offenses is disproportionately high and becoming more so every year. In 2002 Human Rights Watch reported that "out of a total population of 1,976,019 incarcerated in adult facilities, 1,239,946 or 63 percent are black or Latino, though these two groups constitute only 25 percent of the national population.[57]

Human Rights Watch also reports that there are significant differences in the rate of minority incarceration between states. For example:

≫ In 12 states, between 10 and 15 percent of adult black men are incarcerated.

≫ In ten states, between 5 and 10 percent of black adults are incarcerated.

≫ In 12 states, black men are incarcerated at rates between 12 and 16 times greater than those of white women.

≫ In 15 states, black women are incarcerated at rates between 10 and 35 times greater than those of white women.

≫ In six states, black youth under age 18 are incarcerated in adult facilities at rates between 12 and 25 times greater than those of white youth.

≫ In nine states, between 4 and 8 percent of adult Latino men are incarcerated.

≫ In 12 states, between 2 and 4 percent of Hispanic adults (men and women) are incarcerated.

≫ In ten states, Latino men are incarcerated at rates between five and nine times greateer than those of white men.

≫ In eight states, Latina women are incarcerated at rates between four and seven times greater than those of white women.

≫ In four states, Hispanic youth under age 18 are incarcerated in adult facilities at rates between 7 and 17 times greater than those of white youth.[58]

The percentage of state and federal inmates from racial or ethnic minority groups is also growing steadily. This is particularly true in states with three-strikes laws. For example, from 1994, when the three-strikes law was enacted in California, to 1999, African Americans were imprisoned at a rate 15 times that of whites. African Americans comprise only 6 percent of the population in California and yet account for 24 percent of felony arrests, 42 percent of the prison population, and 45 percent of "third strike" defendants sent to state prison. This same pattern holds for other states with three-strikes laws.

The reasons for the link between minorities and crime (especially the African American and Latino populations) are many and complex, and they have less to do with race by itself (although racism plays a role in arrest rates) than with the conditions in which millions of young African Americans, Latinos, and other ethnic or racial groups are growing up: in poverty, broken homes, decaying schools. Such circumstances may lead to criminal behavior for all groups in the population. In addition, low-income people, regardless of race, are often at a disadvantage in the criminal justice system because of such factors as their inability to post bail or to hire an experienced criminal attorney.

The O.J. Simpson trial was a dramatic reminder of how divided the nation is along race lines and how this division gets played out in the justice system. In a decision that shocked millions of white Americans but that elated African Americans, the jury found the former football star not guilty of murdering his former wife, Nicole Brown Simpson, and her friend, Ronald Goldman. After a trial that lasted more than nine months, presented 125 witnesses and 1,105 pieces of evidence, and cost taxpayers an estimated $9 million, the jury took less than four hours to reach its verdict. Reactions to the verdict were divided largely along racial lines. African Americans were more likely to believe the defense's contention that police planted evidence in an attempt to frame Simpson. Most whites, however, believed that a jury composed of eight African American women, one African American man, two white women, and a Latino man simply ignored an overwhelming amount of evidence implicating Simpson. Important to our discussion is the fact that African Americans believe, based largely on experience, that the police routinely discriminate against them and that, in this one case at least, an African American escaped the system. Never mind that this particular African American was rich, famous, and mostly identified with wealthy whites before his arrest and trial.

Social and Economic Class

There is no agreement on whether social class and economic conditions cause criminal behavior. One reason is that some people with similar characteristics commit crimes and others do not. Even so, as a partial answer to the question, Who commits crimes? we will profile offenders based on their social and economic class.

A high proportion of offenders have grown up in homes with one parent. About 48 percent of jail and prison inmates grew up primarily with one parent or other relatives. We have said that many offenders (particularly those who commit violent crimes) have been victims of childhood abuse. People with relatives who have served time in prison are more likely to be arrested. For example, about 40 percent of prison inmates and 34 percent of those in jail have an immediate family member who has been incarcerated.[59]

Most offenders are single and have dependent children. About half of jail and prison inmates have never been married and another 24 percent are divorced or separated. The proportion of divorced and separated white inmates is much higher than in the population; the marital status of African American inmates is closer to their general U.S. population. Women offenders are more likely than men to have dependent children.

The level of education for inmates is far below the national average. Only about 40 percent of jail and 28 percent of prison inmates have completed high school, compared with 85 percent of males aged 20 to 29 in the U.S. population. There are few college graduates in jails or prisons, and of those better educated, the majority are in prison for drug offenses.

The highest arrest and imprisonment rate among males of any age is among those who were unemployed before arrest. About 45 percent of all males in jail were unemployed at the time they entered jail. Among the 55 percent who were working, 22 percent were working only part-time. It follows that the average inmate was at the poverty level before entering jail. For example, nearly half of the males in jail or prison for at least a year had half the annual incomes of the general population. The comparative income levels for women inmates were even lower.[60]

Sex

Most crimes are committed by males, especially by those under age 20. Men also are more likely to be arrested for the more serious crimes. A higher proportion of women, in contrast, are involved in property crimes. More recently, teenage girls have been involved in car hijacking and other violent acts. And as we discussed earlier, a growing number of young women are members of gangs and are more prone to violent and aggressive behavior. Historically, women have been regarded more protectively by both the police and the courts; thus, they have been less likely to be arrested and, if arrested, less likely to be severely punished, especially if they are mothers. This attitude is changing, however, as the patterns of socialization for men and women have changed since the late 1960s.

During the 1990s, for example, the number of women in prison rose by more than 100 percent, while the number of men rose by a little more than 80 percent. By 2000 the growth rates were nearly equal for male and female prison populations. For example, in 2001 the number of women in state and federal prisons increased by 7.1 percent. In the same year, the number of men in state and federal prisons rose by 7.4 percent.

Noncitizens

The number of noncitizens (legal and illegal immigrants) processed in the federal criminal justice system increased an average 10 percent annually from 1984 to 1994. In this time, the number of noncitizens housed in federal prisons increased an average of 15 percent annually; the overall federal prison population, by contrast, increased an average 10 percent annually. A little over half (55 percent) of the noncitizens prosecuted in federal court during 1994 were in the United States legally. During 1984, about 35 percent of noncitizens prosecuted were charged with a drug offense. By 1994 the proportion charged with a drug offense had increased to 45 percent.[61]

In June 2001 the number of noncitizens incarcerated in federal prision had increased a whopping 53 percent since 1994 (18,929 to 35,629). Immigrants comprise 29 percent of all federal inmates; yet they make up only 9.3 percent of the U.S. population. The terrorist attacks on September 11, 2001, the creation of the Office (now Department) of Homeland Security, and the "war on terrorism" are bound to increase these numbers dramatically in the next several years.

IS VIOLENT CRIME A NECESSARY PART OF MODERN SOCIETY?

It is easy, and in a strange way, comforting, to attribute (blame) the violence in our country to (on) industrialization and large-city living conditions. Certainly there are greater concentrations of impoverished and alienated people in inner cities who may be more likely to commit violent crimes. However, how do we explain the rising violence in middle-class suburbs? Or why do we find, when we compare the United States with other industrialized countries, that violent crime rates are much higher in the United States than in these other countries? Comparative data show, for example, that Americans have a seven- to ten-times greater risk of death by homicide than do the people of most European countries and Japan. The nearest competitor to the United States in homicide rates is Great Britain, while we murder one another at more than three times the rate the Finnish do.[62]

Because modern, urbanized living conditions alone do not explain a country's level of violence, additional answers are thought to be found in our cultural, historical, and demographic characteristics. For example, some argue that we are a more violent society in part because of the frontier ethos that is so much a part of the American heritage. Others contend that the easy access to, and proliferation of, guns (especially handguns and military-style weapons) contributes to American violence. Also, our society is far more heterogeneous than most other industrialized countries. This leads to tension between ethnic or racial groups, which may erupt into violence.

Still others say that none of these explanations is sufficient to explain the startling differences in crime rates. For example, Australia and Canada share a common frontier tradition with the United States, yet their murder rates are less than a fourth and a third of ours, respectively. Although roughly the same number of people live in California as live in Canada, Californians kill one another at six times the rate of Canadians. Guns alone cannot explain the differences. More Californians are killed with knives, for example, than are Canadians by all means put together.[63]

The same discrepancy that exists in murder rates holds for other violent crimes as well. For example, American women are more than three times as likely to be raped than are West German women, and U.S. citizens are more than six times as likely to be robbed.[64] If we choose to ignore these differences, then we might fall prey to the more palatable view that violent crime simply is one of the negative trade-offs that comes with modern conveniences. Consequently, we too often focus only on the year-to-year fluctuations of our crime rate and think that we are making progress if they come down slightly each year as they did from 1991 to 2000—ignoring the fact that we still outrank by a substantial margin all other industrial countries and experienced a general upward trend in violent crime from the early 1960s until 1991. This general upward swing in violent crime happened even though we threw substantially more money at the problem and built a great many more prisons and filled them to capacity during that same period.

Considering the comparatively high levels of violent crime in the United States and the tremendous number of dollars and personnel committed to the criminal justice system, the next logical question to ask is whether that system can solve the crime problem. A brief answer is that it can do more to reduce crime than liberal rhetoric implies, but much less than conservatives suggest.

The liberal-conservative rift runs through the justice system. The basic philosophical difference between them is that conservatives are less concerned with the "why" of criminal behavior and are more concerned with social vengeance and punishment for the consequences of behavior. Liberals, in contrast, believe that past "bad" learning can be reversed through education and various rehabilitative programs.

THE JUSTICE SYSTEM: LIBERAL AND CONSERVATIVE MODELS

In 1901, Enrico Ferri, an Italian legal scholar who helped develop criminology as an academic discipline, declared, "We have but to look around us in the realities of contemporaneous life to see that the criminal code is far from being a remedy against crime, that it remedies nothing." Ferri concluded, "Punishment prevents the criminal for a while from repeating his criminal deed," but added, "It is evident that the punishment is not imposed until after the deed has been done. It is a remedy directed against effects, but it does not touch the causes, the roots, of the evil."

Instead of dealing with symptoms, Ferri argued, we should attack the disease itself: "That which has happened in medicine will happen in criminology." The discovery that malaria is transmitted by mosquitoes led not only to the development of new medicines to cure those already infected, but to the draining of swamps to prevent people from contracting the disease in the first place.[65]

Liberals have been addicted to medical metaphors ever since. In dissenting from the 1931 report of the Wickersham Commission (the National Commission on Law Observance and Enforcement), Henry W. Anderson, chairman of the commission's Committee on the Causes of Crime, wrote, "Like eruptions on the human body," criminal acts "are symptoms of more fundamental conditions of personal or social deficiency or imbalance." If "the crime problem is to be solved," Anderson added, "the attack must be made at the sources of the trouble and the remedy must be found in the removal of the causes."[66] It is not a question of either/or; attacking the underlying causes of the problem (favored by liberals) does not preclude an attempt to alleviate the symptoms (favored by conservatives).

Even Band-Aids have their uses; a doctor must treat a symptom, especially if a cure is not immediately at hand. There is no inherent reason why attempts to cut crime through more effective law enforcement must come at the expense of efforts to cure the underlying disease. The reverse may be closer to the truth. Reluctance to invoke the criminal justice system to reduce crime in the short run may create a backlash against the social and economic reforms that are needed for the long run. We saw this happen with the call for harsher law-and-order tactics, such as three-strikes laws, streamlining of the appeals process in capital punishment cases, and prosecuting juveniles as adults.

If liberals have been too preoccupied with underlying causes, conservatives have exaggerated the gains that can be wrung from tougher law enforcement. To read critics such as James Q. Wilson and Ernest van den Haag, one would think that the current level of criminal violence represented a fall from some prior state of grace. Their writings imply that once upon a time, before police officers' and judges' hands were tied by the Supreme Court under Chief Justice Earl Warren (which made many decisions in the 1960s protecting the rights of the accused), criminals were easily and quickly apprehended, rapidly tried and convicted, and promptly sent to prison for an appropriate term.[67]

There never was such a time—at least not in the United States in this century. As the late Dean Roscoe Pound of Harvard Law School, one of the giants of American jurisprudence, told the American Bar Association in 1906, "Dissatisfaction with the administration of justice is as old as law." Dissatisfaction was extremely high when Pound spoke, because urban crime and violence were increasing at an explosive rate. Conservatives of that era, as in our own, thought they knew why: Courts were unduly concerned with the rights of the accused; hence criminals were not being punished the way they used to be. "It is not too much to say that the administration of the criminal law in this country is a disgrace to our civilization," President (later chief justice) William Howard Taft declared in 1909, "and that the prevalence of crime and fraud, which here is greatly in excess of that in European countries, is due largely to the failure of the law to bring criminals to justice. . . . The trial of a criminal seems like a game of chance, with all the chances in favor of the criminal." [68]

The same charge has been voiced many times. In the 1920s, some of the basic safeguards of criminal procedures did not exist; the police routinely held suspects incommunicado for long periods and extracted confessions through physical and psychological torture, often with the prosecutor's knowledge or participation. Yet police chiefs, prosecutors, and other law enforcement officials complained that their hands were being tied. "There has been too much mollycoddling of the criminal population," Edwin Sims, head of the new Chicago Crime Commission, declared in 1920. A few years later, when a state court excluded a defendant's confession because it had been obtained through the use of the third degree, a Chicago police official announced that 95 percent of the department's work would be rendered useless if the decision were allowed to stand. "We are permitted to do less every day," the chief complained. "Pretty soon there won't be a police department." [69]

According to conservatives, we have always been losing the war on crime, and the remedy has always been the same: to unleash the forces of law and order so criminals can be quickly caught, convicted, and punished. Like Richard Nixon 40 years later, Herbert Hoover campaigned for the presidency in 1928 on a law-and-order platform. "Every student of our law enforcement mechanism knows full well . . . that its procedures unduly favor the criminal . . . and that justice must be more swift and sure," he told the Associated Press a month after he took office. "In our desire to be merciful the pendulum has swung in favor of the prisoner and far away from protection of society." Similar thoughts and policies were expressed and enforced by the Reagan and Bush administrations. Although a Democrat and generally thought to be liberal on most social issues, President Clinton's law enforcement policies were little different from those of his Republican predecessors. He too called for a greater police presence, stiffer penalties for violent and drug-related crimes, and greater protections for the rights of victims. The one bone Clinton tossed to liberals was his request for more dollars to support treatment programs, especially for drug- and alcohol-dependent juveniles. We will soon learn that President George W. Bush's position on crime and how best to combat it is very similar to his immediate predecessors, including his father.

It would be helpful if the real world were as simple as the ideologies of both camps suggest. It is not. If the past teaches us anything, it is that there are no quick and easy solutions to the enduring problem of criminal violence—not through social reform and not through law and order. On the contrary, the search for panaceas has often made matters worse. For one thing, the institutions of the criminal justice system are extremely complex: their actual operations often bear little resemblance to the image that people have of them. Hence, attempts to change the police, courts, and prisons often backfire.

Except in the most general sense, moreover, we know remarkably little about the relationship between what the police, courts, and prisoners do, on one hand,

and what criminals do, on the other. We know that punishment deters crime, for example. We do not know whether more punishment, or different punishment, than we now administer will deter crime more effectively. Similarly, the existence of the police undoubtedly leads to less crime than we would have in their absence. There is no evidence, however, that more police will produce less crime; and the police themselves simply do not know what else to do to bring about a reduction in criminal violence. Nor is there any persuasive evidence that correctional officials know how to rehabilitate criminal offenders.

If we are to have any hope of reducing criminal violence to some more tolerable level, we may want to proceed cautiously, and with modest goals and expectations. We also need to shed our ideological blinders. Crime control is a quintessential political issue, for the administration of criminal law poses fundamental questions about the relationship between the individual and the power of the state. All of us, therefore, liberals and conservatives alike, approach the subject with intense emotions and preconceptions.

A Radical Proposal for Fixing the System

Once associated with liberal causes, Judge Harold Rothwax has concluded that the criminal justice system is broken and requires radical change if it is to rediscover the search for truth and the exercise of common sense—neither of which is visible to the casual or expert observer of the American judicial system. Judge Rothwax wrote a book based on his observations of the criminal justice system in New York City after more than 25 years as a judge. In this book, *Guilty: The Collapse of Criminal Justice,* he concludes that nothing less than sweeping change in how we conduct business in the criminal justice system will save us from the (in)justice system that allows so many criminals to go free. He would reform many of the practices we have taken for granted in the past several decades, such as the Miranda warning, the right to counsel, even unanimous jury verdicts.

Judge Rothwax argues, for example, that there is a fundamental difference between the investigative and the trial stages of a case. "The investigative stage is marked by the notion of probable guilt, not the presumption of innocence. Until a defendant goes on trial, he is probably guilty. By the time a person reaches trial he has been deemed 'probably guilty' several times."[70] Rothwax points out that "when a person is arrested, indicted by a grand jury, held in detention or released on bail, it is all based on probable guilt. Once on trial, he is presumed innocent."[71]

A few of the more radical changes Rothwax would like to see made to the criminal justice system include:

THE MIRANDA WARNING　　The Miranda warning requires that the suspect be told he has a right to remain silent, that any statement he makes might be used against him and that he has the right to have a lawyer present. Miranda came about because of abuses such as prolonged custodial interrogation, beatings, and starving in order to get a confession. Rothwax thinks those abuses have been largely dealt with. Now the police officer is put in the position of telling a suspect in a murder or rape, "Look, you don't have to tell us anything, and that may be the best thing for you." And it produces a situation in which a proper confession is thrown out because of the way in which it was read or that it was not read at the right time. Rothwax believes Miranda can be replaced by the recording of an arrest and interrogation through videotapes, tape recorders, and other technology. This would probably show whether a confession or statement was coerced.

THE EXCLUSIONARY RULE   The Supreme Court has consistently ruled that evidence seized in violation of the Fourth Amendment should be excluded from a criminal trial. This ruling has led to countless cases in which key evidence has been excluded on technical grounds from a trial—often resulting in the case being thrown out or, at the very least, the prosecutor's case being gutted, so that convictions often are impossible. Rothwax points out that nowhere in the Fourth Amendment does it say that illegally obtained evidence must be excluded. In his view, when you exclude or suppress evidence, you suppress the truth. Rothwax's solution would be to make the exclusionary rule discretionary instead of mandatory. If it was at the discretion of the judge, there could be a test of reasonableness. A judge could consider factors such as whether a police officer acted with objective reasonableness and subjective good faith. As it is now, the exclusionary rule is irrational and arbitrary and lacks proportion. No wonder that in 90 percent of exclusionary cases, the police do not know what the law is.

THE RIGHT TO COUNSEL   The Sixth Amendment provides for the right to counsel. Rothwax agrees it is essential that there be a right to counsel, but the amendment does not say it has to be during police questioning and investigation. As a result of technicalities over this issue, he has seen murderers go free. Make it clear, he argues, that the right to an attorney should not be a factor in the investigative stage but only in pretrial and trial stages.

INSTRUCTIONS TO THE JURY   In the O.J. Simpson trial, Judge Lance Ito instructed the jury that Simpson's failure to take the stand in his own defense should not be taken to mean anything negative or to draw any other adverse conclusion. This instruction occurs in every trial in which a defendant does not take the stand, based on a Supreme Court ruling in 1981 that said not to do so amounted to a violation of the Fifth Amendment. The Fifth Amendment states that no person shall be forced to testify against him- or herself. Rothwax points out, however, that the Fifth Amendment does not say that one might not draw reasonable inferences from the silence of a defendant. He thinks we must find a way to return to the standard that existed before, that the judge could tell the jury that the failure to explain could amount to an inability to explain.

Rothwax would like to see other changes to the jury system, including:

> Unanimous jury verdicts should no longer be required. Rothwax cites a murder trial he presided over to support his position of not requiring unanimous jury verdicts. He claims that in this one case the evidence of guilt was

overwhelming and yet there was a hung jury. One juror was convinced the defendant was not guilty. How did she know? Well, as she explained it, "Someone that good-looking could not commit such a crime." The case had to be retried and the defendant was quickly found guilty.

Peremptory challenges to prospective jurors should be strictly limited or abolished. Peremptory challenges allow lawyers to knock someone off the jury without giving any reason. Rothwax uses the O.J. Simpson jury to make his point that this process makes it possible to stack a jury so that the most educated juror is excused, and you end up with a jury that can be manipulated to accept innuendo as evidence.[72]

The Limits of Correctional Reform

"The American correctional system today appears to offer minimum protection to the public and maximum harm to the offender," the 1973 Standards and Goals Commission declared in its summary report. "The system is plainly in need of substantial and rapid change."[73] It always has been.

Except for a brief period of euphoria in the early nineteenth century, when penal reformers from around the world came to the United States to study the American invention, the penitentiary, there never has been a time when the correctional system was not in need of rapid and substantial change. Since the republic was founded, historian David Rothman has written, each generation has produced "a dedicated coterie" of prison reformers. Yet each generation "discovers anew the scandals of incarceration, each sets out to correct them and each passes on a legacy of failure. The rallying cries of one period echo dismally into the next."[74]

The Medical Model

The accepted theory of corrections for much of the last century was based on the medical model. In its simplest terms, the medical model assumed offenders to be sick (physically, mentally, and/or socially); offenses were considered a manifestation or symptom of illness, a cry for help. It was believed that early and accurate diagnosis followed by prompt and effective therapeutic intervention ensured a positive prognosis—rehabilitation. Diagnosis was the function of the presentence investigation; therapeutic intervention was decreed in the sentence and made more specific in the treatment plan devised by the correction officers; and the parole board decided (within certain legal constraints) when the patient was to be discharged back into the community as cured.

However, today, in keeping with the trend toward the conservative position, there is a shift away from the medical model to a new approach that says that justice should be based on individual responsibility, with uniform penalties consistently imposed for like crimes. Out would go the indeterminate sentence (in which the number of years to be served is not fixed, as opposed to the determinate sentence, in which the length of the term is set by law), virtually unlimited judicial discretion, parole, and coerced participation in rehabilitation programs. Deterrence, retribution, and incapacitation would be respectable rationalizations for imprisonment; but in general, long prison terms would be reserved only for the habitually violent.

Three-Strikes Laws and Changing Public Attitudes

The shift from rehabilitation is due in part to changed attitudes among professionals. It is also due to changing attitudes of the public and lawmakers. Frightened by rising crime rates, the American public is demanding, in effect, that retribution replace rehabilitation as the purpose of incarceration. Apparently, the public's sense of fairness, fitness, and justice has turned to a punitive mood and a suspicion, bordering on contempt, about the workings of the justice system. The Victims' Bill of Rights passed by California voters in June 1982 was one example of the growing public frustration toward criminal offenders. Since then, many of its provisions have been enacted elsewhere in the country.

In 1996 President Clinton announced his support for a constitutional amendment to give victims a larger role in proceedings against the people accused of harming them. This was the only constitutional amendment Clinton supported while president. "The justice system," he argued, "too often ignores the victims of crime—millions and millions of people who are completely innocent." [75] The proposed Kyle-Feinstein amendment would have guaranteed crime victims and their families the right to be present at all critical stages of a suspect's court proceedings; the right to testify at any parole or probation hearing or plea-bargaining conference; the right to be informed of a defendant's release or escape; the right to full restitution from the offender, if possible; the right to protection from intimidation or retaliation from the accused; the right to a speedy trial; and the right to be informed promptly of these rights.

The Kyle-Feinstein amendment died on the Senate floor, with Vice President Al Gore taking some of the blame during his 2000 presidential campaign. Gore proposed his own constitutional amendment, which called for many of the same rights as those spelled out in the Kyle-Feinstein amendment. President Bush has yet to indicate if he will support a similar amendment. Thirty-two states have enacted some form of victim rights as of 2002.

Certainly, by the mid-1970s and continuing to the present day, the idea of just desserts was enjoying a certain vogue. Punishment, the argument went, should fit the crime and be based on no other criteria. This will, it is argued, increase respect for the law and thus deter crime. Many elected officials used these claims in promoting mandatory sentencing laws. The result has been more people going to jail, resulting in overcrowded prisons and minimal reduction in crime.

An important approach to strengthening the laws on sentencing came in the form of "three strikes and you're out" laws. The target of these laws were repeat offenders, particularly those prone to acts of violence. It is interesting to note that the federal government, not the states, was the first to pass a three-strikes law. It is unusual for the federal government to take the lead on these matters. The federal provision—which is not too different from three-strikes laws at the state level—requires mandatory life in prison for career violent offenders convicted of federal crimes such as bank robbery and smuggling. In 2002, three-strikes laws were on the books in half the states, supported by an electorate fed up with crime. California voted in the nation's toughest three strikes law in 1994. The U.S. Supreme Court agreed to review California's law; the Court's decision is due by the end of June 2003. The Court will hear the case based largely on the question whether the constitutional ban on cruel and unusal punishment as interpreted by the Court in 1991, as a prohibition on sentences that are "grossly disproportionate to the crime," allows a state to impose a tougher sentence for an offense committed by someone with a history of serious crimes.

Clearly, the purpose of these laws was to ensure longer prison sentences and greater punishment for those who have been convicted of serious and violent felonies. In some states, however, the reality is that there is not enough room in existing prisons to house the new influx of repeat offenders. On December 31, 2001, state prisons were operating between 1 percent and 16 percent above capacity, while Federal prisons were operating at 31 percent above capacity.[76] As most state three-strikes laws are not tied to building new prison facilities, local authorities have sometimes been forced to release other inmates early to make room for those convicted under three-strikes laws.

Prisons are not the only element of the criminal justice system overwhelmed by the three-strikes laws. Prosecutors and the courts are feeling the pinch, as well. Literally thousands of cases are cramming an already taxed system. Why? Because defendants charged with their third felony are going to trial rather than enter into plea bargains, knowing they face the possibility of a life sentence. While prosecutors have the authority to decide if a defendant will be charged with a felony (most three-strikes laws require the third strike and at least one of the two previous convictions to be a felony) or a misdemeanor (or request of the court that a previous felony conviction be reduced to a misdemeanor), most are reluctant to appear "soft" on crime and, therefore, go with the more serious charge. Consequently, already understaffed and overworked prosecutors are burdened with even heavier caseloads.

It is still too early to judge the "three strikes and you're out" experiment as a success or failure in reducing violent crime rates. Proponents of the three-strikes laws (and tougher sentencing laws generally) argue that the recent decline in crime rates (particularly violent crimes) is due to three-strikes laws. Critics are skeptical of this claim, suggesting instead that the improved economy and aging population better explain declining crime rates. They argue that, as the next wave of children reach their teenage years, the crime rate will climb once again. Indeed, crime did creep up in 2001—although it is too early to know if this is a trend or an anomaly. Furthermore, those critical of "get tough" laws such as three-strikes point out that the costs associated with these laws far outweigh the benefits to society. The escalating costs to prosecute and imprison offenders is not worth the relatively small reduction in crime rates that we have seen in recent years—even if this reduction in crime can be attributed to tougher sentencing laws.

POLICE: ON THE FRONT LINES AND UNDER FIRE

The greatest loser in the O.J. Simpson trial was the Los Angeles Police Department—and by extension, police around the country. Even before the Simpson trial, Americans had ambivalent feelings about the police. They are necessary to our safety, yet they also threaten us. We see them as threatening because by law they are implementers of violent force and have the potential to wield extraordinary power. The police are the most powerful of all criminal justice actors, largely because of the great amount of discretion available to them. They can deprive individuals of freedom, and under certain circumstances, society permits them to injure and even kill. The police are the most visible, the most pressured, and often, the most maligned actors in the criminal justice system.

After public schools, the police are the best-known agency of government. They are also the least understood. As a result, Americans have come to expect far more of the police than they can possibly deliver. As Robert diGrazia, the once controversial department chief of Montgomery County, Maryland (and former police chief of Boston and St. Louis), told a group of his fellow chiefs, "We are not letting the public in on our era's dirty little secret," namely, "that there is little the police can do about crime."[77] He may have been exaggerating for rhetorical effect—but not by much. The evidence suggests that traditional remedies simply will not work.

For example, short of creating a police state, there was no reason to believe putting 100,000 more officers on the street as required under former President Clinton's Violent Crime Control and Law Enforcement Act of 1994 would affect the amount of street crime. The 58 American cities with populations of more than 250,000 average 3.4 officers per 1,000 residents. Individual departments however, vary in size from 1.7 to 7.0 officers per 1,000 people; there is no observable correlation between the number of police a community has and either the number of crimes that are committed or the proportion of those crimes that are solved. In a controlled experiment conducted in Kansas City, moreover, the Police Foundation found that doubling or tripling the visible police presence had no effect on the number of crimes committed, or on people's feelings of safety.[78]

New technology does not help, either. Since the mid-1960s, police departments have invested huge sums in computerized telecommunication systems designed to cut the period that elapses between the time a citizen calls the police to report a crime and the time a patrol car arrives at the scene. Cutting a police department's response time, however, does little good when, as researchers have discovered, crime victims wait 20 minutes before they call. The emphasis on mobility and rapid response time has kept police officers locked up inside their patrol

A CLOSER LOOK

What is your image of the police? How did you develop your attitudes (positive or negative) about the police? Parents? Television? Personal experience? Experience of friends? Interview classmates to learn if they have a different attitude toward police. Explore any differences of opinion, if they exist. Talk with an international student, an immigrant, or someone of an ethnic minority to learn if he or she is worried about mistreatment as a result of the anti-terrorism laws enacted since September 11, 2001.

cars and reduced person-to-person contact between the police and citizens, thereby hampering police officers' ability to prevent or solve crimes.[79] This is why many police departments in recent years have gone back to neighborhood foot patrols and greater police-citizen interaction.

Contrary to the views of Judge Harold Rothwax discussed earlier, many believe repealing the exclusionary rule would not make the police any more effective in their war against crime.[80] Despite loud and frequent complaints, the police have not been handcuffed by the rulings of the Warren Court. Except for minor drug offenses, there is no evidence to suggest that the police make fewer arrests or that prosecutors secure fewer convictions because of Supreme Court decisions safeguarding the rights of the accused. On the contrary, the evidence runs the other way.

The real message is that for all their macho image, the police are heavily— in some ways, almost totally—dependent on the people being policed. Because they rarely come upon a crime in progress, police depend on members of the public for knowledge that a crime has been committed. They are equally dependent on victims, witnesses, and other informants for knowledge of who offenders are and where they might be found.[81] Think about the many high-profile cases in recent years that were solved because a relative (as in the case of the Unabomber) or other informants identified the suspect to the police.

The closer police are to the people on their beats, the more people they know; and the more these people trust them, the greater their chances of reducing crime. Police cannot solve a crime if they do not know it has been committed—and the majority of Americans do not report the crimes in which they are the victims. Those who do report a crime usually do not do so immediately, thereby giving the offender (and perhaps potential witnesses) time to get away.

The greatest problem facing police today is their tarnished image as a result of cases such as the O.J. Simpson trial and the Rodney King beating in 1991, or the rash of police scandals that have rocked major cities across the country in the past several years. White America became aware of what African Americans have always known—police brutality and abuse of power is not uncommon, at least not in their neighborhoods. White parents, certainly of middle- and upper-middle-class status, traditionally teach their children that the police are their friends in time of trouble. African American parents are much less likely to provide similar advice to their children. An astounding number of African American males have grown up believing that police harassment is a real threat and there is no sure immunity from it—not social status, not wealth, not geography.

Clearly, the videotaped beating of Rodney King (and there have been other videotapes showing police brutality since that fateful day) and the Simpson trial brought into chilling focus the reality of police misconduct and renewed fears that any African American, anywhere, anytime, might be the subject of police abuse. Some people, particularly within the African American community, say that because blacks are more likely to be arrested than any other group, that is evidence of racial bias in the criminal justice system. They also argue that the more African Americans are regarded as potential suspects, the more the innocent fear being on a collision course with police.

However, as we have said, criminals are in many ways worse today than in previous times. The police, particularly inner-city police, are faced with a new, more violent, more death-embracing hatred among many criminals. In fighting these violent forces, police officers must play the role of combat soldiers, referees, psychologists, urban negotiators, social workers, doctors, older brothers or older sisters. This is not an easy task for mere mortals—leading to levels of stress unknown in most other professions. The stress of being a police officer in an increasingly no-win battle causes high rates of alcoholism, heart attacks and other serious health problems, divorce, and suicide.

It is known, however, that some are attracted to police work because they are bullies and/or racists looking for the opportunity to push other people around. These are the rotten apples of law enforcement. Stress-management programs and system reform will not help them. They simply need to be identified and fired. This is not easily done, however, because of the code of silence among police. Also, most police officers agree that brutality would not go on if the department administration did not approve it or at least tolerate it. Civilian review boards are potentially powerful watchdogs over local police forces. Most police review boards consist of citizens appointed by a mayor; they investigate and hear cases of alleged abuses committed by the police. By removing the investigation and hearing outside police departments, it is expected that citizen review boards will bring a measure of objectivity and neutrality to their work. This is essential if they are to win credibility with the general public. Unfortunately, a strong bias in favor of the police has been documented for some review boards, and this casts a negative shadow over the others.[82]

CITIZENS ARE TAKING TO THE FRONT LINES, TOO

Fortunately the police are not alone in fighting the crime battle. For more than two decades, we have seen a growing public awareness of the need to take an active role in helping the police prevent crime. For example, there are many more community crime-stopping programs than in the past. The purpose of these programs is to train neighbors in the best techniques for alerting the police and in protecting each other's property. Other efforts include auxiliary police patrols, taxi radio networks, and other types of voluntary patrol efforts—all of which increase the "eyes on the street." In general these programs have been successful, particularly when local law enforcement agencies have worked with them in support of their efforts. There is evidence that most of the programs have contributed to a slight reduction in crime rates and certainly have gone a long way toward improving public confidence and feelings of security.

One of the more successful crime prevention programs is community policing. This is why former President Clinton increased funding for community policing by $1.3 billion in his Violent Crime Control and Law Enforcement Act of 1994. Community policing is a partnership between the police and the public working together in a joint effort to prevent crime and promote safety. This program is catching on in cities large and small around the country. Its value lies in raising the visibility of police on the streets and in providing residents a voice in setting police priorities and in playing an important role in keeping the peace in their neighborhoods. In Clinton's words:

> At last we have begun to find a way to reduce crime, forming community partnerships with local police forces to catch criminals and prevent crime. This strategy, called community policing, is clearly working. Violent crime is coming down all across America. In New York City murders are down 25 percent; in St. Louis, 18 percent; in Seattle, 32 percent. But we still have a long way to go before our streets are safe and our people are free from fear. The Crime Bill of 1994 is critical to the success of community policing. It provides funds for 100,000 new police in communities of all sizes. We're already a third of the way there. And I challenge the Congress to finish the job. Let us stick with a strategy that's working and keep the crime rate coming down.[83]

In July 1996 Clinton announced that the cellular phone industry had agreed to donate 50,000 phones to help neighborhoods fight crime. Why? Because even though there are citizen watch volunteers working in about 20,000 neighborhoods around the country to keep an eye on their streets and report problems to local police or fire departments, they often are slow in reporting what they see because they are not near a phone. The donated cell phones were preprogrammed to local law enforcement and other emergency numbers. The idea was that any citizen patrollers who encountered an emergency or some other suspicious circumstance could call for help immediately. The phones were provided to groups certified by the Community Policing Consortium (CPC) through the Cellular Telecommunications Industry Association.

Another important area of involvement has been in dispute resolution and crime prevention. Again, we are seeing growing support for citizen involvement in these difficult and time-consuming activities. Perhaps the best example of dispute resolution programs is found in San Francisco. The citizen-run Community

Board Program, founded in 1976, takes on a wide range of simple and complex local mediations. Issues brought before the volunteer mediation forums range from simple nuisance disputes to resolution of gang and racial conflicts. The forums routinely deal with the desire of local groups to rid their neighborhoods of drug pushers and similar local social-control issues. Severe unsolved crimes, of course, remain the province of the professional police and courts. The forums also pay attention to remedying conditions that can lead to victimization.

The lesson to be learned is clear: the more we support community efforts in preventing crime, reforming young offenders, and assisting victims, the more likely it is the crime battle will be won. If history tells us anything, it is that the police and courts cannot do it alone. Certainly citizen involvement in local crime prevention is one of the most promising developments on the anticrime scene today.

Both Democrats and Republicans want to appear tough on crime these days. That is why former President Clinton's crime agenda was similar to the Reagan-Bush agendas in many important respects. We have every reason to think that President George W. Bush's crime policies will reflect those of his immediate predecessors, including his father's. For example, both political parties agree that more police on the streets, stricter sentencing laws, a shorter appeals process for capital offenses, and a greater number of crimes classified as capital offenses are good for the country. Where Clinton differed from his Republican predecessors is on the important issue of gun control and in his nominees for federal judgeships and the Supreme Court. Clinton's support for drug rehabilitation programs and youth-oriented programs also separated his administration from the Reagan-Bush administrations. Understandably, George W. Bush's appointments to the bench and his positions on gun control and drug rehabilitation programs are (except for the Office of Faith-Based Initiatives) more like Reagan's and his father's.

When Clinton was first elected president, the Brady Handgun Violence Prevention Bill had long been blocked in Congress by strong opposition led by the Republican Party and the National Rifle Association. Named after James Brady, the former White House press secretary shot in the head and permanently paralyzed in the 1981 assassination attempt on President Reagan, the act requires a five-day waiting period on all handgun sales in the United States. Not only does the wait serve as a cooling-off period for a new gun owner in the event there is a sinister reason for the purchase, but more important, the act requires all would-be handgun purchasers to submit to a criminal background check. The legislation called for $200 million a year to computerize criminal background information so that an instant-check system could be created by 1998.

Convinced that the Brady Bill could be an effective way to reduce gun-related crimes, Clinton had publicly supported the legislation even before his first election in 1992. That year's statistics on handgun deaths were persuasive indeed. In countries with strong gun laws, the handgun death rates were low: Great Britain, 33 people killed; Sweden, 36; Switzerland, 97; Japan, 60; Australia, 13; and Canada, 128. In the United States 13,220 people were killed by handguns in that same year. In 1993 the total number of people killed in the United States by some type of firearm, including handguns, was 39,595. The Clinton administration helped to finally overcome NRA and Republican opposition to the Brady Bill, and Congress passed it in December 1993. The Bureau of Alcohol, Tobacco, and Fire-arms (BATF) released its "Brady Law First Anniversary Survey" in February 1995. The survey canvassed 30 jurisdictions across the United States and revealed that, since the bill's passage, 3.5 percent of individuals applying for gun purchases had applications denied. Among those stopped from obtaining handguns: 4,365 con-victed felons, 945 fugitives from justice, 649 illegal drug users, 97 persons under indictment, and 63 persons under temporary restraining orders for alleged stalk-ing. The BATF projected from this limited sample that the Brady Law had stopped approximately 70,000 convicted felons, drug offenders, and fugitives from mak-ing over-the-counter purchases of handguns.

A similar survey of 22 law enforcement agencies in 15 states was conducted on the second anniversary of the Brady Law. This 1995 survey found that just in these jurisdictions, nearly 15,000 felons and other prohibited puchasers were stopped from buying handguns.[84] California, which has had at least a five-day waiting period for handgun purchases since 1965, experienced a greater decrease in homicide rates (17.5 percent) in 1998 than the rest of the country (7.4 percent), according to FBI crime reports.

Clinton also waged a successful battle against the NRA and the Republicans in winning approval of the Assault Weapons Ban, a provision in his 1994 Violent Crime Control and Law Enforcement Act. The ban prohibits the sale, transfer, or importation of 19 military-style assault weapons. Banned weapons include the AK-47, Uzi submachine gun, revolving-cylinder shotguns such as the "Street Sweeper" and "Striker 12," as well as the deadly TEC-9 assault pistol, capable of firing more than 50 times before reloading. In answer to the NRA's concern that Americans will be denied access to guns for hunting and self-protection, the As-sault Weapons Ban provision lists 650 legitimate sporting weapons that are pro-tected under the law.[85] Domestic gun manufacturers, under this provision, have been prohibited from producing assault weapons and ammunition clips holding more than ten rounds since September 1994. While it is possible to purchase as-sault weapons and ammunition clips holding more than ten rounds manufactured before September 1994, the price of these weapons has nearly tripled—costing more than $2,000 in some cases. The Assault Weapons Ban resulted in an 18 per-cent decline in assault weapons crimes in 1995.[86]

Proponents of even stronger gun control laws favor creating a national bal-listics database. They believe such a database would have helped law enforce-ment to identify the two snipers who terrorized the Washington, D.C., area and killed at least ten people over a two-month period in 2002. They also would like to see an even stronger background check system that would require checks for all gun sales to keep prohibited people from falling through the cracks. For ex-ample, John Allen Williams (also known as John Allen Mohammad), alleged to be one of the Washington, D.C., snipers, was subject to a domestics violence re-straining order, which makes it illegal for him to own or purchase a firearm. He managed to buy one despite the restraining order. Those who favor stronger gun legislation argue that police need more time to check records and the records need to be updated and computerized. Those opposed to gun control suggest that a national ballistics database would not work because every time a gun is fired, the gun barrel leaves a different "fingerprint" on the bullet, rendering such a database useless.

Political pundits believe that many Republican congressional candidates lost in the 1996 elections because of their strong pro-NRA, pro-gun positions. Bob Dole's support for the NRA and his opposition to the Brady Bill and the Assault Weapons Ban were important reasons why a majority of women supported Clinton for reelection. In recent years, public opinion has swung against the NRA's knee-jerk reaction to any attempt at regulating guns—particularly weapons for which there can be no other purpose but to kill people. That said, one reason given for Gore's defeat to President Bush in 2000 was his strong support for gun control. Gore did not carry many of the states in which there are large numbers of hunters and members of the NRA, including his own state of Tennessee.

Former President Clinton also deviated from Reagan and Bush in his appointment of federal judges and Supreme Court justices. The watchword of the Reagan and Bush administrations was judicial restraint—the view that judges should limit themselves strictly to interpreting the law and avoid more-activist stands, such as telling a country how to run its schools or prisons. Critics, however, saw their administrations as using the justice system as a tool for achieving their social agendas, including such emotionally charged issues as abortion, drug enforcement, and affirmative action while sacrificing basic civil liberties. President George W. Bush nominated 66 individuals to be federal judges by March 2002, all of whom reflected his conservative philosophy on issues such as abortion and stricter law and order. Many of these nominees were very controversial and found their confirmation hearings rough going. If a seat or seats open on the Supreme Court, Bush will very likely choose jurists who favor judicial restraint. Critics of Bush are particularly concerned about attacks on our basic civil liberties as the result of the war on terorrism.

Reagan, Bush I, Clinton, and Bush II Judges: How They Compare

The most potent legacy from the Reagan and Bush presidencies is the literally hundreds of federal judges and six Supreme Court justices (O'Connor, Rehnquist, Scalia, Kennedy, Souter, and Thomas) appointed by them. A rapid court expansion that coincided with their administrations and the high turnover of federal judges enabled Reagan and Bush to nominate more than half of the 761-member U.S. judiciary. Most nominees were conservative white males who have reversed many of the decisions of the more liberal judges they replaced.

In decisions ranging from what schools children should attend to the rights of suspects stopped by police, these judges have played powerful roles in the everyday lives of citizens. For example, a clear turn in the direction of the law occurred in three major areas: criminal justice, civil rights, and business regulation. Sentences for lawbreakers are longer, programs to boost minority jobs have been challenged, and business faces fewer government regulations.

In his first term in office, Clinton made less than half the judicial appointments (147) at the district and appellate levels that Reagan and Bush did. Not surprisingly,

Clinton's appointments differed in many important respects from those made by his two predecessors. The American Bar Association (ABA) gave Clinton's appointees the highest combined competence rating of any group since President Dwight Eisenhower. Clinton's judges were a diverse group, with the largest number of minority and women appointments in history. They were moderate to liberal in political orientation, as opposed to the much more conservative appointments of the Reagan-Bush administrations.[87]

Clinton was the first Democratic president to make a Supreme Court appointment in a generation. The appointment of a Supreme Court justice is one of the most important and certainly the longest-lasting decisions a president makes. Clinton chose a woman, Ruth Bader Ginsburg, in June 1993. First appointed to the court of appeals by President Carter in 1980, she is considered a centrist in her legal philosophy and a consensus builder on an often divided court. As a practicing attorney, she had a strong record as a litigator on behalf of women's rights, including having a role in winning virtually every Supreme Court case in the 1970s that invalidated laws discriminating against women. She is a strong advocate of a woman's right to choose in abortion cases.

In 1994 Clinton was able to make his second appointment to the Supreme Court—Stephen Breyer. Like Justice Ginsburg, Breyer received the ABA's highest rating, and he too was swiftly confirmed by the U.S. Senate. Experts on the Supreme Court agree that Clinton's appointments have moved the court toward the center, providing a balance against the more conservative jurists who joined the court during the Reagan-Bush administrations.[88]

As of January 2002 President George W. Bush had sent 66 judicial nominations to the Senate Judiciary Committee. The Senate had confirmed 28 of them (22 trial level and 6 appellate level). These 66 nominees were strict constructionists and conservative on controversial issues such as abortion. This is in keeping with Bush's judicial appointments as governor of Texas and with his campaign promise that, if elected president, he would appoint judges that would interpret rather than make law. It is reasonable to expect that he will nominate conservative justices to the Supreme Court, if the opportunity presents itself. He may have that opportunity in his first term as president, and definitely would if reelected in 2004. It is predicted that he will be in a position to appoint two to four justices, given the age of several sitting justices. The four Texas Supreme Court justices appointed by Bush favor big business over consumer protection, for example. One of the most telling features of the Bush administration in regard to judicial appointments is the fact that he dispensed with the practice of having the American Bar Association review judicial nominees. No Republican president in modern times has taken that action.

Changes in the Law

Presidents Ronald Reagan, George H. Bush, and Bill Clinton each pressured Congress to pass strong anticrime bills to show the public they were tough on criminals and supportive of victims. In 1984, after years of inaction on reforming U.S. criminal laws, Congress, with pressure from the Reagan administration, passed a tough anticrime bill. The law permits judges to deny bail to suspects whom they consider dangerous, makes it harder to escape conviction by pleading insanity, and sets in motion an overhaul of federal sentencing laws aimed at making penalties more consistent. The law also allows the government to confiscate offenders' property and share proceeds with local agencies.

In 1991, Congress, this time with pressure from the Bush administration, passed an even tougher anticrime bill. However, it was not tough enough to satisfy the conservatives who, in turn, pressured Bush to veto the legislation. The Bush administration sought, among other things, to limit convicts' appeals and allow prosecutors to use evidence seized without a warrant (a 1992 Supreme Court ruling allows for illegally seized evidence to be used in the sentencing phase of a trial). Bush also wanted harsher penalties for drug users, and he stepped up law enforcement as well as stricter death penalty and government seizure laws.

Perhaps the most significant change in the law is the government's right to someone's property if they are suspected of a crime—usually drug related. Under federal seizure law, your cash and belongings are the government's if you fit a vague description of a drug runner (a description that is heavily weighted against minorities), if you have cash tainted by drugs (which is true of most all U.S. currency), or if you have property that was used in the commission of a crime, even if you were not involved. To win back your property, you must sue the government in federal court to prove you are innocent. Cases may take months, if not years, and there is no guarantee you will win. Every crime package passed since 1984 has expanded the uses of forfeiture, and now more than 100 federal and state statutes are on the books. Forfeiture goes beyond drug cases, now covering such things as money laundering, fraud, gambling, importing tainted meats, and carrying intoxicants onto land owned by or under the jurisdiction of Native Americans.

The Reagan and Bush budgets also gave crime a top priority. While spending by most civilian agencies came under the ax, Justice Department funds grew by $1.2 billion between 1982 and 1985. The increase in dollars was double that between 1987 and 1990, with an increase of $2.4 billion. Most of the increased spending went for law enforcement, including a beefed-up counterintelligence force. Clinton continued this commitment to increased spending for the criminal justice system, including funding more prison construction, the hiring of more police officers, and providing for prevention and rehabilitation programs.

Not to be outdone by his Republican predecessors and aware that crime remained Americans' greatest concern, Clinton introduced into Congress and eventually won approval of his own crime bill—the Violent Crime Control and Law Enforcement Act of 1994. Considered by many the most comprehensive crime measure in U.S. history, its features include:

100,000 NEW POLICE OFFICERS   A key provision provides funding for 100,000 new police officers nationwide.

COMMUNITY POLICING   Funding was increased by $1.3 billion for community policing, a partnership between the police and the public working together in a joint effort to prevent crime and promote safety. Catching on in cities large and small around the country, community policing not only increases police visibility in the streets, but also gives residents a voice in setting police priorities and a contributing role in keeping the peace in their neighborhoods.

THREE STRIKES AND YOU'RE OUT   This federal provision requires mandatory life in prison for career violent offenders convicted of federal crimes such as bank robbery and smuggling. Three-strikes laws are on the books in more than a dozen states, pushed forth by an electorate fed up with crime. (See the earlier discussion.)

FEDERAL PRISON CONSTRUCTION   Additional funding was earmarked for the construction of more federal prisons, needed to house the increased inmate population anticipated from the new three-strikes law.

DEATH PENALTY EXPANSION   The number of offenses punishable by the death penalty was expanded by nearly 60 additional categories of violent felons, including terrorists, drug kingpins, and murderers of federal law-enforcement officers.

CREATION OF THE NATIONAL POLICE CORPS   The institution of the National Police Corps helps put military personnel and unemployed veterans to work in law enforcement.

PREVENTION AND REHABILITATION   More money is used to fund drug treatment programs for criminal addicts and boot camps for youthful offenders.

VIOLENCE AGAINST WOMEN ACT   As an integral part of his anticrime legislative package, the president signed this act to provide new grants to bolster local law enforcement and prosecutors and a multitude of victims' services. The act tripled funding for battered women's shelters, improved police and court response to domestic violence crimes, added lighting in public places, and required sex offenders to pay restitution. To coordinate these various new programs, the act provided for the Justice Department to establish a Violence against Women Office.

NATIONAL DOMESTIC VIOLENCE HOTLINE   The Clinton administration established this 24-hour hotline service (800-799-7233) to provide callers with immediate crisis information, counseling, and referrals. Operators offer information on domestic violence, emergency shelters, legal advocacy, assistance programs, and social services. The issue of domestic violence cannot be fully addressed, Clinton stated in July 1996, until the nation's "completely overburdened" 911 emergency number system is fixed. The majority of callers to 911 misuse the system—calling for nonemergencies. At the same time, victims who need immediate police help often receive busy signals. The president recommended that police departments work with local phone companies to come up with another easy-to-remember number for residents to contact police for nonemergency calls.

ASSAULT WEAPONS BAN   Perhaps the hardest-fought provision of Clinton's first-term crime agenda was the Assault Weapons Ban. Like the Brady Bill, it was vehemently opposed by the NRA, which expressed concern for Americans who enjoy hunting. Proponents of the ban claimed that assault weapons are designed and manufactured only to "hurt people." The ban prohibits the sale, transfer, or importation of 19 military-style assault weapons, much like the rifles used in the recent massacres in Scotland and Australia in which the loss of life totaled 42 unsuspecting people, half of whom were children under eight years of age.[89]

While it is still too early to say with certainty which crime policies President George W. Bush's administration will promote, we are able to speculate based on his tenure as governor of Texas and his campaign promises. There is little question that Bush will be a tough "law and order" president, much like Reagan and his father. As governor of Texas, he focused considerable attention on juvenile crime. Bush also sought and signed into law "comprehensive juvenile justice reform, tougher sex offender laws, longer sentences for violent repeat offenders, and zero tolerance for drunk driving."[90] Bush promised to phase out Clinton's initiative to put 100,000 more police officers on the streets—in part to make up for lost revenue due to his massive tax reduction plan adopted by Congress in 2001.

Critics of the Get-Tough Approach to Crime Prevention

Those opposed to the Reagan, Bush, Clinton, and Bush efforts to unhobble prosecutors, stiffen penalties, limit appeals, and compensate crime victims argue that the streets will be no safer and that in the process our civil liberties have been jeopardized. As we said earlier in this chapter, tougher punishment of more criminals is not universally recognized as the best approach to reducing crime. Critics of the punishment approach look to crime data to show that the impact on crime has been extremely modest and not worth the economic and human costs. They argue, for example, that, if the $44 billion spent each year by federal, state, and local governments for prisons and police was used instead for an array of social programs, such as Head Start, there would be less crime. Clinton was sympathetic to this position and therefore supported increased funding for prevention and rehabilitation programs. In effect, he wanted to do it all. As we said earlier, he even supported a constitutional amendment to give victims a larger role in proceedings against the people accused of harming them.

Those who support a social policy approach to crime admit that it is expensive, but not as costly as prison cells costing $90,000 apiece to build, plus thousands of dollars a year to maintain and operate. Social policy experts echo the traditional liberal view that social ills cause the problems that produce crime. They would say that "determining interest rates, allocating tax burdens and setting the minimum wage together have more long-term impact on crime rates than adjusting sentence lengths and putting more police on the street."[91] Critics of the conservative's emphasis on stricter punishment admit, however, that there is little hope in the near term for a debate about the social causes of the problem. The public and, therefore, politicians are preoccupied with the carnage they see everyday on their streets.

A FINAL WORD

There is no doubt that the United States is a violent country. A comparison of U.S. crime statistics with those of other economically developed countries rather dramatically shows our high level of violence and crime. While street crime may be more visible and cause us to be fearful, it is not the only crime that should concern us. Ironically, white collar crime is far more pervasive and costly than street crime, yet it receives far less attention from the justice system, the press, and the public—that is, until 2000 to 2002, when the public learned of corporate corruption on an epidemic scale.

Hundreds of billions of dollars and tens of thousands of jobs were lost because of corrupt practices at the highest levels of America's largest corporations and, in at least the case of Enron, the collusion of its auditors at Arthur Andersen—at the time one of the nation's big five accounting firms. Because so many major corporations were caught in illegal practices of one kind or another and because the cost to individual employees and stockholders reached record levels, law enforcement, politicians, and the public took notice. The most serious and long-term impact of these corporate scandals was the loss of public confidence in our economic system and relevant regulatory agencies. The greatest challenge, therefore, is to restore public trust in our business and political leaders.

With the crime rate still very high (and on the rise again, at least in 2001) and our jails and prisons overflowing with inmates, there is every sign that the justice system remains ineffective. There are those who say the system can never be made effective. Solutions have been proposed, and some have been tried, but few people are optimistic that any of them will make a significant difference in preventing crime or in rehabilitating criminals. In fact, critics say that high levels of crime are virtually built into the nature of our society. Racism, unequal economic opportunity, and poor living conditions breed crime, and unless the basic problems of our socioeconomic system are eliminated, rampant crime will continue. Other observers do not believe that the poverty-leads-to-crime theory is factually correct. They argue that crime skyrocketed during the 1960s, when Americans, including African Americans and other minorities, experienced considerable economic progress and opportunity. If anything, crime appears to be associated with more money and more social progress.

Another view of crime, also emphasizing its inevitability, sees the character of the population as the principle cause. According to this theory, young people (aged 11 to 25) traditionally have been likely to commit crime. Following World War II, the United States experienced a baby boom, and as these postwar children began reaching adolescence in the early 1960s, crime increased dramatically. During the 1960s and 1970s, the 11-to-25-year-old group comprised about a quarter of the population yet accounted for about 75 percent of those arrested for serious crimes. People who argue this theory say the only solution is time. Eventually, as rambunctious youths mature and the birth rate declines, crime will also recede. Even if the theory is true, there remain two problems. First, many of the same adolescents will have developed habitual criminal patterns and will therefore be likely to continue them into adulthood. The other problem is that many of us do not want to wait 15 to 20 years for these children to grow up.

Frequent proposals to reduce crime focus on rehabilitating criminals through such techniques as psychological counseling, behavior modification, job training, work-release programs, halfway houses, and education. Although some programs seem to work fairly well with certain types of people, the overall evaluation of rehabilitation efforts is pessimistic. Especially where hard-core criminals and repeat offenders are involved, rehabilitation efforts have produced meager results. It has proven very difficult to take people who have spent years being criminals and to transform them with a few months of therapy or vocational education. This is, of course, why three-strikes laws are so popular today.

The question on many minds today is, Can we stop or at least greatly reduce crime? The answer is a qualified yes, if we are willing to make some difficult choices. Experience has shown that crime can be drastically reduced if one is willing to bear the costs. For example, China once suffered from widespread opium addiction, but the problem was solved by making addiction a capital offense and then executing thousands of addicts. Opium addiction is no longer a problem. Years ago, city police controlled thefts by keeping poor juveniles out of wealthy neighborhoods because "they had no business being there." Such practices are now politically unacceptable to most people who see them as violations of a citizen's civil rights.

The real issue of effectiveness, then, is how we move between our concerns for freedom and privacy and our desire to eliminate crime. For example, some neighborhoods plagued by drug-related crimes have agreed to allow police cameras to be strategically placed in trees and telephone poles to observe street activities. While some are concerned these cameras could be rotated by the police to peer into the people's bedrooms and bathrooms, most residents are willing to trust that their privacy will not be violated in exchange for drug-free streets. An effective criminal justice system may be incompatible with a free and totally private society. And a free society would probably not last long unless people were reasonably well protected from crime. Obviously, this is not an easy conflict to resolve. The indication is, however, that, as violent crime increases (particularly outside the ghettos), people will sacrifice much of their freedom and privacy in return for protection against crime.

FOR MORE INFORMATION

Federal justice statistics, http://www.ojp.usdoj.gov.
President George W. Bush's public agenda, http://bushsupporter.gov.
Ayers, William. *A Kind and Just Parent: The Children of Juvenile Court.* Boston: Beacon Press, 1998.

Berns, Walter. *For Capital Punishment: Crime and the Morality of the Death Penalty*. New York: Basic Books, 1981.

Mauer, Marc. *Race to Incarcerate*. New York: The New Press, 1999.

Rosenblatt, Elihu. *Criminal Injustice: Confronting the Prison Crisis*. Boston: South End Press, 1996.

NOTES

1. Quoted in Bernard Gavzer, "We're in the Fight of Our Lives," *Parade,* July 28, 1996, 4.
2. *San Francisco Chronicle,* October 29, 2002, A4.
3. Ibid., 4.
4. Bureau of Justice Statistics, U.S. Department of Justice, "Criminal Sentencing Statistics," February 28, 2002, http://www.ojp.usdoj.gov/bjs/sent.htm, 1.
5. Florida Department of Corrections Statistics and Publications, "10-20 Life Criminals Sentenced to Florida's Prisons," May 2002, http://www.dc.state.fl.us/pub/10-20-life/bg .html, 1.
6. Bureau of Justice Statistics, U.S. Department of Justice, "Crime Statistics," September 17, 2002, http://www.dc.state-fl.us/pub/10-20-life/bg.html, 4.
7. Michael de Lourcy Hinds, "Number of Killings Soars in Big Cities Across U.S.," *New York Times,* July 18, 1990. A1, D20; and *San Jose Mercury News,* December 22, 1991, A4.
8. Bureau of Justice Statistics, U.S. Department of Justice, *Crime Statistics,* September 17, 2002, 1.
9. Ibid., 5.
10. Ibid., 4.
11. A longtime friend, who requested that her name not be used. She practices law in Los Angeles.
12. Howard N. Snyder, "Law Enforcement and Juvenile Crime," *Juvenile Offenders and Victims: National Report Series,* National Criminal Justice Reference Service, December 2001, http://www.ncjrs.org/html/ojjdp/nrs_bulletin/nrs_2001_12_1/contents.html, 1.
13. Bureau of Justice Statistics, U.S. Department of Justice, *Data Report,* 1989, 23.
14. *Report to the Nation on Crime and Justice,* 2nd ed., March 1988, 30.
15. David Anderson, "The Aggregate Burden of Crime," *Journal of Law and Economics,* October 1999, 1.
16. Ibid., 2.
17. Ibid.
18. Ibid.
19. Ibid.
20. Ibid.
21. NCS [National Crime Statistics] Data, 1995.
22. Bureau of Justice Statistics, U.S. Department of Justice, "Criminal Offenders Statistics," November 1, 2001, 3.
23. Susan Dentzer, "For Mercy's Sake, Let's Cover Kids," *U.S. News & World Report,* October 21, 1996, 69.
24. Federal Bureau of Investigation (FBI), *White Collar Crime: A Report to the Public* (Washington, DC: U.S. Department of Justice, 1990), 3.
25. FBI Jacksonville, "White-Collar Crime," October 25, 2002, http://jacksonville.fbi.gov/ wcc.htm, 1.
26. John F. Conklin, *Illegal but Not Criminal: Business Crime in America* (Englewood Cliffs, NJ: Prentice-Hall, 1977), 4.

27. Gary F. Glenn, "Crime Doesn't Pay," *Readings in Criminal Justice,* Annual Edition Series (Guilford, CT: Dushkin, 1982), 107.
28. *San Francisco Chronicle,* November 13, 1996, A1.
29. FBI Jacksonville, "White-Collar Crime," 1.
30. *San Francisco Chronicle,* October 27, 2002, G1.
31. Douglas W. Payne, "Drugs into Money into Power: A Global Challenge," *Freedom Review,* July–August 1996, 13.
32. Ibid.
33. *San Francisco Chronicle,* November 17, 1996, A4.
34. *San Francisco Chronicle,* November 5, 1996, A7.
35. Ibid.
36. *Washington Post,* March 14, 1990, A6.
37. Neal Karlen and Susan Agrest, "Assault on the Mafia," *Newsweek,* March 17, 1986, 25.
38. David Connor, "The War on Terrorism: Narco-Terrorism: How the Drug Trade Funds International Terrorism," Entertainment Industries Council, December 2001, http://eiconline.org/creative/spotlighton/newnormal, 1.
39. Svetlana Kolchik, "Exhibit Shows Ties between Terrorism, Drugs," *USA Today,* September 3, 2002, http://www.usatoday.com/travel/news/features/2002/2002-09-04-dea-exhibit.htm, 2.
40. C. S. Taylor, "Female Gangs: A Historical Perspective," in C. S. Taylor, ed., *Girls, Gangs, Women, and Drugs* (East Lansing: Michigan State University Press, 1993), 45.
41. Ibid.
42. C. E. Molidor, "Gender Differences of Psychological Abuse in High School Dating Relationships," *Child and Adolescent Social Work Journal,* October 1996, 238–251.
43. "How Much Does Organized Crime Cost Us," *Forbes,* September 30, 1980.
44. Snyder, "Law Enforcement and Juvenile Crime," http://www.ncjrs.org/pdffiles1/ojjdp/191031.pdf, 1.
45. *San Francisco Chronicle,* August 9, 1996, A2.
46. Richard Zoglin, "Now for the Bad News: A Teenage Time Bomb," *Time,* January 15, 1996, 52.
47. Ibid.
48. Ibid.
49. Ibid.
50. *San Francisco Chronicle,* January 10, 1992, D3.
51. *San Francisco Chronicle,* January 3, 1992, A1.
52. Christian E. Molidor, "Female Gang Members: A Profile of Aggression and Victimization," *Social Work,* vol. 41, no. 3, 1996, 253.
53. Ibid.
54. Emile Durkheim, *Suicide: A Study in Sociology,* trans. John A. Spaulding and George Simpson (1897; reprint, New York: Free Press, 1951). See also Robert K. Merton, *Social Theory and Social Structure,* rev. ed. (New York: Free Press, 1967).
55. The President's Commission on Law Enforcement and Administration of Justice, *Task Force Report: Crime and It's Impact—An Assignment* (Washington, DC: U.S. Government Printing Office, 1967). The relationship of race coupled with age to overall crime rates is so overpowering that Northeastern University criminologist James Alan Fox was able to project crime rates into the future with a model that employed only three exogenous variables. These were (1) the percent of the population that is nonwhite and aged 14 to 17, (2) the percent of the population that is nonwhite and aged 18 to 21, and (3) the consumer price index. Fox's model is not really that simple. In constructing it, he employed other pertinent data, such as previous local crime rates and the

size of area police forces. But the three variables highlighted are important because they are the only factors that have to be estimated for the future in order to make forecasts. Furthermore, the accuracy of the Fox model has been high.

56. Human Rights Watch, "Race and Incaraceration in the United States," Human Rights Watch Press Backgrounder, February 27, 2002, http://www.hrw.org/backgrounder/usa/race, 1.

57. Ibid., 1–2.

58. FBI, U.S. Department of Justice, *Crime in the United States—1995,* Uniform Crime Report, October 13, 1996.

59. Ibid.

60. Bureau of Justice Statistics, U.S. Department of Justice, "Summary Findings," Federal Justice Statistics, October 13, 1996, http://www.ojp.usdoj.gov/bjs/fed.htm, 1.

61. World Health Organization data for 1976–1981, in U.S. Census Bureau, *Statistical Abstract of the United States, 1984* (Washington, DC: Department of Commerce, 1983), 181.

62. Calculated from, Office of Criminal Justice Planning, State of California *Crime in California, 1971–1981* (Sacramento, 1983), A6; and U.S. Census Bureau, *Statistical Abstract of the United States, 1984,* 181.

63. Raymond Teske and Harold Arnold, "Comparison of the Criminal Statistics of the United States and the Federal Republic of Germany," *Journal of Criminal Justice,* vol. 10, 1982, 31.

64. Enrico Ferri, lecture given at the University of Naples, April 24, 1901, reprinted in Stanley E. Grupp, ed., *Theories of Punishment* (Bloomington: University of Indiana Press, 1971), 231–233.

65. Henry W. Anderson, "Separate Report of Henry W. Anderson," in National Commission on Law Observance and Enforcement (Wickersham Commission), Report no. 13, *Report on the Causes of Crime I* (1931; reprint, Montclair, NJ: Patterson Smith Reprint Series, 1968), LXVI, LXVIII.

66. See James Q. Wilson, *Thinking about Crime* (New York: Basic Books, 1975); and Ernest van den Haag, *Punishing Criminals: Concerning a Very Old and Painful Question* (New York: Basic Books, 1974).

67. Quoted in Raymond B. Fosdick, *American Policy System* (1920; reprint Montclair, NJ: Patterson Smith Reprint Series, 1972), 28.

68. Mark H. Haller, "Historical Roots of Police Behavior: Chicago, 1890–1925," *Law and Society Review,* vol. 10, 1976, 317–321. See also Yale Kamisar, "When the Cops Were Not Handcuffed," 1965, reprinted in Arthur Neiderhoffer and Abraham S. Blumberg, eds., *The Ambivalent Force: Perspectives on the Police* (San Francisco: Rhinehard Press, 1973), 312–317. On the nature and extent of policy brutality in the 1920s and early 1930s, see Zechariah Chaffee Jr., Walter N. Pollok, and Carl S. Stern, "The Third Degree," in National Commission on Law Observance and Enforcement (Wickersham Commission), Report no. 11, *Report on Lawlessness in Law Enforcement* (1931; reprint, Montclair, NJ: Patterson Smith Reprint Series, 1968), 13–261.

69. Gavzer, "We're in the Fight of Our Lives," 6.

70. Ibid.

71. Ibid., 5–6.

72. Ibid.

73. National Advisory Commission on Criminal Justice Standards and Goals, *Community Crime Prevention* (Washington, DC: U.S. Government Printing Office, 1973), 9.

74. David Rothman, "Decarcerating Prisoners and Patients," *Civil Liberties Review,* vol. 1, fall 1973, 8–9.

75. *San Francisco Chronicle,* July 10, 1996, A3.

76. Bureau of Justice Statistics, U.S. Department of Justice, "Prisoners in 2001," July 30, 2002, http://www.ojp.usdoj.gov/bjs/abstract/p01.htm, 1.

77. Robert J. diGrazia, "Police Leadership: Challenging Old Assumptions," *Washington Post,* November 10, 1976, 15.

78. See George L. Kelling, et al., *The Kansas City Preventive Patrol Experiment: A Summary Report* (Washington, DC: Police Foundation, 1974), 40–43; Kelling Pate and Tony Pate, "Response to the Davis Knowles Critique of the Kansas City Preventive Patrol Experiment," *The Police Chief,* June 1975, 33–34.

79. See Deborah K. Berman and Alexander Vargo, "Response-Time Analysis Study: Preliminary Findings on Robbery in Kansas City," *The Police Chief* June 1975, 36–41.

80. Under the exclusionary rule, evidence that was obtained illegally cannot be used in court. In a series of controversal decisions during the 1960s, the Supreme Court broadened the scope of the exclusionary rule. In *Miranda v. Arizona,* for example, the court ruled that police officers must inform defendants of their right to counsel. (After the Court's rulling, Miranda was tried and convicted a second time.) The Burger Court reversed many of the Warren Court decisions in this area.

81. David J. Bordua, "Comments on Police-Community Relations," *Law Enforcement Science and Technology, II* (New York: Port City Press, 1969), 118.

82. Jennifer Vogel, "The Pro-Police Review Board," *The Nation,* January 6–13, 1992, 18–22.

83. Bill Clinton, "State of the Union Address," January 23, 1996.

84. Thomas Blood and Bruce Henderson, *State of the Union: A Report on President Clinton's First Four Years in Office* (Santa Monica, CA: W. Quay Hays, 1996), 16–17.

85. Ibid., 19–20.

86. Ibid., 21.

87. Ibid., 25.

88. Ibid., 26.

89. Ibid., 17–19.

90. "Issues in George W. Bush's Vision for America," January 2001, http://bushsupporter.org, 77.

91. Diana R. Gordon, *Justice Juggernaut* (New Brunswick, NJ: Rutgers University Press, 1991).

Five ~

AMERICANS AWAKE TO TERRORISM: THE 21ST-CENTURY WAR

What is terrorism, and who are the terrorists?
Who and what are the biggest threats?
What really happened on September 11, and what led up to it?
What can be done to combat terrorism? What is being done now?

O n September 11, 2001, Americans awoke to a new world and the 21st-century type of war, one caused by the horrendous attacks on the World Trade Center in New York and on the Pentagon in Washington, D.C.

This was far from the first time that terrorism had raised its ugly head—there is a long history of terrorist acts across the world and numerous kinds of terrorism. Below, six different definitions of terrorism by federal agencies or think tanks are provided. Clearly, there are numerous differences between these definitions, but one central element emerges—politically motivated *aggression* manifesting itself in some violent action against noncombatants.

CONGRESSIONAL RESEARCH SERVICE   "Politically motivated violence perpetrated against noncombatant targets by subnational groups or clandestine agents."[1]

U.S. STATE DEPARTMENT   "Premeditated, politically motivated violence against noncombatant targets by subnational groups or clandestine agents, usually intended to influence an audience."[2]

FEDERAL BUREAU OF INVESTIGATION (FBI)   "The unlawful use of violence, committed by a group or two or more individuals against persons or property to intimidate or coerce a government, the civilian population, or any segment thereof, in furtherance of political or social objectives."[3]

FEDERAL EMERGENCY MANAGEMENT AGENCY (FEMA)   "Terrorism is the use of force or violence against persons or property in violation of the criminal laws of the United States for purposes of intimidation, coercion, or ransom. Terrorists often use threats to create fear among the public, to try to convince citizens that their

TABLE 5.1
Categories of Terrorism

	Government Controlled or Directed?	
Scope	No	Yes
National	Domestic terrorism	State terror
Regional/International	International terrorism	State-sponsored terrorism

Source: Terrorism Research Center, Definitions of Terrorism, 2002, http://www.terrorism.com/terrorism/def.shtml.Table.

government is powerless to prevent terrorism, and to get immediate publicity for their causes."[4]

GENERAL ACCOUNTING OFFICE (GAO)   Combat Terrorism includes "the full range of federal programs and activities applied against terrorism, domestically and abroad, regardless of the source or motive."[5]

RAND CORPORATION   "Violence, or the threat of violence, through acts designed to coerce others into action they otherwise would not undertake or into refraining from actions that they desired to take. All terrorist acts are crimes. Many would also be violations of the rules of war, if a state of war existed."[6]

Table 5.1 illustrates the differences in these definitions by identifying several categories of terrorism. Domestic terrorism is not controlled by any government and, obviously, has a limited scope. Examples of this might be the Weather Underground attacks in the United States and the attack on the federal building in Oklahoma City. International terrorism is also not sponsored by a government but has a broader scope, such as that directed against American or Israeli interests abroad. State terror is controlled directly by the government but is focused just upon the citizens of the country itself. It could be argued that the activities of Saddam Hussein against the Kurds in Iraq are state terror activities. Finally, state-sponsored terrorism is violence run by individual nations as a tool of their political and economic interests. The United States considers seven nations to be state sponsors of terrorism: Iran, Iraq, Syria, Libya, Cuba, North Korea, and the Sudan[7]—they either sponsor terrorism or provide safe harbor and assistance to terrorists from outside their country.

HISTORY OF TERRORISM

The history of terrorism is a long one—the term itself goes back to 1795, when it referred to the guillotining of opponents by members of the French Revolution. But acts of terror have been occurring since the first century, when Jewish Zealots publicly executed Romans and their collaborators.[8] Until the twentieth century, the term *terrorism* referred not to acts of violence by nongovernmental entities

FIGURE 5.1

Terrorist Incidents Involving Americans versus Total World Terrorist Incidents, 1987–1999

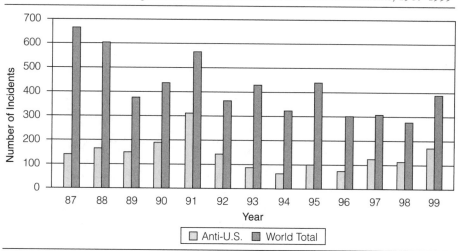

Source: Anthony H. Cordesman, *Terrorism, Asymmetric Warfare, and Weapons of Mass Destruction: Defending the U.S. Homeland* (Westport, CT: Praeger, 2002), 18.

but violence by states themselves, such as acts conducted by the Soviet and Nazi German governments against their citizens.

In the twentieth century, use of the term changed to mean violence against the state itself by individuals and, now, against individual citizens of a state. In the early part of the century, there were numerous examples of the use of violence against the state by those fighting to free individual countries (the Viet Minh against the French in Vietnam, the Irgun and Stern gangs against British rule in Palestine, and the National Liberation Front in Algeria against French rule).[9]

According to Martin Walker, modern terrorism took these activities as examples, but they were honed during the Arab-Israeli Six Day War in 1967 and the student movements in 1968. The first modern terrorist acts were the pro-Palestinian airline hijackings in the early 1970s, leading up to the kidnapping and subsequent murder of Israeli Olympic athletes in 1972.[10]

Since that time, terrorist groups have spread worldwide. These have included the Irish Republican Army in Ireland, the Red Army in Japan, the Red Brigades in Italy, the Weathermen in the United States, and West Germany's Red Army Faction.

Of these and other major terrorist incidents, most of them were aimed at targets around the world, not specifically at the United States or at American interests (see Figure 5.1). Most of the non-U.S. incidents took place in South or Central America. In fact, Figure 5.2 illustrates that the number of terrorist incidents in the United States has declined since the early 1980s. While the attack on the World Trade Center on September 11, 2001, was the deadliest terrorist attack in history, there have actually been fewer terrorist attacks on American soil or on American targets than on other targets worldwide.

FIGURE 5.2
Terrorist Incidents in the United States, 1980–2000

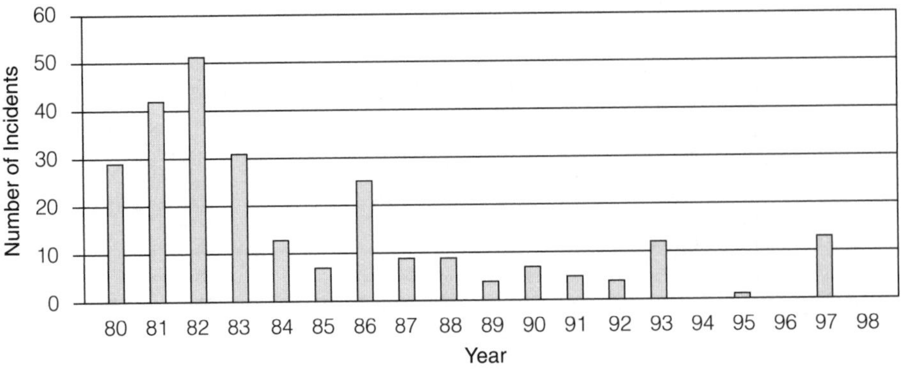

Source: Cordesman, *Terrorism, Asymmetric Warfare, and Weapons of Mass Destruction,* 19.

Table 5.2 provides summary information about the major attacks that have occurred in recent years on American soil. Many other attacks have occurred, yet these are the most prominent, ending with the horrendous attack on September 11, 2001, which took so many lives.

TYPES OF TERRORIST TOOLS AND ATTACKS

Terrorists utilize several different types of tools in their attacks, including the following.

Conventional Weapons

Conventional terrorist attacks involve the use of explosives in pipe bombs, car bombs, shootings, kidnappings, and assassinations. Targets of these attacks could be anything from commercial buildings to water or other utility supplies, information or communication infrastructures, government buildings, transportation links or facilities, or symbolic targets. From the terrorists' point of view, these types of attacks require the least skill and do have some terror effect upon the citizenry of a country yet lack the impact of more advanced weapons of mass destruction (WMD).

Suicide terrorism could utilize any of the tools of terrorism discussed below, but to date, most have utilized conventional means like bombs. While many now associate suicide bombings with Al-Qaeda or Palestinian radicals, many of the recent attacks have come from the Liberation Tigers of Tamil Eelam (also known as the Tamil Tigers), fighting for independence in Sri Lanka, who used the technique to kill Indian prime minister Rajiv Gandhi in 1991 and Sri Lankan president

TABLE 5.2
Major Terrorist Attacks on American Soil or Interests

Attack	Method of Attack	Number of Injuries and Fatalities	Group(s) Responsible	Brought to Justice?
Bombing of PanAm Flight 103 over Lockerbie Scotland 12/21/88	Bomb placed in luggage	270 killed—259 on the plane and 11 on the ground	Two Libyan intelligence officers	1 found guilty (life imprisonment), another acquitted
World Trade Center Bombing, New York City (2/26/93)	Bomb in van	6 killed, over 1,000 injured	Islamic extremist groups	5 found guilty and in prison
Oklahoma City, OK, bombing of federal building (4/19/95)	Truck with explosives	168 killed, over 500 injured	Timothy McVeigh and Terry Nichols	McVeigh executed; Nichols in prison for life
Khobar Towers bombing, Dharan, Saudi Arabia—apartments containing military personnel (6/25/96)	Truck bomb	19 killed, hundreds wounded before evacuation complete	Hezbollah with support from government of Iran	14 indicted
U.S. Embassy bombings in Nairobi, Kenya, and Dar es Salaam, Tanzania (8/7/98)	Coordinated truck bombings	Kenya: 213 killed, over 5,000 injured; Tanzania: 11 killed, 86 injured	Main suspect: Osama bin Laden	U.S. attacked Sudan and Afghanistan to destroy terrorist bases
U.S.S. Cole—destroyer (10/12/00)	Bomb on small boat	17 killed, 39 injured		Still under investigation
World Trade Center, New York City 9/11/01	Hijacked aircraft used as missiles	2,797* killed	Main suspect: Osama bin Laden	War in Afghanistan—removed Taliban from power, still seeking Osama bin Laden, war against Iraq
Pentagon attack (9/11/01)	Hijacked aircraft used as missiles	189 killed		
Flight 93 (9/11/01)	Hijacked aircraft but passengers prevented target damage	45 killed		

Source: Derived from The History Net, "Terrorism through American History," 2002, http://americanhistory.about.com/library/fastfacts/blfterrorism.htm, and Council on Foreign Relations. "Terrorism: An Introduction," 2002, http://www.terrorismanswers.com/terrorism/introduction.html.

*CNNNews, "WTC Victim Toll Drops below 2,800," October 8, 2002, http://www.cnn.com/2002/US/10/08/wtc.toll/index.html.

Ranasinghe Premadasa in 1993. Other groups using suicide tactics include the Kurdistan Workers' Party (PKK) fighting the Turkish government; Hezbollah, a group of radical Shiite Islamists in Lebanon; and Al-Qaeda, Osama bin Laden's group. With the adoption of these tactics by members of the second Palestinian *intifada* in 2000, these tactics have become more common.[11]

Chemical Weapons

Chemical weapons are those chemical substances (made for injury or not) used to kill, injure, or maim citizens. They are considered WMD and include chemical agents like mustard gas and sarin gas. Toxic chemicals that could be used as weapons include pesticides and industrial solvents and dyes, like chlorine and hydrogen cyanide.[12] Chemical weapons include the following:

> Nerve agents, which disrupt the nervous system and can be absorbed through the skin or inhalation. These include tabun, soman, and sarin (used in the Tokyo subway attack discussed below).

> Blister agents, which damage the skin and tissue and can cause blindness and fatal damage through the lungs. These are absorbed through the lungs or skin. They include mustard gases and their relatives.

> Choking agents, which are inhaled, cause blood vessels to hemorrhage until the victim literally drowns in fluid. These include chlorine gases and phosgene.

> Blood agents, which kill when victims breathe them; there is little warning of the presence of these gases. They include hydrogen cyanide and cyanogen chloride.

> Toxins formed by the bacterium *Clostridium botulinum,* which produces very fatal poisoning, typically through respiratory failure.

> Control agents, which temporarily disable the victim but can be survived unless exposure occurs in confined spaces. These include staphylococcus.

> Incapacitating agents, which cause short-term psychoactive effects but rarely kill. They include LSD, mescaline, and psilocybin.

> In addition, other chemically based weapons are being developed, including third- or fourth-generation nerve gases.[13]

Chemical weapons are not easy to handle and even more difficult to obtain and manage, but even small amounts can be damaging and have adverse effects. They would typically be applied in gaseous, aerosol, or vapor form in order to cause harm, which could make it more difficult to distribute and control.

There has already been an example of the use of chemical agents by terrorists—the group Aum Shinrikyo in Japan released sarin gas in a Tokyo subway in 1995. In that attack, 12 people were killed, but more than a thousand residents were injured. The group reportedly had excellent financial resources and sophisticated facilities used to create the weapon and had experimented with numerous chemical weapons but utilized sarin because it was the easiest to make. They purchased the formula from a Russian agent and had attempted several chemical attacks prior to the 1995 attack, including one on a judge involved with a case against them.

Biological Weapons

Biological weapons, which can be far more lethal than chemical weapons, can include either toxins or pathogens. Biological toxins are "toxic substances of natural origin produced by an animal or plant. An example of a toxin is ricin, a poisonous protein extracted from the castor bean."[14] Biological pathogens are "any organism (usually living) such as a bacteria or virus capable of causing serious disease or death. Anthrax is an example of a bacterial pathogen."[15]

Biological weapons can be grouped into the following five categories:

➢ Bacterial agents, like anthrax, plague, and typhoid fever

➢ Rickettsial agents (typhus, Rocky Mountain spotted fever)

➢ Viral agents, like smallpox, influenza, yellow fever, dengue fever, encephalitis, and hemorrhagic fevers like Ebola, Marburg, and Lassa

➢ Toxins (botulinum, shigella toxin, staphylococcus enterotoxin)

➢ Fungal agents, like coccidioidomycosis

The Centers for Disease Control (CDC) further categorize these weapons into three categories—A, B, and C, so that Category A is the high-priority agents that are the most dangerous and easiest to disseminate. Category A includes smallpox, anthrax, plague, botulism, and Ebola and Marburg hemorrhagic fevers. Of these, some estimates are that the first four are the most likely to be used (and of course, we know that anthrax was used in the United States in 2001, although the perpetrators are still unknown).

The use of biological weapons against citizens began with Japan in World War II. During that time, Japan (through its infamous Unit 731) not only experimented with biological agents on Chinese and Russian prisoners but also dropped fleas and rats infected with the plague into China.[16] Since World War II other countries (including the United States) have created or developed biological weapons.

Countries that are known or suspected to still have stockpiles of biological weapons include China, India, Iran, Iraq, Libya, North Korea, and Russia, among others. Pakistan and Syria are both believed to have the capacity to produce biological weapons but are not now known to have them.[17] Many more nations, including the United States, were actively developing and stockpiling these weapons but ceased their activities in 1972, when the Biological Weapons Convention (BWC) was open for ratification; more than 140 countries have now signed this treaty.

There have been 51 reported cases of terrorism utilizing biological weapons of some sort—5 of these are confirmed.[18] Additional cases of simple criminal activity involved biological agents, as well, and the number of hoaxes has been increasing.

Among the cases in which the perpetrators were found were that of the 1984 poisoning of restaurant salad bars with salmonella in a small town in Oregon by one member of the Baghwan Shree Rajneesh group, and of the poisoned oranges sent to Israel by a member of a Palestinian group.[19] A white supremacist associated with the Aryan Nation, Larry Wayne Harris (a microbiologist), was arrested in February of 1998 in Las Vegas when he was found carrying anthrax and threatening to wipe out Las Vegas. Previously he had been arrested while carrying samples of an inert form of the bubonic plague.[20]

There is evidence of numerous attempts by Aum Shinrikyo to use or at least experiment with the use of anthrax and botulinum. However, there is also much evidence emerging of terrorist groups seeking biological weapons. Again, the Aum Shinrikyo group figures prominently here, as they have been rumored to be trying to obtain supplies of anthrax, Ebola virus, and botulinum.

Along with concern about the actual use of these weapons is apprehension about their security, particularly in former Soviet bloc countries. Where are the stores of weapons-grade biological weapons, and how well protected are they? In addition, particularly in the former Soviet bloc, there are thousands of former weapons scientists and other specialists, now under- or unemployed, who could create problems as they possibly seek to sell their skills.[21]

Luckily for citizens of the world, developing and manufacturing biological weapons is not an easy process for most terrorist groups. There are numerous technical issues and problems to be successfully managed; these would require sophisticated labs and skilled and experienced scientists. In addition, the means to deliver biological weapons is also problematic as uncontrollable factors, such as the weather (wind, rain) and the ability of the agent to survive the delivery, are crucial and affect the eventual success of such an attack.

Radiological and Nuclear Weapons

Radiological and nuclear weapons provide another means of terrorist attack. Radiological weapons include the radiological dispersal device (RDD) that spreads radiological materials upon explosion and the simple RDD, or dirty bomb, which spreads radiological materials without the use of explosive materials. These weapons would kill by exposing citizens to radioactive materials when they breathed, touched, or ate them. Damage could be immediate or could be long term.

There is some debate over the difficulty of obtaining the materials and creating these weapons and, thus, the likelihood of successful terrorist attacks using them. But there are many potential sources for these raw materials: other countries, hospital radiation therapy sections, radiopharmaceutical materials, nuclear power plant fuel rods, laboratories, and universities.[22]

Nuclear weapons do present a considerable danger if the weapons are obtained by a terrorist group, although approximate effects of such an attack are very difficult to predict. In order to organize such an attack against the United States or any other target, terrorist groups must first obtain the materials and have the expertise and experience needed to build a bomb or dirty bomb. They must then be able to transport the bomb or materials to the desired site—all without detection. As one way to help reduce the chances of this transport, the United States is working with customs agents in Eastern Europe to help them detect radiological materials crossing the border.[23]

Currently the United States, China, India, Pakistan, and Russia are known to have nuclear weapons capabilities. Iran, Iraq, Libya, North Korea, and Syria are all known to be seeking or to be interested in developing a nuclear capability.

Cyberterrorism

Cyberterrorism is "terrorism that involves computers, networks, and the information they contain."[24] Given the increased reliance of our economy and our entire society upon computers, information, and other technologies, attacks on the infrastructure, computer systems, and computer networks constituting that technology presents an appealing target to many terrorists (as well as other nations interested in cyberwarfare).

As recognized in the Clinton administration's Executive Order 13010,

> Certain national infrastructures are so vital that their incapacity or destruction would have a debilitating impact on the defense or economic security of the United States. These critical infrastructures include telecommunications, electrical power systems, gas and oil storage and transportation, banking and finance, transportation, water supply systems, emergency services (including medical, police, fire and rescue), and continuity of government. Threats to these critical infrastructures fall into two categories: physical threats to tangible property ("physical threats") and threats of electronic, radio frequency, or computer-based attacks on the information or communications components that control critical infrastructures ("cyber-threats"). Because many of these critical infrastructures are owned and operated by the private sector, it is essential that the government and private sector work together to develop a strategy for protecting them and assuring their continued operation.[25]

This critical information and technology infrastructure is now vulnerable to information warfare attacks from, to quote Director of Central Intelligence George Tenet, "national intelligence and military organizations, terrorists, criminals, industrial competitors, hackers and disgruntled or disloyal insiders."[26] Cybercrimes and cyberterrorism have grown at an enormous pace, although there is a wide range between the most serious attacks and the least effective, that is, low-level hacker attacks. This range of attacks can be perpetrated by anyone, from those creating havoc for fun to state terrorists trying to bring down defense systems or entire economies.

The following statement by an army officer studying the problem illustrates the significance of the threat from cyberterrorism and information warfare:

> The Defense Department is heavily dependent upon timely and accurate information and is keenly focused on information operations and information assurance. . . . Over 95% of Department of Defense telecommunications

travel over commercial systems, and the interdependence of our civilian infrastructure and national security grows dramatically on a daily basis. In a few short decades, the global networking of computers via the internet will very likely be viewed as the one invention that had the greatest impact on human civilization—and perhaps the greatest challenge to our national security.

All of these computers and computer-dependent systems are vulnerable to physical and electronic ["cyber"] attack—from the computers on which individuals store and process classified information, privileged attorney-client information, or proprietary data, to our nationwide telecommunication and banking systems. Indeed the year 2000 ["Y2K"] problem demonstrates that we are even vulnerable to our own misfeasance and poor planning. A single non-nuclear, electromagnetic pulse can destroy or degrade circuit boards and chips, or erase all electronic media on Wall Street, in the Pentagon, or your local bank. The loss of a single satellite can terminate service for over 90% of the 45 million pagers in the United States, as well as interrupt thousands of cable television stations and credit card transactions. GPS signals can be spoofed or degraded, or used as part of highly accurate targeting systems. Advanced computer technology can help build nuclear weapons. Internet and computer crime is so simple that two teenagers in Cloverdale, California, with a mentor in Israel can break into sensitive national security systems at the Department of Defense. Information warfare experts can use global television to selectively influence political and economic decisions or produce epileptic-like spasms in viewers. Cyber warfare of the 21st century could significantly impact the daily lives of every man, woman, and child in America.[27]

The first American public response to the threat emerged in President Clinton's Commission on Critical Infrastructure Protection, created in 1997. This commission identified five types of cyberattacks, which could occur at different levels, with very different types of intent and potential for harm:

≫ On a specific database of a specific owner

≫ With the purpose of accessing a network

≫ For espionage purposes

≫ To shut down service (a "denial of service" attack)

≫ To introduce harmful instructions to a computer system[28]

Given the types of databases, networks, and computer systems in use today and what they are used for (emergency, defense, medical, and economic systems), disruption of these systems by any of these means could be extremely damaging to any country.

The types of cyberterrorism weapons include:

Reconnaissance, or sensitive intrusions into systems, is an attempt by a hacker to break into and explore a site with an eye to future intrusions and attacks.

While not damaging in itself, such reconnaissance yields knowledge and experience that are often used to later damage systems.

Root compromise, in which hackers obtain access to the core (top directory) of a system, including administrator authorities and passwords. This allows them to move throughout a system and gives great power and control over it. With the control of root authority, a hacker can cause enormous damage to a system.

Information requests, which can be devised to get around typical security features and allow the hacker inside formerly protected areas.

Malicious codes (viruses, worms, Trojan horses), which are pieces of computer code that are inserted into computer systems without the owner's knowledge; depending on their construction, such codes can wreak havoc on those systems, either taking up available memory, writing over existing programming, attaching themselves to other programs, or accomplishing other damaging tasks. Worms are types of viruses that can replicate themselves, while Trojan horses are dangerous pieces of code that appear to be harmless. Viruses and other malicious codes can cause a great deal of monetary damage to companies and to governments by destroying and damaging systems and software. Already, state-sponsored attacks on other governments, also called information warfare, utilizing these destructive tools, have focused on government and military Web and other servers.[29]

Denial-of-service (DOS) attacks are those brought about by repeated requests for service to a Web site in order to overwhelm the site and shut it down or prevent other users from accessing it. In recent years, several DOS attacks have caused commercial sites to shut down, resulting in the loss of millions of dollars. A terrorist group called the Internet Black Tigers unleashed a denial-of-service attack against Sri Lankan embassy Web servers.

User compromise, in which an individual user password or account is compromised.

Web site defacement is the result of hackers breaking into government agency or private firm Web servers and changing their appearance or content. Several U.S. federal government Web sites (U.S. Senate pages, FBI page, and others) have been recent targets of this type of attack.

Misuse of resources is an attack on a Web site or server that causes attacks on physical information infrastructure, such as cell towers or Internet infrastructure.

A CLOSER LOOK

Have you experienced any of these kinds of cyberattacks, even if on a smaller scale than what might be considered terrorism? How disrupted were your life and your work or play? How disrupted were those of your classmates?

FIGURE 5.3
Summary of Incident Types, Federal Computer Incident Response Capability (FedCIRC)
Survey of Incident Activity, 1999

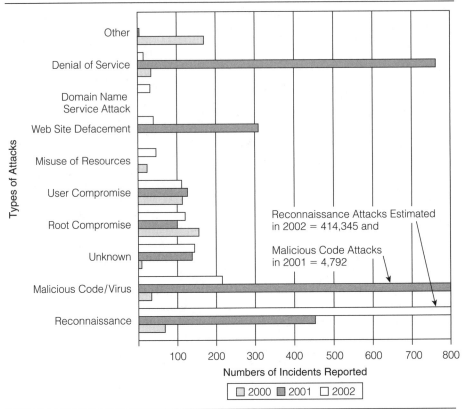

Source: Derived from Federal Computer Incident Response Center, General Services Administration,
FedCIRC Activity Statistics, 2002, http://www.fedcirc.gov/stats.html.

Figure 5.3 describes the types of cybercrime incidents that occurred in 2000
and 2001 and were estimated for 2002. Clearly, the types of attacks have changed
over the years and differ according to some specific attacks that occurred during
this period. Estimates for 2002 are for 414,345 reconnaissance attacks and 215 attacks involving malicious code of some sort (viruses, worms, and the like). The
most common cybercrimes were attempts to check out systems (reconnaissance)
(37 percent) and attempts to gain root, or administrator, authority, which can be
used to manipulate the system (18 percent). Those receiving the most publicity—
viruses (5 percent) and denial-of-service attacks (5 percent)—add up to only 10
percent of the incidents, although at one point the Defense Department alone was
experiencing up to 100 hacker attacks every day.[30] The potential for damage,
however is great.

FIGURE 5.4
Relative Killing Effects of Chemical versus Biological versus Nuclear Weapons

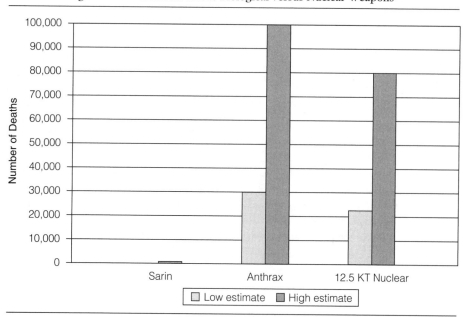

Source: Cordesman, *Terrorism, Asymmetric Warfare, and Weapons of Mass Destruction,* 214.

Summary of Weapons of Terrorism

Clearly, there are numerous ways for terrorists to inflict damage on the public at large. However numerous and however easy to produce, transport, and implement, these various methods also have very differental effects. Figure 5.4 indicates the relative numbers of deaths that could be expected from typical attacks of chemical (sarin) versus biological (anthrax) versus nuclear weapons—the types of weapons that would be most commonly available and easily used. Sarin would create very few fatalities (between 60 and 200) but anthrax could create from 30,000 to 100,000 deaths. A 12.5 kiloton nuclear weapon could create anywhere from 23,000 to 80,000 fatalities.[31]

TERRORIST THREATS

State Sponsors of Terrorism

Seven countries are listed by the U.S. State Department as official sponsors of terrorism. It is clear that the State Department considers statements by other countries criticizing the September 11 attacks as a crucial litmus test in evaluating attitudes toward terrorism. The 2001 Annual Report on Terrorism suggests that several of these seven have begun to move away from their sponsorship of terrorism, with Sudan and Libya leading the way, but that none has totally changed its policies. Iran and Syria have stopped their support for some groups but not for others. According to the State Department, Iran, North Korea, and Syria have made progress in some limited areas, but then North Korea's progress stopped.[32]

IRAN   According to the State Department, Iran continues to be the most active supporter of terrorist groups, although the support and activity has lessened for groups other than Palestinians.

IRAQ   The State Department points out that Iraq was the only Arab-Muslim country that did not condemn the September 11 attacks. The Iraqis continue to support groups like Mujahedin-e-Khalq (MEK), the Kurdistan Workers' Party (PKK), the Palestine Liberation Front (PLF), the Abu Nidal Organization (ANO) and the Popular Front for the Liberation of Palestine (PFLP). The Bush administration claimed in 2002 that Iraq supported Al-Qaeda and harbored weapons of mass destruction (WMD). While United Nations weapons inspectors were unable to find any WMD, the administration's claim was used as justification for the March 2003 war to remove Iraq's Saddam Hussein.

SYRIA   According to the State Department, the government of Syria has not been actively involved in terrorism since 1986, but it has continued to provide safe haven for a number of terrorist groups, including Ahmad Jibril's Popular Front for the Liberation of Palestine–General Command (PFLP-GC), the Palestine Islamic Jihad (PIJ), Abu Musa's Fatah-the-Intifadah, George Habash's Popular Front for the Liberation of Palestine, and HAMAS.

LIBYA   After an agent of Libyan Intelligence was found guilty in January 2001 of planting the bomb on Pan Am Flight 103 that exploded over Lockerbie, Scotland (in 1988) and agents were found guilty in November 2001 of a 1986 disco bombing in West Germany, Libya appears to be trying to distance itself from terrorism and terrorist groups. It even assisted against terrorists by ransoming a hostage held by the Abu Sayyef group in October 2001 and has tried to mediate in recent conflicts.

CUBA   Cuba has provided safety and maintained ties to terrorists, particularly those involved in Latin American issues.

NORTH KOREA   There is evidence that North Korea sold some arms to terrorist groups during 2001. In addition, they are still providing safety to Japanese terrorists from the Japanese Communist League who hijacked a JAL flight to North Korea in 1970.

SUDAN   While some positive steps were taken by Sudan and the United States removed official sanctions, the State Department cites evidence that mem-

> ---
>
> A CLOSER LOOK
>
> Investigate any new information available about state sponsors of ter-
> rorism at the "Terrorism: Questions and Answers" site of the Council on
> Foreign Relations, at http://www.terrorismanswers.com/sponsors.
>
> ---

bers of terrorist groups like Al-Qaeda, the Egyptian Islamic Jihad, the Egyptian al-
Gama'a al-Islamiyya, the Palestine Islamic Jihad, and HAMAS took refuge there
with the assistance of the Sudanese government, although some have probably
left the country since American pressures increased there.[33]

As a result of this designation as state sponsors of terrorism, the United States
has undertaken four actions against these countries:

> ➢ A ban against all arms-related sales and exports
> ➢ Controls against dual-use items (those that could be used as arms or for ter-
>   rorist purposes)
> ➢ A ban on economic assistance to these countries
> ➢ Several other financial restrictions, including U.S. opposition to World Bank
>   loans to these countries and prohibitions against tax credits for individuals or
>   firms working in those countries and against contracts for firms connected to
>   or controlled by those countries.

Terrorist Groups

Box 5.1 describes those organizations declared official terrorist groups by the
U.S. State Department. Box 5.2 describes the criteria used for this designation. The
list itself expresses how widely diverse the issues and goals of these groups are,
but four themes emerge: many of them are focused on overturning the governments in their own countries; many seek to overturn secular governments and
create Islamic states; of course, the Palestinian groups want to overthrow Israel
and establish a Palestinian state; and many are anti–United States and want to reduce U.S. influence overseas (in addition to the influence of other, related bodies, like the North Atlantic Treaty Organization [NATO]).

Among the many reasons terrorist groups have for their actions are the
following:

> ➢ Political beliefs (for example, the Red Army Faction)
> ➢ Religious (Islamic extremism)
> ➢ Ethnic (hate crimes)
> ➢ Social (single-issue, such as anti-abortion, animal rights, or environmentalism)

Box 5.1

STATE DEPARTMENT CURRENT LIST OF DESIGNATED
FOREIGN TERRORIST ORGANIZATIONS

Abu Nidal Organization (ANO)	Split from Palestinian Liberation Organization in 1974. Has carried out attacks in 20 countries, including Pan Am 73 hijacking in 1986. Has received support from Iraq, Libya, and Syria.
Abu Sayyaf Group	Most radical (but smallest) of Islamic groups in the Philippines; conducts bombings and kidnappings.
Al-Aqsa Martyrs Brigade	Group of West Bank militias affiliated with Arafat's al-Fatah faction; started attacks against civilians in 2002.
Armed Islamic Group (GIA)	Islamic extremist groups whose aim is to overthrow the non-Islamic Algerian government; began violence in 1992.
Asbat al-Ansar	Also called the Partisans' League; a Lebanon-based Sunni Muslim extremist group. Wants to overthrow Lebanese government.
Aum Shinrikyo	Japanese cult whose aim is to take over Japan and the world; was responsible for release of sarin gas in Tokyo subway in 1995 and is still active in Japan and elsewhere.
Basque Fatherland and Liberty (ETA)	In existence since 1959, its aim is the establishment of an independent homeland in the Basque region based on Marxist principles. Has killed more than 800 individuals since it began its violence in 1960s.
Gama'a al-Islamiyya (Islamic Group)	Primary goal—overthrow Egyptian government and replace it with Islamic state but issued cease-fire in 1999 and has not attacked targets in Egypt since 1998.
HAMAS (Islamic Resistance Movement)	Created in 1987 from Palestinian branch of the Muslim Brotherhood; goal is to establish Palestinian homeland. Is strong in the West Bank; uses both violent and peaceful means.
Harakat ul-Mujahidin (HUM)	Designated a terrorist group in 1998, an Islamic militant group based in Pakistan but operating primarily in Kashmir.
Hizballah (Party of God)	Also known as the Islamic Jihad, among other names. Formed in Lebanon, wants Islamic republic there, is anti-West and anti-Israel. Involved in several anti-U.S. attacks.
Islamic Movement of Uzbekistan (IMU)	Coalition of Islamic militants; wants Islamic state in Uzbekistan, also anti-West and anti-Israel. Operates in Islamic states of former Soviet Union and in Iran and Afghanistan.
Jaish-e-Mohammed (JEM) (Army of Mohammed)	Islamic group based in Pakistan. Has close ties to Afghan Arabs and to the Taliban.

al-Jihad (Egyptian Islamic Jihad)	Egyptian Islamic extremist group in operation since the late 1970s; wants to overthrow the Egyptian government and replace it with Islamic state. Focuses on high-level individuals.
Kahane Chai (Kach)	Founded by radical Israeli-American rabbi Meir Kahane; goal is to establish biblical state of Israel; declared a terrorist organization by the Israeli government in 1994.
Kurdistan Workers' Party (PKK)	Created in 1974 as a Marx-Leninist group composed of Turkish Kurds; works against Turkish government. Has bombs and has kidnapped foreign tourists.
Lashkar-e Tayyiba (LT) (Army of the Righteous)	Is the armed wing of a Pakistan-based Sunni Muslim group; is anti-U.S; operates in India and Pakistan with many attacks against Indian military and civilian targets.
Liberation Tigers of Tamil Eelam (LTTE)	This most powerful Tamil group works out of Sri Lanka, is involved in armed conflict against the Sri Lankan government, and works for Tamil separatism.
Mujahedin-e Khalq Organization (MEK)	Also known as the National Liberation Army of Iran; is the largest and most active armed Iranian dissident group. Very active and violent against U.S. personnel in the 1970s, but activity has waned in recent years.
National Liberation Army (ELN)	Works in Columbia and is pro-Cuba and anti-U.S. Formed in 1965, primarily rural based. Conducts many kidnappings and bombings.
Palestinian Islamic Jihad (PIJ)	Is not a cohesive group but rather a coalition of factions; wants an Islamic Palestinian state and the destruction of Israel; conducts suicide bombings.
Palestine Liberation Front (PLF)	Has split and split again into various faction. Various of these factions attacked the cruise ship *Achille Lauro* in 1985 and conducted attacks against Israel. In the past, supported by Libya.
Popular Front for the Liberation of Palestine (PFLP)	Founded in 1967 as a Marxist-Leninist group; was part of the PLO but has now broken away. In the 1970s, committed numerous attacks.
PFLP-General Command (PFLP-GC)	Popular Front for the Liberation of Palestine—very opposed to Arafat's PLO and broke off to be more violent; tied to Syria and Iran; conducts border attacks against Israel.
Al-Qaeda	Created by Osama bin Laden in 1990, originally to organize Arabs fighting in Afghanistan against the Soviets. Wants to organize a Muslim state in the world; exceptionally anti-U.S. and is believed responsible for the September 11 terrorist attacks and others following. Prior to that, was active in the 1990s against a series of targets.

Real IRA	Also known as True IRA, was formed in early 1998 as a clandestine military wing of the 32-County Sovereignty Movement; wants to remove the British from Northern Ireland and unify Ireland. Utilizes bombing strategies.
Revolutionary Armed Forces of Colombia (FARC)	Is the best-equipped, largest, and best-trained of the insurgency groups in Columbia. Created in 1964, is rural based and pro-Soviet and anti-U.S. Conducts kidnappings for ransom, bombings against pipelines, and anti-foreign citizen campaigns.
Revolutionary Nuclei (formerly ELA)	Evolved in Greece between 1995 and 1998 as an offshoot of a group that appeared to not be active anymore; this group has filled that void with arsons and bombings against Greek, NATO, and U.S. targets.
Revolutionary Organization 17 November	A largely Greek organization, created in 1975 and named for the Greek student uprising in 1973. Is anti-U.S., anti-Turkey, anti-NATO, wants U.S., NATO, and Turkish military out of Cyprus and Greece. Uses assassinations, bombings, and rocket attacks.
Revolutionary People's Liberation Army/Front (DHKP/C)	Created in 1978, was a splinter group from the Turkish People's Liberation Party/Front. Is Marxist/Leninist, anti-U.S., and anti-NATO. Uses assassinations and has tried to use antitank rockets.
Salafist Group for Call and Combat (GSPC)	Operates in Algeria since it began in 1996; is the most effective remaining revolutionary group in Algeria. Has promised to avoid civilian attacks inside Algeria and has kept to that promise, which brings it some support. Operates against the Algerian government and military.
Shining Path (Sendero Luminoso, SL)	Considered by many to be the most violent terrorist group in the world; was formed as a splinter group from the Communist Party in Peru. Its goal is to destroy the current Peruvian government in favor of an Indian-run government. Since its creation in 1970, has been responsible for the deaths of up 12,000 citizens.
United Self-Defense Forces of Colombia (AUC)	Called the paramilitaries or *autodefensas;* is an umbrella group of other paramilitary organizations 70 percent funded by drug funds. Uses guerilla military tactics against Colombian government.
Communist Party of the Philippines/New People's Army (CPP/NPA)	The military branch of the Communist Party of the Philippines; was formed in 1969 to overthrow the Philippine government.

Source: Library of Congress, "Legislation Related to the Attack of September 11, 2001," Thomas Legislative Information System, 2002, http://thomas.loc.gov/home/terrorleg.htm.

Box 5.2

LEGAL CRITERIA FOR LISTING AS DESIGNATED
TERRORIST ORGANIZATION BY U.S. STATE DEPARTMENT

Legal Criteria

It must be a foreign organization.

The organization must engage in terrorist activity or terrorism, or retain the capability and intent to engage in terrorist activity or terrorism.

The organization's terrorist activity or terrorism must threaten the security of U.S. nationals or the national security of the United States.

Effects of Designation

Supports our efforts to curb terrorism financing and to encourage other nations to do the same.

Stigmatizes and isolates designated terrorist organizations internationally.

Deters donations or contributions to and economic transactions with named organizations.

Heightens public awareness and knowledge of terrorist organizations.

Signals to other governments our concern about named organizations.

Legal Ramifications of Designation

A person in the United States or subject to the jurisdiction of the United States may not knowingly provide "material support or resources," such as financial services, lodging, or expert advice to a designated foreign terrorist organization (FTO).

Members of a designated FTO, if they are aliens, are inadmissible to and, in certain circumstances, removable from the United States.

Any U.S. financial institution that has possession of or control over funds in which a designated FTO has an interest must exert control over the funds and report them to the U.S. Department of the Treasury.

Source: U.S. Department of State, Fact Sheet: Foreign Terrorist Organizations, 2002, http://www.state.gov/coalition/cr/fs/12713.htm.

AL-QAEDA   Al-Qaeda, as the group behind the September 11 terrorist attacks in the United States, deserves additional explanation. They were formed in 1988 by Osama bin Laden, a Saudi whose considerable wealth comes from a family construction business. The group was formed out of those who were recruited to fight against the Soviets in Afghanistan in the 1980s, people who came from a variety of countries and many of whom were radicalized by the process. Many of those stayed to train for terrorist actions in the network of training camps set up by bin Laden or to support the Taliban by fighting in Afghanistan.[34]

The group supports and funds terrorist activities and Islamic extremists across the globe, mainly with bin Laden's funds, and makes wide use of high technology to do so.

A CLOSER LOOK

Controversy: How compelling are the rationales for terrorism listed in this section—would they be enough in your opinion to justify violent acts against civilians? Against anyone?

Al-Qaeda conducts three main activities; it

Attempts to radicalize existing Islamic groups and create Islamic groups where none exist.

Advocates destruction of the United States, which is seen as the chief obstacle to reform in Muslim societies.

Supports Muslim fighters in Afghanistan, Algeria, Bosnia, Chechnya, Eritrea, Kosovo, Pakistan, Somalia, Tajikistan, and Yemen.[35]

To date, the organization is believed responsible for the 1998 bombing of two U.S. embassies in Africa, the bombing of the U.S.S. *Cole* while docked in Yemen, the September 11 attacks on the World Trade Center and the Pentagon, and perhaps also the bombing of a nightclub in Bali in October 2002, which killed 190.

After the September 11 attacks, the Bush administration swore that it would track down and arrest bin Laden. During that war against the Taliban in Afghanistan and since, the United States has

Evicted the Taliban regime from Afghanistan, depriving Al-Qaeda of its training camps and operational headquarters.

Detained or arrested more than one-third of Al-Qaeda's leadership, including top leaders (but not bin Laden).

Established cooperative relationships with 100 countries, where some 3,000 individuals have been detained or arrested.

Blocked some $112 million in Al-Qaeda funds.

Retrieved large amounts of information, including instructional manuals, videos, diaries, CD ROMS, and hard drives from suspected terrorists.[36]

In addition, another six Al-Qaeda members, including one thought to have been responsible for the bombing of the U.S.S. *Cole,* were killed in November 2002 by a Hellfire missile from an unmanned Predator drone.

EXISTING POLICY TOOLS

Prior to 1996, U.S. policy against terrorism focused on the state sponsors of terrorism as opposed to terrorist groups themselves. But in that year, an important piece of legislation, the Anti-Terrorism and Effective Death Penalty Act of 1996,

TABLE 5.3
Policy Tools for Dealing with Terrorism

Policy Tools	Potential Tools
Diplomacy and constructive engagement	International court for terrorism
Economic sanctions	Media self-restraint
Economic inducements	Policy reform
Covert action	
Rewards for information program	
Extradition/law enforcement cooperation	
Military force	
International conventions	
Legislation like USA Patriot Act	

Source: Rensselaer Lee and Raphael Perl, *Terrorism, the Future and U.S. Foreign Policy,* Issue Brief for Congressional Research Service, updated March 26, 2002.

was passed. This created the category of foreign terrorist organization (FTO), seen in Box 5.1 and defined according to the definitions in Box 5.2. The act also banned funding or other support for these organizations. As will be discussed later, the September 11 attacks also elicited much new legislation. Table 5.3 outlines the various policy tools for dealing with terrorism currently available in the United States, all of which will be discussed below.

Diplomacy and Constructive Engagement

Diplomacy with other countries to create effective coalitions against terrorism, not with terrorist groups themselves, is an important policy tool of the current Bush administration. In fact, legislation may specifically prevent the government from engaging in diplomacy with terrorist groups. However, as a result of diplomacy, the United Nations, NATO, and many other countries joined with the United States in condemning the 2001 attacks. The Bush administration is continuing the use of diplomacy in engaging other countries in the war in Afghanistan against the Taliban.[37] In a significant failure of diplomacy, the Bush administration was ultimately unsuccessful in convincing the United Nations to support a war against Iraq to unseat Saddam Hussein. In March 2003 the United States attacked Iraq; as of this writing it appears the war succeeded in removing Hussein from power.

Economic Sanctions

Economic sanctions can be undertaken against terrorist groups themselves or against state sponsors of terrorism. When implemented against nation-states, they fall into any of seven categories:

≫ Restrictions on trading

≫ Restrictions against technology transfers

≫ Restrictions on foreign assistance

≫ Restrictions on export credits and guarantees

≫ Suspension of foreign aid

≫ Restrictions on aircraft or ship traffic

≫ Restrictions on the implementation of some treaties[38]

Economic sanctions can be unilateral, as with those of the United States against Cuba, or they can be multilateral, as they have been after the Pan Am Flight 103 bombing against Libya. In addition, after September 11, sanctions began to be used against terrorist groups themselves, as President Bush signed Executive Order 13324, freezing the assets of the 27 terrorist groups thought to be affiliated with Al-Qaeda and Osama bin Laden. Approval was also given for sanctions against banks known to be providing assistance and services to these known terrorist groups. By January 2002, 168 groups were part of this approach, and another $80 million in assets had been blocked in more than 140 countries.[39]

Other policy support for economic sanctions lies in the International Emergency Economic Powers Act, which allows restrictions on economic relationships when a national emergency exists; the International Trade and Security Act of 1985, which provides legal authority for the Libyan embargo; the Arms Export Control Act; and the Export Administration Act. In addition, any country designated as an official state sponsor of terrorism is prohibited by law (P.L. 104-132) from participating in any arms sales.

Economic Inducements

The other side of economic sanctions is economic inducements. Possible inducements to reduce the potential for terrorism could include support to reduce poverty and enhance education, for instance. The Congressional Research Service suggests as one possibility funding education to provide alternatives to the Madrassahs (Islamic religious schools that have been a source of indoctrination of radical Islamic activists and some terrorists).[40]

Covert Action

Covert action involves "intelligence gathering, infiltration of terrorist groups, and military operations" in order to determine the intentions and actions of terrorist groups.[41] Many believed that the September 11 attacks were the result of colossal failures on the part of the U.S. intelligence community, and there have been congressional hearings on that very topic. Intelligence supporters, in turn, blamed the restrictions placed on them in the reforms of the 1970s and later. As a result, some of these restrictions were removed to make it easier to obtain intelligence information on the possible hostile actions of terrorist groups.

Other covert action could involve sabotaging funding or weapons delivery, kidnapping accused terrorists or criminals, or even assassinating potential terrorists. While the United States is specifically prohibited from assassinations by Executive Order 12333, this has been recently tested. On November 4, 2002, an unmanned Predator drone launched a Hellfire rocket that killed six members of Al-Qaeda in a car in Yemen, including a top member suspected in the U.S.S. *Cole* bombing and an American suspected of being part of an Al-Qaeda terrorist cell in New York. This has created controversy over whether the attack was an assassination or an act of war against combatants. An additional controversy arose when the U.S. military bombed a suspected location for Saddam Hussein prior to the start of the actual war on Iraq in March 2003.

Rewards for Information

Currently a program is in place to provide rewards up to $5 million for information that could prevent or resolve any international terrorism. This policy is covered under the 1984 Act to Combat International Terrorism and is considered at least partly responsible for the arrest of Ramzi Ahmed Yousef, accused of being the leader behind the 1993 World Trade Center bombing, and of Mir Amal Kansi, convicted of murdering several CIA personnel. In addition, in the wake of the 2001 World Trade Center attacks, the U.S. government is offering $25 million for information leading to the arrest of Osama bin Laden. As of March 2003, this policy has not even uncovered direct information about whether he is dead or alive. There continue to be conflicting reports about whether bin Laden is alive, with the head of Interpol saying in early November 2002 that he believes he is.[42]

Extradition/Law Enforcement Cooperation

The Bush administration is relying upon law enforcement cooperation as an integral part of its anti-terrorism program—extradition agreements and the stationing of FBI agents overseas (in 44 different countries) are part of this. The U.S. death penalty laws and other factors (such as the inclusion of an exception for political offenses in many extradition treaties, obviously rendering them useless for most cases of terrorism) have reduced this as a factor at this time, but the administration is attempting to renegotiate treaties so that accused terrorists could be transferred to the United States for trial.[43]

Military Force

The United States has frequently resorted to military force when dealing with terrorism, including in these cases:

≫ The 1986 bombing of Libya for its alleged role in the bombing of a German discotheque.

≫ The 1993 bombing of Iraq's military intelligence headquarters in retaliation for the Iraqi government's attempts to assassinate then president George H. Bush while he was in Kuwait.

≫ The 1998 missile attacks against alleged terrorist bases in Afghanistan and a supposed chemical weapons factory in the Sudan.

≫ The successful military operations in Afghanistan during 2001 and 2002, after the World Trade Center and Pentagon attacks, to remove the Taliban, although the initial goal of finding and destroying Al-Qaeda and bin Laden was not successful.

≫ The November 2002 attack using the unmanned Predator drone with Hellfire missiles that killed the six Al-Qaeda operatives.

As of April 2003, the United States has gone to war against Iraq and has apparently removed the Hussein regime after four weeks of mixed fighting, 148 coalition deaths, and an unknown number of Iraqi military and civilian deaths.

International Conventions

The United States is a signatory to at least three terrorism-related international conventions, or agreements. These are the Convention for the Marking of Plastic Explosives, the U.N. Convention on the Suppression of Terrorist Bombings (since 1999), and the U.N. Anti-Terrorism Financing Convention (in 2000). These agreements often obligate the signatories to prosecute offenders of these crimes or agree to extradite those who are accused of terrorism. After the conventions are signed, they are approved by the Senate and signed into law by the president.

POTENTIAL POLICY TOOLS

There are some other policy tools looming on the horizon that could be helpful in fighting terrorism, as well.

International Court for Terrorism

There has been some support for the creation of an international court for terrorism to try those accused of terrorist acts and sentence and punish those found guilty. There are precedents for the creation of such a body—there is the International Court of Justice in the Hague for disputes between countries, special courts have been convened in cases of genocide, and a new International Criminal Court is being established (although the United States opposes it). It remains to be seen whether a court specifically created to deal with terrorism would deter terrorist activity or could even be created.

Media Self-Restraint

Since obtaining publicity for their cause is a major purpose of many terrorist groups, the role of the media in and around terrorist incidents is an important one. Many have argued that, if the media did not report or sensationalize terrorist incidents, they would decline in number and scope. Others argue that the media have a responsibility to report accurately what is happening at the time, no matter what the consequences—that they are only tools. Two Chicago papers, the *Sun-Times* and *Daily News* have developed standards on how to deal with terrorist incidents—they ban participation of reporters in any negotiations with terrorists, they rewrite terrorist statements to reduce the propaganda possibilities, coverage is coordinated by senior editors in contact with the police, and only senior editors make actual decisions on coverage. Soon after September 11, 2001, five major news organizations agreed to cut and paraphrase video clips by Osama bin Laden. But these are all voluntary, and many news organizations do not follow these or any other principles of self-restraint. Nothing permanent has been adopted.

Policy Reform

Many, many different areas of policy reform have also been explored—the most important of these will be discussed later in this chapter.

THE SEPTEMBER 11 ATTACKS

The attacks were undertaken by 19 terrorists who spent approximately $200,00 to $500,000 to implement their plans.[44] A time line of significant events leading up to the attacks is presented in Table 5.4. These terrorists had been in the United States for some time, taking lessons at flight schools and scouting out possible locations (their interest in some of these sites are still unknown). At several of the flight schools, suspicions were raised (in part since one student had said he was only interested in learning to steer the plane, not to take off or land it), but in some cases, the students were investigated and found to be legitimate, and in others (Arizona) warnings by FBI officials were not heeded in time by FBI headquarters in Washington, D.C.

The U.S. government, during both the Clinton and Bush administrations, had ongoing debates about what to do about Osama bin Laden. Clinton responded, in 1998, with cruise missile attacks against suspected terrorist training camps in Afghanistan but had not been successful in getting rid of bin Laden. With the new administration taking office in January 2001, White House official on terrorism Richard Clarke had prepared a five-point plan on dealing with Al-Qaeda, but with other issues on the agenda (Russia, China, missile defense), the plan was still on National Security Adviser Condoleezza Rice's desk and under review when the attacks occurred.[45]

Warnings and threats continued and the U.S. military went to higher alert, thinking the attack would be similar to the one against the U.S.S. *Cole* in 2000. Clearly, the FBI and the CIA knew attacks were imminent and warned various bodies of this intelligence. After the attacks, there were congressional investigations about what was known and when it was known to determine if the attacks could have been prevented. The time line in Table 5.4 indicates the types and timing of warnings. According to Senator Bob Graham of Florida, chair of the Senate Select

TABLE 5.4

Events Leading up to the September 11 Terrorist Attacks

Early January 2001	During the Clinton-to-Bush transition, White House terrorism czar Richard Clarke briefs Condoleezza Rice on the growing Al-Qaeda threat. But the new Bush team is focused on other foreign-policy priorities: missile defense, relations with Russia and China.
January 25	Clarke presents a plan to his new bosses, urging an aggressive five-point program to take the fight to Al-Qaeda, calling for air attacks on all training camps in Afghanistan and giving full U.S. support to the Northern Alliance.
February	Hani Hanjour raises suspicions at an Arizona flight school with his poor English and mediocre flight skills. The FAA investigates and finds he is a legitimate student.
May–August	The six leading hijackers—Muhammad Atta, Ziad Jarrah, Marwan Al-Shehhi, Hanjour, Khalid Almihdhar, and Nawaf Alhazmi—begin taking cross-country test flights to the West Coast. Afterward they usually meet up in Las Vegas.
May 8	Bush creates a new Office of National Preparedness for terrorism and promises a government review, led by Dick Cheney, into the consequences of a domestic attack. It never happens.
June 22	Because of growing Al-Qaeda threats, the Pentagon puts all U.S. forces in the Middle East and Europe on the highest state of alert—Force Protection Condition Delta—suspends exercises in Jordan, and orders ships from the Fifth Fleet in Bahrain out to sea.
Late June	Bin Laden grants an interview to an Arabic TV station. He says little, offering only pleasantries, while his aides warn that America should expect a new attack in the coming weeks.
June 29	William Milam, the U.S. envoy to Pakistan, in a meeting with Taliban ambassador Abdul Salam Zaeef, warns that the Taliban will be held responsible if bin Laden attacks U.S. targets again.
July 2	The FBI warns law-enforcement agencies of possible Al-Qaeda strikes against overseas targets but also says domestic strikes cannot be ruled out. The next day, CIA Director George Tenet sends a list of Al-Qaeda suspects to 20 foreign intelligence agencies and asks for their immediate arrest.
July 4	Khalid Almihdhar and Nawaf Alhazmi reenter the United States. The CIA knows the two belong to Al-Qaeda but fails to alert the Immigration and Naturalization Service (INS) until Aug. 23.
July 5	Despite a quiet Fourth of July, the CIA warns Bush that imminent strikes are still possible. He asks Rice to find out what the agencies are doing about Al-Qaeda. Clarke holds meetings with CIA, FBI, Pentagon, and State Department officials. He also tells key domestic agencies to be prepared for an attack.
July 10	Phoenix, Arizona: FBI agent Kenneth Williams sends headquarters a memo about Middle Eastern students at an Arizona flight school, theorizing Al-Qaeda could be trying to infiltrate U.S. aviation. Analysts at headquarters defer action on his concerns. The memo never gets past two mid-level unit chiefs.
August 6	Tenet briefs Bush in Crawford, Texas, with an analytic report on Al-Qaeda. It is based largely on old intelligence but raises hijackings as a possible threat while also citing other methods. Tenet meets with a group of senators a few days later and provides them with a similar report.
August 13	Moussaoui begins two days of 747 simulator training at a Minneapolis, Minnesota, flight school. A manager soon reports his suspicious behavior to the FBI. Agents question Moussaoui, and the INS arrests him on August 16.
Late August	Hanjour, Alhazmi, and Almihdhar move into a motel in Maryland. Majed Moqed and Salem Alhazmi join them. Hanjour rents a plane three times for test flights over Washington.

(Continued)

TABLE 5.4 (Continued)

September 4	The Principals' Committee—Cheney, Rice, and other top national security officials—holds its first terrorism meeting. They debate Clarke's plan, decide to implement it in a phased approach, and send it to Bush.
September 9	Al-Shehhi checks out of a Florida motel where he and several other hijackers have been staying. They all fly to Boston. That evening, Alshehri wires $5,215 to Ahmed from Logan Airport. Jarrah is pulled over by police in Maryland for speeding on his way to Newark, New Jersey.
September 9	Two Al-Qaeda assassins, posing as journalists interviewing Massoud (Northern Alliance leader against the Taliban) detonate a bomb, mortally wounding the Northern Alliance commander.
September 9	Donald Rumsfeld threatens to urge a veto if the Senate proceeds with a plan to divert $600 million from missile defense to counterterrorism.
September 11	Ahmed picks up wire transfers of funds, then flies from Dubai to Pakistan. Just before 8 A.M., Atta calls Al-Shehhi from Flight 11 as it sits on a runway. Al-Shehhi is on Flight 175. They confirm the plot is on.

Source: Time/CNN, "A 9/11 Timeline" *The Secret History,* August 12, 2002, http://www.time.com/time/covers/1101020812 and http://www.time.com/time/covers/1101020812/timeline/2.html.

Committee on Intelligence at the time, "intelligence and law enforcement agencies failed to connect the dots of various clues leading up to the catastrophe."[46]

The Attack

The most significant terrorist attacks in American history occurred on September 11, 2001. Table 5.5 presents the timetable of the events of that terrible morning, when four airplanes were hijacked and used as human missiles against the World Trade Center in New York City, the Pentagon in Washington, D.C., and another unknown target, although there was speculation that the target was also somewhere in the Washington area. The last plane's target was unknown since the passengers on that flight, having heard on their cell phones what had happened to the earlier flights, took back the flight, which subsequently crashed in Pennsylvania.

To date, the death toll at the World Trade Center is 2,797, which is down significantly from the highest estimate of over 6,000 individuals and will likely go lower. The number has declined as those listed as missing have been found alive somewhere and duplicate names have been eliminated. Only 1,411 victims' remains have been positively identified. This number is horribly, unacceptably high—and yet there were over 50,000 people working for over 500 companies in the two trade center towers, so the potential for even more carnage was much greater.[47] What is truly amazing is that so many were saved after two airplanes full of jet fuel crashed into the towers. Those who died either worked in the floors above where the planes hit or had not left the buildings when they collapsed.

One reason that so many were saved was the efforts of the rescue workers on that day. And their efforts are seen in the horrible death tolls among the three

TABLE 5.5
Time Line of Events, Morning, September 11, 2001

7:58 A.M.	United Airlines Flight 175 departs Boston for Los Angeles, carrying 56 passengers, two pilots, and seven flight attendants. The Boeing 767 is hijacked after takeoff and diverted to New York.
7:59	American Airlines Flight 11 departs Boston for Los Angeles, carrying 81 passengers, two pilots, and nine flight attendants. This Boeing 767 is also hijacked and diverted to New York.
8:01	United Flight 93, a Boeing 757 carrying 38 passengers, two pilots, and five flight attendants, leaves Newark, New Jersey, for San Francisco.
8:10	American Airlines Flight 77 departs Washington's Dulles International Airport for Los Angeles, carrying 58 passengers, two pilots, and four flight attendants. The Boeing 757 is hijacked after takeoff and eventually crashes into the Pentagon.
8:46	American Flight 11 from Boston crashes into the North Tower at the World Trade Center.
9:03	United Flight 175 from Boston crashes into the South Tower at the World Trade Center. The U.S. Federal Aviation Administration (FAA) shuts down all New York area airports.
9:21	Bridges and tunnels leading into New York City are closed.
9:25	The FAA grounds all domestic flights.
9:45	American Flight 77 crashes into the Pentagon.
10:05	The South Tower at the World Trade Center collapses.
10:05	The White House is evacuated.
10:10	A large section of one side of the Pentagon collapses.
10:10	United Flight 93 crashes in a wooded area in Pennsylvania after passengers confront hijackers.
10:28	The North Tower at the World Trade Center collapses.

Source: September11news.com, Timeline and Images on the Morning of September 11, 2001, 2002,
http://www.september11news.com/AttackImages.htm.

agencies involved—the New York City Fire Department, the New York City Police Department, and the Port Authority of New York and New Jersey. Of these dead, 343 are New York City firefighters, who went into the building to rescue those inside; 84 were New York and New Jersey Port Authority officers; and 23 were New York City police officers. From among those who survived that day and worked in rescue and recovery efforts, many are still suffering lung and other ailments after breathing the air in the area.

Another 45 who were on Flight 93 died in Pennsylvania and 189 died at the Pentagon (both those on Flight 77 itself and those working inside the building).

Estimates of the attacks' impact upon the New York City economy are wide-ranging and serious. A United Way study estimated from $20 billion to $39 billion in lost economic output and 90,000 to 150,000 lost jobs. In December 2001, there were 132,400 fewer jobs in New York City than in December 2000. Most of these jobs were in the hotel/restaurant, securities, general business services, aviation, apparel manufacturing, and retail industries. These losses have, in turn, created even more state and local budgetary problems in a period when state and local governments were already facing increased fiscal pressures. The result—human services and nonprofit organizations, already stressed, are more likely to be budgetarily constrained in the future.[48]

The United Way also identified major and immediate needs for the city in light of the attacks. The most important were helping the victims get back to work, restoring lost housing, and managing the mental health of all those involved still facing traumas. Immigrants were clearly hurt disproportionately to their numbers. Beyond that, there is a need for the physical rebuilding of offices, stores, and restaurants and support for neighborhoods to return to normal.

The Anthrax Attacks

Starting one week after the September 11 attacks, the bacteriological agent anthrax was sent to the offices of NBC in what started a string of such mailings to media and government offices. Letters containing anthrax were then sent the *New York Post,* American Media Inc. (publishers of the *National Enquirer*), senators Tom Daschle and Patrick Leahy in the Hart Senate Office Building, and perhaps the State Department. Due to the timing of the attacks, most assumed these were also part of the plans of the September 11 attacks, but later evidence pointed to domestic terrorism. Altogether, the attacks produced 18 confirmed infections from anthrax: 11 inhalation cases (including five deaths) and seven skin cases. One man died after inhaling anthrax sent to the offices of American Media Inc. in Boca Raton, Florida; two postal workers who handled the letters were killed; one elderly woman in Connecticut was killed, apparently from handling mail that had come into contact with one of the letters; and one hospital supply worker in New York City was also killed. The cutaneous (skin-infected) cases were individuals who had handled or opened the mail. The persons with inhalation anthrax who did not die were practically all postal workers.

The offender or offenders in these cases have not yet been caught, although there are strong suspects who have been publicly identified.

POLICY IMPACTS OF THE ATTACKS

The policy response to the terrorist attacks was immediate and direct. The Thomas legislative information site at the Library of Congress lists 21 bills and joint resolutions signed into law, 27 resolutions approved, and 86 other pieces of legislation

---

A CLOSER LOOK

How was your life, and the lives of your family and friends, changed due to the September 11, 2001, attacks? In what ways? Have things gotten back to "normal"? Why or why not?

260THE PUBLIC AGENDA: ISSUES IN AMERICAN POLITICS

that drew some floor action (this included bills and resolutions). Box 5.3 presents those bills and joint resolutions passed since September 11, 2001, that were in some way related to the attacks. The list shows the incredibly wide range of policy actions that were undertaken after the attacks.

The USA PATRIOT Act

One of the best known of these is the USA PATRIOT Act, signed on October 26, 2001. This act has been very controversial as it gives greater authority for federal law enforcement officials to intercept all kinds of communications either for law-enforcement or foreign intelligence–gathering purposes. It has anti–money laundering provisions, allowing greater powers for the U.S. secretary of the treasury, it attempts to further close United States borders, and creates new crimes and penalties to use against terrorists.[49]

A different view of the Patriot Act is voiced by the Electronic Freedom Foundation, a privacy rights organization organizing mainly around Internet and digital issues. It believes that the act was passed too quickly, is too comprehensive (enacted six weeks after September 11 and altering over 15 statutes). In addition, the foundation believes that the expanded electronic surveillance allowed gives more authority to those who had already abused those powers and that the act focuses too broadly on surveillance authority without enough focus on terrorism and terrorists themselves.[50]

Homeland Security

Another important but controversial initiative is the Office of Homeland Security, created soon after September 11, 2001. President Bush appointed then governor Tom Ridge of Pennsylvania to head the office. With some fanfare, the office soon announced one of its major accomplishments—the creation of a color-coded system to indicate the level of terrorist threats in existence at any one time. A low level is green, "Guarded" is blue, "Elevated" is yellow, "High" is orange, and "Severe" is red.

Other actions taken by the Bush administration under the goal of homeland security since September 11 have been to:

≫ Increase the number of sky marshals on our airlines;

≫ Acquire enough medicine to treat up to 10 million more people for anthrax or other bacterial infection;

≫ Distribute $1.1 billion to States to strengthen their capacity to respond to bioterrorism and other public health emergencies resulting from terrorism;

≫ Deploy hundreds of Coast Guard cutters, aircraft, and small boats to patrol the approaches to our ports and protect them from internal or external threats;

≫ Acquire equipment for certain major mail-sorting facilities to find and destroy anthrax bacteria and other biological agents of terror; and

---

Box 5.3

TERRORISM-RELATED BILLS AND JOINT RESOLUTIONS
PASSED BY THE U.S. CONGRESS SINCE SEPTEMBER 11, 2001

R2882	Public Safety Officer Benefits bill
H.R. 2883	Intelligence Authorization Act for Fiscal Year 2002
H.R. 2884	Victims of Terrorism Relief Act of 2001
H.R. 2888	2001 Emergency Supplemental Appropriations Act for Recovery from and Response to Terrorist Attacks on the United States
H.R. 2926	Air Transportation Safety and System Stabilization Act
H.R. 3162	Uniting and Strengthening America by Providing Appropriate Tools Required to Intercept and Obstruct Terrorism (USA PATRIOT) Act of 2001
H.R. 3275	Terrorist Bombings Convention Implementation Act of 2001
H.R. 3448	Bioterrorism Response Act of 2001
H.R. 3525	Enhanced Border Security and Visa Entry Reform Act of 2002
H.R. 3986	To extend the period of availability of unemployment assistance under the Robert T. Stafford Disaster Relief and Emergency Assistance Act in the case of victims of the terrorist attacks of September 11, 2001
H. J. Res. 71	Designating September 11 as Patriot Day
S. 1372	Export-Import Bank Reauthorization Act of 2002
S. 1424	A bill to amend the Immigration and Nationality Act to provide permanent authority for the admission of "S" visa nonimmigrants
S. 1438	National Defense Authorization Act for Fiscal Year 2002
S. 1447	Aviation and Transportation Security Act
S. 1465	A bill to authorize the President to exercise waivers of foreign assistance restrictions with respect to Pakistan through September 30, 2003, and for other purposes
S. 1573	Afghan Women and Children Relief Act of 2001
S. 1793	Higher Education Relief Opportunities for Students Act of 2001
S. 2431	Mychal Judge Police and Fire Chaplains Public Safety Officers' Benefit Act of 2002
S. J. Res. 22	A joint resolution expressing the sense of the Senate and House of Representatives regarding the terrorist attacks launched against the United States on September 11, 2001
S. J. Res. 23	Authorization for Use of Military Force

Source: Library of Congress, "Legislation Related to the Attack of September 11, 2001," Thomas Legislative Information System, 2002, http://thomas.loc.gov/home/terrorleg.htm.

≫ Station 8,000 National Guard troops at baggage screening checkpoints at 420 major airports.[51]

A major Bush administration initiative now being implemented is the conversion of the Office of Homeland Security into a full-fledged cabinet-level Department of Homeland Security with the same status as the Department of the Interior,

---

A CLOSER LOOK

How do you balance the need for increased security and surveillance and wiretaps to find out information about terrorists with the right to privacy and the right to free speech?

Treasury, or Energy. The proposal involves the largest restructuring of the federal government in several decades. Under the proposal, four divisions were created: Border and Transportation Security; Emergency Preparedness and Response; Chemical, Biological, Radiological and Nuclear Countermeasures; and Information Analysis and Infrastructure Protection.

The controversial part of the proposal is that it moved the Coast Guard from the U.S. Treasury Department, transferred the Immigration and Naturalization Service from the Justice Department, and incorporated the Federal Emergency Management Agency, as well as three national nuclear laboratories, into the new unit, plus many, many more units from around the federal government. This is an enormous shake-up of agencies and personnel. The critically controversial part, however, is that Bush proposed to remove some civil service protections from these individuals, a proposal to which there were enormous objections.

WHAT LOOMS IN THE FUTURE?

This chapter introduces the important points and players within the terrorist and anti-terrorist movements, focusing upon the policy aspects of the fight against terrorism. This fight has clearly just begun, as government workers, health professionals, military personnel, and first-response and other emergency professionals and decision makers learn more about emerging terrorist threats.

Many major issues exist in this area—the enormous threat to free speech that has been created from the existing war on terrorism, the war with Iraq as the Bush administration moved to disarm and remove Saddam Hussein, the potential health problems from the possible use of smallpox or other biological weapons, and many others.

So much is uncertain about the fight against terrorism that the only certainty is just how uncertain the future is at this point. The only answers are to educate ourselves and strive to be involved in the decision-making process as citizens—to truly take advantage of the benefits of our democracy. Only as an informed electorate can we make the kinds of decisions that need to be made in these uncertain times.

FOR MORE INFORMATION

Bergen, Peter. *Holy War, Inc: Inside the Secret World of Osama bin Laden*. New York: Free Press, 2001.

Carr, Caleb. *The Lessons of Terror: A History of Warfare against Civilians: Why It Has Always Failed and Why It Will Fail Again*. New York: Random House, 2002.

Cigler, Allan J. *Perspectives on Terrorism: How 9/11 Changed U.S. Politics*. New York: Houghton Mifflin Company, 2002.

Cordesman, Anthony H. *Terrorism, Asymmetric Warfare, and Weapons of Mass Destruction: Defending the U.S. Homeland*. Westport, CT: Praeger, 2002.

Cordesman, Anthony H., with Justin G. Cordesman. *Cyber-threats, Information Warfare, and Critical Infrastructure Protection: Defending the U.S. Homeland*. Westport, CT: Praeger, 2002.

Council on Foreign Relations, Terrorism Answers. http://www.terrorismanswers.com.

Schweitzer, Glenn E. *A Faceless Enemy: The Origins of Modern Terrorism*. Cambridge, MA: Perseus, 2002.

U.S. Department of State, Office of the Coordinator for Counter-terrorism. http://www.state.gov/s/ct.

NOTES

1. Lee Rensselaer and Raphael Perl, *Terrorism, the Future and U.S. Foreign Policy*, CRS Issue Brief for Congress (Washington, DC: Congressional Research Service, Library of Congress, March 26, 2002).
2. Anthony H. Cordesman. *Terrorism, Asymmetric Warfare, and Weapons of Mass Destruction: Defending the U.S. Homeland* (Westport, CT: Praeger, 2002), 12.
3. Ibid.
4. Ibid., 13.
5. Ibid.
6. Ibid.
7. U.S. Department of State, Office of the Coordinator for Counter-Terrorism, Overview of State-Sponsored Terrorism, 2001, http://www.state.gov/s/ct/rls/pgtrpt/2000/2441.htm.
8. Council on Foreign Relations, "Terrorism: An Introduction," Terrorism: Questions and Answers, 2002, http://www.terrorismanswers.com/terrorism/introduction.html.
9. Martin Walker, "A Brief History of Terrorism," *Europe Magazine* (European Union), no. 410 (October 2001), http://www.eurunion.org/magazine/0110/p26.htm.
10. Ibid.
11. Council on Foreign Relations, "Suicide Terror: Was 9/11 Something New?" Terrorism: Questions and Answers, http://www.terrorismanswers.com/terrorism/suicide.html.
12. Cordesman, *Terrorism, Asymmetric Warfare, and Weapons of Mass Destruction,* 90–91.
13. Ibid., 115–117.
14. Ibid., 90.
15. Ibid.
16. Ibid., 156; Tien-wei Wu, "A Preliminary Review of Studies of Japanese Biological Warfare Unit 731 in the United States," Germ War and Experiments on Humans, 2002, http://www-users.cs.umn.edu/~dyue/wiihist/germwar/731rev.htm; Technology Art-

ist, "Unit 731: A Half-Century of Denial," accessed 2002, http://www.technologyartist .com/unit_731/index.html.; Shane Green, "The Asian Auschwitz of Unit 731," *The Age,* 2002, http://www.theage.com.au/articles/2002/08/28/1030508070534.html.

17. Cordesman, *Terrorism, Asymmetric Warfare, and Weapons of Mass Destruction,* 132–134.

18. Ibid., 147.

19. Ibid., 148.

20. Larry Henry, "*Sun* Profile: Harris' Troubled Past Includes Mail Fraud, White Supremacy," *Las Vegas Sun,* February 28, 1998, http://www.lasvegassun.com/dossier/crime/bio/ harris.html.

21. Cordesman, *Terrorism, Asymmetric Warfare, and Weapons of Mass Destruction,* 143.

22. Ibid., 194.

23. "Catching Nuclear Smugglers," *All Things Considered,* National Public Radio, September 26, 2002 (audio transcript) http://search.npr.org/cf/cmn/cmnpd01fm.cfm?PrgDate= 9%2F26%2F2002&PrgID=2.

24. Council on Foreign Relations, "Cyberterrorism," Terrorism: Questions and Answers, http://www.terrorismanswers.com/terrorism/cyberterrorism.html.

25. Quoted in Anthony H. Cordesman, with Justin G. Cordesman, *Cyber-threats, Information Warfare, and Critical Infrastructure Protection: Defending the U.S. Homeland* (Westport, CT: Praeger, 2002), 56.

26. Ibid., 25.

27. Lieutenant Colonel Jordan, *Information Operations* (Air War College, U.S. Department of Defense), Accessed October 2002, http://www.au.af.mil/au/awc/awcgate/army/ jaoac-io.pdf.

28. Cordesman, *Cyber-threats, Information Warfare, and Critical Infrastructure Protection,* 13.

29. Ibid., 17.

30. Ibid., 16.

31. Cordesman, *Terrorism, Asymmetric Warfare, and Weapons of Mass Destruction,* 214.

32. U.S. Department of State, "Patterns of Global Terrorism," May 2002, http://www.state .gov/s/ct/rls/pgtrpt/2001.

33. Ibid.

34. International Policy Institute for Counter Terrorism, "Al Qa'iad (The Base) in Terrorist Organization Profiles," 2002, http://www.ict.org.il/inter_ter/orgdet.cfm?orgid=74; Richard Engel, "Inside Al-Qaeda: A Window Into the World of Militant Islam and the Afghani Alumni," *Jane's,* September 28, 2001, http://www.janes.com/regional_news/ asia_pacific/news/misc/janes010928_1_n.shtml.

35. International Policy Institute for Counter Terrorism. "Al Qa'iad (The Base) in Terrorist Organization Profiles."

36. Faye Bowers, "Al Qaeda Network Frayed," *Christian Science Monitor,* September 6, 2002, http://www.csmonitor.com/2002/0906/p01s04-uspo.html.

37. Lee Rensselaer and Raphael Perl, *Terrorism, the Future and U.S. Foreign Policy.*

38. Ibid., CRS-9.

39. Ibid.

40. Ibid.

41. Ibid., CRS-10.

42. "'Bin Laden Alive,' Says Interpol," CNN News, November 8, 2002, http://www.cnn .com/2002/WORLD/europe/11/08/interpol/index.html.

43. Lee Rensselaer and Raphael Perl, *Terrorism, the Future and U.S. Foreign Policy.*

44. Ibid., CRS-9.
45. Time/CNN, "A 9/11 Timeline" in "The Secret History," August 12, 2002, *Time,* http://www.time.com/time/covers/1101020812 and http://www.time.com/time/covers/1101020812/timeline/2.html.
46. Quoted in "September 11 Warnings: Who Knew What, and When?" CNN, May 24, 2002, http://www.cnn.com/2002/US/05/22/9.11.warnings.facts/index.html.
47. "WTC Victim Toll Drops below 2,800," CNN News, October 8, 2002, http://www.cnn.com/2002/US/10/08/wtc.toll/index.html.
48. United Way of New York City, *Beyond Ground Zero: Challenges and Implications for Human Services in New York City Post-September 11* (New York, March 2002).
49. Charles Doyle, *The USA PATRIOT Act: A Sketch,* CRS Report for Congress (Washington, DC: Congressional Research Service, Library of Congress, 2002).
50. Electronic Frontier Foundation, "EFF Analysis of the Provisions of the USA PATRIOT Act," 2002,http://www.eff.org/Privacy/Surveillance/Terrorism_militias/20011031_eff_usa_patriot_analysis.html.
51. George W. Bush. "Securing the Homeland Strengthening the Nation," 2002, http://www.whitehouse.gov/homeland/homeland_security_book.html.

INDEX ⌒